ARCO

Everything you need to score high on the

ASVAB BASICS

6th EDITION

ARCO

Everything you need to score high on the

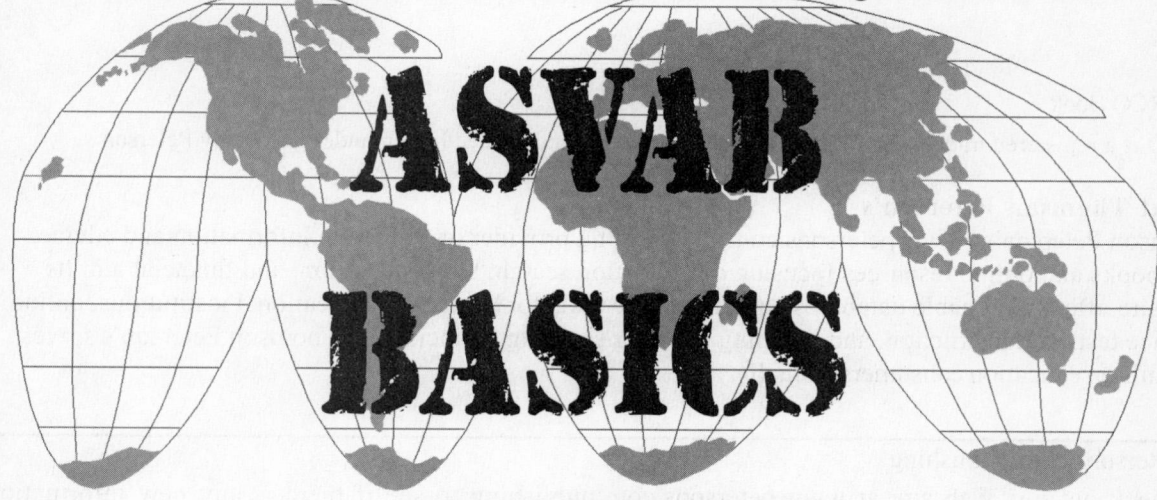

ASVAB BASICS

6th EDITION

Ronald M. Kaprov, Ed.D.
Steffi R. Kaprov, M.A.

THOMSON
★
PETERSON'S ™

Australia • Canada • Mexico • Singapore • Spain • United Kingdom • United States

CONTENTS

PREFACE

You are making some important decisions about your life and are about to embark on an exciting venture—taking the ASVAB in preparation for a possible career in the military.

Why join the U.S. military? Because the military can give you much that is needed in everyone's lives—purpose, direction, vocational and career opportunities, leadership training—and most important, the chance to do something worthwhile for the best country in the world!

Especially now, as our nation encounters new threats and challenges every day, it is of vital importance that our military be prepared with the best young men and women available. Military people are provided with good training and excellent preparation for life in and out of the military.

What is the purpose of the ASVAB? The purpose is to make sure that qualified people are admitted into the military. These young enlistees must be trained using inherent skills and qualities that will enable them to excel and help their country in the process.

What is the ASVAB? ASVAB stands for the Armed Services Vocational Aptitude Battery. The ASVAB consists of a battery of tests that help you and the military determine what your particular skills or talents might be. Can you follow wire circuits to troubleshoot a difficulty? Is dealing with any mechanical problem a piece of cake for you? Can you read directions clearly and understand necessary calculations? All these are examples of abilities that are tested on the ASVAB. The scores you achieve on the ASVAB help you make a decision about what sort of assignment or career plans are good choices for you if you join the Armed Services.

What This Book Will Do for You

ASVAB BASICS has helped thousands of young men and women prepare to take this test. The format is clear and uncluttered, making the book easy to use. The current revised edition contains up-to-date information necessary for success on the current version of the ASVAB. You have made an excellent decision in choosing this book to help you prepare for the ASVAB.

ASVAB BASICS offers you
- Intensive practice in math and verbal areas
- Clear, easy-to-follow instructions
- General tips for taking tests
- Special preparation ideas for improving math and verbal skills
- Specific hands-on instruction
- Clear and detailed solution strategies for the tests
- Interesting information about the great opportunities in the military

To familiarize the reader with the math and verbal questions on the ASVAB, there are twelve practice tests for the four subtests enlistees must take in order to qualify for the Armed Forces, as well as many practice exercises.

The methods of instruction used in this book reflect the authors' understanding of learning styles and the need for clear directions and explanations. The *Mathematics* sections take the reader by the hand and work through concepts that are troublesome to many test-takers. The materials used in the *Paragraph Comprehension* sections are engaging and varied, with the inclusion of many contemporary topics designed to interest and motivate the reader to keep plugging and improve his or her language skills.

About the Authors

The authors of this book, Ronald M. Kaprov, Ed.D., and Steffi R. Kaprov, M.A., have extensive experience working with students in various educational and professional capacities, a lifelong interest in education, a special rapport with young adults, and the ability to help prepare them for qualifying tests. The authors have also written other best-selling test-preparation books.

The writers' special qualifications include experience as master teachers, knowledge of mathematics and English curriculum, experience in test preparation, expertise in educational psychology, and familiarity with learning styles. They have had successful careers in allied fields, such as writing, engineering for the U.S. Army, and school psychology.

INTRODUCTION

The Armed Services Vocational Aptitude Battery (ASVAB) is the selection and classification test used by all branches of the United States Armed Services. The military services use ASVAB scores to determine the qualifications of young people for enlistment and to place them in military occupational programs. For more information, see "Career Opportunities in the Uniformed Forces of the United States" in Part Three of this book.

The ASVAB consists of the following subjects:

Test Subjects

General Science (GS)

Arithmetic Reasoning (AR)

Word Knowledge (WK)

Paragraph Comprehension (PC)

Mathematics Knowledge (MK)

Electronics Information (EI)

Auto & Shop Information (AS)

Mechanical Comprehension (MC)

Assembling Objects (AO)*

Figure 1 on the following page presents the ASVAB tests, the time allowed for the administration of each test, the number of items in each test, and a description of the abilities or knowledge measured. The tests are designed to measure general abilities and information in specific areas covered in the general high school program or acquired through an interest or a hobby.

*NOTE: The Assembling Objects subtest is included only in the paper-and-pencil and the computer-adaptive (CAT) versions of the enlistment ASVAB. It is currently not included in the student ASVAB given in high schools or the AFCT (Armed Forces Classification Test) used when military personnel want to change jobs.

Figure 1.

TEST	TIME	ITEMS	DESCRIPTION
General Science	11 minutes	25	Measures knowledge of the physical and biological sciences.
Arithmetic Reasoning	36 minutes	30	Measures ability to solve arithmetic word problems.
Word Knowledge	11 minutes	35	Measures ability to select the correct meaning of words presented in context and to identify the best synonym for a given word.
Paragraph Comprehension	13 minutes	15	Measures ability to obtain information from written passages.
Mathematics Knowledge	24 minutes	25	Measures knowledge of general mathematics principles, including algebra and geometry.
Electronics Information	9 minutes	20	Measures knowledge of electricity, radio principles, and electronics.
Auto & Shop Information	11 minutes	25	Measures knowledge of automobiles, tools, and shop terminology and practices.
Mechanical Comprehension	19 minutes	25	Measures knowledge of mechanical and physical principles and ability to visualize how illustrated objects work.
Assembling Objects	9 minutes	16	Measures spatial reasoning and speed while performing tasks in a timed context.

ASVAB results are reported as both individual test scores and composite scores, which are combinations of subtest scores. One important composite score derived from the ASVAB is the Armed Forces Qualification Test (AFQT) score, which is used to determine who gets into the armed services. The AFQT score is calculated from the following four subtests:

Arithmetic Reasoning Raw Score

+ Mathematics Knowledge Raw Score

+ 2 × Word Knowledge Raw Score

+ 2 × Paragraph Comprehension Raw Score

= AFQT Raw Score

The AFQT Raw Score is then converted into a Percentile Score, which is used to determine eligibility for entrance into the military.

This book will prepare you for the four ASVAB subtests that form the AFQT score. It provides practice questions and skill reviews designed to help you build your basic math, verbal, and academic abilities up to the level needed to qualify for the armed services branch of your choice. (See Figure 2.)

Figure 2.

ACADEMIC ABILITY	VERBAL ABILITY	MATH ABILITY
Word Knowledge and Paragraph Comprehension + Arithmetic Reasoning and Mathematics Knowledge	Word Knowledge + Paragraph Comprehension	Arithmetic Reasoning + Mathematics Knowledge
Purpose Measures potential for further formal education	*Purpose* Measures capacity for verbal activities	*Purpose* Measures capacity for mathematical activities

How to Use This Book

This easy-to-use book will prepare you to do well on the ASVAB test. It's like studying with your own private tutor. It gives you all the help you need, and it allows you to work at your own pace. There are five different tools in this book that will help you increase your score.

1. Test-Taking Tips

2. General Tips for mathematics and verbal problems

3. Specific Suggestions for all math topics and English skills

4. Solution Strategies for all tests

5. Topic Reviews—a comprehensive summary of each math topic

Four Steps for Success

Step 1   TAKE THE PRETESTS
Take the Mathematics Pretest at the beginning of Part One and the Verbal Pretest at the beginning of Part Two of this book. Check your answers with the answer explanations at the end of each test. Each explanatory answer will refer you to the skill tested by that particular question.

Step 2   PRACTICE NEEDED SKILLS
Turn to the Skills Sections for the items in the Pretests that you missed or that you think need additional study on your part. Follow the directions and pay attention to the suggestions given in each section.

Step 3   TAKE THE FULL-LENGTH TESTS
Take the three full-length Sample Tests at the end of the Arithmetic Reasoning, Mathematics Knowledge, Word Knowledge, and Paragraph Comprehension chapters.

Step 4   REVIEW
Go back and review the sections that still give you trouble. Concentrate on the sections where you made the most errors on the Sample Tests.

How to Prepare for the ASVAB

General Timelines

1. Two months before the test, begin to use this book. Follow steps 1–4, listed above.

2. One month before the test, review this book, concentrating on the sections covering the material that was the hardest for you.

3. One week before the test, review again the hints and suggestions throughout the book and practice doing problems from each of the Mathematics Topics and English Skills sections.

4. The night before the test, go to bed early, try to relax, and have a positive attitude about how well you'll do on the test in the morning.

Study Skills to Increase Retention and Motivation

1. *Get your priorities straight:* Set up your work area in a quiet place and try to leave it ready each day for study. Have your colored markers, pens, pencils, and scrap paper ready so you can work any time you want. Study at least half an hour every day. Make a study plan and follow it.

2. *Be optimistic:* Visualize yourself doing well on the ASVAB. "I am going to do well on this test, and I am going to have a successful career in the military (or in another profession)."

3. *Feel good:* Make sure you get at least 7 to 8 hours of sleep each night. Exercise at least every other day, and eat healthy food. If you stay physically fit, you will be more alert and energetic for studying, for the test, and for doing well in your military career.

4. *As you study:* Try to review occasionally with another person who is also taking the ASVAB; if that's not possible, then talk to yourself as you review this material. This technique improves your memory. Using colored markers when studying increases your retention. Keep a sense of humor if possible.

Test-Taking Suggestions

1. Arrive in plenty of time, and dress in comfortable, layered clothing.

2. Bring a watch to help you keep track of testing time.

3. Follow all oral and written directions carefully.

4. Answer every question:

   • First, answer the questions that are easy for you.

   • Then, go back to answer the ones that need more thought.

   • As a last resort for any question, eliminate all impossible choices, then guess from the choices that remain.

5. Make certain that you record each answer in the right spot on the answer sheet.

GOOD LUCK!

A PREVIEW OF THE ASVAB MATH AND VERBAL TESTS

This section gives you samples of the math and verbal questions in the ASVAB test battery. It will show you what to expect and provide you with a better understanding of the types of questions that appear on the official test battery and on the practice tests in this book.

Sample Test 1

Arithmetic Reasoning (AR)

The Arithmetic Reasoning Test consists of 30 items. It covers basic mathematical problems encountered in everyday life. These questions are designed to measure general reasoning and the ability to solve mathematical problems.

Sample Test Items

1. If three hoses of equal length connected together reach 24 feet, how many hoses would be needed to reach 64 feet?
   1–A   6
   1–B   7
   1–C   8
   1–D   9

2. If 4 feet 5 inches is cut from a 12-foot board, how much of the original board remains?
   2–A   16 feet 5 inches
   2–B   8 feet 7 inches
   2–C   7 feet 10 inches
   2–D   7 feet 7 inches

3. A salesperson earns 30 percent commission on each sale made. How large a commission would the salesperson earn for selling $160 worth of merchandise?
   3–A $36
   3–B $40
   3–C $48
   3–D $50

4. It costs $0.50 per square yard to waterproof canvas. What will it cost to waterproof a canvas truck cover that is 15 feet × 24 feet?

4–A $6.67
4–B $18.00
4–C $20.00
4–D $180.00

5. A box that is 1 foot high, 9 feet wide, and 12 feet long measures how many cubic feet?

5–A   21
5–B   42
5–C   108
5–D   118

6. 30 inches is equal to

6–A $\frac{5}{6}$ yard

6–B   3 feet

6–C $\frac{5}{6}$ feet

6–D   3 yards

Answer Key

1. C	2. D	3. C	4. C	5. C
6. A				

Answers and Explanations

1–C   Make a simple sketch representing the information in the question.

3 hoses: $\longleftrightarrow$ 24 feet

H hoses: $\longleftrightarrow$ 64 feet

Let H be the number of hoses needed to make 64 feet. Set up a proportion:

$$\frac{\text{number of hoses}}{\text{total length}} \quad \frac{3}{24} = \frac{H}{64}$$

$$24H = 192 \ \text{(Cross-multiply.)}$$

$$H = \frac{192}{24} \ \text{(Divide by 24 to find } H\text{.)}$$

$$H = 8 \text{ hoses needed}$$

2–D   Subtract 4'5" from 12'.

12 feet = 11 feet + 12 inches:

$$
\begin{array}{rl}
 & 11\text{ feet} \quad 12\text{ inches} \\
- & \underline{\;4\text{ feet} \qquad 5\text{ inches}} \\
 & 7\text{ feet} \qquad 7\text{ inches}
\end{array}
$$

3–C   Commission = Rate (30%) × Selling Price ($160)

Change 30% to a decimal: $30\% = \dfrac{30}{100} = 0.30 = 0.3$

Therefore, the commission = 0.3 × $160 = $48

4–C   Calculate the area of the canvas in *square yards*. Then change *feet* to *yards*.

Since 1 yard = 3 feet, 15 feet = 5 yards, and 24 feet = 8 yards.

The area of the canvas = [length] × [width] = 5 yards × 8 yards = 40 yards²

The total cost = $0.50/yard² × 40 yards² = $20

5–C   The volume of the box = [length] × [width] × [height] = 12 feet × 9 feet × 1 foot = 108 feet³

6–A   First change *inches* to *feet*, and then change *feet* to *yards*.

$$
30\ \cancel{\text{inches}} \times \frac{1\ \cancel{\text{foot}}}{12\ \cancel{\text{inches}}} \times \frac{1\ \text{yard}}{3\ \cancel{\text{feet}}} = \frac{\overset{10}{\cancel{30}}}{12 \times \underset{1}{\cancel{3}}} = \frac{10}{12} = \frac{5}{6}\ \text{yards}
$$

Sample Test 2

Mathematics Knowledge (MK)

The Mathematics Knowledge Test consists of 25 items. It is designed to measure general mathematical knowledge. It is a test of your ability to solve problems using high school mathematics, including algebra and some basic geometry.

Sample Test Items

1. If $2a + 6 = 5$, then a is equal to

    1–A   0

    1–B $-\dfrac{1}{2}$

    1–C -1

    1–D $\dfrac{7}{6}$

2. What is the area of this square?

    2–A   1 square foot
    2–B   25 square feet
    2–C   .10 square feet
    2–D   .25 square feet

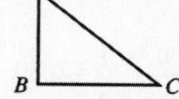

3. If 50% of $B = 66$, then $B =$

    3–A   33
    3–B   66
    3–C   99
    3–D   132

4. In the given triangle, angle B is 90 degrees. Which side of the triangle is the longest?

    4–A $\overline{AB}$
    4–B $\overline{AC}$
    4–C   Neither
    4–D   Can't be determined from the information given

5. If $3x = -5$, then $2x =$

    5–A $\dfrac{3}{5}$

    5–B $-\dfrac{10}{3}$

    5–C $-\dfrac{3}{5}$

    5–D -2

6. If you multiply $x + 3$ by $2x + 5$, what will be the coefficient of x in the product?

    6–A   3
    6–B   6
    6–C   9
    6–D   11

Answer Key				
1. B	2. D	3. D	4. B	5. B
6. D				

Answers and Explanations

1–B   The original equation is $2a + 6 = 5$. Solve:

$$2a\ +\ 6 = 5\ \ \text{(Subtract by 6 on both sides.)}$$
$$2a = -1\ \ \text{(Divide by 2 on both sides.)}$$
$$a = -\frac{1}{2}$$

2–D   The formula for the *area of a square* is: Area = [side] × [side].

Substituting: A = .5 feet × .5 feet = .25 feet^2

3–D   Write the information in the question algebraically and solve for B.

First change 50% to a decimal: $50\% = \dfrac{50}{100} = \dfrac{1}{2} = 0.50 = 0.5$

0.5 of $B = 0.5 \times B = 66$

Divide each side by 0.5 to find the value of B:

$$B = \frac{66}{0.5} = 132$$

4–B   Reason this one out *intuitively*. In a triangle, the larger an angle, the larger is the side opposite it. You can show this to yourself by slowly widening the angle formed by your own index finger and thumb and examining this distance between them.

Since angle B is the largest angle, 90°, side AC must be the largest side.

5–B   Solve algebraically for the value of x; then double your answer to find $2x$.

$$3x = -5\ \ \text{(Divide both sides by 3.)}$$
$$x = -\frac{5}{3}\ \ \text{(Multiply both sides by 2.)}$$
$$2x = 2 \times \left(-\frac{5}{3}\right) = -\frac{10}{3}$$

6–D   Multiply the two binomials and add the two x-terms.

$$\overset{\displaystyle 5x}{(x + 3)(2x + 5)}$$
$$\underset{\displaystyle 6x}{}$$

Adding, we get $5x + 6x = 11x$. Thus, the coefficient of x in the product is 11.

Sample Test 3

Word Knowledge (WK)

The Word Knowledge Test consists of 35 items. It is designed to test your ability to *understand the meaning of words* through the use of synonyms—words having the same or nearly the same meaning as other words in the language. Word Knowledge, or vocabulary, is tested because it is an important factor in assessing a person's reading and verbal comprehension skills.

The words used in these synonym questions are those used in everyday language. The test questions may appear in either of two forms, as follows:

1. The key word appears in the stem and is followed by "most nearly means" (Sample Test items 1–3).

2. The key word is used in a sentence (Sample Test items 4–6).

Sample Test Items

1. Small most nearly means
    - 1–A   cheap
    - 1–B   round
    - 1–C   sturdy
    - 1–D   little

2. Impair most nearly means
    - 2–A   direct
    - 2–B   weaken
    - 2–C   improve
    - 2–D   stimulate

3. Cease most nearly means
    - 3–A   stop
    - 3–B   start
    - 3–C   change
    - 3–D   continue

4. The wind is variable today.
    - 4–A   mild
    - 4–B   steady
    - 4–C   shifting
    - 4–D   chilling

5. The student <u>discovered</u> an error.

    5–A   found

    5–B   entered

    5–C   searched

    5–D   enlarged

6. Do not <u>obstruct</u> the entrance to the building.

    6–A   block

    6–B   enter

    6–C   leave

    6–D   cross

Answer Key

1. D	2. B	3. A	4. C	5. A
6. A				

Answers and Explanations

1–D   The word *small* is a common word meaning tiny in size, short, meager, trivial, or *little*. Therefore, choice D is the correct answer.

2–B   To *impair* something is to make it worse, or to damage it. Choice B, which is *weaken*, is the closest in meaning and the correct answer. Choices C and D are almost opposite in meaning, and choice A, *direct*, is not related at all.

3–A   The word *cease* means to bring an activity to a halt—in other words, to discontinue or *stop* doing something. Therefore, the correct answer is A, *stop*.

4–C   In this question, the context of the sentence can help you figure out the meaning of the underlined word, *variable*. You can eliminate choice A since it doesn't fit in the sentence, which would become "The wind is *mild* today." The word *variable* comes from the verb *vary*, which means to change, shift, or make different. Therefore, the correct answer is choice C, *shifting*, which means that the wind is changeable.

5–A   The word *discovered* means *found*, uncovered, unearthed, or learned. Choice A is correct. If you substitute any of the other choices in the sentence, it loses its meaning.

6–A   Here you can see that only the correct choice, *block*, makes any sense if substituted for *obstruct* in this sentence. To *obstruct* means to *block*, bar, put an obstacle in the way, or impede access to something. Therefore, choice A is the correct answer.

Sample Test 4

Paragraph Comprehension (PC)

The Paragraph Comprehension Test consists of 15 items, each a reading passage of 30 to 120 words presented in one or more paragraphs. This test is given to measure your ability to read and comprehend written material. Most reading passages will have just one question each, while others may have two or more questions. Each question should be answered solely on the basis of information contained in or implied by the reading selection.

Sample Test Items

1. Horses are a unique symbol of the Old West. Ridden by cowboys and Indians, these tough and intelligent animals were the descendents of the sixteenth-century Spanish mustangs brought by the conquistadors as they explored what is now the Southwest. Many of these horses escaped into the wild, where they survive to this day. Currently, in spite of protective laws, these proud and noble wild horses are in serious trouble because of encroachments on their terrain.

    Which of the following is implied by this passage?

    1–A   Horses were not very important in the Old West.

    1–B   Legal protections are no longer needed to protect wild horses.

    1–C   Wild horses are descended from the ones brought from China.

    1–D   America's wild horses need better protection if they are to survive.

2. "Buffalo Bill" Cody did many amazing things even before he became famous. He rode for the Pony Express, scouted for the U.S. Army, guided royalty on big game hunting trips, hunted buffalo, fought in the Civil War, won the Medal of Honor, and also was a star of the American stage. He did all of this before he was 30 years old. If you are interested in knowing more about this remarkable man, visit the *Buffalo Bill Historical Center* in Cody, Wyoming.

    According to the paragraph, "Buffalo Bill"

    2–A   came from a large family.

    2–B   was a movie star.

    2–C   was a man of many talents.

    2–D   liked many sports.

3. The 528 refuges of the National Wildlife Refuge System are among the greatest of America's natural treasures. They total 95 million acres and are spread throughout the United States, providing protection for many diverse forms of wildlife and different kinds of landscapes. Included are such places as the cypress swamps of Okefenokee, the marshes of San Francisco Bay, and the pristine Alaska ANWR preserve.

    As used above, the word *pristine* means
    3–A   pure
    3–B   noisy
    3–C   wild
    3–D   large

4. The great Sahara Desert in North Africa, covering more than 3.5 million square miles, is now considered too hot and dry to inhabit for the most part. However, findings of fossils, rock art, stone artifacts, bone harpoons, and shells suggest that these areas had dense populations of people thousands of years ago. The remains of giraffes, elephants, antelopes, fish, crocodiles, hippopotamuses, and other aquatic animals suggest that water was once abundant as well.

    According to this passage, you can infer that
    4–A   elephants once roamed the desert.
    4–B   hippopotamuses don't require much water.
    4–C   the climate of the Sahara Desert was different thousands of years ago.
    4–D   the Sahara Desert has grown in size.

Answer Key

1. D   2. C   3. A   4. C

Answers and Explanations

1–D   The last sentence of the passage states that these horses are in "serious trouble" because of encroachments, or invasions, into their grazing lands. So the implication is that wild horses need better protection than they are currently receiving, making choice D the correct answer. Choice A is incorrect because, according to the first sentence, horses were a "symbol" of the Old West, thus implying that they were very important. Choice B is contradicted by the passage. Choice C is wrong, since the passage states that these horses were descended from Spanish mustangs, not Chinese horses.

2–C   The general purpose of the paragraph is to tell you of the many accomplishments of "Buffalo Bill" as a young man. The wide variety of activities listed—in the Armed Services, on the stage, hunting, etc.—tell you that he had many talents and capabilities. The correct answer therefore has to be choice C. The remaining choices are not supported by the passage.

3–A   The word *pristine* means *pure*, unspoiled, uncorrupted, fresh, and clean. It means that the Alaska ANWR preserve is not inhabited or changed by humans, that it remains unpolluted by civilization.

4–C   The passage states that the Sahara once had lots of water and abundant animal and human life, as shown by all the fossils that have been found. The implication is that thousands of years ago, the Sahara was not a hot and dry desert but instead must have had a different and better climate. Therefore, the correct answer is C.

PART I

IMPROVING MATH SKILLS

INTRODUCTION TO THE ASVAB MATH TESTS

GENERAL TIPS

Practice math daily in an informal way. Since math skills enter into everything you do, both the military and in civilian life, get into the habit of thinking in terms of numbers. For example, when shopping, mentally add up the cost before coming to the cash register. Or, when driving on a long trip, figure out the cost in terms of gas and tolls. If you are working on a project or creating something, estimate how much material you need and how much it will cost. Think in terms of *using numbers,* and you will become very good at doing mental arithmetic. In this way, you can practice your math skills as you go about your daily routine, and you will be more confident and have an easier time when you study for tests like the ASVAB.

Read and study *Part Two—Improving Verbal Skills* in this book. Taking math tests involves the need for good reading skills. Math examples often require you to read many sentences, and you must understand them in order to answer the questions correctly. While the *Improving Verbal Skills* section is designed to prepare you for the English portions of the ASVAB, it is an important aid in succeeding on the ASVAB math tests as well.

TEST-TAKING TIPS FOR THE ASVAB MATH TESTS

1. *Use Plenty of Scrap Paper*

   • When working out a problem, use scrap paper to organize your thoughts.

   • Number each page (if more than one) and each problem to keep track of your work.

   • Work neatly so your calculations won't run into each other; otherwise the result will be confusion and needless errors.

2. *Manage Your Time During Each Part of the Test*

The test is a timed test. You must stop work when signaled. Therefore, you should work quickly and deliberately.

- Start by approximating how much time you have to solve each problem:

$$\frac{\text{Total Time for That Section}}{\text{Total Number of Problems}} = \text{the approximate time you should spend working on}$$

  any one problem.

- If you are unsure of the answer to a question, eliminate any impossible choices. Then choose the *best* answer from the remaining choices.

- Make a mark (for example a "?" or "*") in the margin of the test paper if you are unsure of a solution. Return to it if you have time at the end of that section.

3. *The Problem and the Solution Should Make Sense*

Especially with word problems, ask yourself, "Does my calculated answer make sense?"

For example, if you have $200 to make purchases, and you buy a few things, then the amount you have left must be *less than* $200. If the estimated purchases are about $120 (after rounding them off), then the correct choice, $80, makes sense.

4. *Try to Approximate the Solution*

Before doing a lot of computations to get the *exact* solution, sometimes you can shorten your efforts. You may be able to quickly arrive at an approximate answer by rounding off numbers and doing the required calculation in your head. You may even be able to eliminate some or all of the incorrect choices to get the correct answer.

Answer Sheet for Pretests and Practice Exercises

Arithmetic Reasoning Pretest

1. Ⓐ Ⓑ Ⓒ Ⓓ   2. Ⓐ Ⓑ Ⓒ Ⓓ   3. Ⓐ Ⓑ Ⓒ Ⓓ   4. Ⓐ Ⓑ Ⓒ Ⓓ   5. Ⓐ Ⓑ Ⓒ Ⓓ
6. Ⓐ Ⓑ Ⓒ Ⓓ   7. Ⓐ Ⓑ Ⓒ Ⓓ   8. Ⓐ Ⓑ Ⓒ Ⓓ   9. Ⓐ Ⓑ Ⓒ Ⓓ   10. Ⓐ Ⓑ Ⓒ Ⓓ

Mathematics Knowledge Pretest

1. Ⓐ Ⓑ Ⓒ Ⓓ   2. Ⓐ Ⓑ Ⓒ Ⓓ   3. Ⓐ Ⓑ Ⓒ Ⓓ   4. Ⓐ Ⓑ Ⓒ Ⓓ   5. Ⓐ Ⓑ Ⓒ Ⓓ
6. Ⓐ Ⓑ Ⓒ Ⓓ   7. Ⓐ Ⓑ Ⓒ Ⓓ   8. Ⓐ Ⓑ Ⓒ Ⓓ

Arithmetic Reasoning Practice Exercise 1

1. Ⓐ Ⓑ Ⓒ Ⓓ   2. Ⓐ Ⓑ Ⓒ Ⓓ   3. Ⓐ Ⓑ Ⓒ Ⓓ   4. Ⓐ Ⓑ Ⓒ Ⓓ   5. Ⓐ Ⓑ Ⓒ Ⓓ
6. Ⓐ Ⓑ Ⓒ Ⓓ   7. Ⓐ Ⓑ Ⓒ Ⓓ   8. Ⓐ Ⓑ Ⓒ Ⓓ   9. Ⓐ Ⓑ Ⓒ Ⓓ   10. Ⓐ Ⓑ Ⓒ Ⓓ
11. Ⓐ Ⓑ Ⓒ Ⓓ   12. Ⓐ Ⓑ Ⓒ Ⓓ   13. Ⓐ Ⓑ Ⓒ Ⓓ

Arithmetic Reasoning Practice Exercise 2

1. Ⓐ Ⓑ Ⓒ Ⓓ   2. Ⓐ Ⓑ Ⓒ Ⓓ   3. Ⓐ Ⓑ Ⓒ Ⓓ   4. Ⓐ Ⓑ Ⓒ Ⓓ   5. Ⓐ Ⓑ Ⓒ Ⓓ
6. Ⓐ Ⓑ Ⓒ Ⓓ   7. Ⓐ Ⓑ Ⓒ Ⓓ   8. Ⓐ Ⓑ Ⓒ Ⓓ

Arithmetic Reasoning Practice Exercise 3

1. Ⓐ Ⓑ Ⓒ Ⓓ   2. Ⓐ Ⓑ Ⓒ Ⓓ   3. Ⓐ Ⓑ Ⓒ Ⓓ   4. Ⓐ Ⓑ Ⓒ Ⓓ   5. Ⓐ Ⓑ Ⓒ Ⓓ
6. Ⓐ Ⓑ Ⓒ Ⓓ   7. Ⓐ Ⓑ Ⓒ Ⓓ   8. Ⓐ Ⓑ Ⓒ Ⓓ   9. Ⓐ Ⓑ Ⓒ Ⓓ   10. Ⓐ Ⓑ Ⓒ Ⓓ
11. Ⓐ Ⓑ Ⓒ Ⓓ   12. Ⓐ Ⓑ Ⓒ Ⓓ

Arithmetic Reasoning Practice Exercise 4

1. Ⓐ Ⓑ Ⓒ Ⓓ   2. Ⓐ Ⓑ Ⓒ Ⓓ   3. Ⓐ Ⓑ Ⓒ Ⓓ   4. Ⓐ Ⓑ Ⓒ Ⓓ   5. Ⓐ Ⓑ Ⓒ Ⓓ

6. Ⓐ Ⓑ Ⓒ Ⓓ   7. Ⓐ Ⓑ Ⓒ Ⓓ   8. Ⓐ Ⓑ Ⓒ Ⓓ   9. Ⓐ Ⓑ Ⓒ Ⓓ   10. Ⓐ Ⓑ Ⓒ Ⓓ

11. Ⓐ Ⓑ Ⓒ Ⓓ   12. Ⓐ Ⓑ Ⓒ Ⓓ

Arithmetic Reasoning Practice Exercise 5

1. Ⓐ Ⓑ Ⓒ Ⓓ   2. Ⓐ Ⓑ Ⓒ Ⓓ   3. Ⓐ Ⓑ Ⓒ Ⓓ   4. Ⓐ Ⓑ Ⓒ Ⓓ   5. Ⓐ Ⓑ Ⓒ Ⓓ

6. Ⓐ Ⓑ Ⓒ Ⓓ   7. Ⓐ Ⓑ Ⓒ Ⓓ   8. Ⓐ Ⓑ Ⓒ Ⓓ   9. Ⓐ Ⓑ Ⓒ Ⓓ   10. Ⓐ Ⓑ Ⓒ Ⓓ

Arithmetic Reasoning Practice Exercise 6

1. Ⓐ Ⓑ Ⓒ Ⓓ   2. Ⓐ Ⓑ Ⓒ Ⓓ   3. Ⓐ Ⓑ Ⓒ Ⓓ   4. Ⓐ Ⓑ Ⓒ Ⓓ   5. Ⓐ Ⓑ Ⓒ Ⓓ

6. Ⓐ Ⓑ Ⓒ Ⓓ   7. Ⓐ Ⓑ Ⓒ Ⓓ   8. Ⓐ Ⓑ Ⓒ Ⓓ   9. Ⓐ Ⓑ Ⓒ Ⓓ   10. Ⓐ Ⓑ Ⓒ Ⓓ

Arithmetic Reasoning Practice Exercise 7

1. Ⓐ Ⓑ Ⓒ Ⓓ   2. Ⓐ Ⓑ Ⓒ Ⓓ   3. Ⓐ Ⓑ Ⓒ Ⓓ   4. Ⓐ Ⓑ Ⓒ Ⓓ   5. Ⓐ Ⓑ Ⓒ Ⓓ

6. Ⓐ Ⓑ Ⓒ Ⓓ   7. Ⓐ Ⓑ Ⓒ Ⓓ   8. Ⓐ Ⓑ Ⓒ Ⓓ   9. Ⓐ Ⓑ Ⓒ Ⓓ   10. Ⓐ Ⓑ Ⓒ Ⓓ

Arithmetic Reasoning Practice Exercise 8

1. Ⓐ Ⓑ Ⓒ Ⓓ   2. Ⓐ Ⓑ Ⓒ Ⓓ   3. Ⓐ Ⓑ Ⓒ Ⓓ   4. Ⓐ Ⓑ Ⓒ Ⓓ   5. Ⓐ Ⓑ Ⓒ Ⓓ

6. Ⓐ Ⓑ Ⓒ Ⓓ   7. Ⓐ Ⓑ Ⓒ Ⓓ   8. Ⓐ Ⓑ Ⓒ Ⓓ   9. Ⓐ Ⓑ Ⓒ Ⓓ   10. Ⓐ Ⓑ Ⓒ Ⓓ

11. Ⓐ Ⓑ Ⓒ Ⓓ

Arithmetic Knowledge Practice Exercise 1

1.Ⓐ Ⓑ Ⓒ Ⓓ   2.Ⓐ Ⓑ Ⓒ Ⓓ   3.Ⓐ Ⓑ Ⓒ Ⓓ   4.Ⓐ Ⓑ Ⓒ Ⓓ   5.Ⓐ Ⓑ Ⓒ Ⓓ
6.Ⓐ Ⓑ Ⓒ Ⓓ   7.Ⓐ Ⓑ Ⓒ Ⓓ   8.Ⓐ Ⓑ Ⓒ Ⓓ   9.Ⓐ Ⓑ Ⓒ Ⓓ   10.Ⓐ Ⓑ Ⓒ Ⓓ

Arithmetic Knowledge Practice Exercise 2

1.Ⓐ Ⓑ Ⓒ Ⓓ   2.Ⓐ Ⓑ Ⓒ Ⓓ   3.Ⓐ Ⓑ Ⓒ Ⓓ   4.Ⓐ Ⓑ Ⓒ Ⓓ   5.Ⓐ Ⓑ Ⓒ Ⓓ
6.Ⓐ Ⓑ Ⓒ Ⓓ   7.Ⓐ Ⓑ Ⓒ Ⓓ   8.Ⓐ Ⓑ Ⓒ Ⓓ   9.Ⓐ Ⓑ Ⓒ Ⓓ   10.Ⓐ Ⓑ Ⓒ Ⓓ

Arithmetic Knowledge Practice Exercise 3

1.Ⓐ Ⓑ Ⓒ Ⓓ   2.Ⓐ Ⓑ Ⓒ Ⓓ   3.Ⓐ Ⓑ Ⓒ Ⓓ   4.Ⓐ Ⓑ Ⓒ Ⓓ   5.Ⓐ Ⓑ Ⓒ Ⓓ
6.Ⓐ Ⓑ Ⓒ Ⓓ   7.Ⓐ Ⓑ Ⓒ Ⓓ   8.Ⓐ Ⓑ Ⓒ Ⓓ   9.Ⓐ Ⓑ Ⓒ Ⓓ   10.Ⓐ Ⓑ Ⓒ Ⓓ

Arithmetic Knowledge Practice Exercise 4

1.Ⓐ Ⓑ Ⓒ Ⓓ   2.Ⓐ Ⓑ Ⓒ Ⓓ   3.Ⓐ Ⓑ Ⓒ Ⓓ   4.Ⓐ Ⓑ Ⓒ Ⓓ   5.Ⓐ Ⓑ Ⓒ Ⓓ
6.Ⓐ Ⓑ Ⓒ Ⓓ   7.Ⓐ Ⓑ Ⓒ Ⓓ   8.Ⓐ Ⓑ Ⓒ Ⓓ   9.Ⓐ Ⓑ Ⓒ Ⓓ   10.Ⓐ Ⓑ Ⓒ Ⓓ

Arithmetic Knowledge Practice Exercise 5

1.Ⓐ Ⓑ Ⓒ Ⓓ   2.Ⓐ Ⓑ Ⓒ Ⓓ   3.Ⓐ Ⓑ Ⓒ Ⓓ   4.Ⓐ Ⓑ Ⓒ Ⓓ   5.Ⓐ Ⓑ Ⓒ Ⓓ
6.Ⓐ Ⓑ Ⓒ Ⓓ   7.Ⓐ Ⓑ Ⓒ Ⓓ   8.Ⓐ Ⓑ Ⓒ Ⓓ   9.Ⓐ Ⓑ Ⓒ Ⓓ   10.Ⓐ Ⓑ Ⓒ Ⓓ

Arithmetic Knowledge Practice Exercise 6

1.Ⓐ Ⓑ Ⓒ Ⓓ   2.Ⓐ Ⓑ Ⓒ Ⓓ   3.Ⓐ Ⓑ Ⓒ Ⓓ   4.Ⓐ Ⓑ Ⓒ Ⓓ   5.Ⓐ Ⓑ Ⓒ Ⓓ
6.Ⓐ Ⓑ Ⓒ Ⓓ   7.Ⓐ Ⓑ Ⓒ Ⓓ   8.Ⓐ Ⓑ Ⓒ Ⓓ   9.Ⓐ Ⓑ Ⓒ Ⓓ   10.Ⓐ Ⓑ Ⓒ Ⓓ

Arithmetic Knowledge Practice Exercise 7

1.(A)(B)(C)(D) 2.(A)(B)(C)(D) 3.(A)(B)(C)(D) 4.(A)(B)(C)(D) 5.(A)(B)(C)(D)
6.(A)(B)(C)(D) 7.(A)(B)(C)(D) 8.(A)(B)(C)(D) 9.(A)(B)(C)(D) 10.(A)(B)(C)(D)

Arithmetic Knowledge Practice Exercise 8

1.(A)(B)(C)(D) 2.(A)(B)(C)(D) 3.(A)(B)(C)(D) 4.(A)(B)(C)(D) 5.(A)(B)(C)(D)
6.(A)(B)(C)(D) 7.(A)(B)(C)(D) 8.(A)(B)(C)(D) 9.(A)(B)(C)(D) 10.(A)(B)(C)(D)

CHAPTER 2

MATHEMATICS PRETEST

This test will show you which mathematical skills will be tested on the ASVAB. Solve each of the following problems and then check your answers against the solutions that follow the test. Each answer is followed by the page numbers where the particular topic area is reviewed.

ARITHMETIC REASONING

This test has 10 questions. Each question has four answer choices lettered A, B, C, and D. Solve each problem. Then mark your choice of the correct answer on the answer sheet. When you have completed the test, check your answers against the answer explanations that follow this sample test.

1. If doughnuts are bought for $6 a dozen and sold for $.60 each, what is the profit on the sale of 2 dozen doughnuts?

    1–A $1.20

    1–B $2.40

    1–C $12.00

    1–D $14.40

2. Josh and Millie have a budget of $3000 to purchase furniture for their new apartment. If they buy a sofa for $1200, two lamps for $120 each, and 3 rugs for $350 each, how much money is left in their furniture budget?

    2–A $510

    2–B $1200

    2–C $2490

    2–D $5000

3. Three fourths of the 160 seniors at Mayberry High School plan to go on to additional education or training after graduation. Of these, 55% plan to attend a four-year college, 25% plan to attend a two-year college, and 20% plan to seek vocational or technical training. How many of these students plan to attend a two-year college?

   3–A   120
   3–B   40
   3–C   30
   3–D   20

4. Daniel, a druggist, wants to know how many antibiotic pills he can make out of 1.5 kilograms of drug X if each pill requires 5 milligrams of drug X.

   4–A   1,500
   4–B   30,000
   4–C   300,000
   4–D   1,500,000

5. John decided to make new swings for the playground. If each swing is 1.8 feet in length, how many swings can John make out of a piece of wood that is 15 feet long?

   5–A   15
   5–B   10
   5–C   9
   5–D   8

6. A special fish tank contains 3 catfish, 5 goldfish, 2 angelfish, and 2 pilot fish. If the special tank contains the same distribution of fish as is found in a large aquarium tank holding 240 fish, how many catfish will be found in the large tank?

   6–A   25
   6–B   60
   6–C   12
   6–D   3

7. Pam, Jeff, and Liz went fishing and caught 8, 20, and 11 fish, respectively. What was the average number of fish caught?

   7–A   9
   7–B   10
   7–C   13
   7–D   14

Questions 8 to 10 refer to the following graph.

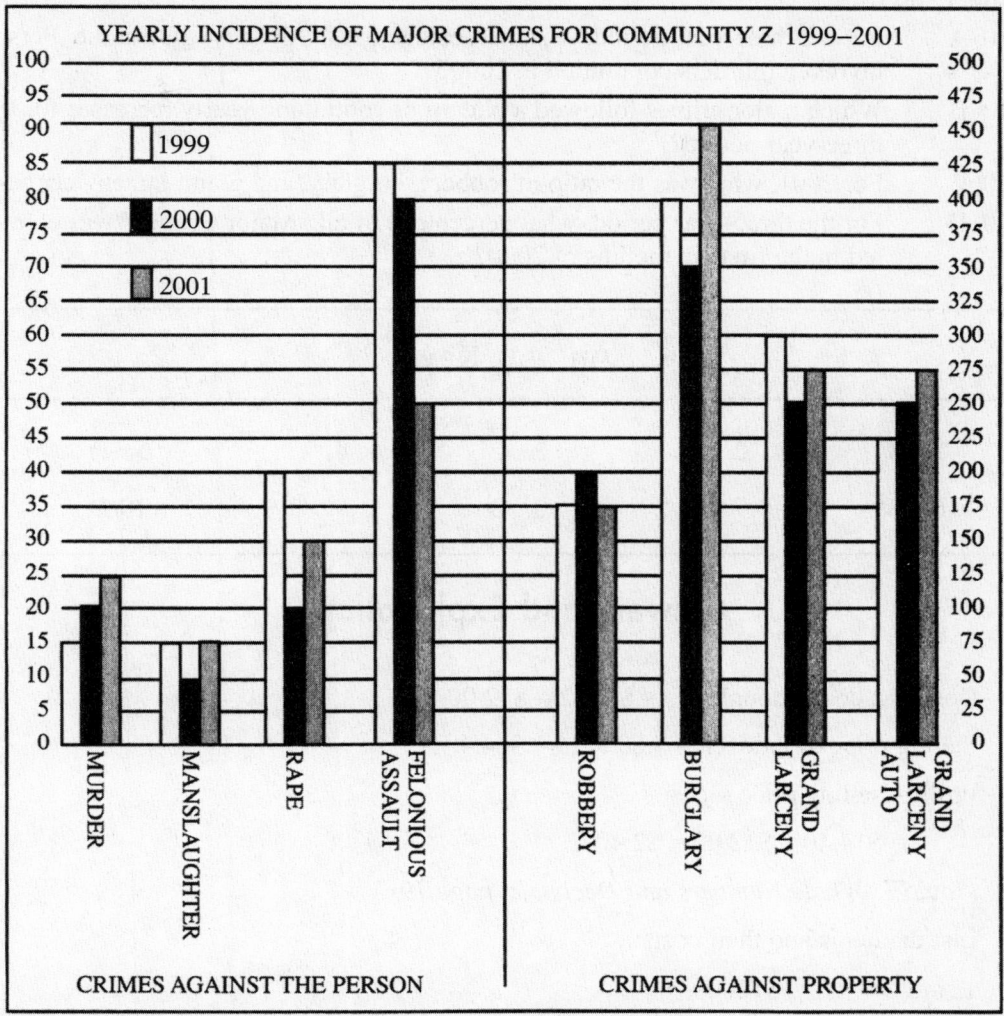

YEARLY INCIDENCE OF MAJOR CRIMES FOR COMMUNITY Z 1999–2001

8. In 2001, the incidence of which of the following crimes was greater than in the previous two years?

   8–A   Grand larceny
   8–B   Murder
   8–C   Rape
   8–D   Robbery

9. The above graph indicates that the *percentage* increase in grand larceny auto from 2000 to 2001 was

   9–A   5%
   9–B   10%
   9–C   15%
   9–D   20%

10. Which of the following cannot be determined because there is not enough information in the graph to do so?

 10–A   For the three-year period, what percentage of all "Crimes Against the Person" involved murders committed in 2000?

 10–B   Which major crimes followed a pattern of continuing yearly increases for the three-year period?

 10–C   For 2001, what was the ratio of robbery, burglary, and grand-larceny crimes?

 10–D   For the three-year period, what percentage of all "Major Crimes" was committed in the first six months of 2000?

Answer Key

1. B	2. A	3. C	4. C	5. D
6. B	7. C	8. B	9. B	10. D

Answers and Explanations

1–B   Cost of 2 dozen doughnuts = $6 × 2 = $12.00

Selling price of 2 dozen = $.60 × 24 = $14.40

Profit = selling price – cost

 = $14.40 – $12.00 = $2.40

(Topic 1: Whole Numbers and Decimals, page 19)

2–A   List the items and their costs:

1 sofa	=	$1200
2 lamps		
2 × $120	=	$240
3 rugs		
3 × $350	=	$1050
Total		$2490

Be careful! This is not the answer.

To find out how much money is left, subtract:

$3000 – $2490 = $510

TIP: Underline what is asked for (how much money is left) so that you give the correct answer and not an intermediate one.

(Topic 2: Making Purchases, page 30)

3–C   Find the number of students who plan to seek additional education or training:

$$\frac{3}{4} \text{ of } 60 = \frac{3}{\overset{}{\underset{1}{4}}} \times \overset{40}{\cancel{160}} = 120$$

Find the number planning to attend a two-year college:

25% of 120 = .25 × 120 = 30

(Topic 3: Fractions and Percents, page 37)

4–C   Make a sketch:

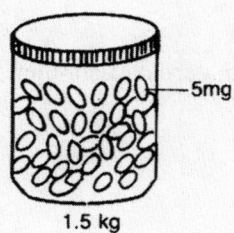

Notice that there are two different units (kilograms and milligrams). That means you must solve this problem in two steps:

Step 1: Convert kilograms and milligrams to grams:

$$1 \text{ kg} = 1000 \text{ gm}$$
$$1.5 \text{ kg} = 1000 \times 1.5 = 1500 \text{ gm}$$
$$1 \text{ mg} = \frac{1}{1,000} \text{ gm} = .001 \text{ gm}$$
$$5 \text{ mg} = .001 \times 5 = .005 \text{ gm}$$

Step 2: Divide total amount of drug X by amount of X in each pill:

$$\frac{\text{total}}{\text{amount per pill}} = \frac{1500}{.005} = \frac{1,500,000}{5} = 300,000 \text{ pills}$$

(Topic 4: Numbers with Units, page 52)

5–D   Plan: Draw a rough sketch:

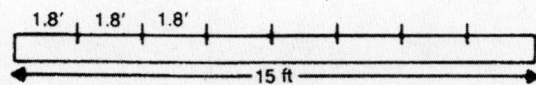

The picture shows that to find the answer, you must divide 1.8 into 15. First, get rid of the decimal point in the divisor by moving it one place to the right. This means you must also move the decimal point in the dividend one place to the right.

$$\frac{15}{1.8} = \frac{150}{18} \approx 8 \quad \text{(Ignore any leftover wood, since it would be too short for another swing.)}$$

Remember: A sketch often helps to make the problem seem easier. Also, it may give you an insight into a problem that you don't know how to start.

(Topic 5: Parts of a Whole, page 65)

6–B   Write a fraction that shows the ratio of catfish to all fish in the special tank:

$$\frac{\text{catfish}}{\text{all fish}} = \frac{3}{3+5+2+2} = \frac{3}{12} = \frac{1}{4}$$

"Same distribution" means if $\frac{1}{4}$ of the fish in the special tank are catfish, then $\frac{1}{4}$ of the fish in the large tank are catfish:

$$\frac{1}{4} \text{ of } 240 = \frac{1}{\cancel{4}} \times \cancel{240}^{60} = 60 \text{ catfish in large tank}$$

(Topic 6: Ratio and Proportion, page 72)

7–C   To find the average, find the sum of the number of fish caught and divide by the number of people fishing:

$$\text{Average} = \frac{8+20+11}{3} = \frac{39}{3} = 13$$

(Topic 7: Averages, page 80)

8–B   The incidence of murder increased from 15 in 1999 to 20 in 2000 to 25 in 2001.

9–B   The incidence of grand-larceny auto went from 250 in 2000 to 275 in 2001, an increase of 25. The percent increase is

$$\frac{25}{250} = .10 = 10\%$$

10–D   This graph gives information by year, not month. It is impossible to determine from the graph the percentage of crimes committed during the first six months of any year.

(Topic 8: Graphs, page 86)

MATHEMATICS KNOWLEDGE

This test has 8 questions. Each question has four answer choices lettered A, B, C, and D. Solve each problem. Then mark your choice of the correct answer on the answer sheet. When you have completed the test, check your answers against the answer explanations that follow this sample test.

1. If 40 miles is 25% of the total distance from Yorkville to Newtown, how many miles apart are these two towns?
   - 1–A   100
   - 1–B   140
   - 1–C   160
   - 1–D   200

2. $5(x + 2) - (2x - 3) =$
   - 2–A $3x$
   - 2–B $3x + 13$
   - 2–C $3x - 7$
   - 2–D $7x + 13$

3. Two cars start from the same point at the same time. One car drives north at 20 miles per hour and the other car drives south at 36 miles per hour. How many miles apart are the two cars after 30 minutes?
   - 3–A   10
   - 3–B   18
   - 3–C   28
   - 3–D   56

4. What is the distance covered in one revolution of a wheel whose diameter is 21 inches?
   (Use $\pi = \dfrac{22}{7}$)
   - 4–A   33 inches
   - 4–B   66 inches
   - 4–C   224 inches
   - 4–D   441 inches

5. What is the perimeter of a square whose area is 49 square inches?
   - 5–A   21 inches
   - 5–B   28 inches
   - 5–C   49 inches
   - 5–D   54 inches

6. What is the area, in square feet, of the triangular plot of land shown below?

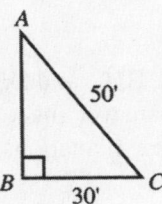

6–A	2400
6–B	150
6–C	1200
6–D	600

7. $\left(3\sqrt{5}\right)^2 =$

7–A	15
7–B	30
7–C	45
7–D	50

8. What is the next number in the following sequence?

7.36, 7.27, 7.18, 7.09, 7.00, _____

8–A	6.95
8–B	7.02
8–C	6.92
8–D	6.91

Answer Key

1. C	2. B	3. C	4. B	5. B
6. D	7. C	8. D		

Answers and Explanations

1–C   Translate the words into an equation and solve.

Let x = total distance between towns. Then 25% of total distance = $.25x$

$$.25x = 40 \qquad \text{(Divide both sides by .25.)}$$

$$x = \frac{40}{.25}$$

$$= 160 \text{ miles}$$

(Topic 1: Writing and Solving Equations, page 135)

2–B   Multiply the first term by 5:

$5(x + 2) = 5x + 10$

Change signs of the second term and follow the rules for addition of signed numbers:

$$5x + 10$$
$$\underline{-2x + 3}$$
$$3x + 13$$

(Topic 2: Signed Numbers and Polynomials, page 143)

3–C   Make a sketch:

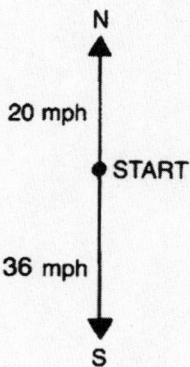

Use distance formula to find how far each car drove. Rate is in miles per hour, so change 30 minutes to $\frac{1}{2}$ hour.

$$D = R \times T \qquad D = R \times T$$
$$= 20 \times \frac{1}{2} \qquad = 36 \times \frac{1}{2}$$
$$= 10 \text{ miles} \qquad = 18 \text{ miles}$$

Since the cars are going in opposite directions, add the two distances to find the number of miles apart.

$10 + 18 = 28$ miles

(Topic 3: Using Formulas, page 150)

4–B   Distance covered in one revolution is the circumference of the wheel.

$$C = \pi d$$
$$= \pi \times 21$$
$$= \frac{22}{\cancel{7}_{1}} \times \frac{\cancel{21}^{3}}{1} = 66 \text{ inches}$$

(Topic 4: Circles, page 159)

5–B   Area of a square $= s^2$

$$49 = s^2$$

$$\sqrt{49} = s$$

$$7 = s$$

Perimeter of a square $= 4s$

$$= 4(7) = 28 \text{ inches}$$

(Topic 5: Quadrilaterals, page 167)

6–D ABC is a 3–4–5 right triangle, with each leg multiplied by 10.

$$\text{Leg } AB = 4 \times 10 = 40 \text{ ft}$$

$$\text{Area of triangle } ABC = \frac{1}{2} bh$$

$$= \frac{1}{2} \times 30 \times 40$$

$$= 600 \text{ square feet}$$

(Topic 6: Triangles, page 178)

7–C $\left(3\sqrt{5}\right)^2 = (3)^2 \times \left(\sqrt{5}\right)^2$

$$= 9 \times 5$$

$$= 45$$

(Topic 7: Powers, Roots, and Radicals, page 188)

8–D   This is a descending arithmetic sequence with a common difference of .09.

$(7.36 - .09 = 7.27)$

The last term is $7.00 - .09 = 6.91$

(Topic 8: Exponents and Sequences, page 195)

ARITHMETIC REASONING

TOPIC 1: WHOLE NUMBERS AND DECIMALS

Model Problem:

The military needed to extend an existing security fence to surround a military base as shown below. What was the total length of fencing material needed if 30 miles of fencing had already been constructed?

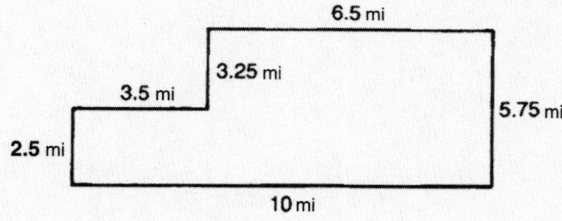

A 31.50

B 3.15

C 2.5

D 1.5

SOLUTION:

1. Add the measurements to find how many miles of fencing are required. Be sure to line up decimal points and add zeros so that each number has the same number of decimal places.

$$
\begin{array}{r}
2.50 \\
3.50 \\
3.25 \\
6.50 \\
5.75 \\
+\ 10.00 \\
\hline
\end{array}
$$

   31.50 miles of fencing needed

2. Subtract to find the difference between what the military needs and what it has.

   Needs   31.50 miles
   Has   − 30.00 miles
   _____
   1.50 miles of fencing to be bought

   Choice D is the correct answer.

> Now try Practice Exercise 1. Check your answers against the answers and explanations that follow and enter your score on the line provided. If your score is 10 or more, go on to Topic 2. If your score is less than 10, study the Topic Review before going on to the next topic area.

Practice Exercise 1

1. Add 37.03, 11.5627, 3.4005, 3423, and 1.141.
   1–A   3476.1342
   1–B   3500
   1–C   3524.4322
   1–D   3424.1342

2. Subtract 4.64324 from 7.
   2–A   3.35676
   2–B   2.35676
   2–C   2.3568
   2–D   11.6432

3. Find the product of 2.7 by 16.9.
   3–A   45.63
   3–B   43.2
   3–C   33.9
   3–D   19.6

4. What is 19.6 divided by 3.2, carried out to 3 decimal places?

    4–A   6.125

    4–B   6.124

    4–C   6.123

    4–D   5.123

5. What is $\dfrac{5}{11}$ in decimal form (to the nearest hundredth)?

    5–A   .44

    5–B   .55

    5–C   .40

    5–D   .45

6. A boy saved up $4.56 the first month, $3.82 the second month, and $5.06 the third month. How much did he save altogether?

    6–A $12.56

    6–B $13.28

    6–C $13.44

    6–D $14.02

7. The diameter of a certain rod is required to be 1.51 ± .015 inches. The rod would not be acceptable if the diameter measured

    7–A   1.490 inches

    7–B   1.500 inches

    7–C   1.510 inches

    7–D   1.525 inches

8. After an employer figures out an employee's salary of $190.57, he deducts $3.05 for Social Security and $5.68 for pension. What is the amount of the check after these deductions?

    8–A $181.84

    8–B $181.92

    8–C $181.93

    8–D $181.99

9. If the outer diameter of a metal pipe is 2.84 inches and the inner diameter is 1.94 inches, the thickness of the metal is

    9–A   .45 inches

    9–B   .90 inches

    9–C   1.94 inches

    9–D   2.39 inches

10. $230 \times 12 =$

    10–A   2300

    10–B   690

    10–C   2760

    10–D   3000

11. $175 \times 130 =$

   11–A   305
   11–B   2275
   11–C   22,000
   11–D   22,750

12. $203 \times 14 =$

   Round off your answer to the nearest tens place.

   12–A   284
   12–B   2840
   12–C   2900
   12–D   812

13. $621 \times 140 =$

   Round off your answer to the nearest thousands place.

   13–A   86,000
   13–B   2484
   13–C   86,940
   13–D   87,000

Your Score _____

Answer Key				
1. A	2. B	3. A	4. A	5. D
6. C	7. A	8. A	9. A	10. C
11. D	12. B	13. D		

Answers and Explanations

1–A   Line up all the decimal points one under the other. Then add:

```
      37.03
      11.5627
       3.4005
    3423.0000
+      1.141
    _____
    3476.1342
```

The correct choice can often be guessed by approximating the solution. Here, by adding the whole numbers only, we get 3475, which is *close* to choice A.

2–B   Add a decimal point and five zeros to the 7. Then subtract:

$$7.00000$$
$$-4.64324$$
$$\overline{2.35676}$$

3–A   To find the product means multiply.

$$\begin{array}{r} 16.9 \\ \times\, 2.7 \\ \hline 1183 \\ 338 \\ \hline 45.63 \end{array}$$

Since there are two decimal places in the multipliers, there must be two decimal places in the product, 45.63.

4–A   Omit the decimal point in the divisor by moving it one place to the right. Move the decimal point in the dividend one place to the right and add three zeros in order to carry your answer out to three decimal places, as instructed in the problem.

$$
\begin{array}{r}
6.125 \\
3.2\,)\overline{19.6,000} \\
\underline{192} \\
40 \\
\underline{32} \\
80 \\
\underline{64} \\
160 \\
\underline{160}
\end{array}
$$

5–D   To convert a fraction to a decimal, divide the numerator by the denominator:

$$
\begin{array}{r}
0.454 \\
11\,)\overline{5.000} \\
\underline{44} \\
60 \\
\underline{55} \\
50 \\
\underline{44} \\
6
\end{array}
$$

6–C   Add the savings for each month:

$4.56
 3.82
+ 5.06
$13.44

7–A

1.51	1.510
+.015	−.015
1.525	1.495

The rod's diameter may be between 1.495 inches to 1.525 inches, inclusive.

8–A   Add to find total deductions:

$3.05
+5.68
$8.73

Subtract total deductions from salary to find amount of check:

$190.57
−   8.73
$181.84

9–A   The difference of the two diameters equals the total thickness of the metal on *both* ends of the inner diameter.

  2.84
−1.94
  .90

.90 ÷ 2 = .45 = thickness of metal

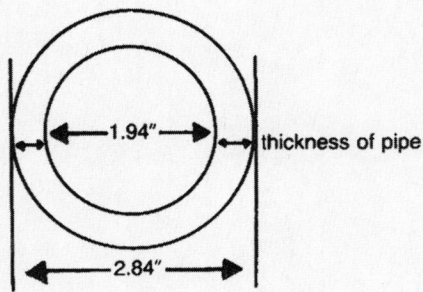

10–C
$$
\begin{array}{r}
230 \\
\times\ 12 \\
\hline
46 \\
23 \\
\hline
2760
\end{array}
$$

Note: In multiplying whole numbers, the final zero(s) may be dropped during computation and simply transferred to the answer. See Topic Review, item #10.

11–D
$$
\begin{array}{r}
175 \\
\times\,130 \\
\hline
525 \\
175 \\
\hline
22750
\end{array}
$$

Note: The last digit must be zero since $5 \times 0 = 0$. Therefore, the answer must be choice C or D.

12–B
$$
\begin{array}{r}
203 \\
\times\ 14 \\
\hline
812 \\
203 \\
\hline
2842
\end{array}
$$

Round off to tens place = 2840

13–D
$$
\begin{array}{r}
621 \\
\times\,140 \\
\hline
2484 \\
621 \\
\hline
86940
\end{array}
$$

Round off to thousands place = 87,000

Topic Review

Decimals

Addition and Subtraction of Decimals

1. Decimals are added and subtracted in the same way that whole numbers are added and subtracted, with the provision that the decimal points must be kept in a vertical line, one under the other. This determines the place of the decimal point in the answer.

    Example: Add 2.31, .037, 4, and 5.0017.

    SOLUTION: 2.3100
                    .0370
                   4.0000
               +5.0017
               11.3487

    Example: Subtract 4.0037 from 15.3.

    SOLUTION: 15.3000
               −4.0037
               11.2963

Multiplication of Decimals

2. Decimals are multiplied in the same way that whole numbers are multiplied.

    The number of decimal places in the product equals the sum of the decimal places in the multiplicand and in the multiplier.

    If there are fewer places in the product than this sum, then a sufficient number of zeros must be added in front of the product to equal the number of places required, and a decimal point is written in front of the zeros.

    Example: Multiply 2.372 by .012.

    SOLUTION: 2.372   (3 decimal places)
            × .012   (3 decimal places)
             4744
            2372
         .028464   (6 decimal places)

3. A decimal can be multiplied by a power of 10 by moving the decimal point to the right as many places as indicated by the power. If multiplied by 10, the decimal point is moved one place to the right; if multiplied by 100, the decimal point is moved two places to the right, etc.

    Example: $235 \times 10 = 2.35$

    $.235 \times 100 = 23.5$

    $.235 \times 1000 = 235$

Division of Decimals

4. When the dividend only is a decimal, the division is the same as that of whole numbers, except that a decimal point must be placed in the quotient exactly above the decimal point in the dividend.

    Example: Divide 12.864 by 32.

    SOLUTION:
    $$32\overline{)12.864}$$
    quotient $.402$

    128

    64

    64

5. When both divisor and dividend are decimals, the decimal point in the divisor is omitted and the decimal point in the dividend must be moved to the right as many decimal places as there were in the divisor. If there are not enough places in the dividend, zeros must be added to make up the difference.

    Example: Divide 2.62 by .131.

    SOLUTION: $.131\overline{)2.62} = 131\overline{)2620}$ quotient 20

    262

6. A decimal can be divided by a power of 10 by moving the decimal to the *left* as many places as indicated by the power. If divided by 10, the decimal point is moved one place to the left; if divided by 100, the decimal point is moved two places to the left; etc. If there are not enough places, add zeros in front of the number to make up the difference and add a decimal point.

    Example: .4 divided by $10 = .04$

    .4 divided by $100 = .004$

Conversion of Fractions to Decimals

7. A fraction can be changed to a decimal by dividing the numerator by the denominator and working out the division to as many decimal places as required.

    Example: Change $\dfrac{5}{11}$ to a decimal of 2 places.

    SOLUTION:

    $$\frac{5}{11} = 11\overline{\smash{)}5.00} \quad .45\tfrac{5}{11}$$

    $$\begin{array}{r} .45\tfrac{5}{11} \\ 11\overline{\smash{)}5.00} \\ \underline{44} \\ 60 \\ \underline{55} \\ 5 \end{array}$$

Conversion of Decimals to Fractions

8. Since a decimal point indicates a number having a denominator that is a power of 10, a decimal can be expressed as a fraction, the numerator of which is the number itself and the denominator of which is the power indicated by the number of decimal places in the decimal.

    Example: $.3 = \dfrac{3}{10}$

    $.47 = \dfrac{47}{100}$

Whole Numbers

Rounding Off Numbers

9. Rounding off a number means substituting an approximately equal number for a given number. Underline the desired "round off place," and then look at the digit to the right of it. If it is less than 5, just drop all the digits to the right of the underlined digit. If it is greater than or equal to 5, add 1 to the underlined digit and drop all the digits to the right of it.

    Let's look at an example to clarify these steps:

    Given the number 12.3456, round it off to the nearest,

a) thousandths place	12.345̲6	12.346
b) hundredths place	12.34̲56	12.35
c) tenths place	12.3̲456	12.3
d) units place	12̲.3456	12
e) tens place	1̲2.3456	10

    Note: In case e), a zero must be left where "2" stood to hold the place.

Final Zeros

10. In multiplying whole numbers, the final zero(s) may be dropped during computation and simply transferred to the answer.

Examples:

$$\begin{array}{r} 2310 \\ \times\ 150 \\ \hline 1155 \\ 231 \\ \hline 346500 \end{array} \qquad \begin{array}{r} 129 \\ \times\ 210 \\ \hline 129 \\ 258 \\ \hline 27090 \end{array} \qquad \begin{array}{r} 1760 \\ \times\ 205 \\ \hline 880 \\ 352 \\ \hline 360800 \end{array}$$

11. When there are final zeros in the divisor but no final zeros in the dividend, move the decimal point in the dividend to the left as many places as there are final zeros in the divisor and omit the final zeros.

Example: $2700.\overline{)37523} = 27.\overline{)375.23}$

TOPIC 2: MAKING PURCHASES

Model Problem:

Amy had a balance of $150 in her checking account, so she decided to pay a few bills. She wrote checks to the telephone company for $35.08, to Bill's Market for $55.23, and to the Corner Drug Store for $23.87. How much money was left in her checking account after these bills were paid?

A $264.18

B $114.18

C $46.82

D $35.82

SOLUTION:

1. Add to find total payments:

    $35.08
      55.23   Be sure to line up decimal points.
      23.87
    $114.18

2. Subtract total payments from amount in checking account:

    $150.00
    −114.18
    $35.82

    Choice D is the correct answer.

    Note: The check for subtraction is to add the answer to the amount subtracted. If correct, the answer will be the amount of Amy's original balance.

    $35.82
    +114.18
    $150.00

Now try Practice Exercise 2. Check your answers against the answers and explanations that follow and enter your score on the line provided. If your score is 6 or more, go on to Topic 3. If your score is less than 6, study the Topic Review before going on to the next topic area.

Practice Exercise 2

1. Irving collects empty cans and returns them to the supermarket for the 5-cent deposit due on each can. He plans to use the money to buy a baseball mitt that costs $35. So far, he has saved $20 toward the mitt. How many more cans must he collect in order to buy the mitt?

    1–A   15
    1–B   150
    1–C   300
    1–D   20

2. Carlos goes shopping and purchases 3 quarts of milk at $1.20 each and 2 dozen eggs at $.95 a dozen. If he gives the cashier $10 and gets $2 back, how much change is still due to Carlos?

    2–A $1.50
    2–B $2.50
    2–C $4.50
    2–D $5.00

3. June collects $150 to purchase equipment for the softball team. If she buys 8 softballs at $5 each, 9 mitts at $15 each, and chalk to line the field at $10, how much more money will she need to pay the bill for these items?

    3–A $35
    3–B $40
    3–C $45
    3–D $50

4. Paula and Pele are going on a canoe trip. They stop for provisions and purchase beef for $12, eggs for $1.20, a frying pan for $17.35, and 2 paddles at $15 each. How much did they spend for the provisions?

    4–A $45.55
    4–B $60.55
    4–C $65.00
    4–D $70.00

5. Alicia bought three items at the candy store for $3.47, $.45, and $2. How much change should she receive if she pays with a $20 bill?

    5–A $3.47
    5–B $5.92
    5–C $14.08
    5–D $15.08

6. Andrew needed some more fruit for his fruit salad. He bought 10 oranges (at 5 for $.75) and a 2-pound melon (at $1.50 per pound). How much change should he receive from $10?

    6–A $4.50

    6–B $5.50

    6–C $3.00

    6–D $1.50

7. Janice bought the following items for which she had "cents off" coupons: 1 double roll of paper towels (with a 40¢ off coupon) at $1.20, 2 quarts of milk (1 coupon for 50¢ off 1 quart) at $.80/quart, 1 box of laundry soap (coupon for $1.50 off) at $3.50. If she used all the coupons, what will Janice have to pay for her purchases?

    7–A $3.10

    7–B $3.40

    7–C $3.90

    7–D $6.80

8. Annisa bought chewing gum for $.45. She handed the cashier a $20 bill. What was the fewest number of bills the cashier could return to Annisa as change? (Assume that the cashier had $1.00s, $5.00s, $10.00s, and $20.00s in the register.)

    8–A $19.55

    8–B $20

    8–C   19

    8–D   6

Your Score _____

Answer Key				
1. C	2. B	3. A	4. B	5. C
6. B	7. C	8. D		

Answers and Explanations

1–C   Total cost for mitt $35

           Amount saved   <u>$20</u>

           Amount still needed $15

           If each can brings .05, then 20 cans will bring $1.00, and 20×15 will bring $15.

           $20 \times 15 = 300$ cans

2–B   The total cost:

3 Milk × $1.20 each $3.60

2 Doz. Eggs × $.95/doz   <u>$1.90</u>

Total Cost $5.50

Expected change from $10:

$10.00

<u>−$5.50</u>

  $4.50

The question asks how much change *is still due*.

  $4.50

<u>−$2.00</u>

  $2.50   is still owed to Carlos.

3–A   Total expenses:

Softballs:

8 × 5 $ 40

Mitts:

9 × 15 $135

Chalk   <u>$ 10</u>

Total $185

Total − $150 = additional money needed

$185 − $150 = $35

4–B   The total cost was:

Beef $12.00

Eggs $ 1.20

Fry Pan $17.35

Paddles

2 × 15   <u>$30.00</u>

Total $60.55   is the total cost.

(Remember to add a decimal point and two zeros for cash values like $12.)

5–C   Write the decimal equivalents under each other. Don't forget to line up the decimals so that the proper place values are added to each other.

$3.47
 $.45   (Fill in the tenths and hundredths with zeros.)
$2.00
$5.92

Subtract to find change due:

$20.00
−$5.92
$14.08

6–B   Oranges 5 for $ .75

10 for 2 × .75 $1.50

Melon   1 lb for $1.50

2 lb for $1.50 × 2 $3.00

Total $4.50

Change: $10.00 − $4.50 = $5.50

7–C   Make an organized list of items:

Paper Towels $1.20 − .40 (coup.) $ .80

2 Milk   2 × .80 = $1.60

              $1.60 − .50 (coup.) $1.10

Soap $3.50 − 1.50 (coup.) $2.00

Total $3.90

8–D $20.00 − $.45 = $19.55

The change could have been returned as $.55 + $10, $5, $1, $1, $1, $1, or 6 total bills (the fewest number of bills).

Topic Review

Money Problems

One very important use for decimals, and one with which you are familiar, is our money system. Our money system is based upon the decimal system. Each cent is a hundredth part of a dollar.

Adding and Subtracting Dollars and Cents

1. To add or subtract amounts expressed as dollars and cents, line up the decimal points so that dollars are under dollars and cents are under cents. Place a decimal point in the answer directly under the decimal point in the other numbers.

   Example: On the way home from work, Jeff did some shopping. He spent $9.85 in the supermarket, $1.75 in the drug store, and $3.65 at the cleaner's. How much money did Jeff spend?

   SOLUTION: $9.85

                           1.75   Line up the decimal points.

                           3.65

                  $15.25   Total the numbers and place the decimal point in the answer.

   Note: If an item has no decimals, as in $5, add a decimal point and 2 zeros to make it conform to the other items in the list. Thus, $5 becomes $5.00.

Multiplying Dollars and Cents

2. When multiplying dollars and cents by a whole number, place the decimal point before the last two figures of the product to separate the dollars from the cents.

   Example: Kim bought 3 blank tapes. Each tape was $2.75. What was the cost of the three tapes?

   SOLUTION: $2.75 × 3 = $8.25

Multiple Purchases

3. When a problem involves multiple purchases, make a list of each item and its cost. If special consideration is made, such as cost per pound or several items at the same cost, enter this information next to the item.

   Example: How much change is expected from $50 if the following items are purchased:

   1 loaf of bread at $1.15

   2 frozen pizzas at $2.40 each

   25 pounds of potatoes at 30 cents a pound

SOLUTION:

1. Make a list.

Item	Cost
1 loaf of bread	$1.15
2 pizzas at $2.40 =	4.80
25 lbs potatoes × $.30 =	7.50
Total Cost	$13.45

2. Subtract to find change due.

$$\begin{array}{r} \$50.00 \\ -13.45 \\ \hline \$36.55 \end{array}$$

CAUTION: Read all problems carefully. If the problem asks how much change is due, do not give the total cost for the items. It might be one of the choices offered, but it is *not* the answer to the problem.

TOPIC 3: FRACTIONS AND PERCENTS

Model Problem:

Carlton's birthday cake contains both brown and white sugar. If sugar accounts for $\frac{2}{5}$ of the weight of the cake, and 45% of the sugar used is brown sugar, how much brown sugar is needed for a cake that weighs 2 pounds?

   A 2.00 lbs

   B .80 lb

   C .45 lb

   D .36 lb

SOLUTION:

1. Make a sketch.

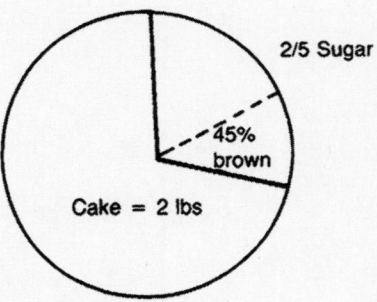

2. Find the weight of all sugar.

$\frac{2}{5}$ of the cake is sugar.

$\frac{2}{5}$ of 2 lbs is sugar.

$\frac{2}{5} \times 2$ (lbs) $= \frac{4}{5}$ (lbs) sugar

Change $\frac{4}{5}$ to a decimal.

$\frac{4}{5} = \frac{8}{10} = .8$ (lbs) sugar

3. Find the weight of the brown sugar.
   45% of the sugar is brown sugar.
   45% of .8 (lbs) = sugar

   Percent means "parts of 100." Therefore, $45\% = \dfrac{45}{100} = .45$

   $.45 \times .8 = .360$ (lbs) brown sugar
   Choice D is the correct answer.

Now try Practice Exercise 3. Check your answers against the answers and explanations that follow and enter your score on the line provided. If your score is 9 or more, go on to Topic 4. If your score is less than 9, study the Topic Review before going on to the next topic area.

Practice Exercise 3

1. 10% written as a decimal is
   1–A   1.0
   1–B   0.01
   1–C   0.001
   1–D   0.1

2. What is 5.37% in fraction form?

   2–A $\dfrac{537}{10,000}$

   2–B $5\dfrac{37}{10,000}$

   2–C $\dfrac{537}{1000}$

   2–D $5\dfrac{37}{100}$

3. What percent of $\dfrac{5}{6}$ is $\dfrac{3}{4}$?

   3–A   75%
   3–B   60%
   3–C   80%
   3–D   90%

4. What percent is 14 of 24?

    4–A $62\frac{1}{4}\%$

    4–B $58\frac{1}{3}\%$

    4–C $41\frac{2}{3}\%$

    4–D $33\frac{3}{5}\%$

5. 200% of 800 equals
    5–A   2500
    5–B   16
    5–C   1600
    5–D   4

6. If John must have a mark of 80% to pass a test of 35 items, the number of items he may miss and still pass the test is
    6–A   7
    6–B   8
    6–C   11
    6–D   28

7. The regular price of a TV set that sold for $118.80 at a 20% reduction sale is
    7–A $148.50
    7–B $142.60
    7–C $138.84
    7–D $ 95.04

8. A circle graph of a budget shows the following expenditures: 26.2% for housing, 28.4% for food, 12% for clothing, 12.7% for taxes, and the balance for miscellaneous items. The percent for miscellaneous items is
    8–A   31.5
    8–B   79.3
    8–C   20.7
    8–D   68.5

9. Two dozen shuttlecocks and four badminton rackets are to be purchased for a playground. The shuttlecocks are priced at $.35 each and the rackets at $2.75 each. The playground receives a discount of 30% from these prices. The total cost of this equipment will be
    9–A $ 7.29
    9–B $11.43
    9–C $13.58
    9–D $18.60

10. A man spent $\frac{15}{16}$ of his entire fortune buying a car for $7500. How much money did he possess?

    10–A $6500

    10–B $7000

    10–C $7500

    10–D $8000

11. The population of a town was 54,000 in the last census. It has increased $\frac{2}{3}$ since then. Its present population is

    11–A   18,000

    11–B   36,000

    11–C   72,000

    11–D   90,000

12. If one third of the liquid contents of a can evaporates on the first day and three fourths of the remainder evaporates on the second day, the fractional part of the original contents remaining at the close of the second day is

    12–A $\frac{5}{12}$

    12–B $\frac{7}{12}$

    12–C $\frac{1}{6}$

    12–D $\frac{1}{2}$

Your Score _____

Answer Key				
1. D	2. A	3. D	4. B	5. C
6. A	7. A	8. C	9. C	10. D
11. D	12. C			

Answers and Explanations

1–D $10\% = .10 = .1$

To change a percent to a decimal, divide the percent by 100; change the fraction to a decimal.

$$10\% = \frac{10}{100} = \frac{1}{10} = .1$$

2–A $5.37\% = .0537 = \dfrac{537}{10,000}$

Divide the percent by 100.

$$5.37\% = \frac{5.37}{100}$$

Multiply numerator and denominator by 100 to get rid of the decimal.

$$\frac{5.37 \times 100}{100 \times 100} = \frac{537}{10,000}$$

3–D   Base (number following "of") $= \dfrac{5}{6}$

Amount (number following "is") $= \dfrac{3}{4}$

$$\text{Rate} = \frac{\text{amount}}{\text{base}}$$
$$= \text{amount} \div \text{base}$$
$$\text{Rate} = \frac{3}{4} \div \frac{5}{6}$$
$$= \frac{3}{\overset{}{\underset{2}{4}}} \times \frac{\overset{3}{6}}{5}$$
$$= \frac{9}{10}$$
$$\frac{9}{10} = .9 = 90\%$$

4–B   Base (number following "of") = 24

Amount (number following "is") = 14

Rate = amount ÷ base

Rate = 14 ÷ 24

$$= .58\frac{1}{3}$$

$$= 58\frac{1}{3}\%$$

5–C   200% of 800 = 2.00 × 800

$$= 1600$$

Remember that 100% of a number is *all* of the number.

6–A   He must answer 80% of 35 correctly. Therefore, he may miss 20% of 35.

20% of 35 = .20 × 35

$$= 7$$

7–A   Since $118.80 represents a 20% reduction, $118.80 = 80% of the regular price.

$$\text{Regular price} = \frac{\$118.80}{80\%}$$

$$= \$118.80 \div .80$$

$$= \$148.50$$

8–C   All the items in a circle graph total 100%. Add the figures given for housing, food, clothing, and taxes:

```
  26.2%
  28.4%
  12.0%
+12.7%
  79.3%
```

Subtract this total from 100% to find the percent for miscellaneous items:

```
 100.0%
 −79.3%
  20.7%
```

9–C Price of shuttlecocks $= 24 \times \$.35 =$ $\$ 8.40$

Price of rackets $= 4 \times \$2.75 =$ $\underline{\$11.00}$

Total price $=$ $\$19.40$

Discount is 30%, and $100\% - 30\%$ $= 70\%$

Actual cost $= 70\%$ of 19.40

$= .70 \times 19.40$

$= 13.58$

10–D $\dfrac{15}{16}$ of fortune is $7500.

Therefore, his fortune $= 7500 \div \dfrac{15}{16}$

$$= \dfrac{\overset{500}{\cancel{7500}}}{1} \times \dfrac{16}{\underset{1}{\cancel{15}}}$$

$$= 8000$$

11–D $\dfrac{2}{3}$ of 54,000 = increase

$$\text{Increase} = \dfrac{2}{\underset{1}{\cancel{3}}} \times \overset{18,000}{\cancel{54,000}}$$

$$= 36,000$$

Present population $= 54,000 + 36,000$

$$= 90,000$$

12–C First day: $\dfrac{1}{3}$ evaporates

$\dfrac{2}{3}$ remains

Second day: $\dfrac{3}{4}$ of $\dfrac{2}{3}$ evaporates

$\dfrac{1}{\underset{2}{\cancel{4}}}$ of $\dfrac{\overset{1}{\cancel{2}}}{3}$ remains

The amount remaining is $\dfrac{1}{4} \times \dfrac{2}{3} = \dfrac{1}{6}$ of original contents.

Topic Review

Fractions

1. A **fraction** is part of a unit.

   A fraction has a **numerator** and a **denominator.**

   Example: In the fraction $\frac{3}{4}$, 3 is the numerator and 4 is the denominator.

   In any fraction, the numerator is divided by the denominator.

   Example: The fraction $\frac{2}{7}$ indicates that 2 is being divided by 7.

   In a fraction problem, the whole quantity is 1, which may be expressed by a fraction in which the numerator and denominator are the same number.

   Example: If the problem involves $\frac{1}{8}$ of a quantity, then the whole quantity is $\frac{8}{8}$, or 1.

2. A **mixed number** is an integer together with a fraction, such as $2\frac{3}{5}, 7\frac{3}{8}$, etc. The integer is the integral part, and the fraction is the fractional part.

3. An **improper fraction** is one in which the numerator is equal to or greater than the denominator, such as $\frac{19}{6}, \frac{24}{5}$, or $\frac{10}{10}$.

4. To change a mixed number to an improper fraction:

   Multiply the denominator of the fraction by the integer.

   Add the numerator to this product.

   Place this sum over the denominator of the fraction.

   Example: Change $3\frac{4}{7}$ to an improper fraction.

   SOLUTION:
   $$7 \times 3 = 21$$
   $$21 + 4 = 25$$
   $$3\frac{4}{7} = \frac{25}{7}$$

5. To change an improper fraction to a mixed number:

Divide the numerator by the denominator. The quotient, disregarding the remainder, is the integral part of the mixed number.

Place the remainder, if any, over the denominator. This is the fractional part of the mixed number.

Example: Change $\dfrac{36}{13}$ to a mixed number.

SOLUTION:
$$13\overline{)36}^{\,2}$$
$$\underline{26}$$
$$10 \text{ remainder}$$
$$\frac{36}{13} = 2\frac{10}{13}$$

6. As a final answer to a problem:

Improper fractions should be changed to mixed numbers.

Fractions should be reduced as far as possible.

Addition of Fractions

7. Fractions cannot be added unless the denominators are all the same.

If the denominators are the same, add all the numerators and place this sum over the common denominator. In the case of mixed numbers, follow the above rule for the fractions and then add the integers.

Example: The sum of $2\frac{3}{8} + 3\frac{1}{8} + \frac{3}{8} = 5\frac{7}{8}$.

If the denominators are not the same, the fractions, in order to be added, must be converted to ones having the same denominator. To do this, it is first necessary to find the lowest common denominator.

8. To add fractions having different denominators:

Find the lowest common denominator (L.C.D.) of the denominators.

Change each fraction to an equivalent fraction having the L.C.D. as its denominator.

When all of the fractions have the same denominator, they may be added.

Example: Add $\frac{1}{4}, \frac{3}{10}$, and $\frac{2}{5}$.

SOLUTION: Find the L.C.D.:

2)	4	10	5
2)	2	5	5
5)	1	5	5
	1	1	1

L.C.D. $= 2 \times 2 \times 5 = 20$

$$\frac{1}{4} = \frac{5}{20}$$

$$\frac{3}{10} = \frac{6}{20}$$

$$\frac{2}{5} = \frac{8}{20}$$

$$\frac{19}{20}$$

9. To add mixed numbers in which the fractions have different denominators, add the fractions by following the rules in item 8 above, then add the integers.

Example: Add $2\frac{5}{7}$, $5\frac{1}{2}$, and 8.

SOLUTION: L.C.D. $= 14$

$$2\frac{5}{7} = 2\frac{10}{14}$$

$$5\frac{1}{2} = 5\frac{7}{14}$$

$$8 = 8$$

$$15\frac{17}{14} = 16\frac{3}{14}$$

Subtraction of Fractions

10. Unlike addition, which may involve adding more than two numbers at the same time, subtraction involves only two numbers.

In subtraction, as in addition, the denominators must be the same.

11. To subtract fractions:

Find the L.C.D.

Change both fractions so that each has the L.C.D. as the denominator.

Subtract the numerator of the second fraction from the numerator of the first, and place this difference over the L.C.D.

Reduce, if possible.

Example: Find the difference of $\frac{5}{8}$ and $\frac{1}{4}$.

SOLUTION:

$$\text{L.C.D.} = 8$$

$$\frac{5}{8} = \frac{5}{8}$$

$$-\frac{1}{4} = -\frac{2}{8}$$

$$\overline{\phantom{-\frac{1}{4} = -}\frac{3}{8}}$$

12. To subtract mixed numbers:

It may be necessary to "borrow," so that the fractional part of the first term is larger than the fractional part of the second term.

Subtract the fractional parts of the mixed numbers and reduce.

Subtract the integers.

Example: Subtract $16\frac{4}{5}$ from $29\frac{1}{3}$.

SOLUTION:

$$\text{L.C.D.} = 15$$

$$29\frac{1}{3} = 29\frac{5}{15}$$

$$-16\frac{4}{5} = -16\frac{12}{15}$$

Note that $\frac{5}{15}$ is less than $\frac{12}{15}$. Borrow 1 from 29, and change that 1 to $\frac{15}{15}$.

$$29\frac{5}{15} = 28\frac{20}{15}$$

$$-16\frac{12}{15} = -16\frac{12}{15}$$

$$\overline{\phantom{-16\frac{12}{15} = -}12\frac{8}{15}}$$

Multiplication of Fractions

13. To be multiplied, fractions need not have the same denominators.

A whole number has the denominator 1 understood.

14. To multiply fractions:

    Change the mixed numbers, if any, to improper fractions.

    Multiply all the numerators, and place this product over the product of the denominators.

    Reduce, if possible.

    Example: Multiply $\dfrac{2}{3} \times 2\dfrac{4}{7} \times \dfrac{5}{9}$

    SOLUTION: $2\dfrac{4}{7} = \dfrac{18}{7}$

    $$\dfrac{2}{3} \times \dfrac{18}{7} \times \dfrac{5}{9} = \dfrac{180}{189}$$
    $$= \dfrac{20}{21}$$

15. **Cancellation** is a device to facilitate multiplication. To cancel means to divide a numerator and a denominator by the same number in a multiplication problem.

    Example: In the problem $\dfrac{4}{7} \times \dfrac{5}{6}$, the numerator 4 and the denominator 6 may be divided by 2.

    $$\dfrac{\overset{2}{\cancel{4}}}{7} \times \dfrac{5}{\underset{3}{\cancel{6}}} = \dfrac{10}{21}$$

    The word "of" is often used to mean "multiply."

    Example: $\dfrac{1}{2}$ of $\dfrac{1}{2} = \dfrac{1}{2} \times \dfrac{1}{2} = \dfrac{1}{4}$

16. To multiply a whole number by a mixed number:

    Multiply the whole number by the fractional part of the mixed number.

    Multiply the whole number by the integral part of the mixed number.

    Add both products.

    Example: Multiply $23\dfrac{3}{4}$ by 95.

    SOLUTION: $\dfrac{95}{1} \times \dfrac{3}{4} = \dfrac{285}{4}$
    $$= 71\dfrac{1}{4}$$
    $$95 \times 23 = 2185$$
    $$2185 + 71\dfrac{1}{4} = 2256\dfrac{1}{4}$$

Dividing Fractions

17. To divide fractions:

    Change all the mixed numbers, if any, to improper fractions.

    Invert the second fraction and multiply.

    Reduce, if possible.

    Example: Divide $\frac{2}{3}$ by $2\frac{1}{4}$.

    SOLUTION:
    $$2\frac{1}{4} = \frac{9}{4}$$
    $$\frac{2}{3} \div \frac{9}{4} = \frac{2}{3} \times \frac{4}{9}$$
    $$= \frac{8}{27}$$

18. A **complex fraction** is one that has a fraction as the numerator, or as the denominator, or as both.

    Example: $\dfrac{\frac{2}{3}}{5}$ is a complex fraction.

19. To clear (simplify) a complex fraction:

    Divide the numerator by the denominator.

    Reduce, if possible.

    Example: Clear $\dfrac{\frac{3}{7}}{\frac{5}{14}}$

    SOLUTION:
    $$\frac{3}{7} \div \frac{5}{14} = \frac{3}{\underset{1}{\cancel{7}}} \times \frac{\overset{2}{\cancel{14}}}{5} = \frac{6}{5}$$
    $$= 1\frac{1}{5}$$

Comparing Fractions

20. If two fractions have the same denominator, the one having the larger numerator is the greater fraction.

Example: $\frac{3}{7}$ is greater than $\frac{2}{7}$.

21. If two fractions have the same numerator, the one having the larger denominator is the smaller fraction.

Example: $\frac{5}{12}$ is smaller than $\frac{5}{11}$.

Fraction Problems

22. Most fraction problems can be arranged in the form: "What fraction of a number is another number?" This form contains three important parts:
   - The fraction part
   - The number following "of"
   - The number following "is"

If the fraction and the "of" number are given, multiply them to find the "is" number.

Example: What is $\frac{3}{4}$ of 20?

SOLUTION: Write the question as " $\frac{3}{4}$ of 20 is what number?" Then multiply the

fraction $\frac{3}{4}$ by the "of" number, 20:

$$\frac{3}{\overset{}{\underset{1}{\cancel{4}}}} \times \overset{5}{\cancel{20}} = 15$$

If the fractional part and the "is" number are given, divide the "is" number by the fraction to find the "of" number.

Example: $\frac{4}{5}$ of what number is 40?

SOLUTION: To find the "of" number, divide 40 by $\frac{4}{5}$:

$$40 \div \frac{4}{5} = \frac{\overset{10}{\cancel{40}}}{1} \times \frac{5}{\underset{1}{\cancel{4}}}$$

$$= 50$$

To find the fractional part when the other two numbers are known, divide the "is" number by the "of" number.

Example: What part of 12 is 9?

SOLUTION:
$$9 \div 12 = \frac{9}{12}$$
$$= \frac{3}{4}$$

Percents

23. The percent symbol (%) means "parts of a hundred." Some problems involve expressing a fraction or a decimal as a percent. In other problems, it is necessary to express a percent as a fraction or a decimal in order to perform the calculations.

24. To change a whole number or a decimal to a percent:

    Multiply the number by 100.

    Affix a % sign.
    Example: Change 3 to a percent.
    SOLUTION: $3 \times 100 = 300$
    $$3 = 300\%$$
    Example: Change .67 to a percent.
    SOLUTION: $.67 \times 100 = 67$
    $$.67 = 67\%$$

25. To change a fraction or a mixed number to a percent:

    Multiply the fraction or mixed number by 100.

    Reduce, if possible.

    Affix a % sign.

    Example: Change $\frac{1}{7}$ to a percent.

    SOLUTION: $\frac{1}{7} \times 100 = \frac{100}{7}$
    $$= 14\frac{2}{7}$$
    $$\frac{1}{7} = 14\frac{2}{7}\%$$

Solving Percent Problems

26. Most percent problems involve three quantities:
    - The rate, R, which is followed by a % sign.
    - The base, B, which follows the word "of."
    - The amount, P, which usually follows the word "is."

If the rate (R) and the base (B) are known, then the amount (P) = $R \times B$.

Example: Find 15% of 50.

SOLUTION:

$$\text{Rate} = 15\%$$
$$\text{Base} = 50$$
$$P = R \times B$$
$$P = 15\% \times 50$$
$$= .15 \times 50$$
$$= 7.5$$

TOPIC 4: NUMBERS WITH UNITS

Model Problems:

1. It is said that he who wastes time, even a second, loses more than gold. If you waste 30 minutes, how many seconds have you wasted?

    1–A   60
    1–B   180
    1–C   1800
    1–D   3600

SOLUTION:

Set up a fraction expressing the relationship between seconds and minutes so that the numerator equals the denominator. Here, $\dfrac{60 \text{ seconds}}{1 \text{ minute}}$.

Multiply by 30 minutes:

$$30\ (\cancel{\text{min}}) \times \frac{60\ (\text{sec})}{1\ (\cancel{\text{min}})} =$$

The minutes cancel, just like numbers when multiplying fractions, and the answer is 30×60 (sec) = 1800 (sec).

The correct answer is choice C.

2. How many seconds are in a day?

    2–A   1440
    2–B   3600
    2–C   8640
    2–D   86,400

SOLUTION:

Use equivalent fractions to express hours per day, minutes per hour, and seconds per minute. Cancel like terms and multiply.

$$1 \text{ day} \times \frac{24 \text{ (hours)}}{1 \text{ (day)}} \times \frac{60 \text{ (minutes)}}{1 \text{ (hour)}} \times \frac{60 \text{ (seconds)}}{1 \text{ (minute)}} =$$

1 day has $24 \times 60 \times 60$ seconds $= 86,400$ seconds.

The correct answer is choice D.

Now try Practice Exercise 4. Check your answers against the answers and explanations that follow and enter your score on the line provided. If your score is 9 or more, go on to Topic 5. If your score is less than 9, study the Topic Review before going on to the next topic area.

Practice Exercise 4

1. Joseph's new overcoat is $4\frac{1}{2}$ feet long. How many meters does this correspond to? (Round off answer to a whole number.)

   1–A   1
   1–B   4
   1–C   12
   1–D   39

2. About how many inches is 1500 millimeters?

   2–A   3
   2–B   59
   2–C   25
   2–D   5

3. The lead elephant in Denver's circus weighs 6 tons. How many grams is this?

   3–A   5,448,000
   3–B   20,000
   3–C   544,800
   3–D   6,000,000

4. "How many miles is it to Washington, D.C.?" asked Frank. "Only 400 kilometers more," replied Fran. How many more miles did they have to travel?

   4–A   40
   4–B   64
   4–C   200
   4–D   250

5. Arthur the astronaut weighed 78 kilograms at launch time. How many pounds did he weigh?

    5–A   78
    5–B   181.60
    5–C   220.6
    5–D   171.60

6. If 7 feet 9 inches is cut from a piece of wood that is 9 feet 6 inches, the piece left is

    6–A   1 foot 9 inches
    6–B   1 foot 10 inches
    6–C   2 feet 2 inches
    6–D   2 feet 5 inches

7. Take 3 hours 49 minutes from 5 hours 13 minutes.

    7–A   1 hour 10 minutes
    7–B   1 hour 18 minutes
    7–C   1 hour 20 minutes
    7–D   1 hour 24 minutes

8. If there are 231 cubic inches in one gallon, the number of cubic inches in 3 pints is closest to which one of the following?

    8–A   24
    8–B   29
    8–C   57
    8–D   87

9. The sum of 5 feet $2\frac{3}{4}$ inches, 8 feet $\frac{1}{2}$ inches, and $12\frac{1}{2}$ inches is

    9–A   14 feet $3\frac{3}{4}$ inches

    9–B   14 feet $5\frac{3}{4}$ inches

    9–C   14 feet $9\frac{1}{4}$ inches

    9–D   15 feet $\frac{1}{2}$ inches

10. Assuming that 2.54 centimeters = 1 inch, a metal rod that measures $1\frac{1}{2}$ feet would most nearly equal which one of the following?

    10–A   380 centimeters
    10–B   46 centimeters
    10–C   30 centimeters
    10–D   18 centimeters

11. To the nearest degree, what is a temperature of 12°C equal to on the Fahrenheit scale?

    11–A   60°

    11–B   57°

    11–C   79°

    11–D   54°

12. A company requires that the temperature in its offices be kept at 68°F. What is this in °C?

    12–A   10°

    12–B   15°

    12–C   20°

    12–D   25°

Your Score _____

Answer Key

1. A	2. B	3. A	4. D	5. D
6. A	7. D	8. D	9. A	10. B
11. D	12. C			

Answers and Explanations

1–A   The conversion from feet to meters is:

1 meter is about 39 inches; 12 inches is 1 foot.

$$4\frac{1}{2}\left(\text{feet}\right) \times \frac{12\left(\text{inch}\right)}{1\left(\text{foot}\right)} \times \frac{1\left(\text{meter}\right)}{39\left(\text{inch}\right)}$$

After cross-multiplying the units,

$$4\frac{1}{2} \times 12 \times \frac{1}{39}\left(\text{meters}\right) = 1.38 \text{ meters; round off to 1 meter.}$$

2–B   The conversion of millimeters to inches is used:

(Note: 1 inch = 2.54 centimeters; 10 millimeters = 1 centimeter)

Method 1:

$$1500\left(\text{mm}\right) \times \frac{1\left(\text{cm}\right)}{10\left(\text{mm}\right)} \times \frac{1\left(\text{in}\right)}{2.54\left(\text{cm}\right)} =$$

After cross-canceling and multiplying the numbers,

$1500 \times \dfrac{1}{10} \times \dfrac{1}{2.54}(\text{in}) = \dfrac{1500}{25.4}(\text{in}) = 59.06 \text{ in}$, which rounds off to 59 inches.

Method 2:

1500 mm is 150 cm because there are 10 mm in 1 cm.

If 2.54 cm = 1 in,

then $\dfrac{2.54}{2.54}\text{cm} = \dfrac{1}{2.54}\text{in}$,

or $1 \text{ cm} = \dfrac{1}{2.54}\text{in}$.

But the problem calls for 150 cm, or $150 \times 1 \text{ cm} = 150 \times \dfrac{1}{2.54}$ in, which equals 59.06 as above.

3–A Use these conversions: 2000 lbs = 1 ton; 454 grams = 1 lb.

$$6 \text{ tons} \times \dfrac{2000 \text{ lbs}}{1 \text{ ton}} \times \dfrac{454 \text{ grams}}{1 \text{ lb}}$$

After canceling the like terms in the numerators and denominators,

$6 \times 2000 \times 454 \text{ grams} = 5,448,000 \text{ grams}$.

4–D Here, convert from kilometers to miles:

$$400 \text{ km} \times \dfrac{1 \text{ mile}}{1.6 \text{ km}}$$

Or, $400 \div 1.6 \text{ [mile]} = 250 \text{ miles}$

5–D Convert kilograms to pounds:

$$78 \text{ kg} \times \dfrac{2.2 \text{ lb}}{1 \text{ kg}}$$

Or, $78 \times 2.2 = 171.60 \text{ pounds}$

6–A
$$
\begin{array}{r}
9 \text{ ft } 6 \text{ in} = \ \ 8 \text{ ft } 18 \text{ in} \\
-7 \text{ ft } 9 \text{ in} = -7 \text{ ft } \ \ 9 \text{ in} \\
\hline
1 \text{ ft } \ \ 9 \text{ in}
\end{array}
$$

7–D
$$
\begin{array}{r}
5 \text{ hours } 13 \text{ minutes} = \ \ 4 \text{ hours } 73 \text{ minutes} \\
-3 \text{ hours } 49 \text{ minutes} = -3 \text{ hours } 49 \text{ minutes} \\
\hline
1 \text{ hour } \ \ 24 \text{ minutes}
\end{array}
$$

8–D

$$1 \text{ gal} = 4 \text{ qt} = 8 \text{ pt}$$

Therefore, $1 \text{ pt} = 231 \text{ cubic inches} \div 8$

$$= 28.875 \text{ cubic inches}$$

$$3 \text{ pts} = 3 \times 28.875 \text{ cubic inches}$$

$$= 86.625 \text{ cubic inches}$$

9–A

$$5 \text{ ft } 2\frac{3}{4} \text{ in} = 5 \text{ ft } 2\frac{3}{4} \text{ in}$$

$$8 \text{ ft } \frac{1}{2} \text{ in} = 8 \text{ ft } \quad \frac{2}{4} \text{ in}$$

$$+ \; 12\frac{1}{2} \text{ in} = \quad 12\frac{2}{4} \text{ in}$$

$$\overline{\qquad\qquad\qquad 13 \text{ ft } 14\frac{7}{4} \text{ in}}$$

$$= 14 \text{ feet } 3\frac{3}{4} \text{ inches}$$

10–B

$$1 \text{ foot} = 12 \text{ inches}$$

$$1\frac{1}{2} \text{ feet} = 1\frac{1}{2} \times 12 \text{ inches} = 18 \text{ inches}$$

Since 1 inch = 2.54 cm, therefore:

$$18 \text{ inches} = 18 \times 2.54 \text{ cm}$$

$$= 45.72 \text{ cm}$$

Round to 46.

11–D

$$°F = \frac{9}{5} \times °C + 32° \text{ (Temperature Conversion Formula)}$$

$$°F = \frac{9}{5} \times 12° + 32°$$

$$= \frac{108°}{5} + 32°$$

$$= 21.6° + 32°$$

$$= 53.6°$$

Round to 54, the closest choice.

12–C $°C = \dfrac{5}{9}(°F - 32°)$

$°C = \dfrac{5}{9}(68° - 32°)$

$= \dfrac{5}{\cancel{9}_1} \times \cancel{36}^{4}$

$= 20°$

Topic Review

Adding and Subtracting Numbers with Units

1.   To add denominate numbers (numbers with units), arrange them in columns by common unit, then add each column. If necessary, simplify the answer, starting with the smallest unit.

   Example: Add 1 yd 2 ft 8 in, 2 yd 2 ft 10 in, and 3 yd 1 ft 9 in.

   SOLUTION:

   ```
        1 yd  2 ft  8 in
        2 yd  2 ft 10 in
      + 3 yd  1 ft  9 in
      ─────────────────────
        6 yd  5 ft 27 in
   ```

   $= 6$ yd 7 ft 3 in (because 27 in $= 2$ ft 3 in)

   $= 8$ yd 1 ft   3 in (because 7 ft $= 2$ yd 1 ft)

2.   To subtract denominate numbers, arrange them in columns by common unit, then subtract each column starting with the smallest unit. If necessary, borrow to increase the number of a particular unit.

   Example: Subtract 2 gal 3 qt from 7 gal 1 qt.

   SOLUTION:

   ```
        7 gal 1 qt =  6 gal 5 qt
      − 2 gal 3 qt = −2 gal 3 qt
      ──────────────────────────
                      4 gal 2 qt
   ```

   Note that 1 gal was borrowed from 7 gal.

   1 gal $= 4$ qt

   Therefore, 7 gal 1 qt $= 6$ gal 5 qt.

Multiplying and Dividing Numbers with Units

3. To multiply a denominate number by a given number:

    If the denominate number contains only one unit, multiply the numbers and write the unit.
    Example: 3 oz × 4 = 12 oz

    If the denominate number contains more than one unit of measurement, multiply the number of each unit by the given number and simplify the answer, if necessary.
    Example: Multiply 4 yd 2 ft 8 in by 2.

    SOLUTION:

    $$4 \text{ yd } 2 \text{ ft } 8 \text{ in}$$
    $$\underline{\times \qquad\qquad 2}$$
    $$8 \text{ yd } 4 \text{ ft } 16 \text{ in}$$
    $$= 8 \text{ yd } 5 \text{ ft } 4 \text{ in (because } 16 \text{ in} = 1 \text{ ft } 4 \text{ in)}$$
    $$= 9 \text{ yd } 2 \text{ ft } 4 \text{ in (because } 5 \text{ ft} = 1 \text{ yd } 2 \text{ ft)}$$

4. To divide a denominate number by a given number, convert all units to the smallest unit, then divide. Simplify the answer, if necessary.
    Example: Divide 5 lb 12 oz by 4.

    SOLUTION:

    $$1 \text{ lb} = 16 \text{ oz, therefore}$$
    $$5 \text{ lb } 12 \text{ oz} = 92 \text{ oz}$$
    $$92 \text{ oz} \div 4 = 23 \text{ oz}$$
    $$= 1 \text{ lb } 7 \text{ oz}$$

Converting One Unit to Another

5. Equivalent fractions may be used to convert one unit to another.
    Example: How many inches are in 3.5 feet?
    SOLUTION:

    Step 1: Write the equivalence between inches and feet.
    1 (foot) = 12 (inch)   Equation 1

    Step 2: Divide left side by right in Equation 1.

    $$\frac{1 \text{ foot}}{12 \text{ inch}} = \frac{12 \text{ inch}}{12 \text{ inch}} = 1 \qquad \text{Equation 2}$$

    Step 3: Divide right side by left in Equation 1.

    $$1 = \frac{1 \text{ foot}}{1 \text{ foot}} = \frac{12 \text{ inch}}{1 \text{ foot}} \qquad \text{Equation 3}$$

    Remember the rule for multiplying fractions and for simplifying by canceling like terms:

    $$\cancel{5} \times \frac{2}{\cancel{5}} = 2 \text{ (We can cancel same numbers in numerator and in denominator.)}$$

This can be done with units, too, so using Equation 3:

$$3.5\left(\cancel{feet}\right) \times \frac{12\ inches}{1\ \cancel{foot}} = 3.5 \times 12\ inches$$

$$= 42\ inches$$

Try these examples:

a. How many inches are in 2 yards?

1 yard = 36 in

$$\boxed{\frac{1\ yard}{36\ in} = 1} \text{ and } \boxed{\frac{36\ in}{1\ yard} = 1}$$

Use $2\ \cancel{yard} \times \dfrac{36\ in}{1\ \cancel{yard}} = 72\ in$ (*Yard* must cancel.)

b. How many grams are in 1.5 kilograms?

1000 grams = 1 kilogram

$$\boxed{\frac{1000\ gram}{1\ kilogram} = 1} \text{ and } \boxed{\frac{1\ kilogram}{1000\ gram} = 1}$$

(Use the fraction in which "kilogram" is in the denominator.)

$$1.5\ \cancel{kilogram} \times \frac{1000\ gram}{1\ \cancel{kilogram}} = 1500\ gram \ \ (\textit{Kilogram}\ must\ cancel.)$$

Metric Measurement

6. The basic units of the metric system are the meter (m), which is used for length; the gram (g), which is used for weight; and the liter (l), which is used for capacity, or volume.

7. The prefixes that are used with the basic units and their meanings are:

Prefix	Abbreviation	Meaning
micro	μ	one millionth (.000001)
milli	m	one thousandth (.001)
centi	c	one hundredth (.01)
deci	d	one tenth (.1)
deka	da *or* dk	ten times (10)
hecto	h	one hundred times (100)
kilo	k	one thousand times (1000)
giga	G	one billion times (1,000,000,000)

8. To convert to a basic metric unit from a prefixed metric unit, multiply by the number indicated in the prefix.

    Example: Convert 72 millimeters to meters.

    $$72 \text{ millimeters} = 72 \times .001 \text{ meters}$$
    $$= .072 \text{ meters}$$

    Example: Convert 4 kiloliters to liters.

    $$4 \text{ kiloliters} = 4 \times 1000 \text{ liters}$$
    $$= 4000 \text{ liters}$$

9. To add, subtract, multiply, or divide using metric measurement, first convert all units to the same unit, then perform the desired operation.

    Example: Subtract 1200 g from 2.5 kg.

    SOLUTION:
    $$
    \begin{aligned}
    2.5\,\text{kg} &= 2500 \text{ g} \\
    -1200\,\text{g} &= \underline{-1200 \text{ g}} \\
    & \ 1300 \text{ g or } 1.3 \text{ kg}
    \end{aligned}
    $$

10. To convert from a metric measure to an English measure, or the reverse:

    In the Table of English-Metric Conversions, find how many units of the desired measure are equal to one unit of the given measure.

    Multiply the given number by the number found in the table.

    Example: Find the number of pounds in 4 kilograms.

    SOLUTION: From the table, 1 kg = 2.2 lb.

    $$4 \text{ kg} = 4 \times 2.2 \text{ lb}$$
    $$= 8.8 \text{ lb}$$

    Example: Find the number of meters in 5 yards.

    $$1 \text{ yd} = .9 \text{ m}$$
    SOLUTION: $$5 \text{ yd} = 5 \times .9 \text{ m}$$
    $$= 4.5 \text{ m}$$

Table of Measures

English Measures	
Length	**Liquid Measure**
1 foot (ft *or* ′) = 12 inches (in *or* ″)	1 cup (c) = 8 fluid ounces (fl oz)
1 yard (yd) = 36 inches	1 pint (pt) = 2 cups
1 yard = 3 feet	1 quart (qt) = 2 pints
1 mile (mi) = 5280 feet	1 gallon (gal) = 4 quarts
1 mile = 1760 yards	1 barrel (bl) = $31\frac{1}{2}$ gallons

Weight

1 pound (lb) = 16 ounces (oz)

1 ton (T) = 2000 pounds

Area

1 square foot (ft^2) = 144 square inches (in^2)

1 square yard (yd^2) = 9 square feet

General Measures

Time

1 minute (min) = 60 seconds (sec)

1 hour (hr) = 60 minutes

1 day = 24 hours

1 week = 7 days

1 year = 52 weeks

1 calendar year = 365 days

Dry Measure

1 quart (qt) = 2 pints (pt)

1 peck (pk) = 8 quarts

1 bushel (bu) = 4 pecks

Volume

1 cubic foot (ft^3 or cu ft) = 1728 cubic inches

1 cubic yard (yd^3 or cu yd) = 27 cubic feet

1 gallon = 231 cubic inches

Angles and Arcs

1 minute (′) = 60 seconds (″)

1 degree (°) = 60 minutes

1 circle = 360 degrees

Counting

1 dozen (doz) = 12 units

1 gross (gr) = 12 dozen

1 gross = 144 units

Table of Metric Conversions

Table of English-Metric Conversions (Approximate)

English to Metric

1 inch = 2.54 centimeters

1 yard = .9 meters

1 mile = 1.6 kilometers

1 ounce = 28 grams

1 pound = 454 grams

1 fluid ounce = 30 milliliters

1 liquid quart = .95 liters

Metric to English

1 centimeter = .39 inches

1 meter = 1.1 yards

1 kilometer = .6 miles

1 kilogram = 2.2 pounds

1 liter = 1.06 liquid quart

1 liter = 1000 cubic centimeters (cm³)

1 milliliter = 1 cubic centimeter

1 liter of water weighs 1 kilogram

1 milliliter of water weighs 1 gram

The Metric System

LENGTH

Unit	Abbreviation	Number of Meters
myriameter	mym	10,000
kilometer	km	1000
hectometer	hm	100
dekameter	dam	10
meter	m	1
decimeter	dm	0.1
centimeter	cm	0.01
millimeter	mm	0.001

AREA

Unit	Abbreviation	Number of Square Meters
square kilometer	sq km *or* km²	1,000,000
hectare	ha	10,000
are	a	100
centare	ca	1
square centimeter	sq cm *or* cm²	0.0001

VOLUME

Unit	Abbreviation	Number of Cubic Meters
dekastere	das	10
stere	s	1
decistere	ds	0.10
cubic centimeter	cu cm *or* cm³ *or* cc	0.000001

CAPACITY

Unit	Abbreviation	Number of Liters
kiloliter	kl	1,000
hectoliter	hi	100
dekaliter	dal	10
liter	l	1
deciliter	dl	0.10
centiliter	cl	0.01
milliliter	ml	0.001

MASS AND WEIGHT

Unit	Abbreviation	Number of Grams
metric ton	MT *or* t	1,000,000
quintal	q	100,000
kilogram	kg	1000
hectogram	hg	100
dekagram	dag	10
gram	g *or* gm	1
decigram	dg	0.10
centigram	cg	0.01
milligram	mg	0.001

TOPIC 5: PARTS OF A WHOLE

Model Problem:

Reynaldo wants to make and sell bamboo flutes. If each flute is 8 inches long, how long a piece of bamboo does Reynaldo need to make 20 flutes?

  A 8 feet

  B 12 feet

  C 13 feet 4 inches

  D 20 feet 8 inches

SOLUTION:

1. Make a sketch:

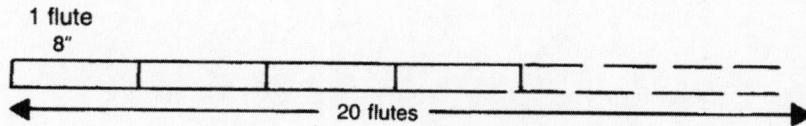

    Notice that you do not have to draw all 20 flutes to see that you must multiply to find the length of bamboo needed.

2. Multiply length of 1 flute times 20.

    $8 \times 20 = 160$ inches

3. Check the answer choices. All are in feet. Divide by 12 to change inches to feet.

    $\dfrac{160}{12} = 13$ feet 4 inches

    The correct answer is choice C.

Now try Practice Exercise 5. Check your answers against the answers and explanations that follow and enter your score on the line provided. If your score is 8 or more, go on to Topic 6. If your score is less than 8, study the Topic Review before going on to the next topic area.

Practice Exercise 5

1. How many pieces of 4-inch pipe can be cut from a 4-foot pipe?
    1–A   3
    1–B   4
    1–C   12
    1–D   16

2. Steffi brought a 1-gallon jug of punch to the picnic. How many 1-cup drinks can she pour? (4 cups = 1 quart)
    2–A   2
    2–B   6
    2–C   12
    2–D   16

3. How many $\frac{1}{2}$-inch markings can be made on a yardstick?
    3–A   72
    3–B   36
    3–C   18
    3–D   6

4. All of the 40 students in Mrs. Gray's class laid their yardsticks end to end outside the school. How far, in feet, did the yardsticks stretch?
    4–A   20 feet
    4–B   40 feet
    4–C   60 feet
    4–D   120 feet

5. The average rainfall for each of the 30 days of April was .24 inches. How many feet of rain fell in April?
    5–A   .24
    5–B   .6
    5–C   12
    5–D   15

6. Len the carpenter has a piece of stock from which he wants to cut 18 equal table legs. If the stock is 21 feet 3 inches, how long will each leg be, to the nearest inch?
    6–A   14 inches
    6–B   18 inches
    6–C   3 inches
    6–D   6 inches

7. A carpenter needs boards for 4 shelves, each 2′9″ long. How many feet of board should he buy?

   7–A   11

   7–B $11\frac{1}{6}$

   7–C   13

   7–D $15\frac{1}{2}$

8. The product of 8 feet 7 inches multiplied by 8 is

   8–A   69 feet 6 inches
   8–B   68.8 feet

   8–C $68\frac{2}{3}$ feet

   8–D   68 feet 2 inches

9. Six gross of special drawing pencils were purchased for use in an office. If the pencils were used at the rate of 24 a week, the maximum number of weeks that the 6 gross of pencils would last is

   9–A   6
   9–B   12
   9–C   24
   9–D   36

10. A piece of wood 35 feet 6 inches long was used to make 4 shelves of equal length. The length of each shelf was

   10–A   8.9 inches
   10–B   8 feet 9 inches

   10–C   8 feet $9\frac{1}{2}$ inches

   10–D   8 feet $10\frac{1}{2}$ inches

Your Score _____

Answer Key				
1. C	2. D	3. A	4. D	5. B
6. A	7. A	8. C	9. D	10. D

Answers and Explanations

1–C   Draw a sketch:

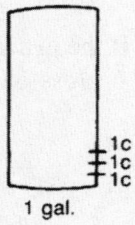

Convert all measurements to inches:

4 ft = 4 × 12 = 48 in

Divide to find number of pipes:

$$\frac{48}{4} = 12 \ \text{(4-inch) pipes}$$

2–D

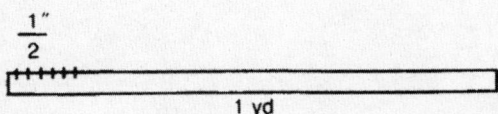

Convert gal to cups:

4 cups = 1 qt

$$1 \ \text{gal} = 4 \ \text{qt} = 4 \times 4 \ \frac{\text{cups}}{\text{qt}} = 16 \ \text{cups}$$

3–A

Convert yards to inches:

$$1 \ \text{yd} = 3 \ \text{ft} = 3 \times 12 \ \frac{\text{in}}{\text{ft}} = 36 \ \text{in}$$

$$36 \ \text{inches} \div \frac{1}{2} = 36 \times \frac{2}{1} = 72 \ \text{half-inch marks}$$

4–D   Multiply: $40 \text{ yd} \times \dfrac{3 \text{ ft}}{\text{yd}} = 40 \times 3 = 120 \text{ ft}$

5–B   Multiply:

$$30 \text{ days} \times \dfrac{.24 \text{ in}}{1 \text{ day}} = 7.2 \text{ in}$$

Since 12 in = 1 ft,

$$7.2 \text{ in} \times \dfrac{1 \text{ ft}}{12 \text{ in}} = \dfrac{7.2}{12} = 0.6 \text{ ft}$$

6–A   Sketch the problem.

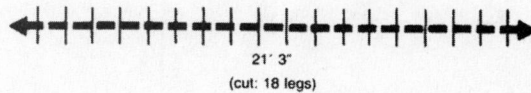

21′ 3″
(cut: 18 legs)

Divide the length of stock by 18. But first, change all units to inches.

$$21 \text{ (ft) } 3 \text{ (in)} = 21\left(\text{ft}\right) \times 12 \dfrac{\text{(in)}}{\left(\text{ft}\right)} + 3 \text{ in} = 252 \text{ (in)} + 3 \text{ (in)} = 255 \text{ in}$$

Dividing by 18, $\dfrac{255}{18} = 18\overline{)255}$

$$14\dfrac{3}{18} = 14\dfrac{1}{6}$$

$$\begin{array}{r} 18 \\ \hline 75 \\ 72 \\ \hline 3 \end{array}$$

Rounding off to the nearest inch, each leg is 14 inches.

7–A   2 ft 9 in
$$\underline{\times \qquad 4}$$
8 ft 36 in = 11 ft   (Since 36 in = 3 ft)

8–C   8 ft 7 in

$\times \quad\quad 8$

64 ft 56 in = 68 ft 8 in

(since 56 in = 4 ft 8 in)

$8 \text{ in} = \dfrac{8}{12} \text{ ft} = \dfrac{2}{3} \text{ ft}$

$68 \text{ ft } 8 \text{ in} = 68\dfrac{2}{3} \text{ ft}$

9–D   Find the number of units in 6 gross:

1 gross = 144 units

6 gross = 6 × 144 units

= 864 units

Divide units by rate of use:

864 ÷ 24 = 36

10–D $8 \text{ feet } 10\dfrac{1}{2} \text{ inches}$

4$)\overline{35 \text{ feet } 6 \text{ inches}}$

$\underline{32 \text{ feet}}$

3 feet = $\underline{36 \text{ inches}}$

42 inches

$\underline{40 \text{ inches}}$

2 inches

Topic Review

1. Many problems involve quantities that must be put together (multiplied) or broken down (divided).

Joining Small Units

2. If you are joining a number of small units to find a larger one, multiply.

   Example: If you set aside 40 minutes each day to learn a new skill, how many hours would you spend learning that skill in 2 weeks?

   SOLUTION: 40 min + 40 min + 40 min . . . for 2 weeks =

   40 (min) × 14 (days) = 560 (min)

   560 min is larger than 60 min (1 hour), so simplify by dividing:

   $\frac{560}{60} = 9\frac{1}{3}$, or 9 hours 20 minutes

Breaking down Large Units

3. If you are breaking down one large unit into a number of smaller ones, divide.

   Example: How many 3-foot broom handles can be made from a pole 25 feet long?

   SOLUTION:

   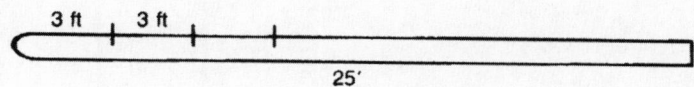

   $\frac{560}{60} = 9\frac{1}{3}$

   Since $\frac{1}{3}$ is not enough for another handle, ignore it. You can make only nine 3-foot handles from a 25-foot pole.

Simplifying Results

4. When multiplying denominate numbers, multiply each of the units, so:

   3 hours 40 minutes

   <u>×   2</u>

   6 hours 80 minutes

   Be sure to simplify the results:

   80 minutes = 1 hour 20 minutes

   Added to the 6 hours, the final answer is

   6 hours + 1 hour 20 minutes = 7 hours 20 minutes.

5. To divide a denominate number, convert all units to the smallest unit, then divide. Simplify if necessary.

    Example: Divide 5 feet 9 inches by 4.

    SOLUTION: Convert 5 feet 9 inches to inches:

    5 ft 9 in = 5 × 12(in) + 9(in) = 60 + 9 = 69 in

    Divide:

    $$\frac{69}{4} = 17\frac{1}{4} \text{ in}$$

    Simplify:

    $$17\frac{1}{4} \text{ in} = 1 \text{ ft } 5\frac{1}{4} \text{ in}$$

TOPIC 6: RATIO AND PROPORTION

Model Problem:

A music store sold the following CDs in 1 week.

Rap	1000
Rock	500
Country	1250
Classical	200
Folk	<u>350</u>
TOTAL	3300

What was the ratio of Classical to non-Classical sales?

A $\dfrac{2}{31}$

B $\dfrac{29}{31}$

C $\dfrac{2}{33}$

D $\dfrac{1}{33}$

SOLUTION:

Determine the ratio of:

$$\frac{\text{Classical}}{\text{non-Classical}}$$

From the chart, the Classical sales = 200

The non-Classical sales = Rap + Rock + Country + Folk = 1000 + 500 + 1250 + 350 = 3100

The ratio $= \frac{200}{3100}$, or $\frac{2}{31}$

The correct answer is choice A.

Now try Practice Exercise 6. Check your answers against the answers and explanations that follow and enter your score on the line provided. If your score is 8 or more, go on to Topic 7. If your score is less than 8, study the topic review before going on to the next topic area.

Practice Exercise 6

1. Wanda's mother wants to make 4 cups of chicken soup from a recipe that makes 16 cups of soup. If the recipe calls for $\frac{1}{4}$ cup of rice, how many tablespoons of rice should be used to make only 4 cups of soup? (16 tablespoons = 1 cup)

    1–A $\frac{1}{16}$

    1–B $\frac{1}{4}$

    1–C $\frac{1}{2}$

    1–D   1

2. The Big Green Club in New Hampshire has decided to throw a Christmas party for its 180 members, but the instructions for Strawberry Fruit Punch are written for 20 people. If the original recipe requires 5 large oranges and 2 quarts of strawberries, how many oranges are required for the party?

    2–A   14

    2–B   20

    2–C   45

    2–D   4

3. *Marchand de vin* sauce, served over broiled steak, requires exactly the right proportion of ingredients in order to obtain the precise delicate flavor. For this reason, Chef Pierre measures all his ingredients in grams. A newly found recipe asks for $\frac{1}{3}$ cup of dry white wine.

   How many grams of wine should Chef Pierre measure out? (1 cup = 8 oz; 1 ounce = 30 grams)

3–A	95
3–B	80
3–C	38
3–D	10

4. Four servings of Maryland Chicken require $3\frac{1}{4}$ pounds of chicken. How many pounds of chicken would be required to make Maryland Chicken for a banquet of 240 people?

4–A	19
4–B	180
4–C	240
4–D	195

5. Mrs. Englebart's recipe for eggplant casserole needs $1\frac{1}{2}$ pounds of chopped meat and 1 cup of tomatoes for 4 servings. If she wanted to serve 20 people, how many pounds should her package of chopped meat and tomatoes weigh? (1 cup = $\frac{1}{2}$ pound)

5–A	10
5–B	$5\frac{1}{2}$
5–C	13
5–D	5

6. A gallon of paint requires 1 pint of thinner before it is spread on the walls. If $1\frac{1}{2}$ gallons of paint are required for one room, how many pints of thinner are required for 7 rooms?

6–A	$10\frac{1}{2}$
6–B	$6\frac{1}{2}$
6–C	7
6–D	9

7. Acid A and Acid B are mixed in the ratio of 1:3 to form a strong cleaning solution. How many gallons of Acid B are required to make $1\frac{1}{2}$ gallons of the cleaning solution?

    7–A $4\frac{1}{2}$

    7–B $1\frac{1}{2}$

    7–C $1\frac{1}{8}$

    7–D   5

8. If 1 quart of iced tea requires 3 tablespoons of sugar, how many tablespoons of sugar are needed for 1 gallon of iced tea?

    8–A   12

    8–B $\frac{3}{4}$

    8–C   16

    8–D   4

9. Anton the artist has a favorite color, which he makes by mixing 3 parts of Deep Brown to 4 parts of Yak Yellow. If Anton needs approximately 35 grams of his special color mixture, how many grams of Deep Brown should he use?

    9–A   50

    9–B   35

    9–C   15

    9–D   3

10. A science teacher mixed 27 grams of hydrochloric acid and 13 grams of nitric acid to use in a demonstration for his class. All of the other teachers liked the demonstration so much that they asked for 1 pound of acid mixture to use in their own classes. How many grams of hydrochloric acid should the science teacher use to make up 1 pound of the acid mixture? (1 pound = 454 grams)

    10–A   27.50

    10–B   306.45

    10–C   327.33

    10–D   454

Your Score _____

Answer Key				
1. D	2. C	3. B	4. D	5. A
6. A	7. C	8. A	9. C	10. B

Answers and Explanations

1–D Let R = cups of rice that Wanda's mother needs.

Set up a proportion as follows:

The Recipe		**Mother's Soup**
$\dfrac{\frac{1}{4} \text{ rice}}{16 \text{ cups}}$	$=$	$\dfrac{R \text{ rice}}{4 \text{ cups}}$

Cross-multiply:

$$16 \times R = \frac{1}{4} \times 4 \qquad \text{Divide both sides by 16.}$$

$$R = \frac{1}{16} \text{ cups of rice}$$

But the problem asks for a measurement in *tablespoons*, NOT in *cups*. To change *cups* to *tablespoons*, recall that 16 tablespoons = 1 cup.

$$\frac{1}{16} \; (\text{cup}) \times \frac{16 \; (\text{tbs})}{1 \; (\text{cup})} = 1 \; (\text{tbs})$$

Note: Remember, after you find an answer, check to see if the units are correct. The types of units are stated either directly in the problem or indirectly in the choices.

2–C The main consideration is that the original recipe is for 20 people and the desired recipe is for 180 people: a factor of 1 to 9. Multiply oranges in original recipe by 9.

$9 \times 5 = 45$ oranges

3–B This problem requires two conversions from cups to grams:

$$\frac{1}{3} \; (\text{cup}) \times \frac{8 \; (\text{oz})}{1 \; (\text{cup})} \times \frac{30 \; (\text{grams})}{1 \; (\text{oz})}$$

Cancel out the units, and then multiply the number-fractions:

$$\frac{1}{3} \times 8 \times 30 = 80 \, (\text{grams})$$

4–D   Notice that the recipe is not for one person, but for 4 people.

$$240 \left(\text{people} \right) \times \frac{1 \left(\text{chicken} \right)}{4 \left(\text{people} \right)} =$$

Cancel out the units (people) since they appear in the numerator and in the denominator; then multiply the two numbers:

$$240 \times \frac{1}{4} = 60 \left(\text{chicken} \right)$$

But each chicken weighs approximately $3\frac{1}{4}$ lb, therefore:

$$60 \left(\text{chicken} \right) \times 3\frac{1}{4} \left(\text{lbs}/\,\text{chicken} \right) =$$

Canceling out the units and multiplying the numbers,

$$60 \times 3\frac{1}{4} = 195 \left(\text{lbs} \right)$$

5–A   Two conversions will be needed: (1) from 4 servings to 20 servings (a factor of 5); and (2) from 1 cup of tomatoes to $\frac{1}{2}$ lb of tomatoes (a factor of $\frac{1}{2}$).

Make a small chart to organize the data:

$$\text{Meat } 5 \times 1\frac{1}{2} = 7\frac{1}{2}\text{lb}$$

$$\text{Tomatoes } 5 \times \frac{1}{2} = 2\frac{1}{2}\text{lb}$$

Note: The problem asks for the total weight of the meat and the tomatoes, so the values must be ADDED:

$$7\frac{1}{2} + 2\frac{1}{2} = 10 \left(\text{pounds} \right)$$

6–A   One pint of thinner is needed for 1 gallon of paint. $1\frac{1}{2}$ pints of thinner are needed for $1\frac{1}{2}$ gallons of paint. Seven rooms need $7 \times 1\frac{1}{2}$ pints of thinner.

$$7 \times 1\frac{1}{2} = 7 \times \frac{3}{2} = \frac{21}{2} = 10\frac{1}{2}$$

$10\frac{1}{2}$ pints of thinner are required.

7–C   If the ratio is 1:3, then the ratio of B to the whole amount is 3:4 (where $4 = 3 + 1$).

Setting up a ratio:

$$\frac{\text{the part of } B}{\text{the whole solution}} = \frac{B}{1\frac{1}{2}} = \frac{3}{4}$$

Cross-multiplying, we find:

$$B \times 4 = 3 \times 1\frac{1}{2} = 4\frac{1}{2}$$

$$B = \frac{4\frac{1}{2}}{4} = \frac{9}{2} \times \frac{1}{4}$$

$$\frac{9}{8} = 1\frac{1}{8} \text{ gallons}$$

8–A   4 cups are in 1 quart of liquid. 4 quarts are in 1 gallon.

Set up a proportion of sugar to cups of iced tea:

$$\frac{\text{original sugar}}{\text{original volume}} = \frac{\text{final sugar}}{\text{final volume}}$$

Let S = final sugar needed in 1 gallon:

$$\frac{3 \text{ tbs}}{4 \text{ cups}} = \frac{S}{16 \text{ cups}}$$

Cross-multiply to find amount of sugar in larger recipe:

$$S \times 4 = 3 \times 16$$

$$S \times \frac{48}{4} = 12 \text{ tbs}$$

9–C   Since 35 represents the total mixture, let B represent the amount of brown used in the mixture, and:

$$\frac{\text{brown}}{\text{total}} = \frac{3}{7} = \frac{B}{35}$$

Cross-multiplying:

$$3 \times 35 = 7 \times B$$

$$\frac{105}{7} = B$$

$$15 \text{ grams} = B$$

10–B   Set up a proportion of hydrochloric acid (HCl) to total mixture:

$$\frac{\text{original HCl}}{\text{original total mix}} = \frac{\text{desired HCl}}{\text{desired total mix}}$$

$$\frac{27 \text{ grams}}{27 \text{ grams} + 13 \text{ grams}} = \frac{\text{HCl}}{454 \text{ grams}}$$

$$(1 \text{ pound} = 454 \text{ grams})$$

Cross-multiply:

$$40 \times \text{HCl} = 27 \times 454$$

$$\text{HCl} = \frac{12258}{40} = 306.45 \text{ grams}$$

Topic Review

Ratio and Proportion Problems

1. A ratio is the quotient of two numbers. The ratio of 2 to 5 may be expressed $2 \div 5$, $\frac{2}{5}$, 2 is to 5, 2:5, or algebraically as $2x{:}5x$.

    The numbers in a ratio are called the terms of the ratio.

2. A **proportion** states that two ratios are equal.

    In the proportion $a{:}b = c{:}d$ (which may also be written $\frac{a}{b} = \frac{c}{d}$), the inner terms, b and c, are called the **means**; the outer terms, a and d, are called the **extremes**.
    Example: In $3{:}6 = 5{:}10$, the means are 6 and 5; the extremes are 3 and 10.

    In any proportion, the product of the means equals the product of the extremes.
    In $a{:}b = c{:}d$, $bc = ad$.

    Example: In $3{:}6 = 5{:}10$, or $= \frac{3}{6} = \frac{5}{10}$, $6 \times 5 = 3 \times 10$.

    In many problems, the quantities involved are in proportion. If three quantities are given in a problem and the fourth quantity is unknown, determine whether the quantities should form a proportion. The proportion will be the equation for the problem.
    Example: A tree that is 20 feet tall casts a shadow 12 feet long. At the same time, a pole casts a shadow 3 feet long. How tall is the pole?

    SOLUTION: Let p = height of pole. The heights of objects and their shadows are in proportion.

$$\frac{\text{tree}}{\text{tree's shadow}} = \frac{\text{pole}}{\text{pole's shadow}}$$ The product of the means equals the product of the extremes.

$$\frac{20}{12} = \frac{p}{3}$$

$$12p = 60$$

$$\frac{12p}{12} = \frac{60}{12}$$

$$p = 5$$

Answer: The pole is 5 feet tall.

Example: The scale on a map is 3 cm = 500 km. If two cities are 15 cm apart on the map, how far apart are they actually?

SOLUTION: Let d = actual distance. The quantities on maps and scale drawings are in proportion to the quantities they represent.

$$\frac{\text{first map distance}}{\text{first actual distance}} = \frac{\text{second map distance}}{\text{second actual distance}}$$

$$\frac{3 \text{ cm}}{500 \text{ km}} = \frac{15 \text{ cm}}{d \text{ km}}$$

$$3d = 7500$$

$$\frac{3d}{3} = \frac{7500}{3}$$

$$d = 2500$$

Answer: The cities are 2500 km apart.

TOPIC 7: AVERAGES

Model Problem:

The first 3 runners to cross the finish line in the first race had the following times:

Merry   1 minute 59 seconds

Marsha   2 minutes 1 second

Maria   2 minutes 6 seconds

What was the average time for these runners in seconds?

A 361

B 207

C 122

D 118

SOLUTION:

1. Convert all times to seconds:
    Merry: 60 sec/min × 1 min + 59 sec = 60 + 59 = 119 sec
    Marsha: 60 sec/min × 2 min + 1 sec = 120 + 1 = 121 sec
    Maria: 60 sec/min × 2 min + 6 sec = 120 + 3 = 126 sec

2. Add to find total time:
    119 + 121 + 126 = 366 sec

3. Divide by number of runners to find average time:

    $$\frac{366}{3} = 122 \text{ seconds}$$

    The correct answer is choice C.

Now try Practice Exercise 7. Check your answers against the answers and explanations that follow and enter your score on the line provided. If your score is 8 or more, go on to Topic 8. If your score is less than 8, study the Topic Review before going on to the next topic area.

Practice Exercise 7

1. The average (arithmetic mean) of 73.8, 92.2, 64.7, 43.8, 56.5, and 46.4 is
    1–A 60.6
    1–B 61.00
    1–C 61.28
    1–D 62.9

2. The median of the numbers 8, 5, 7, 5, 9, 9, 1, 8, 10, 5, and 10 is
    2–A 5
    2–B 7
    2–C 8
    2–D 9

3. The mode of the numbers 16, 15, 17, 12, 15, 15, 18, 19, and 18 is
    3–A 15
    3–B 16
    3–C 17
    3–D 18

4. A clerk filed 73 forms on Monday, 85 forms on Tuesday, 54 on Wednesday, 92 on Thursday, and 66 on Friday. What was the average number of forms filed per day?
    4–A 60
    4–B 72
    4–C 74
    4–D 92

5. The grades received on a test by 20 students were 69, 70, 73, 68, and 75. The average of these grades is

   5–A   70
   5–B   71
   5–C   77
   5–D   80

6. A buyer purchased 75 six-inch rulers costing 15¢ each, 100 one-foot rulers costing 30¢ each, and 50 one-yard rulers costing 72¢ each. What was the average price per ruler?

   6–A $26\frac{1}{8}$¢

   6–B $34\frac{1}{3}$¢

   6–C   39¢
   6–D   42¢

7. What is the average of a student who received 90 in English, 84 in Algebra, 75 in French, and 76 in Music, if the subjects have the following weights: English 4, Algebra 3, French 3, and Music 1?

   7–A   81

   7–B $81\frac{1}{2}$

   7–C   82
   7–D   83

Items 8 to 10 refer to the following information.

A census shows that on a certain block of homes the number of children in each family is 3, 4, 4, 0, 1, 2, 0, 2, and 2, respectively.

8. Find the average number of children per family.

   8–A   2

   8–B $2\frac{1}{2}$

   8–C   3

   8–D $3\frac{1}{2}$

9. Find the median number of children.

   9–A   5
   9–B   4
   9–C   3
   9–D   2

10. Find the mode of the number of children.
    10–A   0
    10–B   1
    10–C   2
    10–D   4

Answer Key

1. D	2. C	3. A	4. C	5. B
6. B	7. D	8. A	9. D	10. C

Answers and Explanations

1–D   Find the sum of the values:

$73.8 + 92.2 + 64.7 + 43.8 + 56.5 + 46.4 = 377.4$

There are 6 values.

Arithmetic mean $= \dfrac{377.4}{6} = 62.9$

2–C   Arrange the numbers in order:

$1, 5, 5, 5, 7, 8, 8, 9, 9, 10, 10$

The middle number, or median, is 8.

3–A   The mode is the number that appears most frequently. The number 15 appears three times.

4–C   Average $= \dfrac{73 + 85 + 54 + 92 + 66}{5} = \dfrac{370}{5} = 74$

5–B $69 + 70 + 73 + 68 + 75 = 355$

$\dfrac{355}{5} = 71$

6–B

$75 \times 15¢ = 1125¢$
$100 \times 30¢ = 3000¢$
$\underline{50} \times 72¢ = \underline{3600¢}$
$225 \qquad\quad = 7725¢$

$\dfrac{7725¢}{225} = 34¢ \text{ (rounded)}$

7–D

Subject	Grade	Weight
English	90	4
Algebra	84	3
French	75	3
Music	76	1

$(90 \times 4) + (84 \times 3) + (75 \times 3) + (76 \times 1)$

$360 + 252 + 225 + 76 = 913$

$\text{Weight} = 4 + 3 + 3 + 1 = 11$

$913 \div 11 = 83 \text{ average}$

8–A $\text{Average} = \dfrac{3 + 4 + 4 + 0 + 1 + 2 + 0 + 2 + 2}{9} = \dfrac{18}{9} = 2$

9–D   Arrange the numbers in order:

0, 0, 1, 2, 2, 2, 3, 4, 4

Of the 9 numbers, the fifth (middle) number is 2.

10–C   The number appearing most often is 2.

Topic Review

1. The averages used in statistics include the arithmetic mean, the median, and the mode.

Average or Arithmetic Mean

2. The most commonly used average of a group of numbers is the arithmetic mean. It is found by adding the numbers given and then dividing this sum by the number of items being averaged.

    Example: Find the arithmetic mean of 2, 8, 5, 9, 6, and 12.

    SOLUTION: There are 6 numbers.

    $\text{Arithmetic mean} = \dfrac{2 + 8 + 5 + 9 + 6 + 12}{6} = \dfrac{42}{6} = 7$

    Answer: The arithmetic mean is 7.

    If a problem calls for simply the "average" or the "mean," it is referring to the arithmetic mean.

Median

3. If a group of numbers is arranged in order, the middle number is called the median. If there is no single middle number (this occurs when there is an even number of items), the median is found by computing the arithmetic mean of the two middle numbers.

   Example: The median of 6, 8, 10, 12, and 14 is 10.

   Example: The median of 6, 8, 10, 12, 14, and 16 is the arithmetic mean of 10 and 12.

   $$\frac{10+12}{2} = \frac{22}{2} = 11$$

Mode

4. The mode of a group of numbers is the number that appears most often.

   Example: The mode of 10, 5, 7, 9, 12, 5, 19, 5, and 9 is 5.

Weighted Average

5. To obtain the average of quantities that are weighted:

   Set up a table listing the quantities, their respective weights, and their respective values.

   Multiply the value of each quantity by its respective weight.

   Add up these products.

   Add up the weights.

   Divide the sum of the products by the sum of the weights.

   Example: Assume that the weights for the following subjects are: English 3, History 2, Mathematics 2, Foreign Languages 2, and Art 1. What would be the average of a student whose marks are: English 80, History 85, Algebra 84, Spanish 82, and Art 90?

   SOLUTION:

Subject	Weight	Mark
English	3	80
History	2	85
Algebra	2	84
Spanish	2	82
Art	1	90

   $$\text{English } 3 \times 80 = 240$$
   $$\text{History } 2 \times 85 = 170$$
   $$\text{Algebra } 2 \times 84 = 168$$
   $$\text{Spanish } 2 \times 82 = 164$$
   $$\text{Art } 1 \times 90 = \underline{90}$$
   $$= 832$$

Sum of the weights: $3 + 2 + 2 + 2 + 1 = 10$

$$832 \div 10 = 83.2$$

Answer: Average = 83.2

TOPIC 8: GRAPHS

Model Problems:

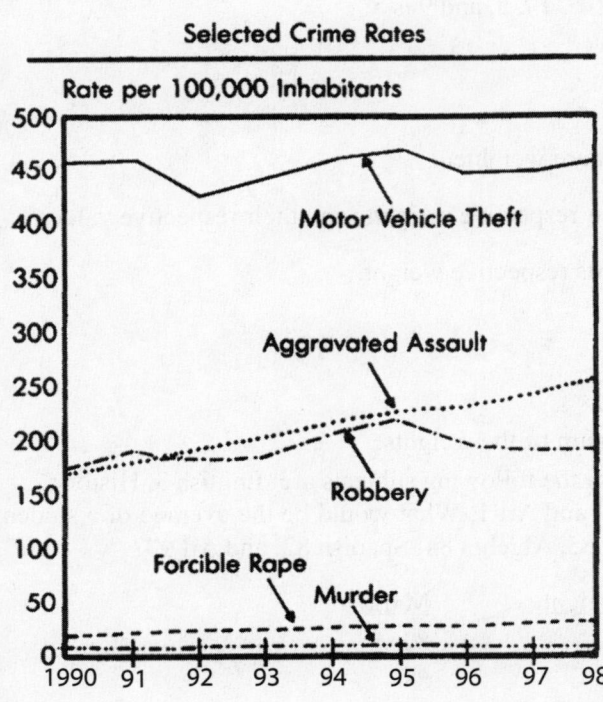

1.   Next to motor vehicle thefts, which crime rate was the highest in 1991?

    1–A   Murder

    1–B   Forcible rape

    1–C   Robbery

    1–D   Aggravated assault

2.   Which crime has steadily increased?

    2–A   Motor vehicle theft

    2–B   Forcible rape

    2–C   Robbery

    2–D   Aggravated assault

3. In a city of 10,000,000, how many motor vehicle thefts would probably have occurred in 1997?

    3–A   4500

    3–B   40,000

    3–C   45,000

    3–D   50,000

SOLUTIONS:

1–C   In 1991, the rate for robbery was about 180, the rate for aggravated assault was about 160, forcible rape was 20, and murder was 30.

2–D   Look at the slope of the graphs. Aggravated assault has an always-increasing slope. Motor vehicle theft and robbery both go up and down. Forcible rape sometimes stays the same.

3–C   In 1997, the rate of motor vehicle thefts was $\dfrac{450 \text{ thefts}}{100,000 \text{ inhabitants}}$.

Set up a proportion and solve for x:

$$\frac{450 \text{ thefts}}{100,000 \text{ people}} = \frac{x \text{ thefts}}{10,000,000 \text{ people}}$$

$$100,000x = 4,500,000,000$$

$$x = \frac{4,500,0\cancel{0}\,\cancel{0},\cancel{0}\,\cancel{0}\,\cancel{0}}{1\cancel{0}\,\cancel{0},\cancel{0}\,\cancel{0}\,\cancel{0}} = 45,000$$

Now try Practice Exercise 8. Check your answers against the answers and explanations that follow and enter your score on the line provided. If your score is less than 9, study the topic review before going on to the review tests.

Practice Exercise 8

Items 1 to 3 refer to the following graph.

In the graph below, the lines labeled A and B represent the cumulative progress in the work of two file clerks, each of whom was given 500 consecutively numbered applications to file in the proper cabinets over a five-day workweek.

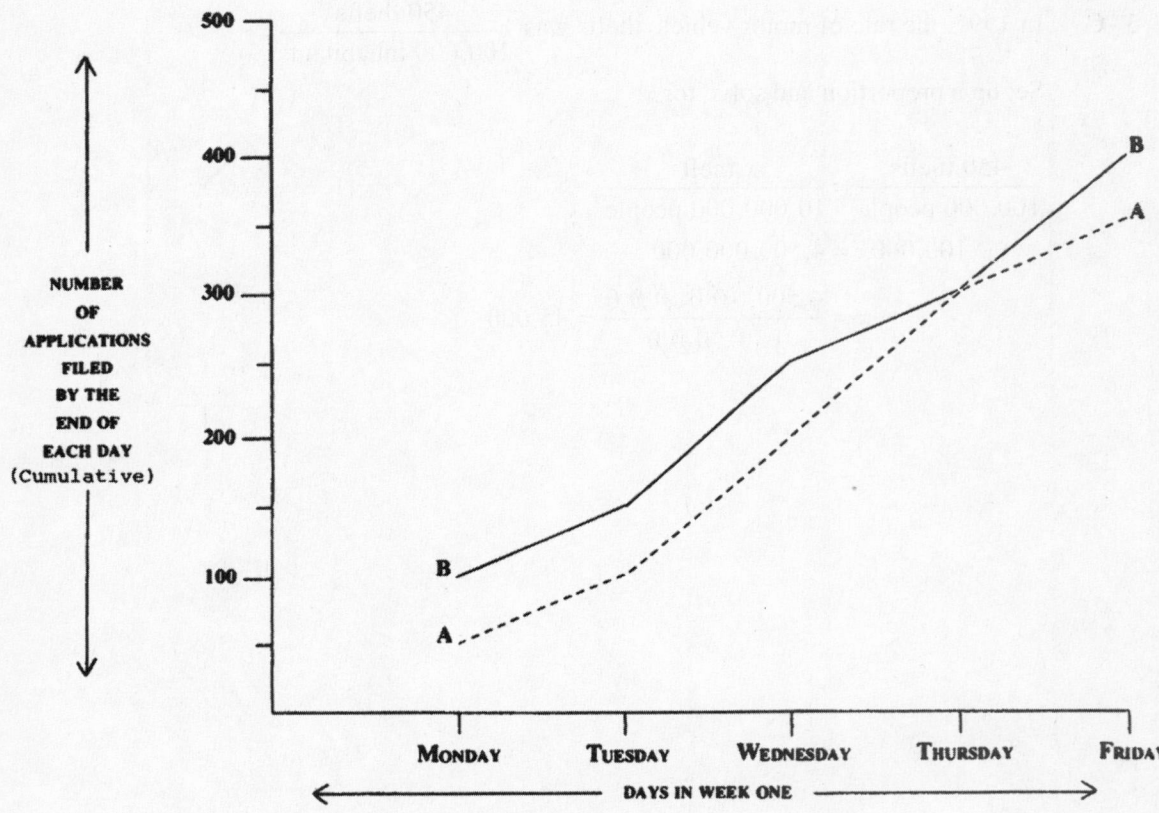

1. The day during which the largest number of applications was filed by both clerks was

    1–A   Monday

    1–B   Tuesday

    1–C   Wednesday

    1–D   Thursday

2. At the end of the second day, the percentage of applications still to be filed was
    2–A   25%
    2–B   50%
    2–C   66%
    2–D   75%

3. Assuming that the production pattern is the same the following week as the week shown in the chart, the day on which Clerk B will finish this assignment will be
    3–A   Monday.
    3–B   Tuesday.
    3–C   Wednesday.
    3–D   Thursday.

Items 4 to 7 refer to the following graph.

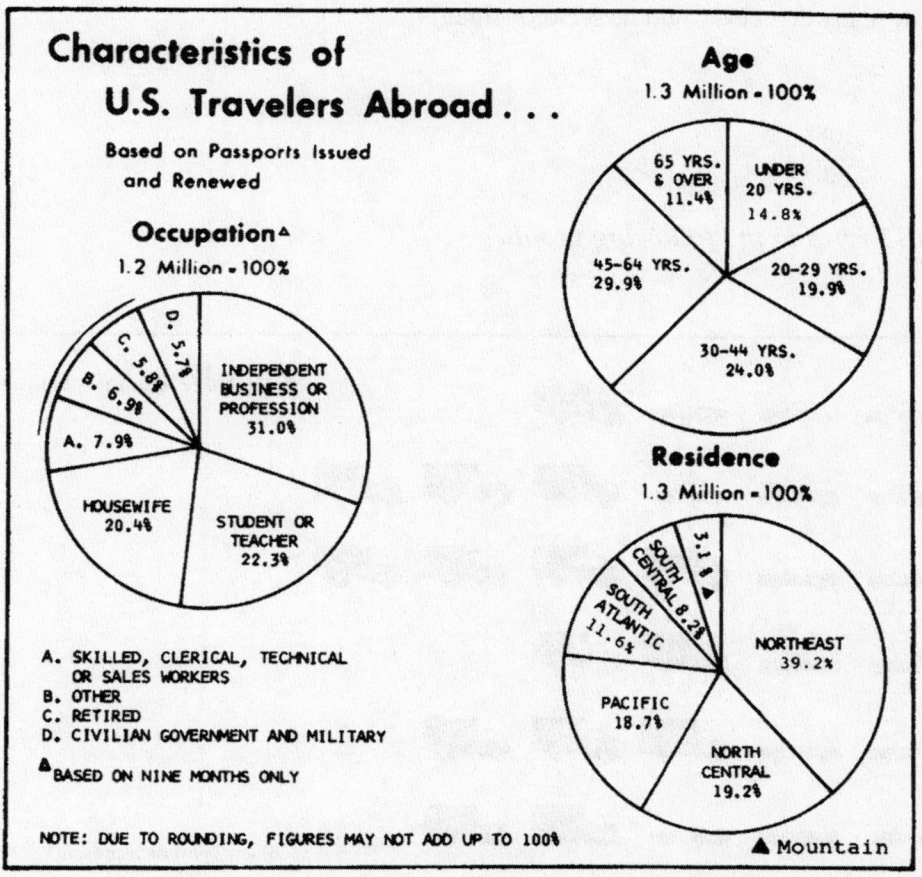

4. Approximately how many persons aged 29 or younger traveled abroad?
    4–A   175,000
    4–B   245,000
    4–C   385,000
    4–D   450,000

5. Of the people who did not live in the Northeast, what percent came from the North Central states?

    5–A   19.2%

    5–B   19.9%

    5–C   26.5%

    5–D   31.6%

6. The fraction of travelers from the four smallest occupation groups is most nearly equal to the fraction of travelers

    6–A   under age 20 and 65 and over, combined.

    6–B   from the North Central and Mountain states.

    6–C   between 45 and 64 years of age.

    6–D   from the Housewife and Other categories.

7. If the South Central, Mountain, and Pacific sections were considered as a single classification, how many degrees would its sector include?

    7–A   30°

    7–B   67°

    7–C   108°

    7–D   120°

Items 8 to 11 refer to the following graph.

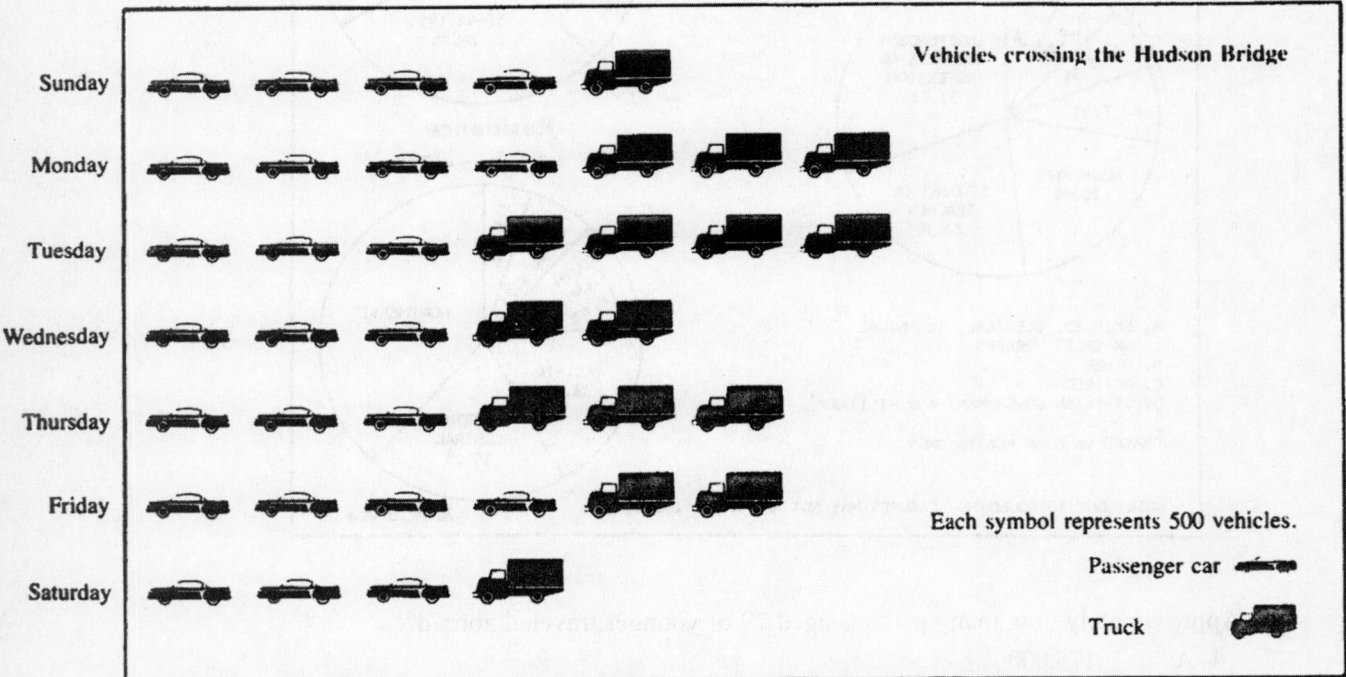

Vehicles crossing the Hudson Bridge

Each symbol represents 500 vehicles.

Passenger car

Truck

8. What percent of the total number of vehicles on Wednesday were cars?

    8–A   30%

    8–B   60%

    8–C   20%

    8–D   50%

9. What was the total number of vehicles crossing the bridge on Tuesday?

    9–A   7

    9–B   700

    9–C   1100

    9–D   3500

10. How many more trucks crossed on Monday than on Saturday?

    10–A   200

    10–B   1000

    10–C   1500

    10–D   2000

11. If trucks paid a toll of $1.00 and cars paid a toll of $.50, how much money was collected in tolls on Friday?

    11–A $600

    11–B $1000

    11–C $1500

    11–D $2000

Answer Key

1. C	2. D	3. A	4. D	5. D
6. A	7. C	8. B	9. D	10. B
11. D				

Answers and Explanations

1–C   For both A and B, the greatest increase in the cumulative totals occurred from the end of Tuesday to the end of Wednesday. Therefore, the largest number of applications was filed on Wednesday.

2–D   By the end of Tuesday, A had filed 100 applications and B had filed 150, for a total of 250. This left 750 of the original 1000 applications.

$$\frac{750}{1000} = .75 = 75\%$$

3–A   During Week One, Clerk B files 100 applications on Monday, 50 on Tuesday, 100 on Wednesday, 50 on Thursday, and 100 on Friday, for a total of 400 applications. On Monday of Week Two, he will file numbers 401 to 500.

4–D   20–29 yrs.:   19.9%

Under 20 yrs.:   +14.8%

34.7%

$34.7\% \times 1.3 \text{ million} = .347 \times 1.3 \text{ million} = .4511 \text{ million}$
$= 451,100$

5–D $100\% - 39.2\% = 60.8\%$ did not live in the Northeast.

19.2% lived in North Central states

$\dfrac{19.2}{60.8} = .316$ approximately $= 31.6\%$

6–A   Four smallest groups of occupation:

$7.9 + 6.9 + 5.8 + 5.7 = 26.3$

Age groups under 20 and over 65:

$14.8 + 11.4 = 26.2$

7–C   South Central: 8.2%

Mountain: 3.1%

Pacific: 18.7%

30.0%

$30\% \times 360° = .30 \times 360° = 108°$

8–B   There are 5 vehicle symbols, of which 3 are cars.

$\dfrac{3}{5} = 60\%$

9–D   On Tuesday, there were $3 \times 500 = 1500$ cars and $4 \times 500 = 2000$ trucks. The total number of vehicles was 3500.

10–B   The graph shows 2 more truck symbols on Monday than on Saturday. Each symbol represents 500 trucks, so there were $2 \times 500 = 1000$ more trucks on Monday.

11–D   On Friday there were

$4 \times 500 = 2000$ cars

$2 \times 500 = 1000$ trucks

Car tolls: $2000 \times \$.50$ = $1000

Truck tolls: $1000 \times \$1.00$ =   +$1000

Total tolls: $2000

Topic Review

1. **Graphs** illustrate comparisons and trends in statistical information. The most commonly used graphs are **bar graphs, line graphs, circle graphs,** and **pictographs.**

Bar Graphs

2. Bar graphs are used to compare various quantities. Each bar may represent a single quantity or may be divided to represent several quantities.

3. Bar graphs may have horizontal or vertical bars.

    Examples:

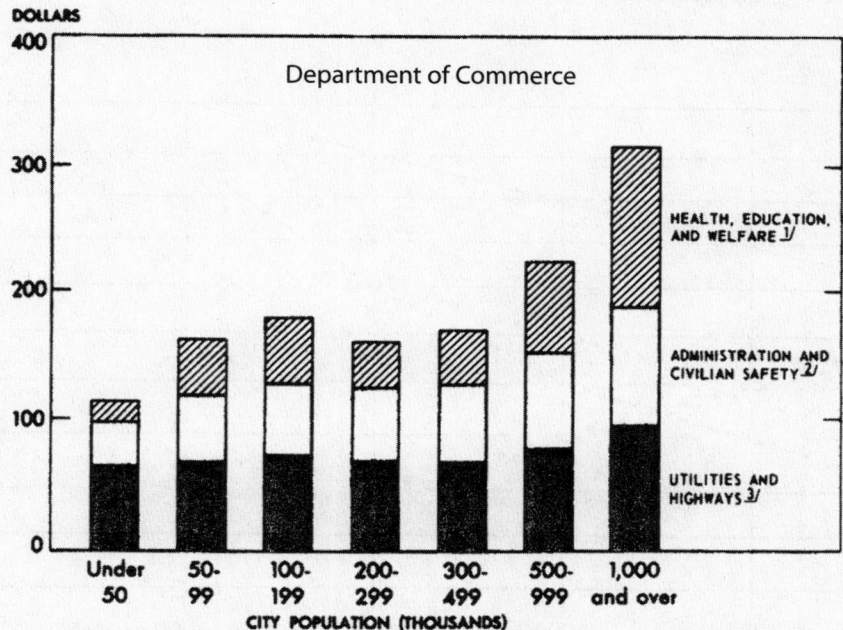

Municipal Expenditures, Per Capita

Question 1: What was the approximate municipal expenditure per capita in cities having populations of 200,000 to 299,000?

Answer: The middle bar of the seven shown represents cities having populations from 200,000 to 299,000. This bar reaches about halfway between 100 and 200. Therefore, the per capita expenditure was approximately $150.

Question 2: Which cities spend the most per capita on health, education, and welfare?

Answer: The bar for cities having populations of 1,000,000 and over has a larger striped section than the other bars. Therefore, those cities spent the most.

Question 3: Of the three categories of expenditures, which was least dependent on city size?

Answer: The expenditures for utilities and highways, the darkest part of each bar, varied least as city size increased.

Line Graphs

4. Line graphs are used to show trends, often over a period of time.

5. A line graph may include more than one line, with each line representing a different item.

    Example:

The graph below indicates at 5-year intervals the number of citations issued for various offenses from the year 1980 to the year 2000.

Question 4: Over the 20-year period, which offense shows an average rate of increase of more than 150 citations per year?

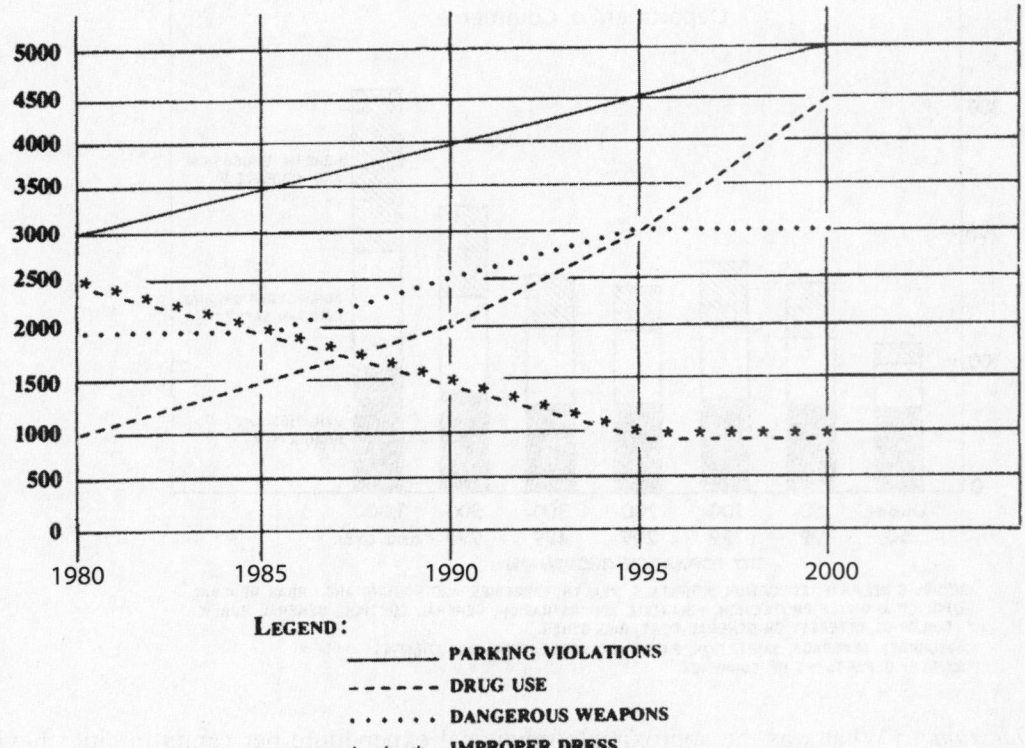

LEGEND:

————— PARKING VIOLATIONS

- - - - - DRUG USE

. . . . . . DANGEROUS WEAPONS

--*- IMPROPER DRESS

Answer: Drug-use citations increased from 1000 in 1980 to 4500 in 2000.

The average increase over the 20-year period is $\dfrac{3500}{20} = 175$.

Question 5: Over the 20-year period, which offense shows a constant rate of increase or decrease?

Answer: A straight line indicates a constant rate of increase or decrease. Of the four lines, the one representing parking violations is the only straight one.

Question 6: Which offense shows a total increase or decrease of 50% for the full 20-year period?

Answer: Dangerous-weapons citations increased from 2000 in 1980 to 3000 in 2000, which is an increase of 50%.

Circle Graphs

6. Circle graphs are used to show the relationship of various parts of a quantity to each other and to the whole quantity.

7. Percents are often used in circle graphs. The 360 degrees of the circle represent 100%.

8. Each part of the circle graph is called a sector.

Example: The following circle graph shows how the federal budget of $300.4 billion was spent.

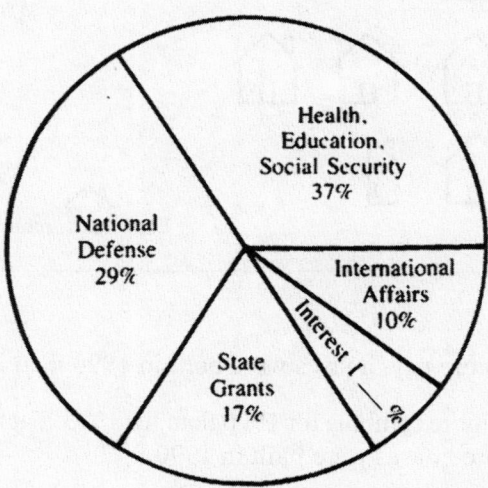

Question 7: What is the value of I?

Answer: There must be a total of 100% in a circle graph. The sum of the other sectors is: 17% + 29% + 37% + 10% = 93%
  Therefore, I = 100% − 93% = 7%.

Question 8: How much money was actually spent on national defense?

Answer: 29% × $300.4 billion = $87.116 billion
                                 = $87,116,000,000

Question 9: How much more money was spent on state grants than on interest?

Answer: $17\% - 7\% = 10\%$

$10\% \times \$300.4 \text{ billion} = .10 \times 300.4 \text{ billion}$

$= \$30.04 \text{ billion}$

$= \$30,040,000,000$

Pictographs

9. Pictographs allow comparisons of quantities by using symbols. Each symbol represents a given number of a particular item.

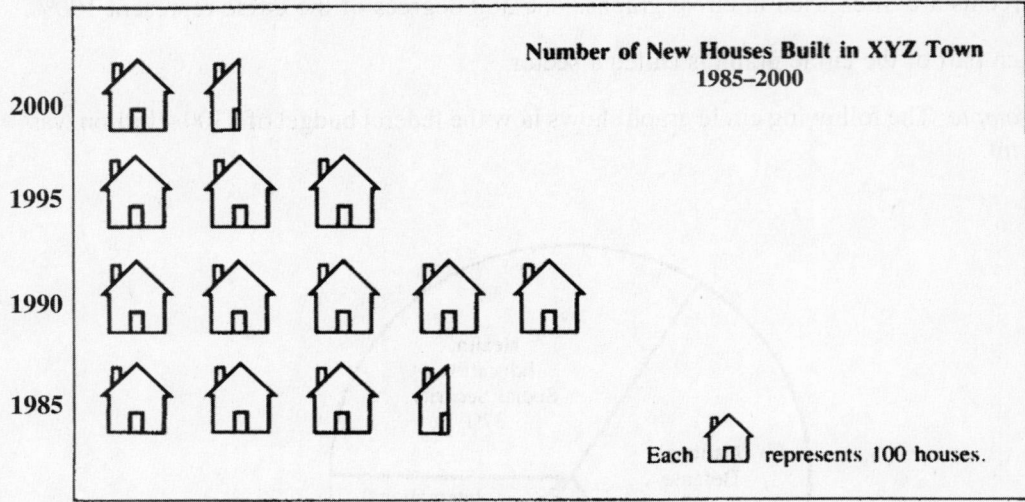

Example:

Question 10: How many more new houses were built in 1990 than in 1995?

Answer: There are two more symbols for 1990 than for 1995. Each symbol represents 100 houses. Therefore, 200 more houses were built in 1990.

Question 11: How many new houses were built in 1985?

Answer: There are $3\frac{1}{2}$ symbols shown for 1985; $3\frac{1}{2} \times 100 = 350$ houses.

Question 12: In which year were half as many houses built as in 1995?

Answer: In 1995, $3 \times 100 = 300$ houses were built. Half of 300, or 150, houses were built in 2000.

THREE SAMPLE ARITHMETIC REASONING TESTS

This section contains three full-length sample Arithmetic Reasoning Tests similar to the ones on the ASVAB. You can tear out this page and use the answer strips below to record your answers to the sample tests, just as you will have to do on the real test. Stick to the time limit for realistic practice. As you finish each sample test, check your answers with the answer key and explanations provided.

Arithmetic Reasoning Test 1

1. Ⓐ Ⓑ Ⓒ Ⓓ   2. Ⓐ Ⓑ Ⓒ Ⓓ   3. Ⓐ Ⓑ Ⓒ Ⓓ   4. Ⓐ Ⓑ Ⓒ Ⓓ   5. Ⓐ Ⓑ Ⓒ Ⓓ
6. Ⓐ Ⓑ Ⓒ Ⓓ   7. Ⓐ Ⓑ Ⓒ Ⓓ   8. Ⓐ Ⓑ Ⓒ Ⓓ   9. Ⓐ Ⓑ Ⓒ Ⓓ   10. Ⓐ Ⓑ Ⓒ Ⓓ
11. Ⓐ Ⓑ Ⓒ Ⓓ   12. Ⓐ Ⓑ Ⓒ Ⓓ   13. Ⓐ Ⓑ Ⓒ Ⓓ   14. Ⓐ Ⓑ Ⓒ Ⓓ   15. Ⓐ Ⓑ Ⓒ Ⓓ
16. Ⓐ Ⓑ Ⓒ Ⓓ   17. Ⓐ Ⓑ Ⓒ Ⓓ   18. Ⓐ Ⓑ Ⓒ Ⓓ   19. Ⓐ Ⓑ Ⓒ Ⓓ   20. Ⓐ Ⓑ Ⓒ Ⓓ
21. Ⓐ Ⓑ Ⓒ Ⓓ   22. Ⓐ Ⓑ Ⓒ Ⓓ   23. Ⓐ Ⓑ Ⓒ Ⓓ   24. Ⓐ Ⓑ Ⓒ Ⓓ   25. Ⓐ Ⓑ Ⓒ Ⓓ
26. Ⓐ Ⓑ Ⓒ Ⓓ   27. Ⓐ Ⓑ Ⓒ Ⓓ   28. Ⓐ Ⓑ Ⓒ Ⓓ   29. Ⓐ Ⓑ Ⓒ Ⓓ   30. Ⓐ Ⓑ Ⓒ Ⓓ

Arithmetic Reasoning Test 2

1. Ⓐ Ⓑ Ⓒ Ⓓ   2. Ⓐ Ⓑ Ⓒ Ⓓ   3. Ⓐ Ⓑ Ⓒ Ⓓ   4. Ⓐ Ⓑ Ⓒ Ⓓ   5. Ⓐ Ⓑ Ⓒ Ⓓ
6. Ⓐ Ⓑ Ⓒ Ⓓ   7. Ⓐ Ⓑ Ⓒ Ⓓ   8. Ⓐ Ⓑ Ⓒ Ⓓ   9. Ⓐ Ⓑ Ⓒ Ⓓ   10. Ⓐ Ⓑ Ⓒ Ⓓ
11. Ⓐ Ⓑ Ⓒ Ⓓ   12. Ⓐ Ⓑ Ⓒ Ⓓ   13. Ⓐ Ⓑ Ⓒ Ⓓ   14. Ⓐ Ⓑ Ⓒ Ⓓ   15. Ⓐ Ⓑ Ⓒ Ⓓ
16. Ⓐ Ⓑ Ⓒ Ⓓ   17. Ⓐ Ⓑ Ⓒ Ⓓ   18. Ⓐ Ⓑ Ⓒ Ⓓ   19. Ⓐ Ⓑ Ⓒ Ⓓ   20. Ⓐ Ⓑ Ⓒ Ⓓ
21. Ⓐ Ⓑ Ⓒ Ⓓ   22. Ⓐ Ⓑ Ⓒ Ⓓ   23. Ⓐ Ⓑ Ⓒ Ⓓ   24. Ⓐ Ⓑ Ⓒ Ⓓ   25. Ⓐ Ⓑ Ⓒ Ⓓ
26. Ⓐ Ⓑ Ⓒ Ⓓ   27. Ⓐ Ⓑ Ⓒ Ⓓ   28. Ⓐ Ⓑ Ⓒ Ⓓ   29. Ⓐ Ⓑ Ⓒ Ⓓ   30. Ⓐ Ⓑ Ⓒ Ⓓ

Arithmetic Reasoning Test 3

1. Ⓐ Ⓑ Ⓒ Ⓓ   2. Ⓐ Ⓑ Ⓒ Ⓓ   3. Ⓐ Ⓑ Ⓒ Ⓓ   4. Ⓐ Ⓑ Ⓒ Ⓓ   5. Ⓐ Ⓑ Ⓒ Ⓓ
6. Ⓐ Ⓑ Ⓒ Ⓓ   7. Ⓐ Ⓑ Ⓒ Ⓓ   8. Ⓐ Ⓑ Ⓒ Ⓓ   9. Ⓐ Ⓑ Ⓒ Ⓓ   10. Ⓐ Ⓑ Ⓒ Ⓓ
11. Ⓐ Ⓑ Ⓒ Ⓓ   12. Ⓐ Ⓑ Ⓒ Ⓓ   13. Ⓐ Ⓑ Ⓒ Ⓓ   14. Ⓐ Ⓑ Ⓒ Ⓓ   15. Ⓐ Ⓑ Ⓒ Ⓓ
16. Ⓐ Ⓑ Ⓒ Ⓓ   17. Ⓐ Ⓑ Ⓒ Ⓓ   18. Ⓐ Ⓑ Ⓒ Ⓓ   19. Ⓐ Ⓑ Ⓒ Ⓓ   20. Ⓐ Ⓑ Ⓒ Ⓓ
21. Ⓐ Ⓑ Ⓒ Ⓓ   22. Ⓐ Ⓑ Ⓒ Ⓓ   23. Ⓐ Ⓑ Ⓒ Ⓓ   24. Ⓐ Ⓑ Ⓒ Ⓓ   25. Ⓐ Ⓑ Ⓒ Ⓓ
26. Ⓐ Ⓑ Ⓒ Ⓓ   27. Ⓐ Ⓑ Ⓒ Ⓓ   28. Ⓐ Ⓑ Ⓒ Ⓓ   29. Ⓐ Ⓑ Ⓒ Ⓓ   30. Ⓐ Ⓑ Ⓒ Ⓓ

ARITHMETIC REASONING TEST 1

TIME: 36 Minutes—30 Questions

This test has 30 questions about arithmetic. Each question is followed by four possible answers. Decide which answer is correct, then blacken the space on your answer form that has the same number and letter as your choice. Use scrap paper for any figuring you need to do.

Your score on this test will be based on the number of questions you answer correctly. You should try to answer every question. Do not spend too much time on any one question.

1. Christine bought 80 shares of stock at $12 per share. If the value of the stock increased by 25%, how many dollars would her stock be worth?

    1–A $960
    1–B $1200
    1–C $1500
    1–D $1000

2. Three identical automobiles are parked, bumper-to-bumper, along a curb. The first car is 40 feet from the corner. How many feet is the farthest part of the third car from the corner, if each car is 14 feet long?

    2–A   42
    2–B   82
    2–C   54
    2–D   75

3. A 12-foot 9-inch flag pole stands on a 6-foot 5-inch base atop a 53-foot building. How far is the top of the flag from the ground?

    3–A   71 feet 9 inches
    3–B   72 feet
    3–C   65 feet 5 inches
    3–D   72 feet 2 inches

4. For her 4-hour daily homework plan, Sonya spends $\frac{1}{2}$ of the time on math, $\frac{1}{8}$ on science, $\frac{1}{8}$ on English, and the rest on history. How much time does she spend on science and English?

    4–A $\frac{1}{2}$ hour

    4–B   1 hour

    4–C   2 hours

    4–D $\frac{1}{8}$ hour

5. The senior class sold plants at a fair. It cost $.65 to grow each plant, but the plants were sold for $2.25 each. How much profit did the class make on 8 plants sold?

    5–A $1.60
    5–B $16.00
    5–C $12.80
    5–D $6.60

6. Pens that cost $1.24 a dozen to manufacture are sold for $2.20 a dozen. How much profit is made on each pen?

    6–A $.96
    6–B $.48
    6–C $.16
    6–D $.08

7. Two hundred and fifty people entered the empty dance hall by 8 p.m. If 70 left by 11 p.m., how many couples still remained? Assume that only couples entered or left.

    7–A   200
    7–B   180
    7–C   100
    7–D   90

8. The Braves baseball team won the ballgame. Their hits were distributed as follows:

    $\frac{2}{5}$ in innings 1–3

    $\frac{1}{5}$ in innings 4–6

    $\frac{2}{5}$ in innings 7–9

    What percent of their hits did they get in innings 7–9?

    8–A   80
    8–B   60
    8–C   40
    8–D   20

9. In Hotel Denver, the owners washed sheets during the week of January as follows:

    250 sheets week 1
    350 sheets week 2
    250 sheets week 3
    400 sheets week 4

What fraction of the sheet-washings were done during the third week?

9–A $\dfrac{1}{2}$

9–B $\dfrac{1}{4}$

9–C $\dfrac{1}{10}$

9–D $\dfrac{1}{5}$

10. Barbara asked her mother at 8:40 a.m. on Sunday, "How much time do I have before the test if the exam begins at 10:20 a.m. tomorrow?" What should her mother answer?
    10–A   25 hours
    10–B   25 hours 40 min
    10–C   30 hours 20 min
    10–D   28 hours

11. Roberta wanted to make a large fruit salad for her Fourth of July party. Her register receipt showed the following:

    Apples $1.75
    Grapes $2.75
    Peaches $2.50
    Watermelon $8.50

    How much change should Roberta get back if she hands the cashier a $20 bill?
    11–A $4.50
    11–B $5.00
    11–C $15.50
    11–D $20.00

12. Steven weighed 271.50 pounds when he decided to go on a diet. A year later, he weighed 161.61 pounds. Approximately how many pounds did Steven lose?
    12–A   162
    12–B   100
    12–C   110
    12–D   112

13. The empty bus started out from the terminal, picking up 5 passengers at Market Street, unloading 3 passengers at Broadway, picking up 12 at Main Street, and unloading 5 at Logan Avenue. How many passengers were still on the bus after the Logan Avenue stop?
    13–A   25
    13–B   18
    13–C   10
    13–D   9

14. In preparation for football season, Tony increased his weight from 135 lbs 6 oz to 168 lbs 4 oz. How much weight did he gain?

    14–A   32 lbs
    14–B   35 lbs 6 oz
    14–C   33 lbs
    14–D   32 lbs 14 oz

15. Two cups of warm water were added to the 8 cups of boiling water in the soup pot. If Mrs. Katz added 2 cups of cold water to cool the soup for her son Timmy, how many total cups of water made up the soup?

    15–A   16
    15–B   18
    15–C   12
    15–D   6

16. "When will supper be ready, Mom?" cried Helen. "I told you 10 minutes ago that it would be ready in 15 minutes," replied her mother. When will Helen's supper be ready?

    16–A   In 10 minutes

    16–B   In $7\frac{1}{2}$ minutes

    16–C   In 5 minutes
    16–D   In 15 minutes

17. The baseball team scored 5, 8, 6, 7, and 4 runs in their last 5 games respectively. What was their average number of runs for these games?

    17–A   30
    17–B   5
    17–C   6
    17–D   11

18. Paul wishes to cut cylindrical discs for checkers out of a 6′ 3″ long pole. How many discs can he get if each disc is $\frac{1}{2}''$ wide?

    18–A   75
    18–B   80
    18–C   100
    18–D   150

19. Ms. Jones, of Jones's Travel Bureau, received a 15% commission on all sales. If her sales were $3000 in March and $8000 in April, how much commission did she earn for March and April?

    19–A $450
    19–B $1650
    19–C $750
    19–D $1000

20. One salami sandwich requires $\frac{1}{4}$ lb of salami. How many pounds of salami are required to make 72 sandwiches?

    20–A   72

    20–B   18

    20–C   36

    20–D   24

21. If each hot dog and each hamburger requires a roll, how many rolls will be needed to serve 50 people if each person eats 1 hot dog and 2 hamburgers?

    21–A   50

    21–B   150

    21–C   100

    21–D   300

22. How many pieces of 4-inch pipe can be cut from a piece of 4-foot stock?

    22–A   6

    22–B   4

    22–C   24

    22–D   12

23. Fred goes to Europe, where he must weigh himself in kilograms. How much will 150-pound Fred weigh in kilograms on a European scale? (Note: 2.2 pounds = 1 kilogram)

    23–A   75

    23–B   68.2

    23–C   65.2

    23–D   60.8

24. Police officer Polz started Monday with a new book of 200 summonses. For the first three days of the week, he wrote the following summonses:

Monday   25

Tuesday   43

Wednesday   42

How many summonses did he have left when he started work on Thursday?

    24–A   90

    24–B   310

    24–C   210

    24–D   110

25. Pens that normally sell for $2 each were on sale for 2 for $3. How much would Gary save if he bought 10 pens at the sale price?

    25–A $10

    25–B $20

    25–C $5

    25–D $35

26. Nancy needed a 29-cent pencil but had only a $10 bill. How much change should she get?

    26–A $9.51

    26–B $10.29

    26–C $10.71

    26–D $9.71

27. Calculate 3×16^2.

    27–A   256

    27–B   512

    27–C   768

    27–D   800

28. Calculate $\dfrac{4^2}{4^3}$.

    28–A $\dfrac{1}{40}$

    28–B $\dfrac{1}{2}$

    28–C $\dfrac{1}{8}$

    28–D $\dfrac{1}{4}$

Items 29 and 30 refer to the following graph.

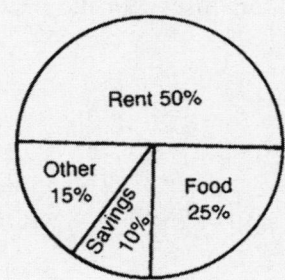

Bob's Monthly Budget

29. How much does Bob spend each month on food and rent if he earns $800 per month?

    29–A $400

    29–B $600

    29–C $800

    29–D $250

30. How much could Bob save each month if he went on a diet and reduced his food expenses to 19% of his monthly budget?

    30–A $25

    30–B $30

    30–C $36

    30–D $48

Answer Key

1. B	2. B	3. D	4. B	5. C
6. D	7. D	8. C	9. D	10. B
11. A	12. C	13. D	14. D	15. C
16. C	17. C	18. D	19. B	20. B
21. B	22. D	23. B	24. A	25. C
26. D	27. C	28. D	29. B	30. D

Answers and Explanations

1–B   Value of 1 stock = original cost + percentage increase of original cost

$12 + ($12 × .25) = $12 + $3 = $15

Multiplying by 80 gives total worth:

80 × $15 = $1200

2–B   Sketch the parked cars:

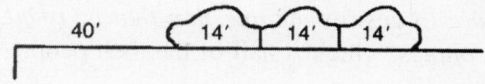

40 + (3 × 14) = 40 + 42 = 82 feet

3–D   Make a sketch:

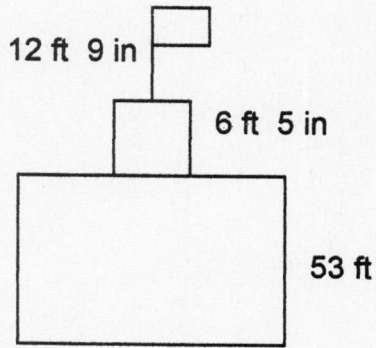

To find total distance, line up the feet and inches and add:

flag:	12 ft	9 in
base:	6 ft	5 in
building:	53 ft	
TOTAL:	71 ft	14 in

4–B Draw a circle graph:

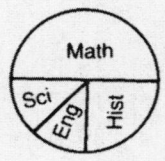

Science: $\dfrac{1}{8}$ of 4 hours $= \dfrac{1}{2}$ hour

English: $\dfrac{1}{8}$ of 4 hours $= \dfrac{1}{2}$ hour

Total   1 hour

5–C Individual Profit = Selling Price – Cost

$8 \times [2.25 - .65] = 8 \times \$1.60 = \$12.80$

6–D For 12 pens, profit is $\$2.20 - \$1.24 = \$.96$

To find the profit on each pen, divide by 12:

$\$.96 \div 12 = \$.08$

7–D $250 - 70 = 180$ people were left. *Be sure to answer the question that is asked.* Here, you are asked for the number of *couples*, which is half of the total people

remaining, or $\dfrac{180}{2} = 90$ couples.

8–C $\frac{2}{5}$ = .40; to change a decimal to a percent, move the decimal point to the right two places, 40%.

9–D   Fraction = $\frac{\text{number washed week 3}}{\text{total washed}}$

$$\frac{250}{250+350+250+400} = \frac{250}{1250} = .20 = \frac{20}{100} = \frac{1}{5}$$

10–B   Break the problem into different time segments:

8:40 a.m. Sunday to 8:40 a.m. Monday = 24 hr

8:40 a.m. Monday to 9 a.m. Monday = 20 min

9 a.m. to 10:20 a.m. = 1 hr 20 min

Adding the hours and the minutes = 25 hours 40 minutes

11–A   Add the prices of the fruits:

1.75 + 2.75 + 2.50 + 8.50 = 15.50

Subtract the total from $20.

$20.00 – $15.50 = $4.50

12–C   Find the difference: before – after

271.50 – 161.61 = 109.89 lbs = 110 lbs (rounded off to nearest pound)

13–D   You must account for all of the passengers at each stop:

Let + mean passengers enter the bus and let – mean they leave.

Before the terminal	0
at Market Street	+ 5
at Broadway	– 3
at Main	+ 12
at Logan	– 5
After Logan	+ 9 passengers

14–D   6 ounces (oz) = 1 pound (lb); 168 lbs 4 oz = 167 lbs 20 oz (In subtracting, borrow 1 pound from the 168 lbs, making it 167 lbs, and add 16 oz to the 4 oz, making it 20 oz)

167 lbs 20 oz
–135 lbs 6 oz
———————
  32 lbs 14 oz

15–C   Add the cups of water:

$$
\begin{array}{r}
2 \text{ cups warm} \\
+8 \text{ cups boiling} \\
+\underline{2 \text{ cups cold}} \\
12 \text{ cups water total}
\end{array}
$$

16–C   Read the dialogue carefully.

10 minutes ago, her mother said that it would be ready in 15 minutes. If she had said that it would be ready in 10 minutes, it would be ready "now." But she said 15 minutes, so it will be ready in 5 minutes.

17–C $\text{Average} = \dfrac{\text{the sum}}{\text{the number of values}}$

$\text{Average} = \dfrac{(5+8+6+7+4)}{5} = \dfrac{30}{5} = 6 \text{ runs per game}$

18–D   Divide: Length of pole $\div \dfrac{1}{2}$

Change the length into inches: $6'3'' = (12 \times 6) + 3 = 75''$

$75'' \div \dfrac{1}{2} = 75 \times \dfrac{2}{1} = 150 \text{ checkers}$

19–B   "15% commission on all sales" is $.15 \times$ (each sale).

March:	$.15 \times 3000$	$= \$450$
April:	$.15 \times 8000$	$= \underline{1200}$
Total Commissions		$\$1650$

20–B   Make a ratio to solve this problem. Let P be the number of pounds of salami required for 72 sandwiches. Then,

$$\frac{\frac{1}{4} \text{ lb}}{1 \text{ sandwich}} = \frac{P \text{ lb}}{72 \text{ sandwiches}}$$

Cross-multiply:

$$\frac{1}{4} \times 72 = P \times 1$$

Solving for P:

$18 \text{ lb} = P$

21–B If each hamburger uses 1 roll, and each person orders 2 hamburgers, and each hot dog uses 1 roll, and each person orders 1 hot dog, then each person gets 3 rolls total. Therefore, 50 people need $50 \times 3 = 150$ rolls.

22–D Draw the picture:

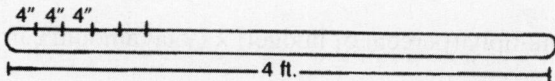

Put both measurements into the same units:

4 [feet] length

$4 \text{ in} = \frac{4}{12} \text{ ft} = \frac{1}{3} \text{ ft individual length}$

Divide:

$4 \div \frac{1}{3} = 4 \times \frac{3}{1} = 12 \text{ pieces}$

23–B **Method 1:** 2.2 pounds is 1 kilogram.

1 pound is $\frac{1}{2.2}$ kilograms.

150 pounds is $150 \times \frac{1}{2.2} = 68.2$ kilograms.

Method 2:

Using unit cancellations:

$150 \left(\cancel{\text{pounds}} \right) \times \dfrac{1 \text{ (kilogram)}}{2.2 \left(\cancel{\text{pounds}} \right)}$

After canceling all units, we arrive at 68.2 kilograms.

24–A The total of summonses (tickets) issued was $25 + 43 + 42 = 110$.

The number left on Thursday was $200 - 110 = 90$ summonses.

25–C Normally, 10 pens would cost $10 \times \$2 = \$20$. On sale, they would be $5 \times \$3 = \$15$, since he would buy 5 sets of two pens to get 10 pens.

The question asks how much Gary would save, not what he paid. (Be sure to answer what is asked for.)

Regular Price – Sale Price = Savings

$\$20 - \$15 = \$5$

26–D $\$10.00 - .29 = \$9.71$

27–C $3 \times 16^2 = 3 \times (16 \times 16) = 3 \times 256 = 768$

28–D $\dfrac{4^2}{4^3} = \dfrac{\overset{1}{\cancel{4}} \times \overset{1}{\cancel{4}}}{4 \times \underset{1}{\cancel{4}} \times \underset{1}{\cancel{4}}} = \dfrac{1}{4}$

29–B   To find the amount Bob spends, multiply (percent of budget) × (total amount earned).

Food: 25% × $800 = .25 × 800   = $200

Rent: 50% × $800 = .50 × 800   = $<u>400</u>

Total (Food & Rent)   = $600

30–D   Bob will save 25 − 19 = 6%

The amount of money is determined as follows: (percent saved) × (total amount earned) = 6% × $800 = .06 × 800 = $48

ARITHMETIC REASONING TEST 2

TIME: 36 Minutes—30 Questions

This test has 30 questions about arithmetic. Each question is followed by four possible answers. Decide which answer is correct, then blacken the space on your answer form that has the same number and letter as your choice. Use scrap paper for any figuring you wish to do.

Your score on this test will be based on the number of questions you answer correctly. You should try to answer every question. Do not spend too much time on any one question.

1. How many 8-ounce cups of coffee can be served from a 2-gallon coffee urn? (4 cups = 1 quart)

    1–A   4
    1–B   16
    1–C   32
    1–D   40

2. A shipment consists of 340 ten-foot pieces of conduit with a coupling on each piece. If the conduit weighs 0.85 lb per foot and each coupling weighs 0.15 lb, the total weight of the shipment is

    2–A   340 lb
    2–B   628 lb
    2–C   2941 lb
    2–D   3400 lb

3. Jeff finished the marathon in 2 hours 28 minutes 32 seconds, and Josh finished it in 2 hours 32 minutes 30 seconds. What was the difference in their times?

    3–A   3 minutes 58 seconds

    3–B   3 minutes

    3–C   2 minutes 2 seconds

    3–D   4 minutes

4. Richard sold 45 newspapers at 25 cents each, making a profit of 11 cents on each paper sold. What was his profit for the day's sales?

    4–A $4.50

    4–B $4.95

    4–C $5.25

    4–D $4.61

5. How many feet are in a 100-yard football field?

    5–A   300

    5–B   250

    5–C   100

    5–D   50

6. At the San Diego Zoo, a ride on Jerry the Giraffe costs $1.50; a book of 5 rides costs $5.00. What percent of the regular ride cost is saved by purchasing the book?

    6–A   25

    6–B $33\frac{1}{3}$

    6–C   75

    6–D   100

7. Mrs. Fletcher cried angrily, "You boys owe me $8.50 for the broken window pane, $6.50 for the damaged rosebush, and $5.50 for the flat tire on my car. You gave me only $10.00!" How much more do the boys owe Mrs. Fletcher?

    7–A $19.50

    7–B $10.00

    7–C $8.50

    7–D $10.50

8. Last week, the trip to school on the bus lasted:

Monday	43 minutes
Tuesday	48 minutes
Wednesday	51 minutes
Thursday	1 hr 2 minutes
Friday	56 minutes

What was the average time in minutes of the bus trip to school?

8–A   52

8–B   58

8–C   62

8–D   260

9. Calculate $\dfrac{4^3}{4^2}$.

9–A $\dfrac{1}{4}$

9–B   40

9–C   4

9–D   400

10. Max's Appliance Mart marked a television set down to $375, which was 25% off the regular price. What was the regular price of the TV?

10–A $93.75

10–B $350.00

10–C $375.25

10–D $500.00

11. If it is 10:38 a.m. now and the swimming meet begins at 3:05 p.m., how much time does the team have to prepare for the big event?

11–A   4 hours 30 minutes

11–B   4 hours 27 minutes

11–C   4 hours 5 minutes

11–D   1 hour 27 minutes

12. Charlie was hungry after the football game, so he stopped at the diner and ordered:

2 eggs and toast	$1.40
2 chocolate milks	$1.50
1 melon	$1.25
3 doughnuts	$1.50

If he left a 15 percent tip, how much did Charlie spend for his meal?

12–A $6.65

12–B $6.50

12–C $5.65

12–D $5.50

13. A collision one morning involved 5 blue cars, 3 red cars, and 2 blue trucks. What percentage of the vehicles involved in this collision were NOT blue?

13–A   30%

13–B   50%

13–C   70%

13–D   3%

14. Arty's $8\frac{1}{4}$ -minute rock song had $3\frac{1}{2}$ minutes left to play. How many minutes of the song had already been played?

    14–A   5

    14–B $11\frac{3}{4}$

    14–C $5\frac{1}{2}$

    14–D $4\frac{3}{4}$

15. Admission to the movies costs $3.00 for adults and $1.50 for children. How much does Mr. Ruiz pay to take his wife and 3 children to the movies?

    15–A $1.50
    15–B $4.50
    15–C $10.50
    15–D $8.50

16. An average tennis match at South Shore High School runs 1 hour 25 minutes. How long would 3 average matches take?

    16–A   1 hour 15 minutes
    16–B   4 hours 15 minutes
    16–C   3 hours
    16–D   4 hours 45 minutes

Items 17 to 19 refer to the following graph, which illustrates the unemployment rate by age and amount of education.

Unemployment Rate in New City

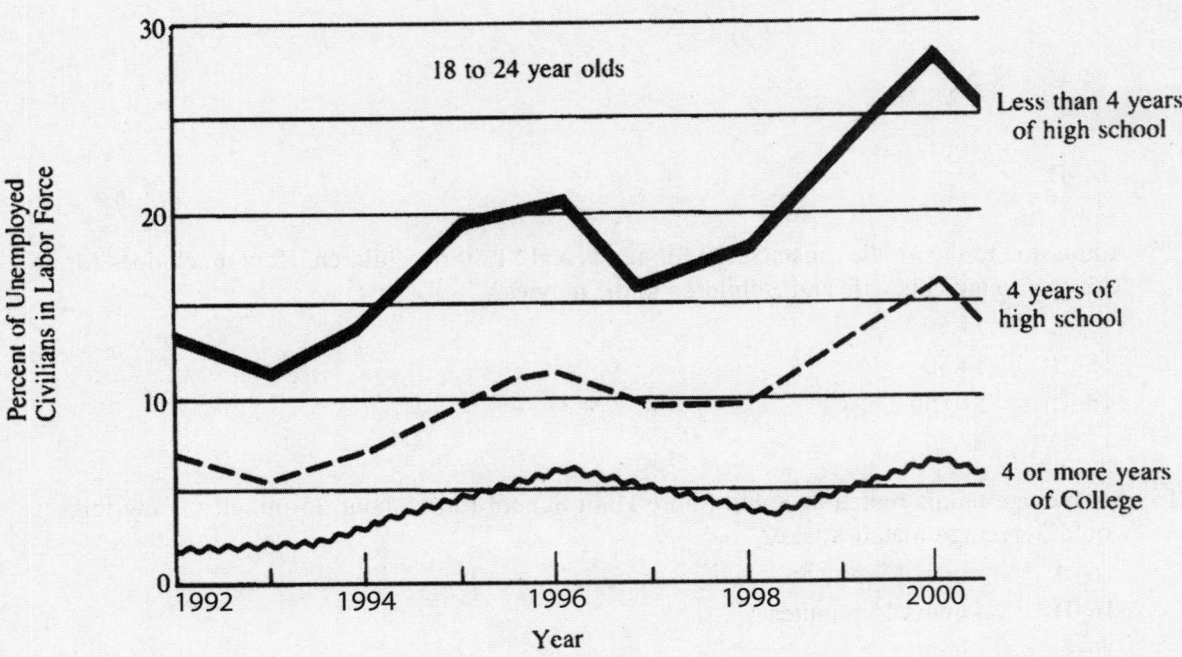

17. According to the graph, in which year was unemployment the highest?

    17–A   1997
    17–B   1998
    17–C   1999
    17–D   2000

18. What was the difference in percent of unemployment between those with 4 years of high school and those with fewer than 4 years of high school in 1997?

    18–A   6%
    18–B   10%
    18–C   12%
    18–D   15%

19. For people with *fewer than 4 years of high school,* what was the total change in percent of unemployment between 1993 and 2000?

    19–A   6
    19–B   12
    19–C   16
    19–D   26

20. The scale on a blueprint is $\frac{1}{4}$ inch equals 12 inches. What is the actual length in feet of a steel

bar that is represented on the blueprint by a line $3\frac{3}{8}$ inches long?

    20–A $3\frac{3}{8}$

    20–B $6\frac{3}{4}$

    20–C $13\frac{1}{2}$

    20–D $27\frac{1}{2}$

21. Coach Rogers bought 8 baseball bats for $6 each, 12 balls for $4 each, and 2 batting helmets for $24 each from his sports fund of $200. How much was left in the fund after making these purchases?
    21–A $48
    21–B $144
    21–C $200
    21–D $56

22. A bag of nickels and dimes contains $11.50. If there are 73 dimes, how many nickels are there?
    22–A   78
    22–B   80
    22–C   82
    22–D   84

23. If candies are bought at $1.10 per dozen and sold at 3 for 55 cents, the total profit on $5\frac{1}{2}$

dozen is
    23–A $5.55
    23–B $6.05
    23–C $6.55
    23–D $7.05

24. Sandra received a 20% commission for each newspaper subscription of $2.50. If she sold 50 subscriptions, how much did she earn?
    24–A $25.00
    24–B $50.00
    24–C $30.00
    24–D $52.50

25. The newspaper advertised the following airfares:

New York to Paris $309 each way
New York to Los Angeles $179 each way

How much will Ted save if he buys the round-trip to Los Angeles instead of the roundtrip to Paris?

25–A $618
25–B $358
25–C $260
25–D $130

26. How many 1-inch slices can be cut from a 5-foot hero sandwich?

26–A   50
26–B   60
26–C   64
26–D   72

27. How many round-trips must the shuttle bus make to transport 254 passengers if the bus can carry 38 passengers at a time?

27–A   6

27–B $6\frac{3}{4}$

27–C   7

27–D $7\frac{1}{2}$

28. Normal daily mean temperatures for January to June in Juneau, Alaska, are as follows:

January   21.8°
February   27.8°
March   31.2°
April   39.1°
May   46.5°
June   52.7°

What is the average daily mean temperature in Juneau for the first six months of the year?

28–A   38.6°
28–B   36.5°
28–C   35°
28–D   34.3°

29. Ron, who is 6 feet 3 inches tall, is standing next to his son Christopher. If Ron's shadow is 50 inches long and Christopher's shadow is 20 inches long, how tall is Christopher?

29–A   20 inches
29–B   30 inches
29–C   40 inches
29–D   50 inches

30. A recipe calls for $1\frac{1}{2}$ cups of sugar. It is necessary to make 8 times the recipe for a Fourth of July party. If 2 cups of sugar equal 1 pound, how many pounds of sugar will be needed to make the recipe for the party?

    30–A   2

    30–B $4\frac{1}{2}$

    30–C   6

    30–D   8

Answer Key

1. C	2. C	3. A	4. B	5. A
6. B	7. D	8. A	9. C	10. D
11. B	12. B	13. A	14. D	15. C
16. B	17. D	18. A	19. C	20. C
21. D	22. D	23. B	24. A	25. C
26. B	27. C	28. B	29. B	30. C

Answers and Explanations

1–C   1 gallon = 4 quarts = 16 cups

        2 gallons = 16×2 = 32 cups

2–C   Each 10-foot piece weighs:

$$10 \times .85 \text{ lb} = 8.50 \text{ lb}$$
$$+ \underline{0.15 \text{ lb}}$$
$$8.65 \text{ lb}$$

The entire shipment weighs:

$$340 \times 8.65 \text{ lb} = 2941 \text{ lb}$$

3–A   2 hr 32 min 30 sec Josh

        – $\underline{\text{2 hr 28 min 32 sec}}$ Jeff

Borrowing for subtractions with Josh's values:

    32 min = 31 min + 60 sec

    2 hr 31 min 90 sec Josh

    – $\underline{\text{2 hr 28 min 32 sec}}$ Jeff

           3 min 58 sec

4–B   The profit for the entire 45 newspapers is $45 \times .11 = \$4.95$.

5–A $100\left(\text{yards}\right) \times \dfrac{3\left(\text{feet}\right)}{1\left(\text{yard}\right)} = 300 \text{ feet}$

6–B   Using the book, each ride costs $1.00, a savings of $.50 a ride ($1.50 – $1.00 = $0.50).

Fraction of regular cost $= \dfrac{.50}{1.50} = \dfrac{50}{150} = \dfrac{1}{3}$

Percent of regular cost $= 100 \times \dfrac{1}{3} = 33\dfrac{1}{3}\%$

7–D   Add the costs:

Window	$ 8.50
Roses	6.50
Tire	5.50
Total Owed	$20.50

If the boys paid $10.00 already, they still owe $20.50 – 10.00 = $10.50

8–A   To find the average, all values must be in the same units, so change Thursday's to 62 minutes. Then add all minutes and divide by 5.

Average $= \dfrac{43+48+51+62+56}{5} = \dfrac{260}{5} = 52$ minutes

9–C $4^3 = 4 \times 4 \times 4 = 64$

$4^2 = 4 \times 4 = 16$

Dividing, we get $\dfrac{64}{16} = 4$

10–D $375 is 75% of original price (100% – 25% = 75%).

Original price $= \$375 \div 75\%$

$= \$375 \div .75$

$= \$500$

11–B

10:38 to 11	=	22 minutes
11 to noon	=	1 hour
noon to 3:05	=	3 hours 5 minutes
Total		4 hours 27 minutes

12–B   Add the individual prices to get:

Cost of food = $1.40 + 1.50 + 1.25 + 1.50 = $5.65

Tip = $5.65 × .15 = $0.847 = $0.85

Total = $5.65 + .85 = $6.50

13–A
$$\text{Vehicles Involved} = \quad 5 \quad \text{blue cars}$$
$$3 \quad \text{red cars}$$
$$2 \quad \text{blue trucks}$$

Total   = 10 vehicles

Total NOT blue = 3 red cars

Percentage NOT blue = 3 red cars/10 vehicles × 100

= .3 × 100 = 30%

14–D   Music played + music not played = total length of song

Music played = total music – music not played

$$8\frac{1}{4} - 3\frac{1}{2}$$
$$= 8\frac{1}{4} - 3\frac{2}{4}$$
$$= 7\frac{5}{4} - 3\frac{2}{4}$$
$$= 4\frac{3}{4} \text{ minutes played}$$

15–C   Adults $3.00

Children $1.50

2 Adults + 3 Children = (2 × $3.00) + (3 × $1.50) = $6.00 + $4.50 = $10.50

16–B   3 × (1 hour + 25 minutes) = 3 hours + 75 minutes

But this is an improper number of minutes since it is greater than 60 minutes. In fact, 75 minutes = 1 hour and 15 minutes, which, when added to 3 hours, becomes 4 hours and 15 minutes.

17–D   The highest peaks for all three groups occur in 2000.

18–A   In 1997, the high school graduate line is at about 10%, while the line for those with fewer than 4 years of high school is at 15%. The difference then is about 5%. 6% is the closest choice given.

19–C   Look at the line graph: *Fewer than 4 years of high school*. The difference between the values at 2000 (28) and at 1993 (12) is 28 – 12 = 16.

20–C   12 inches = 1 foot, therefore each $\dfrac{1}{4}$ inch on the blueprint represents 1 foot.

$3\dfrac{3}{8}$ inches represent:

$$3\dfrac{3}{8}\ \text{in} \div \dfrac{1}{4}\ \text{in} = \dfrac{27}{\overset{}{\underset{2}{8}}} \times \dfrac{\overset{1}{4}}{1}\ \text{ft}$$

$$= \dfrac{27}{2}\ \text{ft}$$

$$= 13\dfrac{1}{2}\ \text{feet}$$

21–D   Add up each item individually. Find the total cost.

Baseball bats $6 × 8 = $48
Baseballs $4 × 12 = $48
Helmets $24 × 2 = $48
                Total = $144

Subtract from $200: 200 − 144 = $56 left in fund.

22–D   73 dimes = 73 × $.10

                       = $7.30

$11.50 − $7.30 = $4.20

There is $4.20 worth of nickels in the bag.

$4.20 ÷ $.05 = 84 nickels

23–B   The cost of $5\dfrac{1}{2}$ dozen is:

$$5\dfrac{1}{2} \times \$1.10 = 5.5 \times \$1.10$$

$$= \$6.05$$

The candies sell at 3 for $.55. A dozen sell for 4 × $.55, or $2.20. The selling price

of $5\dfrac{1}{2}$ dozen is:

$$5\frac{1}{2} \times \$2.20 = 5.5 \times \$2.20$$

$$= \$12.10$$

$$\text{Profit} = \$12.10 - \$6.05$$

$$= \$6.05$$

24–A Move the (intended) decimal two places to the left: 20% = .20

50 subscriptions × \$2.50 / subscription × .20 = \$25.00

25–C

New York to Paris	\$309
New York to LA	179
Difference	\$130 each way

Multiply by 2 to find the difference for a round-trip ticket:

\$130 × 2 = \$260

26–B 1 foot = 12 inches

5 feet = 5 × 12 = 60 inches

27–C Divide total passengers by number of passengers per busload:

$$\begin{array}{r} 6 \\ 38\overline{)254} \\ \underline{228} \\ 26 \end{array}$$

Because there is a remainder, the bus will have to make 1 more trip, for a total of 7 round-trips.

28–B $\text{Average} = \dfrac{\text{total of all terms}}{\text{number of terms}}$

$$= \frac{21.8 + 27.8 + 31.2 + 39.1 + 46.5 + 52.7}{6} = \frac{219.1}{6} = 36.5$$

29–B Set up a proportion of their actual heights to the lengths of their shadows. All measurements should be in the same units, *inches*.

$$\frac{\text{height}}{\text{length of shadow}} =$$

$$\frac{\overset{3}{\cancel{75}}}{\underset{2}{\cancel{50}}} = \frac{C}{20} \quad \text{(Cross-multiply.)}$$

$$2C = 60 \quad \text{(Divide by 2 to find } C.)$$

$$C = 30 \text{ inches}$$

30–C $1\dfrac{1}{2}$ cups $\times\, 8 = 12$ cups sugar needed

2 cups sugar = 1 pound

$$\dfrac{12\,(\text{cups})}{2\,(\text{cups/pound})} = 6 \text{ pounds}$$

ARITHMETIC REASONING TEST 3

TIME: 36 Minutes—30 Questions

This test has 30 questions about arithmetic. Each question is followed by four possible answers. Decide which answer is correct, then blacken the space on your answer form that has the same number and letter as your choice. Use scrap paper for any figuring you wish to do.

Your score on this test will be based on the number of questions you answer correctly. You should try to answer every question. Do not spend too much time on any one question.

1. Of the 123 points scored by the Lakers basketball team, 28 points were scored in the first quarter, 36 points in the second quarter, 45 points in the third quarter, and the rest in the fourth quarter. How many points were scored in the last quarter?

    1–A   36
    1–B   62
    1–C   26
    1–D   14

2. Mr. Graham, the druggist, measured out 1362 grams of Vitamin C during the day. If 454 grams equal 1 pound, how many pounds of Vitamin C did Mr. Graham measure out that day?

    2–A   1
    2–B   3
    2–C   2
    2–D   4

3. From a 20-foot board, Ernie cut 3 sections measuring $4\frac{1}{2}$ feet, $3\frac{1}{2}$ feet, and $2\frac{1}{2}$ feet each. How many feet of the original board remained?

    3–A $10\frac{1}{2}$

    3–B   10

    3–C $9\frac{1}{2}$

    3–D   8

4. At the salon, Lisa spent $5.00 for a manicure, $4.00 for a shampoo, and $18.50 for haircut. How much change should Lisa get if she hands the cashier $40.00?
    4–A $12.50
    4–B $13.50
    4–C $22.50
    4–D $27.50

5. If you know the cost of one ice cream cone and wish to buy 8 cones, how do you find the total cost?
    5–A   cost of one cone ÷ 8
    5–B   cost of one cone × 8
    5–C   cost of one cone + 8
    5–D   cost of one cone − 8

6. How long a piece of wood is required to make 3 steps, each measuring 1 foot 8 inches?
    6–A   3 feet
    6–B   3 feet 8 inches
    6–C   4 feet
    6–D   5 feet

7. Harry discovered that his test scores represent 15 points for each half hour he spends studying up to 3 hours. At that rate, if Harry spends 3 hours studying for the next math test, what grade should he expect to receive?
    7–A   90
    7–B   45
    7–C   50
    7–D   30

Questions 8 and 9 refer to the following graph.

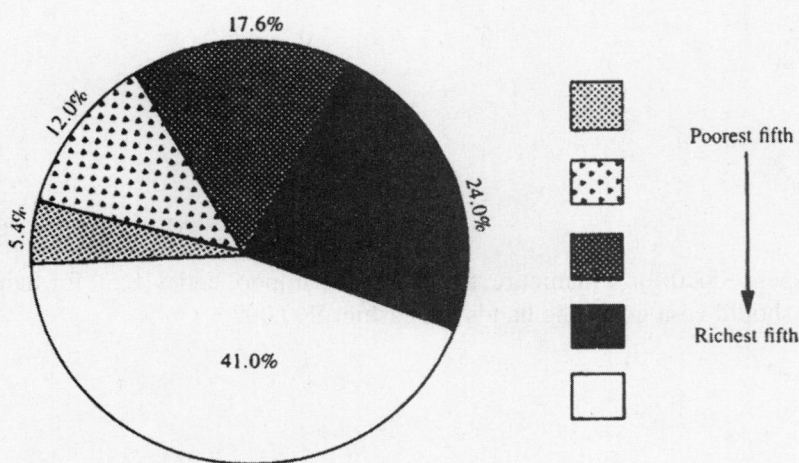

On the circle graph, the distribution of available income in the United States for a particular year is represented. The population has been divided into 5 equal parts, starting from the poorest fifth and ending with the richest.

8. What is the difference between the income available to the poorest $\frac{3}{5}$ of the population and

    that available to the richest $\frac{1}{5}$?

    8–A   11%
    8–B   6%
    8–C   18%
    8–D   12.9%

9. Which of the following ratios best illustrates the relationship in income distribution between

    the poorer $\frac{4}{5}$ of the population and the richest $\frac{1}{5}$?

    9–A   41:59
    9–B   76:24
    9–C   6:4
    9–D   59:41

10. If 50 gallons of water fall over a waterfall in 1 minute, how many gallons of water tumble over it in one day?

    10–A   72,000
    10–B   36,000
    10–C   5000
    10–D   3600

11. The Eastlands spent $535 for roundtrip tickets from Nashville to New Orleans, $325 for three nights in a hotel, $275 for food and entertainment, and $175 for a rental car. What was the total cost of their trip?

    11–A $1310
    11–B $1200
    11–C $1420
    11–D $1350

12. The heights of the 4 new members of the basketball team are as follows:

    Tom   6 ft 2 in
    Duncan   6 ft 4 in
    Troy   6 ft 4 in
    Vinnie   6 ft 10 in

    What is the average height of these 4 players?

    12–A   6ft
    12–B   6 ft 3 in
    12–C   6 ft 5 in
    12–D   6 ft 8 in

13. Maria had one coupon good for 75 cents off a half-gallon of orange juice. If she bought 2 half-gallons of orange juice at $1.95 each, how much did she have to pay?

    13–A $4.65
    13–B $3.90
    13–C $3.15
    13–D $4.00

14. Jack can lift 110 pounds. If his barbell weighs 20 pounds, how many pounds are in each of the two equal weights added to the barbell to make it weigh 110 pounds?

    14–A   90
    14–B   45
    14–C   95
    14–D   40

15. Tires regularly priced at $44 each are on sale for $37. How much would a car owner save by buying four tires at the sale price?

    15–A $7
    15–B $28
    15–C $49
    15–D $81

16. To check the quality of a shipment of 500 articles, a sampling of 50 articles was carefully inspected. Of this sample, 4 were found to be defective. On this basis, what is the probable percentage of defective articles in the original shipment?

    16–A   .04%

    16–B   4%

    16–C   8%

    16–D   40%

17. If one quart of floor wax covers 400 square feet, how many gallons of wax are needed to wax the floor of an office of 6400 square feet?

    17–A   4

    17–B   8

    17–C   12

    17–D   16

18. The 1988 National League Pennant winner won 94 games and lost 67 games. What percentage of games did the team win that year?

    18–A   50

    18–B   96

    18–C   58

    18–D   42

19. How many seasons (1 season per year) did Cy Young pitch, if he played baseball from 1890 to 1911?

    19–A   21

    19–B   22

    19–C   10

    19–D   11

20. During a competition, a javelin was thrown 280 feet, 260 feet, and 282 feet on three successive throws. What was the average distance for the three javelin throws?

    20–A   822 feet

    20–B   540 feet

    20–C   400 feet

    20–D   274 feet

21. For his birthday, Frank received a $15.00 gift certificate to Ramble's Department Store. If he used the gift certificate to purchase a shirt for $18.75, how much money did he have to add?

    21–A $3.75

    21–B $4.25

    21–C $5.75

    21–D $33.75

22. A $150 fund is available for a holiday party. If 60% of the available money is spent for food and beverages, how much is left for other expenses?

    22–A $60

    22–B $70

    22–C $80

    22–D $90

23. A book of 20 tickets for the city bus costs $15.00. Individually purchased tickets cost $1.25 each. John made 25 trips on the bus. What is the minimum amount he must pay?

    23–A $6.25

    23–B $20.00

    23–C $21.25

    23–D $25.00

24. A 500-foot ribbon was tied around the school for the homecoming football game. If 750 students attend the game and each receives an equal share of the ribbon as a souvenir, how many inches of ribbon should each student receive?

    24–A   5

    24–B   8

    24–C $\dfrac{2}{3}$

    24–D   4

25. A $\dfrac{1}{2}$-gram specimen of tropical soil was divided into samples for each of 50 biology students to examine under individual microscopes. If equal portions were prepared for each student, how many grams of soil should each student receive?

    25–A   .5

    25–B   1.0

    25–C   .1

    25–D   .01

26. The value of 32 nickels, 73 quarters, and 156 dimes is

    26–A $26.10

    26–B $31.75

    26–C $35.45

    26–D $49.85

27. The wage rate in a certain trade is $8.60 an hour for a 40-hour week and $1\dfrac{1}{2}$ times the base pay for overtime. An employee who works 48 hours in a week earns

    27–A $447.20

    27–B $498.20

    27–C $582.20

    27–D $619.20

28. The population of Stormville has increased from 80,000 to 100,000 in the last twenty years. What is the percent of increase in the population?

    28–A   20
    28–B   25
    28–C   60
    28–D   80

29. Fifty men and 40 women started the 10-mile hike. Five men and 4 women dropped out. What percentage of people dropped out of the hike?

    29–A   10
    29–B   9
    29–C   2
    29–D   90

30. The 100-meter freestyle swimming competition was won by Roosevelt High School in 50 seconds. How many meters/second did the Roosevelt High swimmer swim?

    30–A $\dfrac{1}{2}$

    30–B $1\dfrac{1}{2}$

    30–C   4
    30–D   2

Answer Key

1. D	2. B	3. C	4. A	5. B
6. D	7. A	8. B	9. D	10. A
11. A	12. C	13. C	14. B	15. B
16. C	17. A	18. C	19. B	20. D
21. A	22. A	23. C	24. B	25. D
26. C	27. A	28. B	29. A	30. D

Answers and Explanations

1–D   Total score = first quarter + second quarter + third quarter + fourth quarter

123 = 28 + 36 + 45 + fourth quarter

Total score – points in first 3 quarters = points in 4th quarter

123 – (28 + 36 + 45) = 123 – 109 = 14 points in 4th quarter

2–B $1362\left(\cancel{\text{grams}}\right) \times \dfrac{1(\text{pound})}{454\left(\cancel{\text{grams}}\right)} = 3(\text{pounds})$

3–C   Sum the sections and subtract the total from 20 feet.

$$4\frac{1}{2}+3\frac{1}{2}+2\frac{1}{2}=10\frac{1}{2}$$

Subtracting: $20-10\frac{1}{2}=9\frac{1}{2}$ feet

4–A   Add up the individual prices:

Manicure	$5.00
Shampoo	$4.00
Haircut	$18.50
Total Cost	$27.50

Subtract from $40 to find change:

$$\begin{array}{r} \$40.00 \\ -\ 27.50 \\ \hline \$12.50 \end{array}$$

5–B   Multiply: Cost of one × 8

6–D   Multiply: 1 ft 8 in × 3 = 3 ft 24 in

Simplify by changing 24 into 2 ft:

3 ft + 2 ft = 5 ft

7–A   15 points for each $\frac{1}{2}$ hour = 30 points per hour

30 points per hour × 3 hours = 90 points

8–B   To find the income available to the poorest $\frac{3}{5}$, add 5.4 + 12.0 + 17.6 and get 35%.

That is 6% less than the 41% available to the richest $\frac{1}{5}$.

9–D   The poorest $\frac{4}{5}$ received 59% while the richest $\frac{1}{5}$ got 41%. In that order, the ratio is 59:41.

10–A $\dfrac{50\,(\text{gallons})}{(\text{minute})}\times\dfrac{60\,(\text{minutes})}{(\text{hour})}\times\dfrac{24\,(\text{hours})}{(\text{day})}=\dfrac{72{,}000\,(\text{gallons})}{(\text{day})}$

11–A   Add up the individual costs:

Tickets	$535
Total	$325
Food & Enter.	$275
Car	<u>$175</u>
Total Cost	$1310

12–C   Add the individual heights and divide by 4:

6ft	2in
6ft	4in
6ft	2in
<u>6ft</u>	<u>10in</u>
24ft	20in

$$\frac{24\text{ft } 20\text{in}}{4} = 6\text{ft } 5\text{in}$$

13–C   2 Orange Juice = 2 × $1.95 = $3.90

   (minus coupon)   <u>− $0.75</u>

                            $3.15

14–B   Make a sketch:

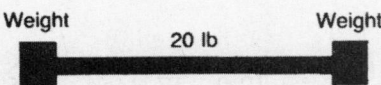

Weight desired − weight of barbell = weight to be added

110 lb − 20 lb = 90 lb

90 lb in 2 equal weights = $\frac{90}{2}$ = 45 lb per weight

15–B   Regular price − sale price = savings per tire

$44 − $37 = $7

Savings per tire × 4 = total savings

$7 × 4 = $28

16–C   Fraction of defective articles = $\frac{4}{50} = \frac{8}{100}$

Percent of defective articles = 8%

17–A   1 quart waxes 400 sq. ft. Since 4 quarts = 1 gallon, 1 gallon waxes 400 × 4 = 1600 sq. ft.

$$\frac{6400}{1600} = 4 \text{ gallons needed}$$

18–C   Percent won = $\dfrac{\text{number won}}{\text{number won} + \text{number lost}}$

Substituting, percent won = $\dfrac{94}{(94+67)} = \dfrac{94}{161} = .58$

Move the decimal over to the right two places to get 58%.

19–B   Break up the problem into two steps. Be sure to count the first season, and remember there is one season per year.

1890 to 1900	11 seasons
1901 to 1911	<u>11 seasons</u>
Total	22 seasons

20–D   To find the average, add the throws and divide by the number of tries, 3.

$$\frac{(280 + 260 + 282)}{3} = \frac{822}{3} = 274 \text{ feet}$$

21–A   Cost of shirt – gift certificate = money paid

$18.75 – $15.00 = $3.75

22–A   100% – 60% = 40% left for other expenses

40% of $150 = .40 × 150 = $60

23–C

1 book of 20 tickets	= $15.00
5 tickets at $1.25	= <u> 6.25</u>
total cost	= $21.25

24–B   Cutting the ribbon into 750 parts requires dividing:

$$\frac{500\,(\text{feet})}{750\,(\text{students})} = \frac{2\,(\text{feet})}{3\,(\text{students})}$$

Convert feet to inches:

$$\frac{2}{\cancel{3}_{1}}\left(\cancel{\text{feet}}\right) \times \cancel{12}^{\,4}\,\frac{(\text{inches})}{\left(\cancel{\text{foot}}\right)} = 8 \text{ inches}$$

25–D   Dividing the sample of $\frac{1}{2}$ gram by 50 students,

$$\frac{1}{2}(\text{gram}) \div 50(\text{students}) =$$

$$\frac{1}{2}(\text{gram}) \times \frac{1}{50}(\text{students}) =$$

$$\frac{1}{100}\frac{\text{grams}}{\text{student}} \text{ or } .01 \frac{\text{grams}}{\text{student}}$$

26–C

32 nickels	$= 32 \times \$.05 =$	$ 1.60
73 quarters	$= 73 \times \$.25 =$	18.25
156 dimes	$= 156 \times \$.10 =$	15.60
Total	$=$	35.45

27–A $48 - 40 = 8$ hours overtime.

Salary for 8 hours overtime:

$$1\frac{1}{2} \times \$8.60 \times 8 = \frac{3}{\underset{1}{2}} \times \$8.60 \times \overset{4}{8}$$

$$= \$103.20$$

Salary for 40 hours regular time:

$\$8.60 \times 40 = \$344.00$

Total salary $= \$344.00 + \$103.20$

$= \$447.20$

28–B   Amount of increase $= 100,000 - 80,000 = 20,000$

$$\text{Fraction of increase} = \frac{20,000}{80,000} = \frac{1}{4}$$

Percent of increase $= 25\%$

29–A   The percentage is found from the fraction of dropouts compared to the total number of hikers:

$$\frac{\text{dropouts}}{\text{total}} = \frac{5+4}{50+40} = \frac{9}{90} = .1$$

Move the decimal two places to the right $(.\underset{\smile}{10}.)$. Therefore, 10% dropped out.

30–D Watch the units in the problem and the answer will come out.

The problem wants "meters/second," therefore,

$$\frac{100\left(\text{meters}\right)}{50\left(\text{seconds}\right)} = 2\left(\text{meters/second}\right)$$

CHAPTER

MATHEMATICS KNOWLEDGE

TOPIC 1: WRITING AND SOLVING EQUATIONS

Model Problem:

There are 6 more women than men in a group of 26 people. How many women are in the group?

    A 6
    B 10
    C 16
    D 20

SOLUTION:

1.   Translate the words into an equation.

     Let m = number of men

     There are 6 more women than men; therefore, $m + 6$ = number of women.

     Total group = 26

     $m + (m + 6) = 26$

2.   Solve the equation.

$$m + m + 6 = 26$$ Remove parentheses.
$$2m + 6 = 26$$ Combine like terms.
$$\underline{\quad -6 \;\; -6 \quad}$$ Subtract 6 from both sides of equation.
$$2m \quad\quad = 20$$
$$\frac{2m}{2} \quad = \frac{20}{2}$$ Divide both sides of equation by 2.
$$m \quad\quad = 10$$ There are 10 men in the group.
$$m + 6 \quad = 10 + 6 = 16$$ There are 16 women in the group.

Choice C is the correct answer.

Now try Practice Exercise 1. Check your answers against the answers and explanations that follow and enter your score on the line provided. If your score is 8 or more, go on to Topic 2. If your score is less than 8, study the Topic Review before going on to the next topic area.

Practice Exercise 1

For items 1 and 2, choose the correct mathematical statement.

1.   Five times a number minus one third of the number equals 28.

   1–A $5N - \dfrac{N}{3} = 28$

   1–B $3N + 5 = 28$

   1–C $5N + \dfrac{N}{3} = 28$

   1–D $3N - 5 = 28$

2.   24 added to a number is 52.
   2–A $N + 24 = 25$
   2–B $24 - 52 = N$
   2–C $24 + N = 52$
   2–D $N - 24 = 52$

For items 3 to 6, write the equation for each problem and then solve for the number.

3.   If 3 is subtracted from a given number, the difference is 3.
   3–A   3
   3–B   4
   3–C   5
   3–D   6

4. The product of 5 and a number is 70.

    4–A   7

    4–B   14

    4–C   5

    4–D   350

5. $\frac{1}{3}$ of a number decreased by 3 is 18.

    5–A   3

    5–B   21

    5–C   18

    5–D   63

6. When 3 is subtracted from 3 times a number, the result is 3.

    6–A   0

    6–B   9

    6–C   6

    6–D   2

7. Solve for C: $.3C - 6 = 9$

    7–A   3

    7–B   15

    7–C   50

    7–D   15

8. Solve for x: $3x - 4 = 5$

    8–A   9

    8–B   3

    8–C   2

    8–D   1

9. $Y = 8x - 4$

    Find Y when x is -2.

    9–A   –20

    9–B   20

    9–C   –4

    9–D   4

10. Solve for B: $B - 4.5 = 3$

    10–A   1.5

    10–B   7.5

    10–C   5.5

    10–D   12

Your Score _____

Answer Key				
1. A	2. C	3. D	4. B	5. D
6. D	7. C	8. B	9. A	10. B

Answers and Explanations

1–A   Let N be the number.

$$5N - \frac{N}{3} = 28$$

2–C   Let N be the number.

$$24 + N = 52$$

3–D   Let N be the given number.

$$
\begin{array}{ll}
N - 3 = 3 & \\
\underline{+3 \ +3} & \text{Add 3 to both sides.} \\
N \quad = 6 &
\end{array}
$$

4–B   Let N be the number.

$$
\begin{array}{ll}
5N = 70 & \\
\dfrac{\cancel{5}N}{\cancel{5}} = \dfrac{70}{5} & \text{Divide both sides by 5.} \\
N = 14 &
\end{array}
$$

5–D   Let N be the number.

$$
\begin{array}{ll}
\dfrac{N}{3} - 3 = 18 & \\
\underline{\phantom{\dfrac{N}{3}}+3 \ +3} & \text{Add 3 to both sides of the equation.} \\
\dfrac{N}{3} = 21 & \\
\cancel{3}\left(\dfrac{N}{\cancel{3}}\right) = (21)3 & \text{Multiply both sides of equation by 3.} \\
N \quad = 63 &
\end{array}
$$

6–D   Let N be the number.

$$3N - 3 = 3 \qquad \text{Add 3 to both sides of the equation.}$$
$$\underline{+3\ +3}$$
$$3N = 6$$
$$\frac{1}{3}(3N) = \frac{1}{3}(6) \qquad \text{Divide both sides of equation by 3.}$$
$$N = 2$$

7–C $.3C - 6 = 9$
$$\underline{+6+6} \qquad \text{Add 6 to both sides.}$$
$$.3C = 15$$
$$\frac{\cancel{.3}C}{\cancel{.3}} = \frac{15}{.3} \qquad \text{Divide both sides by .3.}$$
$$C = 50$$

8–B $3x - 4 = 5$
$$\underline{+4\ +4} \qquad \text{Add 4 to both sides.}$$
$$3x = 9$$
$$\frac{\cancel{3}x}{\cancel{3}} = \frac{9}{3} \qquad \text{Divide both sides by 3.}$$
$$x = 3$$

9–A   Substitute the value for x into the equation and perform the indicated operations:

$Y = 8x - 4$

$Y = (8)\,(-2) - 4$

$Y = -16 - 4$

$Y = -20$

10–B $B - 4.5 = 3$
$$\underline{+4.5+4.5} \qquad \text{Add 4.5 to both sides}$$
$$B = 7.5$$

Topic Review

Solving Problems Using Algebra

1. Many types of problems can be solved by using algebra. To solve a problem:
   a. Read it carefully. Determine what information is given and what information is unknown and must be found.
   b. Represent the *unknown* quantity with a letter.
   c. Write an equation that expresses the relationship given in the problem.
   d. Solve the equation.

Example: If 7 is added to twice a number, the result is 23. Find the number.

SOLUTION: Let x = the unknown number, and write the equation:

$$7 + 2x = 23$$
$$\underline{-7 \qquad\quad -7}$$
$$\frac{2x}{2} = \frac{16}{2}$$
$$x = 8$$

2. An **equation** states that two quantities are equal.

   The solution to an equation is a number that can be substituted for the letter, or **variable,** to give a true statement.

Example: In the equation $x + 7 = 10$, if 5 is substituted for x, the equation becomes $5 + 7 = 10$, which is false. If 3 is substituted for x, the equation becomes $3 + 7 = 10$, which is true. Therefore, $x = 3$ is a solution for the equation $x + 7 = 10$.

   To **solve an equation** means to find all solutions for the variables.

Transforming Equations

3. An equation has been solved when it is transformed or rearranged so that a variable is isolated on one side of the equal sign and a number is on the other side.

   Two basic principles are used to transform equations:
   a. The same quantity may be added to, or subtracted from, both sides of an equation.

Example: To solve the equation $x - 3 = 2$, add 3 to both sides:

$$x - 3 = 2$$
$$\underline{+3 \quad +3}$$
$$x = 5$$

Adding 3 isolates x on one side and leaves a number on the other side. The solution to the equation is $x = 5$.

Example: To solve the equation $y + 4 = 10$, subtract 4 from both sides (adding –4 to both sides will have the same effect):

$$\begin{aligned} y + 4 &= 10 \\ \underline{-4 \quad\ \ } &\ \underline{-4\ } \\ y &=\ \ 6 \end{aligned}$$

The variable has been isolated on one side of the equation. The solution is $y = 6$.

b. Both sides of an equation may be multiplied or divided by the same quantity.

Example: To solve $2a = 12$, divide both sides by 2:

$$\begin{aligned} 2a &= 12 \\ \frac{2a}{2} &= \frac{12}{2} \\ a &= 6 \end{aligned}$$

Example: To solve $\dfrac{b}{5} = 10$, multiply both sides by 5:

$$\frac{b}{5} = 10$$

$$\begin{aligned} 5 \bullet \frac{b}{5} &= 10 \bullet 5 \\ b &= 50 \end{aligned}$$

4. To solve equations containing more than one operation:

   a. First eliminate any number that is being added to or subtracted from the variable.

   b. Then eliminate any number that is multiplying or dividing the variable.

Example: Solve $3x - 6 = \quad 9$

$$\begin{aligned} \underline{+6 \quad\ } &\ \underline{+6\ } \qquad \text{Adding 6 eliminates } -6. \\ 3x \quad &= 15 \\ \frac{\cancel{3}x}{\cancel{3}} &= \frac{15}{3} \qquad \text{Dividing by 3 eliminates the 3 that multiplies the } x. \\ x &= 5 \qquad \text{The solution to the original equation is } x = 5. \end{aligned}$$

5. The variable term may be added to, or subtracted from, both sides of an equation. This is necessary when the variable appears on both sides of the original equation.

Example: Solve

$$6y + 9 = 2y + 1$$ Eliminate the *y*-term from the right side by
$$\underline{-2y \qquad -2y}$$ subtracting $2y$ from both sides.
$$4y + 9 = \quad +1$$ Eliminate 9 from the left side by subtracting 9
$$\underline{\quad -9 \qquad -9}$$ from both sides.
$$4y \quad = \quad -8$$
$$\frac{\cancel{4}y}{\cancel{4}} = \frac{-8}{4}$$ Divide both sides by 4 to eliminate the multiplication
$$y \quad = \quad -2$$ by 4 and isolate the *y*.

6. It may be necessary to first **simplify** the expression on each side of an equation by removing parentheses or combining like terms.

Example: Solve $5z - 3(z - 2) = 8$ Remove parentheses first.
$$5z - 3z + 6 = 8$$
$$2z + 6 = 8$$ Combine like terms.
$$\underline{\quad -6 \quad -6}$$ Subtract 6 from both sides.
$$\frac{\cancel{2}z}{\cancel{2}} = \frac{2}{2}$$ Divide by 2 to isolate the *z*.
$$z = 1$$

7. To check the solution to any equation, replace the variable with the solution in the original equation, perform the indicated operations, and determine whether a true statement results.

Example: Earlier it was found that $x = 5$ is the solution for the equation $3x - 6 = 9$. To check, substitute 5 for *x* in the equation:

$$3 \cdot 5 - 6 = 9$$ Perform the operations on the left side.
$$15 - 6 = 9$$
$$9 = 9$$ A true statement results; therefore, the solution is correct.

Evaluating Algebraic Expressions

8. To evaluate algebraic expressions and formulas:
    a. Substitute the given values for the letters in the expression.
    b. Perform the arithmetic in the following order: First, perform the operations within parentheses (if any). Second, compute all powers and roots. Third, perform all multiplications and divisions in order, from left to right. Fourth, perform all additions and subtractions in order, from left to right.

Example: If $P = 2(L + W)$, find *P* when $L = 10$ and $W = 5$

SOLUTION: Substitute 10 for *L* and 5 for *W*:

$$P = 2(L + W)$$
$$P = 2(10 + 5) \quad\quad \text{First, add numbers in parentheses.}$$
$$= 2(15) \quad\quad\quad \text{Then multiply 2 by 15.}$$
$$= 30$$

Answer: 30

Example: Evaluate $5a^2 - 2b$ if $a = 3$ and $b = 10$

SOLUTION: Substitute 3 for *a* and 10 for *b*:

$$5a^2 - 2b$$
$$= 5 \cdot 3^2 - 2 \cdot 10 \quad\quad \text{First, calculate } 3^2.$$
$$= 5 \cdot 9 - 2 \cdot 10 \quad\quad \text{Next, multiply } 5 \times 9 \text{ and } 2 \times 10.$$
$$= 45 - 20 \quad\quad\quad \text{Then subtract 20 from 45.}$$
$$= 25$$

Answer: 25

TOPIC 2: SIGNED NUMBERS AND POLYNOMIALS

Model Problem:

The product of $(x + 4)$ and $(2x - 1)$ is

    A $2x^2 - 4$
    B $3x^2 - 4$
    C $2x^2 - 7x + 4$
    D $2x^2 + 7x - 4$

SOLUTION:

Multiply each term of the first polynomial by each term of the second polynomial:

$$(x + 4)(2x - 1) = 2x^2 - x + 8x - 4$$

Add like terms:

$$2x^2 - x + 8x - 4 = 2x^2 + 7x - 4$$

The correct answer is choice D.

Now try Practice Exercise 2. Check your answers against the answers and explanations that follow and enter your score on the line provided. If your score is 8 or more, go on to Topic 3. If your score is less than 8, study the Topic Review before going on to the next topic area.

Practice Exercise 2

1. When +4 is added to –6, the sum is
    1–A   –10
    1–B   +10
    1–C   –2
    1–D   +2

2. At 8 a.m. the temperature was –4°. If the temperature rose 7 degrees during the next hour, what was the thermometer reading at 9 a.m.?
    2–A   –11°
    2–B   +11°
    2–C   –3°
    2–D   +3°

3. Find the product of (–6), (–4), (–4), and (–2).
    3–A   –16
    3–B   +96
    3–C   –192
    3–D   +192

4. The temperatures reported at hour intervals on a winter evening were + 4°, 0°, –1°, –5°, and –8°. Find the average temperature for these hours.
    4–A   – 10°
    4–B   – 2°
    4–C   +2°
    4–D $-2\frac{1}{2}°$

5. Evaluate the expression $5a - 4x - 3y$ if $a = -2$, $x = -10$, and $y = 5$.
    5–A   +15
    5–B   +25
    5–C   –65
    5–D   –35

6. If $3x - 1$ is multiplied by $2x$, the product is
    6–A $4x$
    6–B $5x^2$
    6–C $6x^2 - 2x$
    6–D $6x^2 - 1$

7. The sum of $3x^2 - 5x + 2$ and $x^2 - x - 7$ is
   - 7–A $-7x$
   - 7–B $-2x - 5$
   - 7–C $3x^2 - 5x - 5$
   - 7–D $4x^2 - 6x - 5$

8. The product of $(x + 5)$ and $(x + 5)$ is
   - 8–A $2x + 10$
   - 8–B $x^2 + 25$
   - 8–C $x^2 + 10x + 25$
   - 8–D $x^2 + 5x + 10$

9. $2(a - b) + 4(a + 3b) =$
   - 9–A $6a + 10b$
   - 9–B $6a + 2b$
   - 9–C $6a - 10b$
   - 9–D $8a^2 + 2b^2$

10. $3(x + 4) - (2x - 4) =$
   - 10–A $5x$
   - 10–B $5x + 8$
   - 10–C $x + 8$
   - 10–D $x + 16$

Your Score _____

Answer Key

1. C	2. D	3. D	4. B	5. A
6. C	7. D	8. C	9. A	10. D

Answers and Explanations

1–C   To add numbers with different signs, subtract the magnitude of the numbers and use the sign of the number with the greatest magnitude.

-6
$\underline{+4}$
-2

2–D   Add +7 to –4.

–4

+7
___

+3

Alternatively, using a number line:

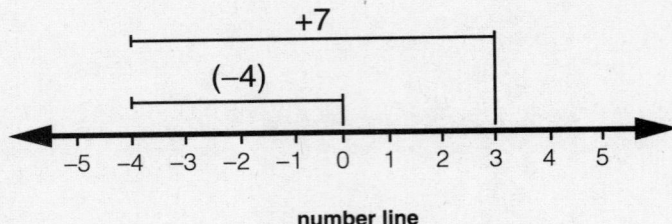

number line

3–D   Multiply the numbers:

$6 \times 4 \times 4 \times 2 = 192$

An even number of negative signs gives a positive product; therefore, the correct answer is +192.

4–B   Add all the terms and then divide by the number of terms.

$$\frac{(+4) + (0) + (-1) + (-5) + (-8)}{5}$$

$$= \frac{-10}{5} = -2$$

5–A   Substitute the values for a, x, and y in the original equation and then solve.

$$5a - 4x - 3y = 5(-2) - 4(-10) - 3(5)$$
$$= -10 + 40 - 15$$
$$= +15$$

6–C   Multiply each term by $2x$.

$3x - 1$

$\times \quad 2x$
_____

$6x^2 - 2x$

7–D   Line up like terms and add.

$3x^2 - 5x + 2$

$x^2 - x - 7$
_____

$4x^2 - 6x - 5$

8–C   Multiply each term of the first polynomial by each term of the second polynomial. Then combine like terms.

$$\begin{array}{r} x+5 \\ \times\ x+5 \\ \hline x^2+5x \\ +\ \ 5x+25 \\ \hline x^2+10x+25 \end{array}$$

9–A   Clear the parentheses by multiplying $(a-b)$ by 2 and $(a+3b)$ by 4. Line up like terms and add.

$$\begin{array}{l} 2(a-b)+4(a+3b)= \\ 2a-2b \\ +4a+12b \\ \hline 6a+10b \end{array}$$

10–D   Multiply $x+4$ by 3. Then subtract $2x-4$.

$$\begin{array}{r} 3(x+4)=3x+12 \\ -2x\ +4 \\ \hline x\ +16 \end{array}$$ To subtract signed numbers, change the signs and add

$$-(2x-4)=-2x+4$$

Topic Review

Signed Numbers

The rules for operations with signed numbers are basic to successful work in algebra. Be sure you know, and can apply, the following rules.

1. **Addition:** To add numbers with the same sign, add the magnitudes of the numbers and keep the same sign. The *magnitude* of a signed number is also called its absolute value. The symbol for absolute value is | |. To add numbers with different signs, subtract the magnitudes of the numbers and use the sign of the number with the greater magnitude.

Example: Add the following:

$$\begin{array}{rrrr} +4 & -4 & -4 & +4 \\ \underline{+7} & \underline{-7} & \underline{+7} & \underline{-7} \\ +11 & -11 & +3 & -3 \end{array}$$

2. **Subtraction:** Change the sign of the number to be subtracted and proceed with the rules for addition. Remember that subtracting is really adding the additive inverse.

Example: Subtract the following:

$$
\begin{array}{cccc}
+4 & -4 & -4 & +4 \\
\underline{+7} & \underline{-7} & \underline{+7} & \underline{-7} \\
-3 & +3 & -11 & +11
\end{array}
$$

3. **Multiplication:** If there is an odd number of negative factors, the product is negative. An even number of negative signs gives a positive product.

Example: Find the following products:

$$(+4)(+7) = +28 \quad (+4)(-7) = -28 \quad (-4)(-7) = +28 \quad (-4)(+7) = -28$$

4. **Division:** If the signs are the same, the quotient is positive. If the signs are different, the quotient is negative.

Example: Divide the following:

$$\frac{+28}{+4} = +7 \qquad \frac{-28}{-4} = +7 \qquad \frac{-28}{+4} = -7 \qquad \frac{+28}{-4} = -7$$

Polynomials

A **polynomial** is an algebraic expression that has one or more terms. The terms are separated by + or − signs.

Example: The polynomial $5x^3 + x^2 - 4x + 7$ has four terms.

The coefficients of the terms are +5, +1, −4, and +7, in that order.

5. To add polynomials, add the coefficients of like terms. Like terms have identical variables and exponents.

Example: Add $4x^2 - 3x + 2$

$$
\begin{array}{l}
4x^2 - 3x + 2 \\
\underline{2x^2 - 7x - 5} \\
6x^2 - 10x - 3
\end{array}
$$

6. To subtract polynomials, subtract the coefficients of like terms.

Example: Subtract $7a - 2b + 4c$

$$
\begin{array}{l}
7a - 2b + 4c \\
\underline{9a + 6b - 2c} \\
-2a - 8b + 6c
\end{array}
$$

7. To multiply two monomials (single terms), multiply their coefficients and add the exponents of like variables.

Examples:

$$2x^5 \bullet 3x^4 = 6x^9$$

$$y^4 \bullet y^{10} = y^{14}$$

$$9b^3 \bullet 2b = 18b^4 \qquad \left(\text{Note that } 2b = 2b^1.\right)$$

$$\left(-4a^2b^3\right)\left(-3a^{11}b^8\right) = +12a^{13}b^{11}$$

8. To multiply a polynomial by a monomial, use the distributive property to multiply each term of the polynomial by the monomial.

Examples:

$$3(2x + 4y) = 6x + 12y$$

$$y^2\left(5y - 3y^5\right) = 5y^3 - 3y^7$$

9. To multiply a polynomial by a polynomial, multiply each term of the first polynomial by each term of the second polynomial, then add any like terms in the answer.

Examples:

$$(x + 3)(x + 4) = x^2 + 4x + 3x + 12$$
$$= x^2 + 7x + 12$$
$$(a - 1)(b + 5) = ab + 5a - 1b - 5$$
$$(y + 4)\left(y^2 + 2y - 3\right) = y^3 + 2y^2 - 3y + 4y^2 + 8y - 12$$
$$= y^3 + 6y^2 + 5y - 12$$

10. To divide two monomials, divide their coefficients and subtract the exponents of like variables.

Examples:

$$\frac{12a^5}{3a^2} = 4a^3$$

$$\frac{ac^7}{ac^5} = c^2 \qquad \text{Note that } \frac{a}{a} = 1.$$

$$\frac{-6b^{10}c^7}{+2bc^2} = 3b^9c^5$$

11. To divide a polynomial by a monomial, divide each term of the polynomial by the monomial.

Examples:

$$\frac{15a^2 - 12a}{3} = 5a^2 - 4a$$

$$\left(12x^3 - 8x^2 + 20x\right) \div 4x = 3x^2 - 2x + 5$$

Simplifying Expressions by Removing Parentheses

Parentheses may be removed by using these rules:

12. If a positive sign appears right before the parentheses, simply drop the parentheses.

Example: $3x^2 + (5x + 2) = 3x^2 + 5x + 2$

13. If a negative sign appears right before the parentheses, change the sign of each term inside the parentheses, then drop the parentheses.

Example: $4 - (2x - y + z) = 4 - 2x + y - z$

14. If a number or variable is indicated as a multiplier right before the parentheses, multiply each term inside by the multiplier, then drop the parentheses.

Example: $5x - 2(3y - 4) = 5x - 6y + 8$

15. Combine like terms after parentheses have been removed.

Example:
$$3(x - y) + (6x - 4y) - (5x + 2y)$$
$$= 3x - 3y + 6x - 4y - 5x - 2y$$
$$= 4x - 9y$$

TOPIC 3: USING FORMULAS

Model Problem (Distance):

If a passenger train leaves Terminal A at 10 a.m. and travels at an average speed of 55 miles per hour, what time will it arrive at Terminal B, 275 miles away?

A Noon
B 2 p.m.
C 3 p.m.
D 5 p.m.

SOLUTION:

1. First find the time the train traveled using the distance formula:
    Distance = Rate × Time

    $D = R \times T$ Divide both sides of equation by R.

    $$\frac{D}{R} = \frac{\cancel{R} \times T}{\cancel{R}}$$

    $$\frac{D}{R} = T$$

2. Substitute values in equation for time and solve for time:

$$\frac{275}{55} = T$$

$T = 5$ hours

3. Add 5 hours to starting time to find arrival time:

10 a.m. + 5 = 3 p.m.
10 a.m. to noon = 2 hours
noon to 3 p.m. = 3 hours
Total time = 5 hours

The correct answer is choice C.

Model Problem (Interest):

What is the difference between the amount of interest paid on a $500 deposit in an account

that pays 5% interest and another account that pays $5\frac{1}{2}\%$ interest?

A $2.50
B $5.00
C $25.00
D $27.50

SOLUTION:

1. Find the amount of interest paid on each account using the interest formula:
Interest = Principal × Rate

In 5% Account (5% = .05):   **In $5\frac{1}{2}\%$ Account** ($5\frac{1}{2}\%$ = .055):

$I = P \times R$ $I = P \times R$
  = $500 × .05   = $500 × .055
  = $25.00   = $27.50

2. Subtract to find the difference.
$27.50 – $25.00 = $2.50
Choice A is the correct answer.

Now try Practice Exercise 3. Check your answers against the answers and explanations that follow and enter your score on the line provided. If your score is 8 or more, go on to Topic 4. If your score is less than 8, study the Topic Review before going on to the next topic area.

Practice Exercise 3

1. During the month of February, 25% of the class of 32 students forgot their lunches. How many students forgot their lunches in February?

   1–A   25
   1–B   6
   1–C   32
   1–D   8

2. Whitey Ford got 220 hits after being at bat for 660 times. What was his percentage of hits?

   2–A   40
   2–B   50

   2–C $33\frac{1}{3}$

   2–D   25

3. A dealer buys a TV set for $550 and wishes to sell it at a 20% profit. What should his selling price be?

   3–A $570
   3–B $600
   3–C $660
   3–D $672

4. Paul received a bonus of $750, which was 5% of his annual salary. His annual salary was

   4–A $37,500
   4–B $25,000
   4–C $22,500
   4–D $15,000

5. A man travels a distance of 20 miles at 60 miles per hour and returns over the same route at 40 miles per hour. What is his average rate for the round-trip in miles per hour?

   5–A   50
   5–B   48

   5–C $47\frac{1}{2}$

   5–D $33\frac{1}{3}$

6. A store reduced the price of eggs from $1.00 per dozen to 2 dozen for $1.60. What was the percent decrease per dozen?

  6–A 16

  6–B 20

  6–C $25\frac{1}{2}$

  6–D $37\frac{1}{2}$

7. Michael earns $50 for 8 hours of work. At the same rate of pay, how much will he earn for 28 hours of work?

  7–A $150

  7–B $175

  7–C $186

  7–D $232

8. Jean sells cosmetics, earning a 12% commission on all sales. How much will she need in sales to earn $300 in commission?

  8–A $1800

  8–B $2500

  8–C $3600

  8–D $4000

9. A driver traveled 100 miles at the rate of 40 mph, then traveled 80 miles at 60 mph. The total number of hours for the entire trip was

  9–A $1\frac{3}{20}$

  9–B $1\frac{3}{4}$

  9–C $2\frac{1}{4}$

  9–D $3\frac{5}{6}$

10. Two people start at the same point and walk in opposite directions. If one walks at the rate of 2 miles per hour and the other walks at the rate of 3 miles per hour, in how many hours will they be 20 miles apart?

  10–A 2

  10–B 3

  10–C 4

  10–D 5

Your Score _____

Answer Key

1. D	2. C	3. C	4. D	5. B
6. B	7. B	8. B	9. D	10. C

Answers and Explanations

1–D   Translate the word problem into a mathematical problem:

"25%" "of" "the class of 32" means $.25 \times 32 = 8$ students

2–C   Write a fraction that shows ratio of hits to "at bats":

$$\frac{\text{hits}}{\text{at bats}} = \frac{220}{660} = \frac{1}{3}$$

Convert to a percentage:

$$\frac{1}{3} = 33\frac{1}{3}\%$$

3–C   His selling price will be (100% + 20%) of his cost price.

$$120\% \text{ of } \$550 = 1.20\,(\$550)$$
$$= \$660$$

4–D   Let s = Paul's annual salary

$$5\% \text{ of } s = \$750$$
$$.05s = \$750$$
$$\frac{.05s}{.05} = \frac{\$750}{.05}$$
$$s = \$15,000$$

5–B $\text{Time} = \dfrac{\text{Distance}}{\text{Rate}}$

Time for 20 miles at 60 miles per hour $= \dfrac{20}{60} = \dfrac{1}{3}$ hour

Time for 20 miles at 40 miles per hour $= \dfrac{20}{40} = \dfrac{1}{2}$ hour

Total distance = 40 miles

Total time $= \dfrac{1}{3} + \dfrac{1}{2} = \dfrac{5}{6}$ hour

$$\text{Rate} = \frac{\text{Distance}}{\text{Time}}$$

$$= \frac{40 \text{ miles}}{\frac{5}{6} \text{ hour}}$$

$$= 40 \div \frac{5}{6} \text{ miles per hour}$$

$$= 40 \bullet \frac{6}{5} \text{ miles per hour}$$

$$= 48 \text{ miles per hour}$$

6–B
Original price = $1.00 per dozen
New price = $1.60 per 2 doz = $.80 per doz
Decrease = $1.00 − $.80 = $.20

Percent of decrease = $\dfrac{\text{amount of decrease}}{\text{original price}}$

$$= \frac{.20}{1.00} = 20\%$$

7–B The amount earned is proportional to the number of hours worked.

Let m = unknown pay

$$\frac{m}{28} = \frac{50}{8}$$
$$8m = 28 \bullet 50$$
$$\frac{8m}{8} = \frac{1400}{8}$$
$$m = 175$$

8–B Let s = needed sales. 12% of sales will be $300.

$$.12s = 300$$

$$\frac{.12s}{.12} = \frac{300}{.12} \quad \text{Divide both sides by .12.}$$
$$s = 2500$$

9–D The first part of the trip took:

$$100 \text{ mi} \div 40 \text{ mph} = 2\frac{1}{2} \text{ hours}$$

The second part of the trip took:

$$180 \text{ mi} \div 60 \text{ mph} = 1\frac{1}{3} \text{ hours}$$

$$2\frac{1}{2} = 2\frac{3}{6}$$
$$+1\frac{1}{3} = 1\frac{2}{6}$$
$$\overline{\hspace{1cm}}$$
$$3\frac{5}{6}$$

10–C In 1 hour they are 5 miles apart.

20 mi ÷ 5 mph = 4 hours

It will take 4 hours to be 20 miles apart.

Topic Review

Motion Problems

1. **Motion problems** are based on the following relationship:

    Rate • Time = Distance

    Rate is usually given in miles per hour. Time is usually given in hours and distance is given in miles.

    Example: A man traveled 225 miles in 5 hours. How fast was he traveling (what was his rate)?

    SOLUTION: Let r = rate

    Rate • Time = Distance
    $$r \bullet 5 = 225$$
    $$\frac{5r}{5} = \frac{225}{5}$$

    Answer: $r = 45$ miles per hour

    Example: John and Henry start at the same time from cities 180 miles apart and travel toward each other. John travels at 40 miles per hour and Henry travels at 50 miles per hour. In how many hours will they meet?

SOLUTION: Let h = number of hours. Then, $40h$ = distance traveled by John, and $50h$ = distance traveled by Henry. The total distance is 180 miles.

$$40h + 50h = 180$$
$$\frac{90h}{90} = \frac{180}{90}$$
$$h = 2 \text{ hours}$$

Answer: They will meet in 2 hours.

Percent Problems

2.   **Percent** problems may be solved algebraically by translating the relationship in the problem into an equation. The word "of" means multiplication, and "is" means equal to.

Example: 45% of what number is 27?

SOLUTION: Let n = the unknown number. 45% of n is 27.

$$.45n = 27 \qquad \text{Change the \% to a decimal} (45\% = .45).$$
$$45n = 2700 \qquad \text{Multiply both sides by 100 to eliminate the decimal.}$$
$$\frac{45n}{45} = \frac{2700}{45}$$
$$n = 60$$

Example: Mr. Jones receives a salary raise from \$15,000 to \$16,200. Find the percent of increase.

SOLUTION: Let p = percent. The increase is $16,200 - 15,000 = 1200$. What percent of 15,000 is 1200?

$$p \bullet 15,000 = 1200$$
$$\frac{15,000p}{15,000} = \frac{1200}{15,000}$$
$$p = .08$$
$$p = 8\%$$

Interest Problems

3. **Interest** is the price paid for the use of money in loans, savings, and investments. Interest problems are solved using the formula $I = prt$, where:

I = interest

p = principal (amount of money bearing interest)

r = rate of interest, in %

t = time, in years

Example: How long must $2000 be invested at 6% to earn $240 in interest?

SOLUTION: Let t = time

$$I = \$240$$
$$p = \$2000$$
$$r = 6\% \text{ or } .06$$
$$240 = 2000(.06)t$$
$$\frac{240}{120} = \frac{120t}{120}$$
$$2 = t$$

Answer: The $2000 must be invested for 2 years.

Profit and Loss Problems

4. **Profit** is the amount of money added to the dealer's cost of an item to find the selling price. The cost price is considered 100% of itself. If the profit is 20% of the cost, the selling price must be 100% + 20%, or 120% of the cost.

Example: A furniture dealer sells a sofa at $870, which represents a 45% profit over the cost. What was the cost to the dealer?

SOLUTION: Let c = cost price. 100% + 45% = 145%. The selling price is 145% of the cost.

$$145\% \text{ of } c = \$870$$
$$1.45c = 870 \quad \text{(Multiply both sides by 100 to eliminate decimal.)}$$
$$\frac{145c}{145} = \frac{87,000}{145}$$
$$c = 600$$

Answer: The sofa cost the dealer $600.

5. If an article is sold at a loss, the amount of the loss is deducted from the cost price to find the selling price. An article that is sold at a 25% loss has a selling price of 100% – 25%, or 75%, of the cost price.

Example: Mr. Charles bought a car for $8000. After a while he sold it to Mr. David at a 30% loss. What did Mr. David pay for the car?

SOLUTION: The car was sold for 100% – 30%, or 70%, of its cost price.

$$70\% \text{ of } \$8000 = .70\,(\$8000)$$
$$= \$5600$$

Answer: Mr. David paid $5600 for the car.

6. A discount is a percent that is deducted from a marked price. The marked price is considered to be 100% of itself. If an item is discounted 20%, its selling price is 100% – 20%, or 80%, of its marked price.

Example: A radio is tagged with a sale price of $42.50, which is 15% off the regular price. What is the regular price?

SOLUTION: Let r = regular price. The sale price is 100% – 15%, or 85%, of the regular price.

$$85\% \text{ of } r = \$42.50$$
$$.85r = \$42.50$$
$$\frac{85r}{85} = \frac{4250}{85} \quad \text{(Multiply by 100 to eliminate the decimals.)}$$
$$r = 50$$

Answer: The regular price was $50.

TOPIC 4: CIRCLES

Model Problem:

If the circumference of a wheel is 44 inches, what is the diameter of the wheel? (Use $\pi = \dfrac{22}{7}$).

A 7 inches
B 14 inches
C 22 inches
D 138 inches

SOLUTION:

Use the formula for circumference:

$$C = \pi d$$

$$\frac{C}{\pi} = d \qquad\qquad \text{Divide both sides by } \pi.$$

$$\frac{44}{\frac{22}{7}} = d \qquad\qquad \text{Substitute values and solve for diameter.}$$

$$44 \div \frac{22}{7} = \overset{2}{\cancel{44}} \times \frac{7}{\underset{1}{\cancel{22}}} = 14 \text{ inches}$$

The correct answer is choice B.

Now try Practice Exercise 4. Check your answers against the answers and explanations that follow and enter your score on the line provided. If your score is 8 or more, go on to Topic 5. If your score is less than 8, study the Topic Review before going on to the next topic area.

Practice Exercise 4

1. Find the circumference to the nearest centimeter of a circle whose radius is 12 centimeters. (Use $\pi = 3.14$)

1–A	27
1–B	24
1–C	75
1–D	80

2. Find the radius of a circle whose circumference is 20π.

2–A	10π
2–B	10
2–C	40π
2–D	40

3. The hour hand of a clock is 3 feet long. How many feet does the tip of this hand move between 8 a.m. and 12 noon?

3–A	π
3–B	2π
3–C	3π
3–D	4π

4. If the radius of a circle is increased by 3, the circumference is increased by

4–A	3
4–B	3π
4–C	6
4–D	6π

5. The radius of a wheel is 18 inches. Find the number of feet covered by this wheel in 20 revolutions.

    5–A 60π

    5–B   360

    5–C 360π

    5–D   720

6. If the area of a circle of radius x is 5π, find the area of a circle of radius $3x$.

    6–A 15π

    6–B 20π

    6–C 30π

    6–D 45π

7. The area of one circle is 9 times as great as the area of another. If the radius of the smaller circle is 3, find the radius of the larger circle.

    7–A   9

    7–B   12

    7–C   18

    7–D   24

8. If the radius of a circle is doubled, then the circumference

    8–A   and area are both doubled.

    8–B   is doubled and the area is multiplied by 4.

    8–C   is multiplied by 4 and the area is doubled.

    8–D   and area are each multiplied by 4.

9. The circumference of a circle whose area is 16π is

    9–A 8π

    9–B 16π

    9–C   8

    9–D   16

10. Water is poured into a cylindrical tank at the rate of 9 cubic inches a minute. How many minutes will it take to fill the tank if its radius is 3 inches and its height is 14 inches?

(Use $\pi = \dfrac{22}{7}$)

    10–A $14\dfrac{2}{3}$

    10–B   44

    10–C   30

    10–D $27\dfrac{2}{9}$

Your Score _____

Answer Key				
1. C	2. B	3. B	4. D	5. A
6. D	7. A	8. B	9. A	10. B

Answers and Explanations

1–C Use the formula for circumference:

$C = 2 \times \pi \times r$

Substitute 12 cm for r:

$C = 2 \times \pi \times 12 \text{(cm)}$

$C = 24\pi \text{ (cm)}$

Using $\pi = 3.14$:

$C = 24 \times 3.14 = 75.36 \text{ cm}$

Rounded to the nearest centimeter, 75.36 becomes 75 (because the number after 75 is less than 5).

2–B
$$C = 2 \times \pi \times r$$
$$\frac{C}{2\pi} = r$$
$$\frac{20\pi}{2\pi} = r$$
$$10 = r$$

3–B In 4 hours, the hour hand moves through one third of the circumference of the clock.

$$C = 2\pi r = 2\pi(3) = 6\pi$$
$$\frac{1}{3} \cdot 6\pi = 2\pi$$

4–D Compare $2\pi r$ with $2\pi(r + 3)$:

$2\pi(r + 3) = 2\pi r + 6\pi$

Circumference was increased by 6π. Trying this with a numerical value for r will give the same result.

5–A In one revolution, the distance covered is equal to the circumference.

$C = 2\pi r = 2\pi(18) = 36\pi \text{ inches}$

To change this to feet, divide by 12.

$$\frac{36\pi}{12} = 3\pi \text{ feet}$$

In 20 revolutions, the wheel will cover $20(3\pi)$ or 60π feet.

6–D If the radius is multiplied by 3, the area is multiplied by 3^2 or 9.

$$5\pi \times 9 = 45\pi$$

7–A If the area ratio is 9:1, the linear ratio is 3:1. Therefore, the larger radius is 3 times the smaller radius.

$$3 \times 3 = 9$$

8–B Ratio of circumference is the same as ratio of radii, but the area ratio is the square of this.

9–A Area of circle = $\pi r^2 = 16\pi$

Therefore, $r^2 = 16$ or $r = 4$

Circumference of circle = $2\pi r = 2\pi(4) = 8\pi$

10–B $V = \pi r^2 h = \dfrac{22}{7} \cdot 9 \cdot 14 = 396$ cubic inches

To find minutes, divide by 9:

$$\frac{396 \ \cancel{\text{cubic inches}}}{9 \ \dfrac{\cancel{\text{cubic inches}}}{\text{minute}}} = 44 \text{ minutes}$$

Topic Review

Circles

1. A **circle** is a closed plane curve, all points of which are equidistant from a point within called the center.

2. A **complete circle** contains 360°.
    A **semicircle** contains 180°.

3. A **chord** is a line segment connecting any two points on the circle.
    A **radius** of a circle is a line segment connecting the center with any point on the circle.
    A **diameter** is a chord passing through the center of the circle.
    A **secant** is a chord extended in either one or both directions.
    A **tangent** is a line touching a circle at only one point.
    The **circumference** is the curved line bounding the circle.
    An **arc** of a circle is any part of the circumference.

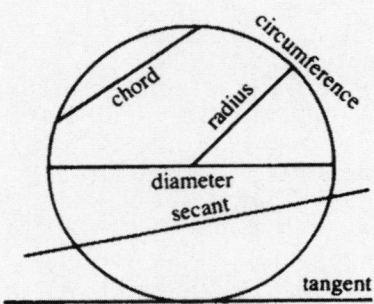

4. A **central angle**, as ∢ AOB in the figure below, is an angle whose vertex is the center of the circle and whose sides are radii. A central angle is equal in degrees to (or has the same number of degrees as) its intercepted arc.

    An **inscribed angle**, as ∢ MNP, is an angle whose vertex is on the circle and whose sides are chords. An inscribed angle is equal in degrees to one half its intercepted arc. ∢ MNP equals one half the degrees in arc MP.

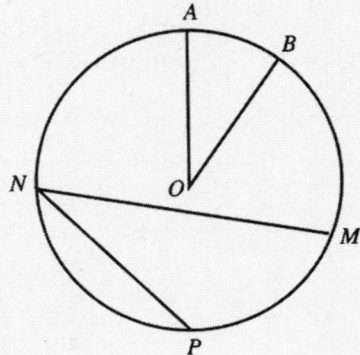

Circumference

5. The **circumference** of a circle is equal to the product of the diameter multiplied by π. The formula is $C = \pi d$.

The number π ("pi") is approximately equal to $\frac{22}{7}$, or 3.14 (3.1416 for greater accuracy). The problem will state which value to use; otherwise, express the answer in terms of "pi," π.

Example: The circumference of a circle whose diameter is 4 inches = 4π inches; or, if it is stated that $\pi = \frac{22}{7}$, then the circumference $= 4 \times \frac{22}{7} = \frac{88}{7} = 12\frac{4}{7}$ inches.

Since the diameter is twice the radius, the circumference equals twice the radius multiplied by π. The formula is $C = 2\pi r$.

Example: If the radius of a circle is 3 inches, then the circumference = 6π inches.

The diameter of a circle equals the circumference divided by π.

Example: If the circumference of a circle is 11 inches, then assuming $\pi = \frac{22}{7}$,

$$\text{diameter} = 11 \div \frac{22}{7} \text{ inches}$$

$$= \overset{1}{\cancel{11}} \times \frac{7}{\underset{2}{\cancel{22}}} \text{ inches}$$

$$= \frac{7}{2} \text{ inches, or } 3\frac{1}{2} \text{ inches}$$

Area

6. The area of a circle is equal to the radius squared multiplied by π. The formula is $A = \pi r^2$.

Example: If the radius of a circle is 6 inches, then the area = 36π square inches.

To find the radius of a circle given the area, divide the area by π and find the square root of the quotient.

Example: To find the radius of a circle of area 100π:

$$\frac{100\pi}{\pi} = 100$$

$$\sqrt{100} = 10 = \text{radius}$$

Volume

7. The volume of a circular cylinder is equal to the product of π, the radius squared, and the height.

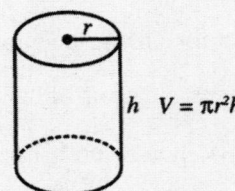

$h \quad V = \pi r^2 h$

Example: A circular cylinder has a radius of 7 inches and a height of $\frac{1}{2}$ inch.

Using $\pi = \frac{22}{7}$, its volume is:

$$\frac{22}{7} \times 7 \times 7 \times \frac{1}{2} = 77 \text{ cubic inches}$$

8. The volume of a sphere is equal to $\frac{4}{3}$ the product of π and the radius cubed.

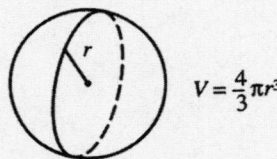

$V = \frac{4}{3}\pi r^3$

Example: If the radius of a sphere is 3 cm, its volume in terms of π is:

$$\frac{4}{3} \times \pi \times 3 \times 3 \times 3 = 36\pi \text{ cubic centimeters}$$

TOPIC 5: QUADRILATERALS

Model Problem:

How many square feet of carpet will be needed to cover the entire floor of the of[f]
below?

  A 1000
  B 1400
  C 800
  D 1200

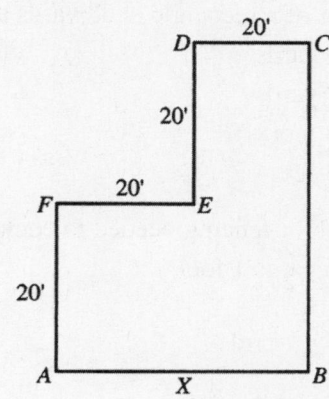

SOLUTION:

1. Find the missing dimensions:

    $AB = FE + DC = 20 + 20 = 40$

    $CB = DE + FA = 20 + 20 = 40$

2. Draw a line from E to x. Now there are two figures: A rectangle measuring 20×40 and a square measuring 20×20.

3. Find the area of each figure:

    Area of rectangle $=$ $l \times w$

                   $=$ 20×40

                   $=$ 800 sq ft

    Area of square $=$ $l \times w$

                   $=$ 20×20

                   $=$ 400 sq ft

4. Add the two areas to find the total:

    $800 + 400 = 1200$ sq ft

    The correct answer is choice D.

Now actice Exercise 5. Check your answers against the answers and explanations
and enter your score on the line provided. If your score is 8 or more, go on to
the If your score is less than 8, study the Topic Review before going on to the next
area.

ctice Exercise 5

If the perimeter of a rectangle is 68 yards and the width is 48 feet, the length is

1–A   10 yards

1–B   18 yards

1–C   20 feet

1–D   56 feet

2. The total length of fencing needed to enclose a rectangular area 46 feet by 34 feet is

2–A   26 yards 1 foot

2–B $26\frac{2}{3}$ yards

2–C   52 yards 2 feet

2–D $53\frac{1}{3}$ yards

3. A square is equal in area to a rectangle whose length is 9 and whose width is 4. Find the perimeter of the square.

3–A   36

3–B   26

3–C   13

3–D   24

4. The dimensions of a rectangular living room are 18 feet by 20 feet. How many square yards of carpeting are needed to cover the floor?

4–A   360

4–B   42

4–C   40

4–D   240

5. A piece of wire is shaped to enclose a square, whose area is 121 square inches. It is then reshaped to enclose a rectangle whose length is 13 inches. The area of the rectangle, in square inches, is

5–A   64

5–B   96

5–C   117

5–D   144

6. The area of a 2-foot-wide walk around a garden that is 30 feet long and 20 feet wide is
    6–A   104 square feet
    6–B   120 square feet
    6–C   180 square feet
    6–D   216 square feet

7. The figure below is composed of 5 equal squares. If the area of the figure is 125, find its perimeter.

    7–A   60
    7–B   100
    7–C   80
    7–D   75

8. If the area of a square with side x is 5, what is the area of a square with side $3x$?
    8–A $3\sqrt{5}$
    8–B $9\sqrt{5}$
    8–C   15
    8–D   45

9. What will it cost to carpet a room 12 feet wide and 15 feet long if carpeting costs $20.80 per square yard?
    9–A $334.60
    9–B $374.40
    9–C $416.00
    9–D $504.60

10. A rectangular bin 4 feet long, 3 feet wide, and 2 feet high is solidly packed with bricks whose dimensions are 8 inches, 4 inches, and 2 inches. The number of bricks in the bin is
    10–A   54
    10–B   648
    10–C   1296
    10–D   1300

Your Score _____

Answer Key

1. B	2. D	3. D	4. C	5. C
6. D	7. A	8. D	9. C	10. B

Answers and Explanations

1–B Make a sketch:

$P = 68$yd	$w = 48$ ft.

Perimeter $= 2(l + w)$. Let the length be x yards.

$$\text{Each width} = 48 \text{ ft}$$
$$= 16 \text{ yd}$$
$$2(x + 16) = 68$$
$$2x + 32 = 68$$
$$\underline{-32 \quad -32}$$
$$\frac{2x}{2} = \frac{36}{2}$$
$$x = 18$$

2–D Make a sketch:

$l = 46$ ft.	
	$w = 34$ ft.

$$\text{Perimeter} = 2(l + w)$$
$$= 2(46 + 34) \text{ feet}$$
$$= 2 \times 80 \text{ feet}$$
$$= 160 \text{ feet}$$
$$160 \text{ feet} \times \frac{1 \text{ yard}}{3 \text{ feet}} = 53\frac{1}{3} \text{ yards}$$

3–D   Make a sketch:

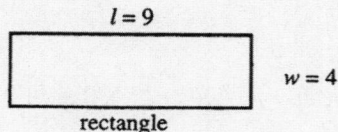

rectangle

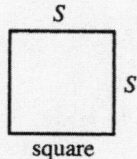

square

$$\text{Area of rectangle} = l \times w$$
$$= 9 \times 4 = 36$$
$$\text{Area of square} = s^2 = 36$$
$$s = \sqrt{36} = 6$$
$$\text{Perimeter of square} = 4s$$
$$= 4 \times 6 = 24$$

4–C   Make a sketch:

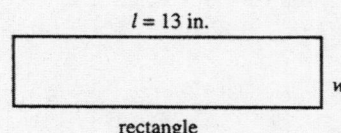

Find the area in square feet and then convert to square yards by dividing by 9. Remember there are 9 square feet in one square yard.

$(18 \bullet 20) \div 9 = 360 \div 9 = 40$ square yards.

5–C   Make a sketch:

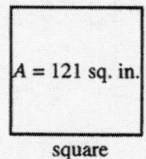

rectangle

square

If the area of the square is 121 square inches, each side is $\sqrt{121} = 11$ inches and the perimeter is $4 \times 11 = 44$ inches. The perimeter of the rectangle is then 44 inches. If the two lengths are each 13 inches, their total is 26 inches. $44 - 26 = 18$ inches remain for the two widths. Therefore, each width is equal to $18 \div 2 = 9$ inches.

The area of a rectangle with length 13 inches and width 9 inches is $13 \times 9 = 117$ square inches.

6–D The walk consists of:

a) 2 rectangles of length 30 ft and width 2 ft.

    Area of each   = $2 \times 30 = 60$ sq ft

    Area of both   =   120 sq ft

b) 2 rectangles of length 20 ft and width 2 ft.

    Area of each   = $2 \times 20 = 40$ sq ft

    Area of both   =   80 sq ft

c) 4 squares, each having a side of 2 ft.

    Area of each square = $2^2 = 4$ sq ft

    Area of 4 squares   =   16 sq ft

    Total area of walk   = $120 + 80 + 16$

                             =   216 sq ft

Alternatively, you may solve this problem by finding the area of the garden and the area of the garden plus the walk, then subtracting to find the area of the walk alone:

Area of garden = $20 \times 30 = 600$ sq ft

Area of garden + walk:

$(20 + 2 + 2) \times (30 + 2 + 2) = 24 \times 34 = 816$ sq ft

Area of walk alone:

$816 - 600 = 216$ sq ft

7–A Area of each square = $\frac{1}{5} \bullet 125 = 25$

Side of each square = 5

Perimeter is made up of 12 sides. $12(5) = 60$

8–D $x^2 = 5$

$(3x)^2 = 9x^2 = 9 \bullet 5 = 45$

9–C   The room is 4 yards by 5 yards, or 20 square yards.

($20.80)(20) = $416.00

10–B   Convert the dimensions of the bin to inches:

4 feet	=	48 inches
3 feet	=	36 inches
2 feet	=	24 inches
Volume of bin	=	48 × 36 × 24 cubic inches
	=	41,472 cubic inches
Volume of each brick	=	8 × 4 × 2 cubic inches = 64 cubic inches
41472 ÷ 64	=	648 bricks

Topic Review

Quadrilaterals

1. A **quadrilateral** is a closed, four-sided figure in two dimensions. Common quadrilaterals are the **parallelogram, rectangle,** and **square**.

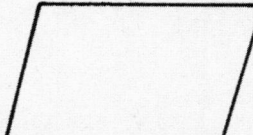  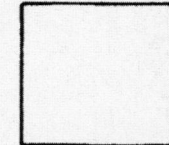

The sum of the four angles of a quadrilateral is 360°.

2. A **parallelogram** is a quadrilateral in which both pairs of opposite sides are parallel.
    Opposite sides of a parallelogram are equal.
    Opposite angles of a parallelogram are equal.

Example:

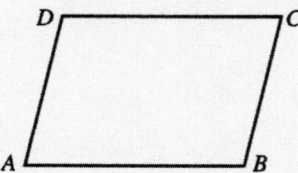

In parallelogram ABCD:

AB ∥ CD, AB = CD, ∢A = ∢C

AD ∥ BC, AD = BC, ∢B = ∢D

(Note: The symbol for *parallel* is " ∥ ".)

3. A **rhombus** is a parallelogram that has all sides equal.
    A **rectangle** is a parallelogram that has all right angles.
    A **square** is a rectangle that has all sides equal. A square is also a rhombus.

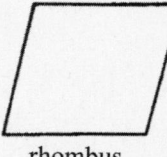 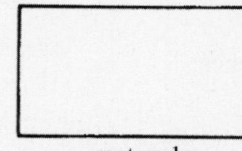 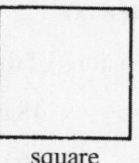

     rhombus   rectangle   square

4. A **trapezoid** is a quadrilateral with one and only one pair of opposite sides parallel.

    In trapezoid ABCD, AB ∥ CD

Perimeter

5. The **perimeter** of a two-dimensional figure is the distance around the figure.

Example: The perimeter of the figure below is $9 + 8 + 4 + 5 + 3 = 29$

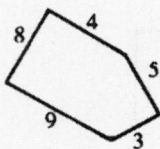

6. The perimeter of a triangle is found by adding all of its sides.

Example: If the sides of a triangle are 4, 5, and 7, its perimeter is $4 + 5 + 7 = 16$.

           If the perimeter and two sides of a triangle are given, the third side is found by adding the two given sides and subtracting this sum from the perimeter.

Example: Two sides of a triangle are 12 and 15. The perimeter is 37.

           Find the other side.

SOLUTION: $12 + 15 = 27$

                $37 - 27 = 10$

                The third side is 10.

Perimeter Problems

7. To solve a perimeter problem, express each side of the figure algebraically. The **perimeter** of the figure is equal to the sum of all of the sides.

Example: A rectangle has four sides. One side is the length and the side next to it is the width. The opposite sides of a rectangle are equal. In a particular rectangle, the length is one less than twice the width. If the perimeter is 16, find the length and the width.

SOLUTION:

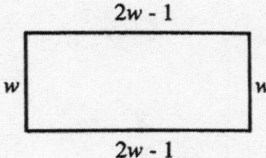

$$\text{Let } w = \text{width}$$
$$\text{Then } 2w - 1 = \text{length}$$

The sum of the four sides is 16.

$$w + (2w - 1) + w + (2w - 1) = 16$$
$$w + 2w - 1 + w + 2w - 1 = 16$$
$$6w - 2 = 16$$
$$\underline{+2 = +2}$$
$$\frac{6w}{6} = \frac{18}{6}$$
$$w = 3$$
$$2w - 1 = 2(3) - 1 = 5$$

The width is 3 and the length is 5.

Area

8. In a figure of two dimensions, the total space within the figure is called the **area.** Area is expressed in square denominations, such as **square inches, square centimeters,** and **square miles.** When computing area, all dimensions must be in the same denomination.

9. The area of a square is equal to the square of the length of any side. The formula is $A = s^2$.

Example: The area of a square one side of which is 6 inches is $6 \times 6 = 36$ square inches.

10. The area of a rectangle equals the product of the length multiplied by the width. The formula is $A = l \times w$.

Example: If the length of a rectangle is 6 feet and its width is 4 feet, then the area is $6 \times 4 = 24$ square feet.

If given the area of a rectangle and one dimension, you can find the other dimension by dividing the area by the given dimension.

Example: If the area of a rectangle is 48 square feet and one dimension is 4 feet, then the other dimension is $48 \div 4 = 12$ feet.

11. The altitude, or **height**, of a parallelogram is a line drawn from a vertex perpendicular to the opposite side, or **base**.

Example:

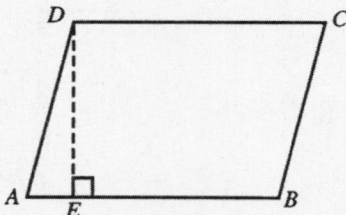

DE is the height.
AB is the base.

The area of a parallelogram is equal to the product of its base and its height. The formula is $A = b \times h$.

Example: If the base of a parallelogram is 10 centimeters and its height is 5 centimeters, its area is $10 \times 5 = 50$ square centimeters.

To find the base or the height of a parallelogram given one of these dimensions and given the area, divide the area by the given dimension.

Example: If the area of a parallelogram is 40 square inches and its height is 8 inches, its base is $40 \div 8 = 5$ inches.

Volume

12. A rectangular solid is a figure of three dimensions having six rectangular faces meeting each other at right angles. The three dimensions are **length, width,** and **height.** The figure below is a rectangular solid; "*l*" is the length, "*w*" is the width, and "*h*" is the height.

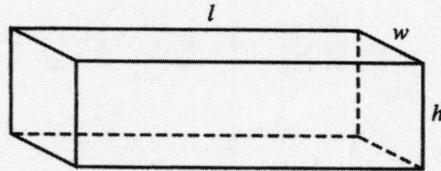

The volume of a rectangular solid is the product of the length, width, and height: $V = l \times w \times h$.

Example: The volume of a rectangular solid whose length is 6 ft, width 3 ft, and height 4 ft is $6 \times 3 \times 4 = 72$ cubic ft.

13. A **cube** is a rectangular solid whose edges are equal. The figure below is a cube; the length, width, and height are all equal to "*e*."

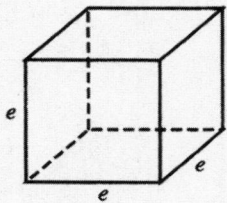

The volume of a cube is equal to the edge cubed: $V = e^3$.

Example: The volume of a cube whose height is 6 inches equals $6^3 = 6 \times 6 \times 6 = 216$ cubic inches.

The surface area of a cube is equal to the area of any side multiplied by 6.

Example: The surface area of a cube whose length is 5 inches = $5^2 \times 6 = 25 \times 6 = 150$ square inches.

TOPIC 6: TRIANGLES

Model Problem:

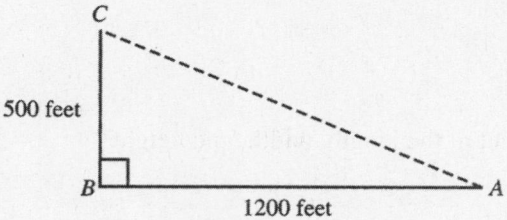

A road runs 1200 feet from A to B, and then makes a right angle going to C, a distance of 500 feet. A new road is being built directly from A to C. How much shorter will the new road be?

A   400 feet

B   609 feet

C   850 feet

D   1300 feet

SOLUTION:

The new road is the hypotenuse of a right triangle whose legs are the old road. Using the Pythagorean theorem,

$$(AC)^2 = 500^2 + 1200^2$$
$$= 250,000 + 1,440,000$$
$$= 1,690,000$$
$$AC = \sqrt{1,690,000}$$
$$= \sqrt{169} \bullet \sqrt{10,000}$$
$$= 13 \bullet 100$$
$$= 1300$$

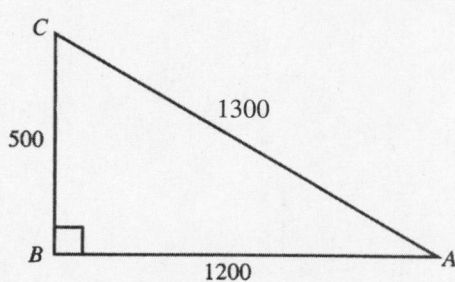

If you remember the 5-12-13 right triangle, you can see right away that the new road will be 1300 feet.

Old road	=	500 ft + 1200 ft
	=	1700 ft
New road	=	1300 ft
Difference	=	400 ft

The correct answer is choice A.

Now try Practice Exercise 6. Check your answers against the answers and explanations that follow and enter your score on the line provided. If your score is 8 or more, go on to Topic 7. If your score is less than 8, study the Topic Review before going on to the next topic area.

Practice Exercise 6

1. If the area of rectangle *ABCD* is 1200 square feet, what is the length of diagonal *AC*?

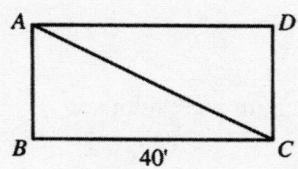

1–A	250 feet
1–B	500 feet
1–C	50 feet
1–D	25 feet

2. If the angles of a triangle are in the ratio of 1:2:3, what is the measure of the largest angle?

2–A	30°
2–B	45°
2–C	60°
2–D	90°

3. What is the area of the figure shown below?

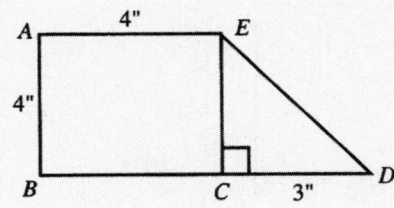

3–A	12 square inches
3–B	16 square inches
3–C	22 square inches
3–D	28 square inches

4. Find the area of a triangle whose base is 8 cm and whose height is 3.5 cm less than the base.

    4–A   36 cm²

    4–B   22 cm²

    4–C   18 cm²

    4–D   14 cm²

5. In isosceles triangle *ABC*, the measure of angle *C* is 30° more than the measure of each base angle. Find the number of degrees in each base angle.

    5–A   30

    5–B   50

    5–C   60

    5–D   75

6. Two boats leave the same dock at the same time, one traveling due west at 8 miles per hour and the other due north at 15 miles per hour. How many miles apart are the boats after three hours?

    6–A   17

    6–B   69

    6–C   75

    6–D   51

7. An umbrella 50″ long can lie on the bottom of a trunk whose length and width are respectively

    7–A   36 inches, 30 inches

    7–B   42 inches, 24 inches

    7–C   42 inches, 36 inches

    7–D   39 inches, 30 inches

8. Find the perimeter of right triangle *ABC* if the area of square *AEDC* is 100 and the area of square *BCFG* is 36.

    8–A   22

    8–B   24

    8–C $16+\sqrt{3}$

    8–D $16+6\sqrt{2}$

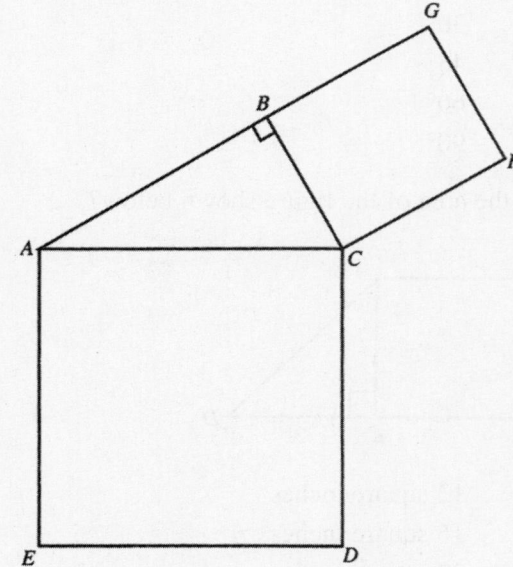

9. A certain triangle has sides that are, respectively, 6 inches, 8 inches, and 10 inches long. A rectangle equal in area to that of the triangle has a width of 3 inches. The perimeter of the rectangle, expressed in inches, is

    9–A   11

    9–B   16

    9–C   18

    9–D   22

10. The angles of a triangle are in the ratio 1:5:6. This triangle is

    10–A   right.

    10–B   acute.

    10–C   isosceles.

    10–D   obtuse.

Your Score _____

Answer Key

1. C	2. D	3. C	4. C	5. B
6. D	7. C	8. B	9. D	10. A

Answers and Explanations

1–C   Area of rectangle $ABCD = AB \times BC$

$$1200 = AB \times 40$$

$$\frac{1200}{40} = AB$$

$$30 = AB$$

Diagonal AC is the hypotenuse of right triangle ABC.

$$AC^2 = AB^2 + BC^2$$
$$= (30)^2 + (40)^2$$
$$= 900 + 1600$$
$$= 2500$$
$$AC = \sqrt{2500} = 50$$

2–D   Let x = smallest angle

$2x$ = second angle

$3x$ = largest angle

The sum of the angles of a triangle is 180°, therefore

$$x + 2x + 3x = 180°$$
$$6x = 180°$$
$$x = 30°$$

Largest angle = $3x = 3(30°) = 90°$

3–C   Area of $ABCE = 4 \times 4 = 16$ in²

Area of $ECD = \dfrac{1}{2}bh = \dfrac{1}{2}(3 \times 4) = \dfrac{1}{2}(12) = 6$ in²

Total area = 16 + 6 = 22 in²

4–C   Base of triangle = 8 cm

Height of triangle = 8 cm − 3.5 cm = 4.5 cm

$$\text{Area of triangle} = \dfrac{1}{2}bh = \dfrac{1}{2}(8 \times 4.5)$$
$$= \dfrac{1}{2}(36) = 18 \text{ cm}^2$$

5–B   Let x = base angle (Base angles of an isosceles triangle are equal.)

Then angle $C = x + 30°$

$$x + x + x + 30° = 180° \quad\text{(The sum of the angles of}$$
$$3x + 30° = 180° \quad\quad\text{a triangle} = 180°.)$$
$$3x = 150°$$
$$x = 50°$$

6–D

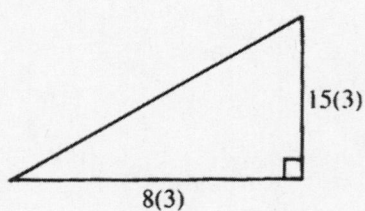

This is an 8–15–17 right triangle, making the missing side (3)17, or 51.

7–C   The umbrella would be the hypotenuse of a right triangle whose legs are the dimensions of the trunk. According to the Pythagorean theorem, in any right triangle the square of the hypotenuse equals the sum of the squares of the legs. Therefore, the sum of the dimensions squared must at least equal the length of the umbrella squared: $(50)^2 = 2500$.

The only set of dimensions that fills this condition is choice C.

$$(42)^2 + (36)^2 \quad = \quad 1764 + 1296$$
$$= \quad 3060$$

8–B   Area of square $AEDC = S^2 = 100$
$$S = \sqrt{100} = 10$$
Area of square $BCFG = S^2 = 36$
$$S = \sqrt{36} = 6$$

Therefore, right triangle ABC is a 6–8–10 triangle.

Perimeter = 6 + 8 + 10 = 24

9–D   Since $6^2 + 8^2 = 10^2$, or $36 + 64 = 100$, the triangle is a right triangle. Its area is

$$\frac{1}{2} \times 6 \times 8 = 24 \text{ sq in} \quad (\text{area of a triangle} = \frac{1}{2} \bullet b \bullet h).$$

Therefore, the area of the rectangle is also 24 square inches. If the width of the rectangle is 3 inches, the length is $24 \div 3 = 8$ inches. Then, the perimeter of the rectangle is $2(3 + 8) = 2 \times 11 = 22$ inches.

10–A   Represent the angles as x, $5x$, and $6x$.

They must add up to 180°.

$$12x = 180$$
$$x = 15$$

The angles are 15°, 75°, and 90°.

A triangle with a 90°-angle is a right triangle.

Topic Review

Triangles

1. A triangle is a closed, three-sided figure. The following figures are triangles.

    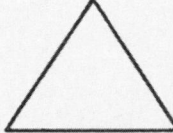 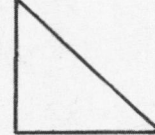 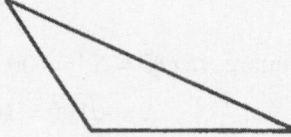

2. The sum of the three angles of a triangle is 180°.

    To find an angle of a triangle given the other two angles, add the given angles and subtract their sum from 180°.

    Example: Two angles of a triangle are 60° and 40°. Find the third angle.

    SOLUTION: 60° + 40° = 100°

    180° − 100° = 80°
    The third angle is 80°.

3. A triangle with two equal sides is called an **isosceles triangle**.

    In an isosceles triangle, the angles opposite the equal sides are also equal.

    Example:

    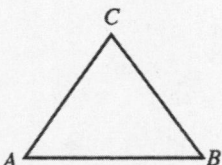

    If $AC = BC$, then $\angle A = \angle B$

4. A triangle with all three sides equal is called an **equilateral triangle**.

    Each angle of an equilateral triangle is 60°.

5. A triangle with a right angle is called a **right triangle**.

    In a right triangle, the two acute angles are complementary.

    In a right triangle, the side opposite the right angle is called the **hypotenuse** and is the longest side. The other two sides are called **legs**.

Example:

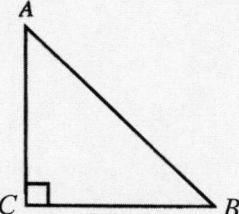

In a right triangle *ABC*, *AB* is the hypotenuse. *AC* and *BC* are the legs.

Pythagorean Theorem

6. The **Pythagorean theorem** states that in a right triangle, the square of the hypotenuse equals the sum of the squares of the legs.

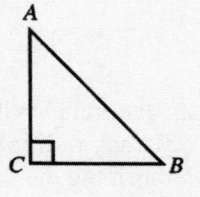

$$(AC)^2 + (BC)^2 = (AB)^2$$

Example: Find the hypotenuse (*h*) in a right triangle that has legs 6 and 8.

SOLUTION:

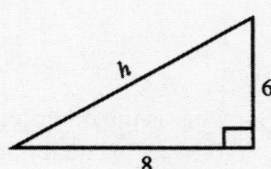

$$6^2 + 8^2 = h^2$$
$$36 + 64 = h^2$$
$$100 = h^2$$
$$\sqrt{100} = h$$
$$10 = h$$

Example: One leg of a right triangle is 5. The hypotenuse is 13. Find the other leg.

SOLUTION: Let the unknown leg be represented by x.

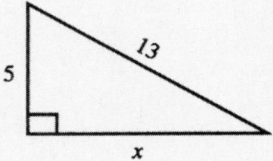

$$5^2 + x^2 = 13^2$$
$$25 + x^2 = 169$$
$$\underline{-25 \qquad -25}$$
$$x^2 = 144$$
$$x = \sqrt{144}$$
$$x = 12$$

The other leg is 12.

7. **Pythagorean triples** are sets of numbers that satisfy the Pythagorean theorem. When a given set of numbers such as 3, 4, 5 form a Pythagorean triple ($3^2 + 4^2 = 5^2$), any multiples of this set, such as 6, 8, 10 or 30, 40, 50, also form a Pythagorean triple. Memorizing the sets of Pythagorean triples that follow will save you valuable time in solving problems because if you recognize given numbers as multiples of Pythagorean triples, you do not have to do any arithmetic at all. The most common Pythagorean triples that should be memorized are

    3–4–5
    5–12–13
    8–15–17
    7–24–25

Example: If one leg of a right triangle is 16 and the hypotenuse is 34, what is the other leg?

SOLUTION: Squaring these numbers to apply the Pythagorean theorem would take too much time. Instead, recognize the hypotenuse as 2(17). Suspect an 8–15–17 triangle. Since the given leg is 2(8), the missing leg will be 2(15) or 30, without any computation at all.

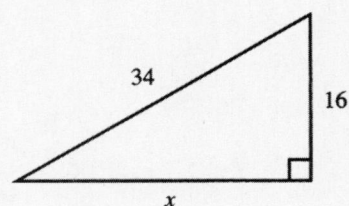

8. In a right triangle with equal legs (an isosceles right triangle), each acute angle is equal to 45°. There are special relationships between the legs and the hypotenuse:

$$\text{each leg} = \frac{1}{2}(\text{hypotenuse}) \sqrt{2}$$

$$\text{hypotenuse} = (\text{leg}) \sqrt{2}$$

$$AC = BC = \frac{1}{2}(AB) \sqrt{2}$$

$$AB = (AC)\sqrt{2} = (BC) \sqrt{2}$$

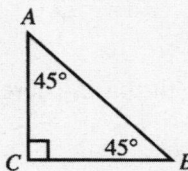

Example: In isosceles right triangle *RST*,

$$RT = \frac{1}{2}(10) \sqrt{2}$$

$$= 5 \sqrt{2}$$

$$ST = RT = 5 \sqrt{2}$$

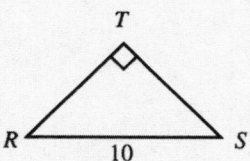

In a right triangle with acute angles of 30° and 60°, the leg opposite the 30° angle is one half the hypotenuse. The leg opposite the 60° angle is one half the hypotenuse multiplied by $\sqrt{3}$.

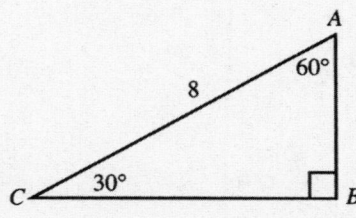

Example:

$$AB = \frac{1}{2}(8) = 4$$

$$BC = \frac{1}{2}(8)\sqrt{3} = 4\sqrt{3}$$

Area of a Triangle

9. The altitude, or height, of a triangle is a line drawn from a vertex perpendicular to the opposite side, called the base.

    The area of a triangle is equal to one half the product of the base and the height. The formula is $A = \frac{1}{2}b \times h$.

Example: The area of a triangle that has a height of 5 inches and a base of 4 inches is

$\frac{1}{2} \times 5 \times 4 = \frac{1}{2} \times 20 = 10$ square inches.

In a right triangle, one leg may be considered the height and the other leg the base. Therefore, the area of a right triangle is equal to one half the product of the legs.

Example: The legs of a right triangle are 3 and 4. Its area is $\frac{1}{2} \times 3 \times 4 = 6$ square units.

TOPIC 7: POWERS, ROOTS, AND RADICALS

Model Problems:

1. Find the side of a square whose area is 64.
     1–A   8
     1–B   16
     1–C   32
     1–D   40

SOLUTION:

Area of a square $= s^2$

$$64 = s^2$$

$$s = \sqrt{64} = 8$$

The correct answer is choice A.

2. If $\frac{2}{x} = \sqrt{.16}$, then x equals
     2–A   50
     2–B   5
     2–C   .5
     2–D   .05

SOLUTION:

$$\sqrt{.16} = .4$$

$$\frac{2}{x} = .4 \quad \text{(Multiply by } x.\text{)}$$

$$2 = .4x \,\text{(Divide by .4.)}$$

$$x = 5$$

The correct answer is choice B.

Now try Practice Exercise 7. Check your answers against the answers and explanations that follow and enter your score on the line provided. If your score is 8 or more, go on to Topic 8. If your score is less than 8, study the Topic Review before going on to the next topic area.

Practice Exercise 7

1. The square of 10 is
    1–A   1
    1–B   2
    1–C   5
    1–D   100

2. The cube of 9 is
    2–A   3
    2–B   27
    2–C   81
    2–D   729

3. The fourth power of 2 is
    3–A   2
    3–B   4
    3–C   8
    3–D   16

4. In exponential form, the product $7 \times 7 \times 7 \times 7 \times 7$ may be written
    4–A 5^7
    4–B 7^5
    4–C 2^7
    4–D 7^2

5. The value of 3^5 is
    5–A   243
    5–B   125
    5–C   35
    5–D   15

6. Find $\sqrt{\dfrac{1}{4}}$.

    6–A   2

    6–B $\dfrac{1}{2}$

    6–C $\dfrac{1}{8}$

    6–D $\dfrac{1}{16}$

7. The sum of 2^2 and 2^3 is
    7–A   9
    7–B   10
    7–C   12
    7–D   32

8. The square root of 2704 is exactly
    8–A   52
    8–B   53
    8–C   54
    8–D   56

9. The sum of $\sqrt{18}$ and $\sqrt{72}$ is

    9–A $18\sqrt{2}$

    9–B $9\sqrt{2}$

    9–C $3\sqrt{10}$

    9–D   40

10. Simplify $\dfrac{20\sqrt{3}}{\sqrt{5}}$.

    10–A $4\sqrt{3}$

    10–B $4\sqrt{15}$

    10–C $100\sqrt{3}$

    10–D $10\sqrt{3}$

Your Score _____

Answer Key

1. D	2. D	3. D	4. B	5. A
6. B	7. C	8. A	9. B	10. B

Answers and Explanations

1–D $10^2 = 10 \times 10 = 100$

2–D $9^3 = 9 \times 9 \times 9$
$= 81 \times 9$
$= 729$

3–D $2^4 = 2 \times 2 \times 2 \times 2$
$= 4 \times 2 \times 2$
$= 8 \times 2$
$= 16$

4–B $7 \times 7 \times 7 \times 7 \times 7 = 7^5$

5–A $3^5 = 3 \times 3 \times 3 \times 3 \times 3$
$= 243$

6–B $\sqrt{\dfrac{1}{4}} = \dfrac{\sqrt{1}}{\sqrt{4}} = \dfrac{1}{2}$

7–C $2^2 + 2^3 = 4 + 8 = 12$

8–A The correct answer must be a number that, when multiplied by itself, will end in 4. This happens only with 52 ($2 \times 2 = 4$).

$52 \times 52 = 2704$

9–B $\sqrt{18} + \sqrt{72} = \sqrt{9} \cdot \sqrt{2} + \sqrt{36} \cdot \sqrt{2}$
$= 3\sqrt{2} + 6\sqrt{2}$
$= 9\sqrt{2}$

10–B $\dfrac{20\sqrt{3}}{\sqrt{5}} = \dfrac{20\sqrt{3}}{\sqrt{5}} \cdot \dfrac{\sqrt{5}}{\sqrt{5}}$
$= \dfrac{20\sqrt{15}}{\sqrt{5}}$
$= 4\sqrt{15}$

Topic Review

Powers and Roots

1. The numbers that are multiplied to give a product are called the **factors** of the product.

    Example: In $2 \times 3 = 6$, 2 and 3 are factors.

2. If the factors are the same, an **exponent** may be used to indicate the number of times the factor appears.

    Example: In $3 \times 3 = 3^2$, the number 3 appears as a factor twice, as is indicated by the exponent 2.

3. When a product is written in exponential form, the number the exponent refers to is called the **base.** The product itself is called the **power.**

    Example: In 2^5, the number 2 is the base and 5 is the exponent.

    $2^5 = 2 \times 2 \times 2 \times 2 \times 2 = 32$, so 32 is the power.

4. If the exponent used is 2, we say that the base has been **squared,** or raised to the second power.

    Example: 6^2 is read "six squared" or "six to the second power."

    If the exponent used is 3, we say that the base has been **cubed**, or raised to the third power.

    Example: 5^3 is read "five cubed" or "five to the third power."

    If the exponent is 4, we say that the base has been raised to the fourth power. If the exponent is 5, we say the base has been raised to the fifth power, etc.

    Example: 2^8 is read "two to the eighth power."

5. A number that is the product of a number squared is called a **perfect square.**

    Example: 25 is a perfect square because $25 = 5^2$.

6. If a number has exactly two equal factors, each factor is called the **square root** of the number.

    Example: $9 = 3 \times 3$; therefore, 3 is the square root of 9.

    The symbol $\sqrt{}$ is used to indicate square root.

    Example: $\sqrt{9} = 3$ means that the square root of 9 is 3, or $3 \times 3 = 9$.

Perfect Squares

7. The square root of the most common perfect squares may be found by using the following table, or by trial and error; that is, by finding the number that, when squared, yields the given perfect square.

NUMBER	PERFECT SQUARE	NUMBER	PERFECT SQUARE
1	1	10	100
2	4	11	121
3	9	12	144
4	16	13	169
5	25	14	196
6	36	15	225
7	49	20	400
8	64	25	625
9	81	30	900

Example: To find $\sqrt{81}$, note that 81 is the perfect square of 9, or $9^2 = 81$. Therefore, $\sqrt{81} = 9$.

Finding Square Roots

8. To find the square root of a number, first pair off the digits in the square root sign in each direction from the decimal point. If there is an odd number of digits *before* the decimal point, insert a zero at the *beginning* of the number in order to pair digits. If there is an odd number of digits *after* the decimal point, add a zero at the *end*. It should be clearly understood that these zeros are placeholders only and in no way change the value of the number. Every *pair* of numbers in the radical sign gives one digit of the square root.

Example: The square root of 328,329 is exactly

> A   249
> B   573
> C   650
> D   1267

SOLUTION: First pair the numbers beginning at the decimal point.

$$\sqrt{\overline{32}\,\overline{83}\,\overline{29}.}$$

Each pair will give one digit in the square root. Therefore, the square root of 328,329 has three digits.

Next, look among the answer choices for a three-digit number. If there is more than one, look for one which, when multiplied by itself, ends in 9. Going through the digits from 0 to 9, this could be 3 ($3 \times 3 = 9$) or 7 ($7 \times 7 = 49$). Choice B is a three-digit number that ends in 3, and it is the correct answer.

9. To find the square root of a fraction, find the square root of its numerator and of its denominator.

Example: $\sqrt{\dfrac{4}{9}} = \dfrac{\sqrt{4}}{\sqrt{9}} = \dfrac{2}{3}$

Cube Roots

10. If a number has exactly three equal factors, each factor is called the **cube root** of the number.

The symbol $\sqrt[3]{}$ is used to indicate the cube root.

Example: $8 = 2 \times 2 \times 2$; therefore, $\sqrt[3]{8} = 2$

Radicals

11. The symbol $\sqrt{x}$ means the positive square root of x. The $\sqrt{}$ is called the **radical sign** and the x is called the **radicand**.

Any positive number has two square roots, one positive and one negative. $\sqrt{x}$ indicates the positive root and $-\sqrt{x}$ indicates the negative root.

Example: The square roots of 100 are 10 and –10, since $(10)^2 = 100$ and $(-10)^2 = 100$.

$$\sqrt{100} = 10$$
$$-\sqrt{100} = -10$$

12. Many radicals may be simplified by using the principle $\sqrt{ab} = \sqrt{a} \cdot \sqrt{b}$

Example: $\sqrt{100} = \sqrt{25} \cdot \sqrt{4} = 5 \cdot 2 = 10$
$\sqrt{18} = \sqrt{9} \cdot \sqrt{2} = 3\sqrt{2}$
$\sqrt{75} = \sqrt{25} \cdot \sqrt{3} = 5\sqrt{3}$

Note: The factors chosen must include at least one perfect square.

13. Radicals with the same radicands may be added or subtracted as like terms.

Example: $3\sqrt{5} + 4\sqrt{5} = 7\sqrt{5}$
$$10\sqrt{2} - 6\sqrt{2} = 4\sqrt{2}$$

Radicals with different radicands may be combined only if they can be simplified to have like radicands.

Example: $\sqrt{50} + \sqrt{32} - 2\sqrt{2} + \sqrt{3} = \sqrt{25} \cdot \sqrt{2} + \sqrt{16} \cdot \sqrt{2} - 2\sqrt{2} + \sqrt{3}$
$$= 5\sqrt{2} + 4\sqrt{2} - 2\sqrt{2} + \sqrt{3}$$
$$= 7\sqrt{2} + \sqrt{3}$$

14. To multiply radicals, first multiply the coefficients. Then multiply the radicands.

Example: $2\sqrt{3} \cdot 4\sqrt{5} = 8\sqrt{15}$

15. To divide radicals, first divide the coefficients. Then divide the radicands.

Example: $\dfrac{14\sqrt{20}}{2\sqrt{2}} = 7\sqrt{10}$

TOPIC 8: EXPONENTS AND SEQUENCES

Model Problems:

1. Calculate $\dfrac{3^6}{3^4}$.

1–A	$\dfrac{1}{9}$
1–B	9
1–C	27
1–D	81

SOLUTION:

$$\frac{3^6}{3^4} = 3^{(6-4)} = 3^2 = 9$$

The correct answer is choice B.

2. Find the missing term in the following series: 6 $8\frac{1}{2}$ 11   ____   16

2–A	12
2–B	$12\frac{1}{4}$
2–C	$13\frac{1}{2}$
2–D	14

SOLUTION:

This is an arithmetic progression with a difference of $2\frac{1}{2}$ between terms:

$$6 \;(+ 2\tfrac{1}{2} =)\; 8\tfrac{1}{2} \;(+ 2\tfrac{1}{2} =)\; 11 \;(+ 2\tfrac{1}{2} =)\; 13\tfrac{1}{2} \;(+ 2\tfrac{1}{2} =)\; 16$$

The missing term is $13\frac{1}{2}$.

Choice C is the correct answer.

Now try Practice Exercise 8. Check your answers against the answers and explanations that follow and enter your score on the line provided. If your score is 8 or more, go on to the Mathematics Knowledge Review Tests. If your score is less than 8, study the topic review before you go on to the review tests.

Practice Exercise 8

1. $(b^2)^{-3} =$

1–A	b^{-8}
1–B	b^{-6}
1–C	b^{-5}
1–D	b^{-1}

2. $\left(\dfrac{-6\,x^2}{2\,x}\right)^0 =$

2–A	0
2–B	1
2–C	$-3x$
2–D	-6

3. Solve for x: $2^x = \dfrac{1}{8}$

    3–A   3

    3–B   2

    3–C   −1

    3–D   −3

4. $5^{2a} \div 25 =$

    4–A $\left(\dfrac{1}{5}\right)^{2a}$

    4–B 5^a

    4–C $\left(\dfrac{1}{5}\right)^{a-2}$

    4–D 5^{2a-2}

5. Simplify $\dfrac{\left(x^{-2}\bullet x^{3}\right)^{4}}{x^{-5}}$

    5–A x^{9}

    5–B x^{-3}

    5–C x^{-9}

    5–D x^{4}

Find the missing term in each of the following sequences.

6. __, 7, 10, 13

    6–A   5

    6–B   4

    6–C   3

    6–D   2

7. 5, 10, 20, __, 80

    7–A   25

    7–B   30

    7–C   40

    7–D   50

8. 49, 45, 41, __, 33, 29

    8–A   37

    8–B   44

    8–C   36

    8–D   30

9. 1.002, 1.004, 1.006, __

    9–A   1.007

    9–B   1.08

    9–C   1.010

    9–D   1.008

10. 1, 4, 9, 16, __

    10–A   20

    10–B   25

    10–C   23

    10–D   32

Your Score _____

Answer Key

1. B	2. B	3. D	4. D	5. A
6. B	7. C	8. A	9. D	10. B

Answers and Explanations

1–B $(b^2)^{-3} = b^{(2)(-3)} = b^{-6}$

2–B   Any number raised to the zero power is one.

3–D $2^3 = 8; \ 2^{-3} = \dfrac{1}{8}$

4–D $5^{2a} \cdot \dfrac{1}{25} = 5^{2a} \cdot 5^{-2} = 5^{2a-2}$

5–A $\dfrac{\left(x^{-2} \cdot x^3\right)^4}{x^{-5}} = \dfrac{\left(x^1\right)^4}{x^{-5}} = \dfrac{x^4}{x^{-5}} = x^9$

6–B   This is an ascending arithmetic sequence in which the common difference is $10 - 7$, or 3. The first term is $7 - 3 = 4$.

7–C   This is a geometric sequence in which the common ratio is $10 \div 5$, or 2. The missing term is $20 \times 2 = 40$.

8–A   This is a descending arithmetic sequence in which the common difference is $49 - 45$, or 4. The missing term is $41 - 4 = 37$.

9–D This is an ascending arithmetic sequence in which the common difference is 1.004 – 1.002, or .002. The missing term is 1.006 + .002 = 1.008.

10–B This sequence is neither arithmetic nor geometric. However, if the numbers are rewritten as 1^2, 2^2, 3^2, and 4^2, it is clear that the next number must be 5^2, or 25.

Topic Review

Exponents

1. Zero, negative, and fractional exponents are defined as follows:

$$x^0 = 1 \qquad \text{(for } x \neq 0)$$

$$x^{-a} = \frac{1}{x^a} \qquad \text{(for } x \neq 0)$$

$$x^{\frac{1}{a}} = \sqrt[a]{x}$$

Examples: $5^0 = 1$

$$6^{-2} = \frac{1}{6^2} = \frac{1}{36}$$

$$8^{\frac{1}{3}} = \sqrt[3]{8} = 2$$

2. Laws of exponents: These laws apply to all real exponents, except where zero denominators may result.

LAW	EXAMPLE
I. $x^a \bullet x^b = x^{a+b}$	$x^2 \bullet x^3 = x^5$
II. $\dfrac{x^a}{x^b} = x^{a-b}$	$\dfrac{x^6}{x^2} = x^4 ; \dfrac{y^9}{y^{10}} = y^{-1}$
III. $(x^a)^b = x^{ab}$	$(x^2)^3 = x^6$
IV. $(xy)^a = x^a y^a$	$(5x)^2 = 25x^2$
V. $\left(\dfrac{x}{y}\right)^a = \dfrac{x^a}{y^a}$	$\left(\dfrac{x}{3}\right)^2 = \dfrac{x^2}{9}$

3. More than one law may be applied in a problem.

Examples:

$$\left(x^2 y^3\right)^4 = x^8 y^{12} \qquad \text{(Laws III and IV)}$$

$$\frac{\left(x^{-2}\right)^{-1} \cdot x^5}{x^4} = \frac{x^2 \cdot x^5}{x^4} = \frac{x^7}{x^4} = x^3 \qquad \text{(Laws I, II, and III)}$$

$$\left(\frac{x^{3a} \cdot x^{a+1}}{y^b}\right)^2 = \left(\frac{x^{4a+1}}{y^b}\right)^2 = \frac{x^{8a+2}}{y^{2b}} \qquad \text{(Laws I, III, and V)}$$

4. To solve an equation that has the variable in an exponent, express both sides of the equation as powers of the same base, then set the exponents equal to each other.

Example: Solve $2^x = 32$.

SOLUTION: Write 32 as a power of 2.

$$2^x = 2^5$$
$$x = 5$$

Example: Solve $125^x = \dfrac{1}{25}$.

SOLUTION: Write both sides as powers of 5.

$$125^x = \frac{1}{25}$$
$$\left(5^3\right)^x = \frac{1}{5^2}$$
$$5^{3x} = 5^{-2}$$
$$3x = -2$$
$$x = -\frac{2}{3}$$

Sequences

5. A sequence is a list of numbers based on a certain pattern. There are three main types of sequences.
   - If each term in a sequence is being increased or diminished by the same number to form the next term, then it is an arithmetic sequence. The number being added or subtracted is called the common difference.

Examples: 2, 4, 6, 8, 10 . . . is an arithmetic sequence in which the common difference is 2.

14, 11, 8, 5, 2 . . . is an arithmetic sequence in which the common difference is 3.

- If each term of a sequence is being multiplied by the same number to form the next term, then it is a geometric sequence. The number multiplying each term is called the common ratio.

Examples: 2, 6, 18, 54 . . . is a geometric sequence in which the common ratio is 3.

64, 16, 4, 1 . . . is a geometric sequence in which the common ratio is $\frac{1}{4}$.

- If the sequence is neither arithmetic nor geometric, it is a miscellaneous sequence. Such a sequence may have each term a square or a cube, or the difference may be squares or cubes; or there may be a varied pattern in the sequence that must be determined.

6. A sequence may be ascending, that is, the numbers increase; or descending, that is, the numbers decrease.

7. To determine whether the sequence is arithmetic:
   - If the sequence is ascending, subtract the first term from the second, and the second term from the third. If the difference is the same in both cases, the sequence is arithmetic.
   - If the sequence is descending, subtract the second term from the first, and the third term from the second. If the difference is the same in both cases, the sequence is arithmetic.

8. To determine whether the sequence is geometric, divide the second term by the first, and the third term by the second. If the ratio is the same in both cases, the sequence is geometric.

Finding Missing Terms

9. To find a missing term in an arithmetic sequence that is ascending:
   - Subtract any term from the one following it to find the common difference.
   - Add the common difference to the term preceding the missing term.
   - If the missing term is the first term, it may be found by subtracting the common difference from the second term.

Example: In this sequence, what number follows $16\frac{1}{3}$?

$$3, \ 6\frac{1}{3}, \ 9\frac{2}{3}, \ 13, \ 16\frac{1}{3}, \ \underline{\qquad}$$

SOLUTION: $6\frac{1}{3} - 3 = 3\frac{1}{3}, \ 9\frac{2}{3} - 6\frac{1}{3} = 3\frac{1}{3}$

The sequence is arithmetic; the common difference is $3\frac{1}{3}$.

$$16\frac{1}{3} + 3\frac{1}{3} = 19\frac{2}{3}$$

The missing term, which is the term following $16\frac{1}{3}$, is $19\frac{2}{3}$.

10. To find a missing term in an arithmetic sequence that is descending:
    • Subtract any term from the one preceding it to find the common difference.
    • Subtract the common difference from the term preceding the missing term.
    • If the missing term is the first term, it may be found by adding the common difference to the second term.

Example: Find the first term in the sequence:

$$\_\_, 16, 13\frac{1}{2}, 11, 8\frac{1}{2}, 6, \_\_\_$$

SOLUTION: $16 - 13\frac{1}{2} = 2\frac{1}{2}, 13\frac{1}{2} - 11 = 2\frac{1}{2}$

The sequence is arithmetic; the common difference is $2\frac{1}{2}$.

$$16 + 2\frac{1}{2} = 18\frac{1}{2}$$

The term preceding 16 is $18\frac{1}{2}$.

11. To find a missing term in a geometric sequence:
    • Divide any term by the one preceding it to find the common ratio.
    • Multiply the term preceding the missing term by the common ratio.
    • If the missing term is the first term, it may be found by dividing the second term by the common ratio.

Example: Find the missing term in the sequence:

$$2, 6, 18, 54, \_\_\_\_$$

SOLUTION: $6 \div 2 = 3, 18 \div 6 = 3$

The sequence is geometric; the common ratio is 3.

$54 \times 3 = 162$

The missing term is 162.

Example: Find the missing term in the sequence:

____, 32, 16, 8, 4, 2

$$16 \div 32 = \frac{1}{2} \text{ (common ratio)}$$

SOLUTION: $32 \div \frac{1}{2} = 32 \times \frac{2}{1}$

$$= 64$$

The first term is 64.

12. If, after trial, a sequence is neither arithmetic nor geometric, it must be one of a miscellaneous type.

   • Test to see whether it is a sequence of squares or cubes or whether the difference is the square or the cube of the same number; or the same number may be first squared, then cubed, etc.

   • Other sequences are:

   1, 2, 4, 7,____, 16

   [First term + 1 = second term; second term + 2 = third term; third term + 3 = fourth term, etc.]

   1, 2, 3, 5, 8, ____, 21

   [First term + second term = third term; second term + third term = fourth term; third term + fourth term = fifth term, etc.]

THREE SAMPLE MATHEMATICS KNOWLEDGE TESTS

This section contains three full-length sample Mathematics Knowledge Tests similar to the ones on the ASVAB. Tear out this page and use the answer strips below to record your answers to the sample tests, just as you will have to do on the real test. Stick to the time limit for realistic practice. As you finish each sample test, check your answers with the answer key and solutions provided.

Mathematics Knowledge Test 1

1. Ⓐ Ⓑ Ⓒ Ⓓ   2. Ⓐ Ⓑ Ⓒ Ⓓ   3. Ⓐ Ⓑ Ⓒ Ⓓ   4. Ⓐ Ⓑ Ⓒ Ⓓ   5. Ⓐ Ⓑ Ⓒ Ⓓ
6. Ⓐ Ⓑ Ⓒ Ⓓ   7. Ⓐ Ⓑ Ⓒ Ⓓ   8. Ⓐ Ⓑ Ⓒ Ⓓ   9. Ⓐ Ⓑ Ⓒ Ⓓ   10. Ⓐ Ⓑ Ⓒ Ⓓ
11. Ⓐ Ⓑ Ⓒ Ⓓ   12. Ⓐ Ⓑ Ⓒ Ⓓ   13. Ⓐ Ⓑ Ⓒ Ⓓ   14. Ⓐ Ⓑ Ⓒ Ⓓ   15. Ⓐ Ⓑ Ⓒ Ⓓ
16. Ⓐ Ⓑ Ⓒ Ⓓ   17. Ⓐ Ⓑ Ⓒ Ⓓ   18. Ⓐ Ⓑ Ⓒ Ⓓ   19. Ⓐ Ⓑ Ⓒ Ⓓ   20. Ⓐ Ⓑ Ⓒ Ⓓ
21. Ⓐ Ⓑ Ⓒ Ⓓ   22. Ⓐ Ⓑ Ⓒ Ⓓ   23. Ⓐ Ⓑ Ⓒ Ⓓ   24. Ⓐ Ⓑ Ⓒ Ⓓ   25. Ⓐ Ⓑ Ⓒ Ⓓ

Mathematics Knowledge Test 2

1. Ⓐ Ⓑ Ⓒ Ⓓ   2. Ⓐ Ⓑ Ⓒ Ⓓ   3. Ⓐ Ⓑ Ⓒ Ⓓ   4. Ⓐ Ⓑ Ⓒ Ⓓ   5. Ⓐ Ⓑ Ⓒ Ⓓ
6. Ⓐ Ⓑ Ⓒ Ⓓ   7. Ⓐ Ⓑ Ⓒ Ⓓ   8. Ⓐ Ⓑ Ⓒ Ⓓ   9. Ⓐ Ⓑ Ⓒ Ⓓ   10. Ⓐ Ⓑ Ⓒ Ⓓ
11. Ⓐ Ⓑ Ⓒ Ⓓ   12. Ⓐ Ⓑ Ⓒ Ⓓ   13. Ⓐ Ⓑ Ⓒ Ⓓ   14. Ⓐ Ⓑ Ⓒ Ⓓ   15. Ⓐ Ⓑ Ⓒ Ⓓ
16. Ⓐ Ⓑ Ⓒ Ⓓ   17. Ⓐ Ⓑ Ⓒ Ⓓ   18. Ⓐ Ⓑ Ⓒ Ⓓ   19. Ⓐ Ⓑ Ⓒ Ⓓ   20. Ⓐ Ⓑ Ⓒ Ⓓ
21. Ⓐ Ⓑ Ⓒ Ⓓ   22. Ⓐ Ⓑ Ⓒ Ⓓ   23. Ⓐ Ⓑ Ⓒ Ⓓ   24. Ⓐ Ⓑ Ⓒ Ⓓ   25. Ⓐ Ⓑ Ⓒ Ⓓ

Mathematics Knowledge Test 3

1. Ⓐ Ⓑ Ⓒ Ⓓ   2. Ⓐ Ⓑ Ⓒ Ⓓ   3. Ⓐ Ⓑ Ⓒ Ⓓ   4. Ⓐ Ⓑ Ⓒ Ⓓ   5. Ⓐ Ⓑ Ⓒ Ⓓ
6. Ⓐ Ⓑ Ⓒ Ⓓ   7. Ⓐ Ⓑ Ⓒ Ⓓ   8. Ⓐ Ⓑ Ⓒ Ⓓ   9. Ⓐ Ⓑ Ⓒ Ⓓ   10. Ⓐ Ⓑ Ⓒ Ⓓ
11. Ⓐ Ⓑ Ⓒ Ⓓ   12. Ⓐ Ⓑ Ⓒ Ⓓ   13. Ⓐ Ⓑ Ⓒ Ⓓ   14. Ⓐ Ⓑ Ⓒ Ⓓ   15. Ⓐ Ⓑ Ⓒ Ⓓ
16. Ⓐ Ⓑ Ⓒ Ⓓ   17. Ⓐ Ⓑ Ⓒ Ⓓ   18. Ⓐ Ⓑ Ⓒ Ⓓ   19. Ⓐ Ⓑ Ⓒ Ⓓ   20. Ⓐ Ⓑ Ⓒ Ⓓ
21. Ⓐ Ⓑ Ⓒ Ⓓ   22. Ⓐ Ⓑ Ⓒ Ⓓ   23. Ⓐ Ⓑ Ⓒ Ⓓ   24. Ⓐ Ⓑ Ⓒ Ⓓ   25. Ⓐ Ⓑ Ⓒ Ⓓ

MATHEMATICS KNOWLEDGE TEST 1

TIME: 24 Minutes—25 Questions

This is a test of your ability to solve 25 general mathematical problems. You are to select the correct response from the choices given. Then mark the space on your answer form that has the same number and letter as your choice. Use the scrap paper that has been given to you to do any figuring that you wish.

Your score on this test will be based on the number of questions you answer correctly. You should try to answer every question. Do not spend too much time on any one question.

1. The sum of two numbers is 512. If one number is 420, how much is the other?
   - 1–A   920
   - 1–B   932
   - 1–C   92
   - 1–D   100

2. If the owner of a store is required to collect an 8% sales tax, what was the total amount of sales for a day in which she collected $280 in taxes?
   - 2–A $350
   - 2–B $2240
   - 2–C $3500
   - 2–D $4200

3. Add: $(2x^2 + 4x + 6) + (3x^2 - 5x + 7)$
   - 3–A $5x^2 - x + 13$
   - 3–B $5x^2 + 12$
   - 3–C $5x^2 + 9x + 13$
   - 3–D $5x^2 - x - 1$

4. The value of $[7 - (1 - 4)] + [(2 - 8) -(7 - 6)]$ is
   - 4–A   3
   - 4–B   9
   - 4–C   11
   - 4–D   17

5. If $3x + 3x - 3x = 12$, find $3x + 1$.
   - 5–A   4
   - 5–B   5
   - 5–C   10
   - 5–D   13

6. Two ships leave from the same port at 11:30 a.m. If one sails due east at 20 miles per hour and the other due south at 15 miles per hour, how many miles apart are the ships at 2:30 p.m.?

    6–A   25

    6–B   50

    6–C   75

    6–D   80

7. The next term in the sequence 27, 9, 3, 1, _____ is

    7–A -3

    7–B -1

    7–C $\dfrac{1}{3}$

    7–D $-\dfrac{1}{3}$

8. A clerk's weekly salary is $140 after a 25% raise. What was his weekly salary before the raise?

    8–A $112

    8–B $110

    8–C $125

    8–D $105

9. $(7x - 3) + (4x^2 - 5x + 8) - (3x^2 - 4x + 5) =$

    9–A $7x^3$

    9–B $x^2 + 6x$

    9–C $x^2 + 6x - 10$

    9–D $x^2 - 2x - 10$

10. If the area of each circle enclosed in rectangle $ABCD$ is 9π, the area of $ABCD$ is

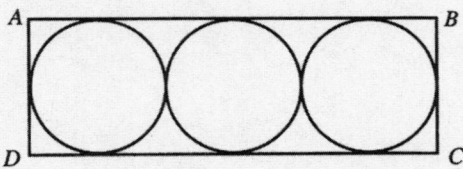

    10–A   108

    10–B   27

    10–C   54

    10–D 54π

11. If $5x + 6 = 10$, then x equals

    11–A $\dfrac{16}{5}$

    11–B $\dfrac{5}{16}$

    11–C $-\dfrac{5}{4}$

    11–D $\dfrac{4}{5}$

12. If the area of a square of side x is 5, what is the area of a square of side $3x$?

    12–A   15
    12–B   45
    12–C   95
    12–D   75

13. From 9 a.m. to 2 p.m., the temperature rose at a constant rate from $-14°F$ to $+36°F$. What was the temperature at noon?

    13–A $-4°$
    13–B $+6°$
    13–C $+16°$
    13–D $+26°$

14. If $7x = 3x + 12$, then $2x + 5 =$

    14–A   10
    14–B   11
    14–C   12
    14–D   13

15. If a discount of 20% off the marked price of a suit saves a woman $15, how much did she pay for the suit?

    15–A $60
    15–B $75
    15–C $120
    15–D $150

16. Divide: $\dfrac{3xy^2 - 4x^2y}{xy}$

    16–A $3xy - 4xy$
    16–B $3y - 4x$
    16–C $3x^2y - 4xy^2$
    16–D $3x - 4y$

17. If the diameter of a circle is increased by 50%, the area is increased by

    17–A   50%

    17–B   100%

    17–C   225%

    17–D   200%

18. If $a = x^2$ and $x = \sqrt{8}$, then $a =$

    18–A $2\sqrt{2}$

    18–B   4

    18–C   64

    18–D   8

19. What number added to 40% of itself is equal to 84?

    19–A   33.6

    19–B   60.0

    19–C   64.0

    19–D   40.6

20. Mr. Prince takes his wife and two children to the county fair. If the price of a child's ticket is $\frac{1}{2}$ the price of an adult ticket and Mr. Prince pays a total of $12.60, find the price of a child's ticket.

    20–A $4.20

    20–B $3.20

    20–C $2.10

    20–D $1.60

21. The value of $(-3) + (-2)(-4) \div (-1) + (-1)$ is

    21–A   4

    21–B   10

    21–C   −10

    21–D   −12

22. If $3x + y = 6$, what is the value of y when $x = -2$?

    22–A   0

    22–B   4

    22–C   8

    22–D   12

23. If $2^{n-3} = 32$, then n equals

    23–A   6

    23–B   7

    23–C   8

    23–D   9

24. If the cost of digging a trench is $2.12 a cubic yard, what would be the cost of digging a trench 2 yards by 5 yards by 4 yards?

    24–A $21.20

    24–B $40.00

    24–C $64.00

    24–D $84.80

25. $(2y - 1)(3y + 4) =$

    25–A $6y^2 + 5y - 4$

    25–B $6y^2 - 5y + 8$

    25–C $6y^2 + 3y - 4$

    25–D $6y^2 + 4$

Answer Key

1. C	2. C	3. A	4. A	5. D
6. C	7. C	8. A	9. B	10. A
11. D	12. B	13. C	14. B	15. A
16. B	17. C	18. D	19. B	20. C
21. D	22. D	23. C	24. D	25. A

Answers and Explanations

1–C Let n = missing number

$$n + 420 = 512$$
$$n = 512 - 420$$
$$n = 92$$

2–C Let x = total sales

8% of total sales = $280

$$.08x = 280$$

$$x = .08\overline{)280.00}\quad \$3500$$

3–A Add like terms:

$$2x^2 + 4x + 6$$
$$\underline{3x^2 - 5x + 7}$$
$$5x^2 - x + 13$$

4–A $[7 - (1 - 4)] + [(2 - 8) - (7 - 6)]$

$$= \left[7 - (-3)\right] + \left[(-6) - 1\right]$$
$$= 10 + (-7)$$
$$= 3$$

5–D
$$3x = 12$$
$$x = 4$$
$$3x + 1 = 13$$

6–C   11:30 a.m. to 2:30 p.m. = 3 hours. In 3 hours, one ship went 60 miles, the other 45 miles. This is a 3–4–5 right triangle as 45 = 3(15), 60 = 4(15). The hypotenuse will be 5(15), or 75.

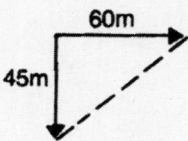

7–C   The sequence is geometric with a common ratio of $\dfrac{9}{27} = \dfrac{1}{3}$. The term after 1

is $1 \cdot \dfrac{1}{3} = \dfrac{1}{3}$.

8–A $140 is 125% of his former salary.

$$140 = 1.25x$$
$$14000 = 125x$$
$$\$112 = x$$

9–B $(7x - 3) + (4x^2 - 5x + 8) - (3x^2 - 4x + 5)$

$$= 7x - 3 + 4x^2 - 5x + 8 - 3x^2 + 4x - 5$$
$$= x^2 + 6x$$

10–A   Area of circle = $\pi r^2 = 9\pi$

Radius of each circle = $\sqrt{9} = 3$

Therefore, $AB = 6 \times 3 = 18$ and $AD = 2 \times 3 = 6$

Area of rectangle $ABCD = 18 \times 6 = 108$

11–D $5x + 6 = 10$

$$5x = 4$$
$$x = \dfrac{4}{5}$$

12–B   Area = s^2

$$\text{Area}_1 = x^2$$
$$\text{Area}_2 = (3x)^2 = 9x^2$$
$$x^2 : 9x^2 = 1 : 9$$
$$9 \times 5 = 45$$

13–C   Total rise in temperature:

$$36 - (-14) = 36 + 14 = 50°$$

9 a.m. to 2 p.m. = 5 hours

Hourly rise in temperature = $\dfrac{50}{5} = 10°$ per hour

At noon temperature = $-14 + 3(10) = -14 + 30 = +16°$

14–B   Solve for x:

$$7x = 3x + 12$$
$$4x = 12$$
$$x = 3$$
$$2x + 5 = 2(3) + 5 = 11$$

15–A   Let x = amount of marked price. Then

$$\frac{1}{5}x = 15$$
$$x = 75$$
$$75 - 15 = \$60$$

16–B   Divide the coefficients and subtract exponents of the same base:

$$\frac{3xy^2 - 4x^2y}{xy} = \frac{3xy^2}{xy} - \frac{4x^2y}{xy} = 3y - 4x$$

17–C   If the linear ratio is 1:1.5, then the area ratio is $(1)^2:(1.5)^2$ or 1:2.25. The increase is 1.25 or 225% of the original area.

18–D $\left(\sqrt{8}\right)^2 = 8$

19–B   Let x = the number

$$x + .40x = 84$$
$$1.40x = 84$$
$$14x = 840$$
$$x = 60$$

20–C   The two children's tickets equal one adult ticket. Mr. Prince pays the equivalent of 3 adult tickets.

$$3a = 12.60$$
$$a = 4.20$$

Child's ticket = $\dfrac{1}{2}(4.20) = \$2.10$

21–D $(-3)+(-2)(-4)\div(-1)+(-1)$

$=(-3)+(8)\div(-1)+(-1)$

$=(-3)+(-8)+(-1)$

$=-12$

22–D $3(-2)+y=6$

$-6+y=6$

$y=12$

23–C $2^{n-3}=32=2^5$

$n-3=5$

$n=8$

24–D The trench contains:

$2\text{ yd}\times5\text{ yd}\times4\text{ yd}=40\text{ cubic yards}$

$40\times\$2.12=\$84.80$

25–A $(2y-1)(3y+4)=6y^2+8y-3y-4=6y^2+5y-4$

MATHEMATICS KNOWLEDGE TEST 2

TIME: 24 Minutes—25 Questions

This is a test of your ability to solve 25 general mathematical problems. You are to select the correct response from the choices given. Then mark the space on your answer form that has the same number and letter as your choice. Use the scrap paper that has been given to you to do any figuring that you wish.

Your score on this test will be based on the number of questions you answer correctly. You should try to answer every question. Do not spend too much time on any one question.

1. Door *ABCD* is to be reinforced by 2 metal wires, *AC* and *BD*. If the dimensions of the door are 5 feet × 12 feet, how many feet of wire will be required to reinforce the door?

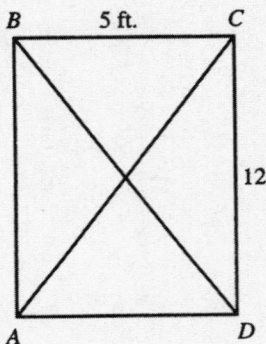

    1–A   26
    1–B   17
    1–C   13
    1–D   8

2. Solve for *C*:

    $C + 2 = Y$ and $Y = 2$

    2–A   2
    2–B   −1
    2–C   1
    2–D   0

3. What is the next number in the following series:

   25, 30, 24, 31, 23, ____

   3–A   32
   3–B   30
   3–C   25
   3–D   35

4. Subtract: $(2x^2 + 4x + 6) - (3x^2 + 5x + 7)$

   4–A $x^2 + 1$
   4–B $-x^2 + x + 1$
   4–C $x^2 - 1$
   4–D $-(x^2 + x + 1)$

5. At an average speed of 65 miles per hour, how many hours will it take a train to travel 390 miles?

   5–A   3
   5–B   6
   5–C   8
   5–D   10

6. Find the value of $\left(3\sqrt{2}\right)^2$.

   6–A $9\sqrt{2}$
   6–B $6\sqrt{2}$
   6–C   18
   6–D   36

7. Solve for k: $\dfrac{k}{3} + \dfrac{k}{4} = 1$

   7–A $\dfrac{11}{8}$

   7–B $\dfrac{8}{11}$

   7–C $\dfrac{7}{12}$

   7–D $\dfrac{12}{7}$

8. If the angles of a triangle are in the ratio 2:3:7, the triangle is

    8–A   acute

    8–B   isosceles

    8–C   obtuse

    8–D   right

9. The surface of a cube is 96 square feet. How many cubic feet are there in the volume of the cube?

    9–A   16

    9–B   4

    9–C   12

    9–D   64

10. The Bears played 78 games last season. If they won 8 games more than they lost, how many games did they lose?

    10–A   70

    10–B   43

    10–C   35

    10–D   33

11. $\sqrt{18} + \sqrt{50} =$

    11–A $\sqrt{68}$

    11–B $3\sqrt{2}$

    11–C $8\sqrt{2}$

    11–D $5\sqrt{3}$

12. The perimeter of a rectangle is 40 feet. The length is 2 more than 5 times the width. Find the width of the rectangle.

    12–A   3 feet

    12–B   4 feet

    12–C   6 feet 4 inches

    12–D   12 feet

13. If $.23m = .069$, $m =$

    13–A   .003

    13–B   .03

    13–C   .3

    13–D   3

14. As shown in the figure, a circular metal disc wears down to one half of its original radius. What percent of the original area remains?

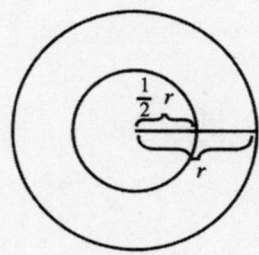

      14–A   50%
      14–B   25%
      14–C   75%
      14–D   40%

15. Multiply: $(3a^2b^3)\,(4a^3b^4)$
      15–A $7a^5b^7$
      15–B $12a^5b^7$
      15–C $12ab^5$
      15–D $12ab$

16. A train traveled 90 miles in $1\frac{1}{2}$ hours. At the same rate, how long will it take the train to travel 330 miles?
      16–A   4 hours

      16–B $4\frac{1}{2}$ hours

      16–C $5\frac{1}{2}$ hours

      16–D   6 hours

17. If $\dfrac{a}{b} = \dfrac{3}{5}$, then $15a =$
      17–A $3b$
      17–B $5b$
      17–C $6b$
      17–D $9b$

18. How many digits are in the square root of 15,129?
      18–A   2
      18–B   3
      18–C   4
      18–D   5

19. Find the value of $\left(5\sqrt{2}\right)^2$.

    19–A   20
    19–B   25
    19–C   40
    19–D   50

20. Multiply $(x-9)(x+9)$.

    20–A $(x-81)^2$
    20–B $x^2 - 81$
    20–C $x+9$
    20–D $x-9$

21. A rectangular table, 6 feet by 3 feet, has six placemats, each 2 feet by 1 foot, arranged 3 placemats to a side. How many square feet of the table is not covered by the placemats?

    21–A   12
    21–B   18
    21–C   6
    21–D   3

22. 8 is 8% of what number?

    22–A   64
    22–B   1
    22–C   10
    22–D   100

23. The area of circle O is 64π. The perimeter of square $ABCD$ is

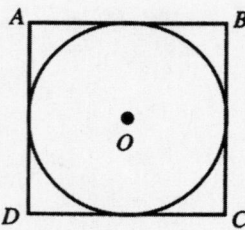

    23–A   32
    23–B 32π
    23–C   64
    23–D   16

24. If $x = -1$, then $x^2 + 2x - 1 =$

    24–A -2
    24–B -1
    24–C   0
    24–D $+1$

25. At the end of one year, a $2000 savings certificate earning $6\frac{1}{2}\%$ interest per year will be worth

    25–A $2013

    25–B $2113

    25–C $2130

    25–D $2230

Answer Key

1. A	2. D	3. A	4. D	5. B
6. C	7. D	8. C	9. D	10. C
11. C	12. A	13. C	14. B	15. B
16. C	17. D	18. B	19. D	20. B
21. C	22. D	23. C	24. A	25. C

Answers and Explanations

1–A   From the diagram you can see that there are two right triangles (*BAD* and *BCD*), each having legs of 5 feet and 12 feet, with a supporting wire as the hypotenuse of each triangle. Using the Pythagorean theorem,

$$BD^2 = AD^2 + AB^2$$
$$= 5^2 + 12^2 = 25 + 144 = 169$$
$$BD = \sqrt{169} = 13$$
$$BD = AC$$

Therefore, the door requires $13 + 13 = 26$ feet of wire.

If you recognize this as a 5–12–13 right triangle, you can see immediately that each wire must be 13 feet.

2–D $C + 2 = Y$

Substitute 2 for *Y:*

$C + 2 = 2$

$C = 2 - 2 = 0$

3–A   Look at the differences between consecutive terms:

$+5, -6, +7, -8, +9 \ldots$

The next term will be $23 + 9 = 32$.

4–D   Change the signs of the second term and add:

$$2x^2 + 4x + 6$$
$$\underline{-3x^2 - 5x - 7}$$
$$-x^2 - x - 1 \text{ or } -\left(x^2 + x + 1\right)$$

5–B

$$D = R \times T$$

$$T = \frac{D}{R}$$

$$= \frac{390 \text{ (miles)}}{65 \text{ (mph)}} = 6 \text{ (hours)}$$

6–C $\left(3\sqrt{2}\right)\left(3\sqrt{2}\right) = 9 \cdot 2 = 18$

7–D   Multiply by 12: $4k + 3k = 12$

$$7k = 12$$

$$k = \frac{12}{7}$$

8–C   Represent the angles as $2x$, $3x$, and $7x$.

$$2x + 3x + 7x = 180°$$

$$12x = 180°$$

$$x = 15°$$

The angles are 30°, 45°, and 105°. Since one angle is between 90° and 180°, the triangle is called an obtuse triangle.

9–D   There are 6 equal squares in the surface of a cube. Each square will have an area of

$\dfrac{96}{6}$ or 16.

Area of a square $= s^2 = 16$

$$s = \sqrt{16} = 4$$

Volume of a cube $= e^3 = 4^3 = 64$

10–C   Let x = games lost

$x + 8$ = games won

$$x + x + 8 = 78$$

$$2x + 8 = 78$$

$$2x = 70$$

$$x = 35$$

11–C $\sqrt{18} = \sqrt{9 \cdot 2} = \sqrt{9} \cdot \sqrt{2} = 3\sqrt{2}$

$\sqrt{50} = \sqrt{25 \cdot 2} = \sqrt{25} \cdot \sqrt{2} = 5\sqrt{2}$

$3\sqrt{2} + 5\sqrt{2} = 8\sqrt{2}$

12–A Let x = width of rectangle

Length of rectangle = $5x + 2$

Perimeter = $2l + 2w = 40$

$2(x) + 2(5x + 2) = 40$

$2x + 10x + 4 = 40$

$12x = 36$

$x = 3$ feet

13–C Multiply by 100 to make the coefficient an integer.

$23x = 6.9$

$x = .3$

14–B Original area = πr^2

Reduced area = $\pi \left(\dfrac{1}{2}r\right)^2 = \dfrac{1}{4}\pi r^2$

Hence, 25% of the original area remains.

15–B Multiply the coefficients and add the exponents of the same base.

$3 \times 4 = 12$

$a^2 \times a^3 = a^{(2 + 3)} = a^5$

$b^3 \times b^4 = b^{(3 + 4)} = b^7$

16–C Use a proportion:

Short Trip		**Longer Trip**
$\dfrac{\text{Distance}}{\text{Time}}$	=	$\dfrac{\text{Distance}}{\text{Time}}$
$\dfrac{90}{1\frac{1}{2}}$	=	$\dfrac{330}{x}$
$90x$	=	495
x	=	$\dfrac{495}{90} = 5\frac{1}{2}$ hours

17–D $\dfrac{a}{b} = \dfrac{3}{5}$

$5a = 3b$

Multiply both sides by 3.

$15a = 9b$

18–B   Pair off the numbers starting at the decimal point. Add a zero if necessary to complete a pair.

01 / 51 / 29

Each pair of numbers represents 1 digit in the square root.

19–D $\left(5\sqrt{2}\right)^2 = 5\sqrt{2} \times 5\sqrt{2} = 25 \cdot 2 = 50$

20–B

$$\begin{array}{r}
x - 9 \\
\times\ x + 9 \\
\hline
x^2 - 9x \\
+9x - 81 \\
\hline
x^2 - 81 = x^2 - 81
\end{array}$$

21–C   Make a sketch.

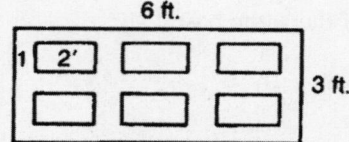

Area of 1 placemat = 2 ft × 1 ft = 2 ft²

Area of 6 placemats = 6 × 2 ft² = 12 ft²

Area of table = 6 × 3 = 18 ft²

Area of table – area of placemats = 18 – 12 = 6 ft²

22–D   Let x = the number

$8 = .08x$ (Multiply by 100.)

$800 = 8x$

$100 = x$

23–C   Area of circle = $64\pi = \pi r^2$

Radius of circle = 8

Side of square = 16

Perimeter of square = 64

24–A $x^2 + 2x - 1$

$$= (-1)^2 + 2(-1) - 1$$
$$= +1 \quad - 2 \quad - 1$$
$$= -2$$

25–C Interest = principal × rate × time

$$I = \$2000 \times .065 \times 1 = \$130$$

Add interest to principal: $2000 + $130 = $2130

MATHEMATICS KNOWLEDGE TEST 3

TIME: 24 Minutes—25 Questions

This is a test of your ability to solve 25 general mathematical problems. You are to select the correct response from the choices given. Then mark the space on your answer form that has the same number and letter as your choice. Use the scrap paper that has been given to you to do any figuring that you wish.

Your score on this test will be based on the number of questions you answer correctly. You should try to answer every question. Do not spend too much time on any one question.

1. Solve for A:
   $A - 2 = 2 - A$

   1–A   2
   1–B   0
   1–C   1
   1–D   8

2. When 3 is added to 3 times a number, the result is 3. What is the number?

   2–A   −3
   2–B   0
   2–C   9
   2–D   6

3. In a laboratory experiment, a mouse ran through a maze at the rate of 20 feet per minute. If it took $2\frac{1}{2}$ minutes for the mouse to complete the maze, how many feet did the mouse run?

   3–A   50
   3–B   40
   3–C   20
   3–D   10

4. Four is what percent of 32?

    4–A   1.25

    4–B   125

    4–C   12.5

    4–D   10

5. What is the next term in the following sequence?

    4.5, 8, 11.5, 15, ____

    5–A   17

    5–B   18

    5–C   18.5

    5–D   20

6. What is the sum of $(6x^2 + 7x + 8) + (9x^2 - 8x - 7)$?

    6–A $15x^2 - x + 1$

    6–B $x - 1$

    6–C $15x^2 + x + 1$

    6–D $x^2 - x + 1$

7. How many inches will the perimeter of a rectangle increase if the length increases by 2 inches and the width by 3 inches?

    7–A   4

    7–B   7

    7–C   10

    7–D   12

8. One sixth of the audience of parents and children at the Saturday movie consisted of boys, and one third of it consisted of girls. What percent of the audience consisted of children?

    8–A $66\frac{2}{3}\%$

    8–B   50%

    8–C $33\frac{1}{3}\%$

    8–D   40%

9. $(2x + 4)(3x + 5) =$

    9–A $6x^2 + 20$

    9–B $22x + 20$

    9–C $6x^2 + 22x + 20$

    9–D $6x^2 + 22x - 20$

10. Ellen and Warren left the service area on Highway 1 at the same time. Ellen drove east on the highway at 45 miles per hour and Warren drove west at 50 miles per hour. How many miles apart will they be in 2 hours?

    10–A   10

    10–B   90

    10–C   100

    10–D   190

11. Divide: $\dfrac{24a^5}{3a^2}$

    11–A $8a$

    11–B $8a^7$

    11–C $8a^3$

    11–D $\dfrac{a^3}{8}$

12. A circle is inscribed in a square whose side is 6. Express the area of the circle in terms of π.

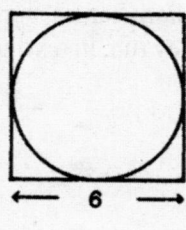

    12–A 6π

    12–B 3π

    12–C 9π

    12–D 36π

13. A classified ad in *Metro Magazine* costs $100 for the first 3 lines, $75 for the next 3 lines, and $40 for each additional line. Find the cost of an 8-line ad.

    13–A $255

    13–B $210

    13–C $180

    13–D $175

14. 8% of 8% of 8 is what number?

    14–A   .005

    14–B   .08

    14–C   .0512

    14–D   .0256

15. If $1 - A = A - 1$, then find $\dfrac{2}{A}$.

    15–A   4
    15–B   2
    15–C   1
    15–D   0

16. Find the first term in the following series: ____, 10, 50, 250.

    16–A   1
    16–B   2
    16–C   5
    16–D   −5

17. If $(4x + 4)$ is multiplied by 4, the result is 48. What is the value of x?

    17–A   2
    17–B   4
    17–C   16
    17–D   32

18. A pulley having a 9-inch diameter is belted to a pulley having a 6-inch diameter, as shown in the figure. If the large pulley runs at 120 rpm, how fast does the small pulley run, in revolutions per minutes?

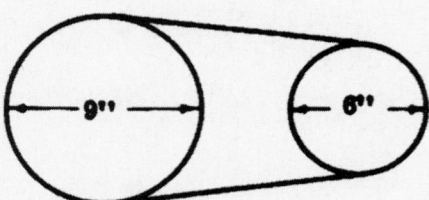

    18–A   80 rpm
    18–B   100 rpm
    18–C   160 rpm
    18–D   180 rpm

19. If an item costs $4.20 after a 40% discount, what was its original price?

    19–A $4.60
    19–B $5.33
    19–C $7.00
    19–D $10.50

20. The base of a rectangular tank is 6 feet by 5 feet and its height is 16 inches. Find the number of cubic feet of water in the tank when it is $\frac{3}{4}$ full.

    20–A   10
    20–B   30
    20–C   40
    20–D   50

21. $2\sqrt{3} + \sqrt{27} =$

    21–A $2\sqrt{30}$

    21–B $3\sqrt{3}$

    21–C $3\sqrt{2}$

    21–D $5\sqrt{3}$

22. A farmer uses 140 feet of fencing to enclose a rectangular field. If the ratio of length to width is 3:4, find the diagonal, in feet, of the field.

    22–A   50
    22–B   100
    22–C   20
    22–D   10

23. If a car uses $1\frac{1}{2}$ gallons of gas for 30 miles, how many miles can be driven with 6 gallons of gas?

    23–A   60
    23–B   80
    23–C   100
    23–D   120

24. In triangle ABC, $AC = BC$. If angle $A = (4x - 30)°$ and angle $B = (2x + 10)°$, find the number of degrees in angle C.

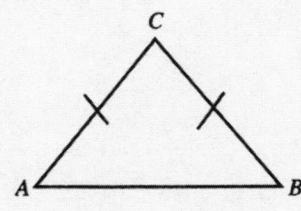

    24–A   40
    24–B   50
    24–C   100
    24–D   80

25. Which of the following represents the distance traveled in 3 hours by a car traveling at $3x - 7$ miles per hour?

   25–A $3x - 7$

   25–B $3x^2 - 21$

   25–C $9x - 21$

   25–D $\dfrac{3x - 7}{3}$

Answer Key

1. A	2. B	3. A	4. C	5. C
6. A	7. C	8. B	9. C	10. D
11. C	12. C	13. A	14. C	15. B
16. B	17. A	18. D	19. C	20. B
21. D	22. A	23. D	24. D	25. C

Answers and Explanations

1–A

$$A - 2 = 2 - A$$
$$\underline{+A \qquad +A} \qquad \text{(Add } A \text{ to both sides.)}$$
$$2A - 2 = 2$$
$$\underline{+2 = +2} \qquad \text{(Add 2 to both sides.)}$$
$$\frac{2A}{2} = \frac{4}{2} \qquad \text{(Divide both sides by 2.)}$$
$$A = 2$$

2–B

$$3x + 3 = 3$$
$$3x = 0 \qquad \text{(Subtract 3 from both sides.)}$$
$$x = 0 \qquad \text{(Divide both sides by 3.)}$$

3–A   Distance = Rate × Time

Substitute values:

$$\text{Distance} = \frac{20 \text{ feet}}{\cancel{\text{minute}}} \times 2\frac{1}{2} \cancel{\text{ minutes}}$$
$$= 20 \times 2\frac{1}{2} = 50 \text{ feet}$$

4–C $\dfrac{4}{32} = \dfrac{x}{100}$

$32x = 400$ (Cross-multiply.)

$x = \dfrac{400}{32} = 12.5$ (Divide by 32.)

5–C   Add 3.5 to each term to get the next term:

$15 + 3.5 = 18.5$

6–A $\quad 6x^2 + 7x + 8$

$\quad \underline{+9x^2 - 8x - 7}$

$\quad 15x^2 - x + 1$

7–C   Make a sketch:

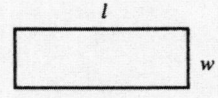

Original rectangle $= l \times w$

Perimeter $= 2l + 2w$

New rectangle $= (l + 2) \times (w + 3)$

$\qquad$ Perimeter $= 2(l + 2) + 2(w + 3)$

$\qquad\qquad = 2l + 4 + 2w + 6$

$\qquad\qquad = 2l + 2w + 10$

Difference is $(2l + 2w + 10) - (2l + 2w) = 10$.

8–B   Let $x =$ number of people in audience

Then, $\dfrac{1}{6}x =$ number of boys

$\dfrac{1}{3}x =$ number of girls

$\dfrac{1}{6}x + \dfrac{1}{3}x = \dfrac{1}{6}x + \dfrac{2}{6}x = \dfrac{3}{6}x = \dfrac{1}{2}x =$ number of children

$\dfrac{1}{2} = 50\%$

9–C
$$2x + 4$$
$$\times\ \underline{3x + 5}$$
$$10x + 20$$
$$\underline{6x^2 + 12x}$$
$$6x^2 + 22x + 20$$

10–D Make a sketch:

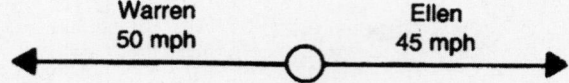

Since they are going in opposite directions, their distances are added.

Ellen: 45 mph × 2 hours = 90 miles

Warren: 50 mph × 2 hours = 100 miles

Distance apart = 90 + 100 = 190 miles

11–C Divide the coefficients and subtract the exponents:

$$\frac{24a^5}{3a^2} = 8a^{(5-2)} = 8a^3$$

12–C If the side of the square is 6, then the diameter of the circle is also 6 and the radius of the circle is $\dfrac{1}{2}$ of 6, which is 3.

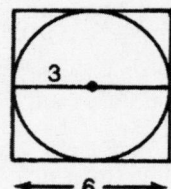

Area of a circle = $\pi r^2 = \pi 3^2 = 9\pi$

13–A

3 lines at $100	$100
3 lines at $75	75
2 lines at $40 each	80
Total for 8 lines	$255

14–C .08 × .08 × 8 = .0064 × 8 = .0512

15–B Solve for A:

$$1 - A = A - 1$$
$$1 = 2A - 1$$
$$2 = 2A$$
$$1 = A$$

$$\frac{2}{A} = \frac{2}{(1)} = 2$$

16–B Each term is the previous term times 5. The first term will be $\dfrac{10}{5} = 2$.

17–A $4(4x + 4) = 48$

$$16x + 16 = 48$$
$$16x = 32$$
$$x = 2$$

18–D One revolution on the larger wheel causes more than one revolution on the smaller. This is an inverse proportion; that is:

$$\frac{9}{6} = \frac{x}{120}$$
$$6x = 1080$$
$$x = 180$$

19–C Let x = original price

$$.60x = \$4.20$$
$$\text{or } 6x = \$42.00$$
$$x = \$7.00$$

20–B Change 16 inches to feet: $\dfrac{16}{12} = 1\dfrac{4}{12} = 1\dfrac{1}{3}$ feet

$$Volume = l \times w \times h$$
$$= 6 \times 5 \times 1\frac{1}{3}$$
$$= 40 \text{ cubic feet (when tank is full)}$$

$\dfrac{3}{4} \times 40 = 30$ cubic feet (when $\dfrac{3}{4}$ full)

21–D $2\sqrt{3} + \sqrt{27}$

$\sqrt{27} = \sqrt{9 \cdot 3} = \sqrt{9} \cdot \sqrt{3} = 3\sqrt{3}$

$2\sqrt{3} + 3\sqrt{3} = 5\sqrt{3}$

22–A   Perimeter $= 2l + 2w = 140$ ft

$$2(3x) + 2(4x) = 140$$
$$6x + 8x = 140$$
$$14x = 140$$
$$x = 10$$
$$3x = 30$$
$$4x = 40$$

The rectangle is 30′ by 40′. This is a 3–4–5 right triangle, so the diagonal is 50′.

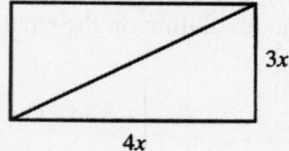

23–D   Use a proportion comparing gallons to miles.

$$\frac{1\frac{1}{2}}{30} = \frac{6}{x}$$
$$1\frac{1}{2} \cdot x = 180$$
$$x = 120$$

24–D Triangle ABC is an isosceles triangle; therefore, angle A = angle B.

$$4x - 30 = 2x + 10$$
$$2x = 40$$
$$x = 20$$
$$4x - 30 = 4(20) - 30 = 80 - 30 = 50°$$

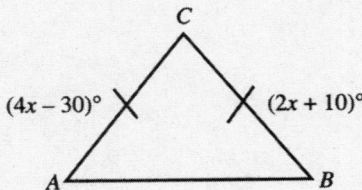

Angle A + Angle B + Angle C = 180°

50°   +   50°   +   Angle C = 180°

Angle C = 180° − 100° = 80°

25–C Distance = Rate × Time
$$= (3x - 7) \times (3)$$
$$= 9x - 21 \text{ miles}$$

PART II

IMPROVING VERBAL SKILLS

INTRODUCTION TO THE ASVAB VERBAL TESTS

GENERAL TIPS

In order to become a skillful reader and fluent in language, get used to doing some reading each and every day—at least for a half-hour. Whatever catches your eye is fine, such as a good newspaper, magazine, or book. Word games, like Scrabble™ or crossword puzzles, are excellent for improving your vocabulary and having a good time.

Notice the spellings and meanings of words and phrases, the way sentences are put together, and the usage of familiar and unfamiliar words. If possible, use a dictionary to look up words you don't know. You can also infer the meanings of a lot of unfamiliar words by guessing from the context.

Visit your local bookstore or library. Ask your teachers or the librarian to help you find books on whatever topics you might be interested in. Walk around and browse. The majority of knowledge and understanding is picked up casually. Relax and take your time. Don't overlook the sections that feature practical everyday topics, such as carpentry, home repair, gardening, home decorating, and relationships. The Internet is also a great resource for finding stories and newspaper articles, as well as magazines from all over the world.

If you can follow any of these suggestions on a regular basis, you'll have a lot of fun and improve your chances of success on tests such as the ASVAB verbal tests at the same time.

TEST-TAKING TIPS FOR THE ASVAB VERBAL TESTS

The following tips are important, so read them carefully. Keep them in mind when you take the ASVAB Word Knowledge and Paragraph Comprehension Tests.

1. *Keep an eye on your watch.*

    Be aware of the time. Use all the time you've got but don't spend more than necessary on any one item. Some questions will take you longer than others, so keep moving along. Don't waste valuable time re-reading directions once you know what is required.

2. *Concentrate.*

    Position yourself so that you won't be distracted by your surroundings and by other test-takers. Discipline yourself not to think about other topics, but only think about the test before you. Try to work up your interest in the topic. This will improve concentration.

3. *On the Paragraph Comprehension Test, glance at the question first.*

    Before reading the passage, quickly look at the question. This will give you an idea of what you need to think about as you're going through the paragraph(s).

4. *Answer based on what's before you.*

    Often, the sentences or passages are about easy-to-understand everyday topics that you have heard or thought about before. Remember to base your answer *strictly* on what's stated or inferred in the item, not on your own ideas about the topic.

5. *Narrow the odds by eliminating obviously incorrect choices.*

    Whether you're taking the Paragraph Comprehension or Word Knowledge Test, you will often see answer choices that are unrelated to the question, nonsensical, silly sounding, or obviously incorrect. By eliminating these choices, you can zero in on the correct answer. Also remember that an answer choice that is only *partly* right is incorrect.

6. *If necessary, guess. You will not be penalized for incorrect answers.*

    Your test score is based on how many questions you answer correctly, so take a guess even if you are clueless as to the correctness of your answer. If you have already eliminated the obviously wrong choices, your chances of guessing a correct answer are good.

CHAPTER

6

VERBAL PRETEST

ollowing are two short pretests that show which verbal skills you will need to master for the ASVAB. First, you will take the Word Knowledge Test, then the Paragraph Comprehension Test. Read the directions, then take the tests.

After you check your answers against the Answer Key and Explanations, look at the brief *Finding Help in This Book* sections that follow. They will refer you to the pages in this book where the skill that is tested is reviewed.

WORD KNOWLEDGE

This test has 10 questions about the meanings of words. Each question has an underlined word. You must decide which of the four choices (A, B, C, or D) is closest in meaning to the underlined word. Mark down your answer choice. Then check your answers against the Answer Key and Explanations that follow this Verbal Pretest.

First, look at the two sample questions below.

Sample 1. Extract most nearly means

    1–A   paper

    1–B   doorway

    1–C   excerpt

    1–D   history

1–C   *Extract*, when used as a noun, means an *excerpt*, or a short section or part of something, such as a couple of lines from a poem. Choices A and D are unrelated. Choice B, *doorway*, is related to the word exit, not *extract*.

Sample 2. He <u>devoted</u> two hours a week to helping students learn to read.

  2–A dedicated

  2–B exercised

  2–C wasted

  2–D thought

2–A *Dedicated* is a synonym for *devoted* and is therefore the correct answer. *Devoted* means to have given *effort*, *attention*, or *time* to something important and seriously believed in. The words *devotion* and *devotee* are related to *devoted*. Choices B, C, and D are unrelated and incorrect.

Now try the pretest that follows.

1. <u>Paddle</u> most nearly means

  1–A row

  1–B enclose

  1–C mess

  1–D bother

2. <u>Sloppy</u> most nearly means

  2–A lengthy

  2–B slippery

  2–C careless

  2–D dangerous

3. <u>Urban</u> most nearly means

  3–A mountainous areas

  3–B farmland acreage

  3–C related to a city

  3–D coastal regions

4. It is illegal to <u>tamper</u> with a jury during a trial.

  4–A interfere

  4–B touch

  4–C lock

  4–D circle

5. They looked <u>vigorous</u> because they exercised regularly.

  5–A clever

  5–B timid

  5–C weak

  5–D strong

6. The line will <u>originate</u> at the barracks.

  6–A start

  6–B leave

  6–C postpone

  6–D detour

7. Advanced education and wealth <u>uplifted</u> their social status.

  7–A turned

  7–B continued

  7–C elevated

  7–D overfed

8. <u>Revise</u> most nearly means

  8–A tighten

  8–B unscrew

  8–C damage

  8–D improve

9. <u>Unravel</u> most nearly means

  9–A whip up

  9–B untangle

  9–C dance

  9–D bind

10. <u>Reflect</u> most nearly means

  10–A throw back

  10–B anger

  10–C divide

  10–D injure

Answer Key

1. A	2. C	3. C	4. A	5. D
6. A	7. C	8. D	9. B	10. A

Answers and Explanations

1–A To *paddle* means to *row* or move through water with the use of an oar, which pushes the water aside.

2–C The word *sloppy* means to be *careless,* slovenly, or messy. For example, someone who makes *careless* mistakes on tests is *sloppy* in his ability to concentrate and do serious work.

3–C *Urban* refers to something having to do with a city. For example, *urban renewal* means the rebuilding of decayed or substandard buildings in a city. Or, the expression *urban sprawl* refers to a city's housing or shopping centers spreading out into nearby land.

4–A To *tamper* with something, like a jury, is to meddle, or *interfere* with it. In other words, contacting a jury and trying to influence its thinking or decision-making would be considered the illegal act of jury *tampering.*

5–D To be *vigorous* is to be *strong, healthy,* and *robust.* Also, the word means doing something with *vigor* and with force and energy.

6–A To *originate* a line is to *start* or to *begin* it. The word *originate* comes from the word *origin,* meaning the beginning of something. The line *originated,* or began, or was formed, at the barracks.

7–C *Uplifted* means *elevated.* The sentence implies that their social status or prestige improved or was *elevated* as they became better-educated and gained greater wealth. In this sentence, *uplifted* means to have raised, increased, or *elevated* their status.

8–D To *revise* something is to *improve,* amend, review, and redo it for the better. For example, the *revised* bible was an effort to *improve,* update, and correct some errors in the earlier edition.

9–B To *unravel* something is to *untangle* it, to clear something up, like a mysterious story, by solving the complexity of it and separating all the elements. To *unravel* something is to open it up, to make it understandable. Choices A and C are unrelated, and choice D is almost the opposite.

10–A The only possible synonym for *reflect* is choice A, *throw back.* For example, a radiator can *reflect* or *throw back* heat. When you look into a mirror, it *reflects* or *throws back* your image.

Finding Help in This Book

If you missed 1, 2, or 3, see Word Skill 1: Recognizing Familiar Words, page 251.

If you missed 4, 5, 6, or 7, see Word Skill 2: Context Clues, page 262.

If you missed 8, 9, or 10, see Word Skill 3: Word Parts, page 273.

PARAGRAPH COMPREHENSION

This test consists of a series of passages, each one followed by a question or incomplete statement. Read each item carefully and select the one of the lettered choices (A, B, C, or D) that best completes the statement or answers the question.

First, look at the two sample questions below.

Sample 1. The Jim Walter Resources No. 5 Mine, located in Brookwood, Alabama, extends 2,140 feet beneath the surface, making it North America's deepest vertical-shaft coal mine. The mine experienced a tragic explosion in 2001 in which 13 workers were killed. Its remaining 400 workers lost their jobs late in 2004 because the mine closed permanently at that time.

The No. 5 mine probably closed because

  1–A   it was too dangerous to operate any longer.
  1–B   it had been losing money for its owners.
  1–C   there was probably no longer any coal to be found.
  1–D   people in Alabama started using oil instead of coal.

1–A   The passage does not tell you exactly why the mine is closed. But based on information given in the second sentence about the explosion, you can infer, or take an educated guess, that the mine closed because it was dangerous. Choices B, C, and D are on topics not discussed in the passage, so this is a further clue that choice A is the correct answer.

Sample 2. Antarctica, referred to as the White Continent, is known as the forbidden and dangerous territory explored by Sir Ernest Shackleton many years ago. Not that well known is the fact that now anyone can visit the area as a tourist. Expedition boats go to Antarctica regularly, allowing tourists to experience the adventure of a lifetime—kayaking among giant icebergs, or watching scores of penguins and other wildlife from the safety of a ship!

According to this passage

  2–A   Shackleton was the first to take tourists to Antarctica.
  2–B   expeditions to Antarctica continue to be dangerous.
  2–C   there are no longer any icebergs.
  2–D   tourists can now go kayaking in Antarctica.

2–D   The last sentence tells you that choice D is correct—tourists can now visit and go kayaking in Antarctica. Choice A is incorrect—according to the first sentence, Shackleton explored the Antarctic; nothing is stated about his taking tourists there. Choice B is an incorrect inference—if tourists are able to go there, Antarctica is obviously no longer dangerous. Choice C is contradicted by the last sentence.

Now try the pretest that follows.

1.   Lt. Gen. Matthew Ridgway is widely considered to be one of the two or three greatest American soldiers of the twentieth century. He was the battlefield commander who took over the conduct of the Korean War in December 1950. Because of his fierce leadership, Ridgway was able to transform the Eighth Army into an effective fighting force and turn the tide of battle in just a few short months.

From this passage, you can infer that

    1–A   the Korean War had been going badly before Ridgway took over.

    1–B   Ridgway was obviously a graduate of West Point.

    1–C   General MacArthur was the senior commander.

    1–D   All of the above are true.

Questions 2 and 3 are based on the following passage.

Redoing a small room, like a bathroom, requires good planning and the careful use of space. Using light colors, carefully selecting compact sinks and cabinets, installing small shelves and a mirror, and even building a skylight to open up the area to light can do wonders! By carefully choosing its features, and with the avoidance of clutter, you can make even a tiny room cheerful and functional.

2.   The author of this passage would probably agree that

    2–A   a large vanity is essential for any bathroom.

    2–B   small spaces should be turned into closets.

    2–C   you can make even a small space feel larger.

    2–D   tiny bathrooms cannot be altered.

3.   Which of the following makes a good title for this piece?

    3–A   "Interior Decorating"

    3–B   "Installing Shelves and Mirrors"

    3–C   "Decorating Small Rooms"

    3–D   "Avoiding Clutter"

4. While Americans generally rely on their cars to get from one place to another, people in Europe often depend on trains for both work and leisure travel. These trains, which are generally government owned and run, are the "highways" of Europe, reaching most large as well as small destinations. They are luxurious, speedy and convenient, and have reasonable fares. They also often run through particularly beautiful scenic areas, thus providing good sightseeing opportunities.

Which of the following can be inferred according to this passage?

  4–A   In the United States, there is probably a higher proportion of people who own cars than in Europe.

  4–B   Trains in Europe run on highways.

  4–C   American trains are luxurious, speedy, convenient, and reasonable.

  4–D   Gas is much cheaper in Europe than in the United States.

5. Tests show that a few injured college football players still have some impairment of mental functioning after suffering a concussion even though they may feel fine. In order to be sure that an athlete is fully recuperated and ready to return to the field, trainers and coaches are now being advised by doctors to keep their athletes on the sidelines for at least a week *after* their concussion symptoms disappear.

The author's primary message is that

  5–A   it is important for injured players not to return to the field too soon.

  5–B   concussions can take a month to heal.

  5–C   headaches are a sign of concussion.

  5–D   football is a dangerous sport.

6. In September 1938, before the era of modern satellite communications and accurate weather predictions, a violent hurricane hit the East Coast of the United States. It was a devastating storm that gave no warning and killed 700 people. Because of wind gusts that measured 186 miles per hour, the damage to property was also very severe. It was estimated that approximately 20,000 dwellings were destroyed.

According to the passage, the hurricane of 1938

  6–A   struck Florida first.

  6–B   was unexpected.

  6–C   barely touched the East Coast.

  6–D   destroyed only tall buildings.

7. Often, large fleets of fishing boats use giant nets spanning many miles of ocean waters. These nets sweep up everything in their path, endangering whales, sharks, and giant sea turtles. With these methods, some fish species, such as cod and salmon, are also being caught in such large numbers that they may soon die out. International agreements will have to be worked out to limit fishing of some species so as to preserve them for the future.

According to this passage, which of the following is a TRUE statement?

  7–A   Most fishing is done by small, individual boats.

  7–B   Fishermen use radar to avoid sharks and whales.

  7–C   There is no ecological danger in using large nets.

  7–D   Large fishing nets often catch unwanted fish.

8. In 1991, a couple of surprised hikers came across a highly unusual person lying face down in the melting snows of the Alps in northern Italy. The person they found, later called the "Ice Man," was a 5,000-year-old man from ancient times who had been buried in the ice for all these years. His well-preserved body, weapons, clothing, and other belongings can be seen in the Archaeological Museum in Bolzano. They are being studied to determine where the Ice Man came from and what he was doing at such a high altitude.

Which of the following statements is TRUE according to this passage?

　　　8–A　　　The "Ice Man" lived 5,000 years ago.
　　　8–B　　　The Archaeological Museum has many weapons from the area.
　　　8–C　　　The Ice Man was a well-known mountain climber.
　　　8–D　　　Hikers often come across many strange findings.

Questions 9 and 10 are about the following passage.

The United States Department of Agriculture–Forest Service reminds us of the rules that must be remembered when making campfires.

Keep the campfire small. Build it away from overhanging branches, steep slopes, dry grass, leaves, and any burnable materials. Scrape away litter within a 10-foot circle of the fire. Never leave the fire unattended, because even a small breeze can quickly cause it to spread. Keep plenty of water handy, and have a shovel close by for throwing dirt on the fire if it gets out of control.

When you're ready to put it out, drown all the embers, sticks, and logs of the fire with plenty of water. Make sure you've wet everything thoroughly, even the rocks, which may have some hidden burning embers underneath.

9. Which of the following statements would the author agree with?

　　　9–A　　You can often read your newspaper by a campfire.
　　　9–B　　Cooking outdoors stimulates the appetite.
　　　9–C　　An outdoor fire can restart if it isn't properly extinguished.
　　　9–D　　It's all right to go fishing while the steak is cooking on the campfire.

10. As used in the last sentence, the word *embers* probably means

　　　10–A　　the burning remains of a fire.
　　　10–B　　sticks and stones.
　　　10–C　　cold ashes and dirt.
　　　10–D　　All of the above.

Answer Key				
1. A	2. C	3. C	4. A	5. A
6. B	7. D	8. A	9. C	10. A

Answers and Explanations

1–A   The last sentence of the passage, which states that Ridgway was able "to turn the tide of battle," is your clue that things had been going badly for the Eighth Army before Ridgway stepped in. Choices B and C are incorrect because we are told nothing about the background of Ridgway, and General MacArthur is not mentioned. Since choices B and C are wrong, choice D is incorrect also.

2–C   The main idea is that a small space, like a tiny bathroom, can be brightened up and made really functional. It will then not seem so small, so choice C is the correct answer. The author would *not* agree that a large vanity should be used, so choice A is incorrect. Choice B is incorrect because alternative uses for small bathrooms are not dealt with in the passage, which also contradicts choice D.

3–C   All the choices have something to do with this passage, but the best title is choice C, *Decorating Small Rooms,* because the main message is about the skills involved in doing this successfully. Choice A is too general. Choice B is too specific—shelves and mirrors are only a couple of the suggestions mentioned. Choice D is on a topic mentioned in the passage, but not its main point.

4–A   Since the passage states that "Americans generally rely on their cars," you can assume that car ownership in the U.S. is greater than it is in Europe. Choice B is incorrect, since the author is just *comparing* European trains to the highways of America, not saying that they *run* on highways. Choice C is incorrect, because the paragraph is about European, not American, trains. Choice D is incorrect because cheaper gas in Europe would favor the use of cars instead of trains.

5–A   The main idea is that football players may return to the field too quickly after suffering a concussion, and that they should be prevented from doing so. The fact that doctors are advising a longer rest means that this is important, so choice A is correct. No evidence is given for choices B, C, or D.

6–B   The second sentence tells you that the hurricane gave no warning. Thus, it was unexpected.

7–D   According to the last two sentences of the passage, the only correct statement is choice D, *large fishing nets often catch unwanted fish.* Choices A and B are not supported by the passage. Choice C is incorrect because it is contradicted by the passage. The danger to some species like cod and salmon is spelled out—the passage states that *they may soon die out.*

8–A   In the second sentence, we are told that the "Ice Man" lived 5,000 years ago. You can assume that this was determined by the scientists who have been studying his remains. There is no evidence for choice B. Choices C and D are not supported by this passage.

9–C   You can infer that the author would agree with choice C, *an outdoor fire can restart if it isn't properly extinguished.* The last paragraph tells you that it is important to *drown* a campfire completely once you're finished using it, implying that it can restart if you don't. Choice A is contradicted by the second sentence of the second paragraph—burnables like newspapers must be kept from the fire. Choice B is not related to the passage. Choice D is contradicted by the statement that fires shouldn't be left unattended. If you go fishing while the dinner is cooking, you're doing just that.

10–A   The only correct answer is choice A, *the burning remains of a fire*. *Embers* are the remains of the fire after the flames have subsided. Choice B is incorrect because these things would need to be burning in order to be called *embers*. The same reason makes choice C incorrect. Because there is only one correct answer, choice D, *all of the above*, is incorrect.

Finding Help in This Book

If you missed 2, 3, or 5, see Comprehension Skill 1: Finding Main Ideas, page 303.

If you missed 6, 7, or 8, see Comprehension Skill 2: Looking for Details, page 314.

If you missed 1, 4, or 9, see Comprehension Skill 3: Making Inferences, page 324.

If you missed 10, see Comprehension Skill 4: Finding Word Meanings, page 335.

WORD KNOWLEDGE

WORD SKILL 1: RECOGNIZING FAMILIAR WORDS

n important skill you need for success on the Word Knowledge Test is the ability to *recognize familiar words*. Most of the words on this test will already be familiar to you. You use them every day, and you read them in newspapers, magazines, or work-related material.

Practice Exercises 1 through 3 will help you sharpen your skills in *recognizing familiar words* by looking for synonyms. A *synonym* is a word that is the same or *nearly* the same as the test word. For each question, choose the word that is closest in meaning to the underlined word.

Each exercise is followed by an Answer Key and Explanations. You should study the Explanations carefully, because they clearly explain the answers, present many pointers, and show additional related familiar words you can easily review to expand your vocabulary.

Practice Exercise 1

1. <u>Massive</u> most nearly means
   - 1–A   large
   - 1–B   instructional
   - 1–C   slippery
   - 1–D   loud

2. <u>Cease</u> most nearly means
   - 2–A   stop
   - 2–B   curse
   - 2–C   liquefy
   - 2–D   bend

3. <u>Rapid</u> most nearly means
   - 3–A   torn
   - 3–B   crazy
   - 3–C   fast
   - 3–D   slow

4. <u>Decoy</u> most nearly means
   - 4–A   lure
   - 4–B   trick
   - 4–C   duck
   - 4–D   disturbance

5. Obsolete most nearly means
   5–A   jumbled
   5–B   new
   5–C   outdated
   5–D   tiny

6. Mimic most nearly means
   6–A   laugh
   6–B   scold
   6–C   raise
   6–D   imitate

7. Jolly most nearly means
   7–A   silly
   7–B   cheerful
   7–C   weak
   7–D   hungry

8. Erosion most nearly means
   8–A   blotting
   8–B   wearing away
   8–C   dislike and fear
   8–D   overpowering

9. Dismantle most nearly means
   9–A   put together
   9–B   douse a fire
   9–C   take apart
   9–D   disrobe

10. Insist most nearly means
    10–A   waiver
    10–B   stop quickly
    10–C   shout loudly
    10–D   demand firmly

11. Expire most nearly means
    11–A   grow
    11–B   sweat
    11–C   die
    11–D   referee

12. Pamper most nearly means
    12–A   spoil
    12–B   complain
    12–C   cry
    12–D   enlarge

13. Galoshes most nearly means
    13–A   stops
    13–B   trash
    13–C   boots
    13–D   tall ships

14. Nullify most nearly means
    14–A   postpone
    14–B   polish
    14–C   inform
    14–D   cancel

15. Rely most nearly means
    15–A   stagger
    15–B   depend
    15–C   race
    15–D   switch

16. Precise most nearly means
    16–A   steep
    16–B   vague
    16–C   exact
    16–D   pinpointed

17. Anonymous most nearly means
    17–A   confused
    17–B   drunken
    17–C   sleepy
    17–D   unknown

18. Vicious most nearly means
    18–A   malicious
    18–B   rebellious
    18–C   virtuous
    18–D   ridiculous

19. Sinister most nearly means
    19–A   container
    19–B   evil
    19–C   wavering
    19–D   comical

20. Shrivel most nearly means
    20–A   upset
    20–B   pitch
    20–C   shrink
    20–D   turn

Answer Key

1. A	2. A	3. C	4. A	5. C
6. D	7. B	8. B	9. C	10. D
11. C	12. A	13. C	14. D	15. B
16. C	17. D	18. A	19. B	20. C

Answers and Explanations

1–A The word *massive* comes from the familiar word *mass*, which refers to the expanse, bulk, or *large size* of something. Something that is bulky, weighty, heavy, and impressively large is *massive*.

2–A To *cease* means to bring an activity to an end, to discontinue or *stop* doing something, so choice A, *stop*, is the correct answer. For example, when there is a *cease-fire* during a conflict, it means fighting has stopped.

3–C *Rapid* is another familiar word, which relates to something marked by a *fast* rate of activity. A *rapid* transit refers to a metro or urban train that moves people quickly. A *rapid* is also a part of a river where the current is *fast*. When gunshots are fired quickly, that is call *rapid*-fire. Choice D, *slow*, is the opposite in meaning.

4–A The word *decoy* is often related to hunting, where it refers to something used as a *lure* to attract an animal or bird into a trap. For example, an artificial bird can be a *lure* or *decoy* to fool live birds into coming within shooting range. Choice C is a misleading choice, a trap to fool you, since ducks are often hunted.

5–C Something that is *obsolete* is old-fashioned, *outdated*, no longer in use. For example, computer models become *obsolete* or *outdated* very quickly as new features are developed. Choice B, *new*, is the opposite in meaning.

6–D To *mimic* someone is to *imitate*, simulate, or ape him or her. The word *mimic* is related to a *mime*, who is an actor using *mimicry* to entertain the audience. While this may cause you to laugh, choice A is incorrect as it is not a synonym for *mimic*.

7–B Someone who seems *jolly* is *cheerful*, happy, merry, and gay in mood, so choice B is the correct answer. He may or may not be *silly*, so choice A is incorrect, as are the other choices.

8–B *Erosion* is a common word often used in agriculture, or when speaking of the environment. It refers to the *wearing away*, decrease, or destruction of something. For example, heavy rains can cause the *erosion* of topsoil. *Erosion* is a noun derived from the verb *erode*.

9–C To *dismantle* something like a car, for example, is to *take it apart*, demolish it, strip it down, or destroy it. Choice A, *put together*, is the opposite in meaning; choice B is unrelated; and choice D, *disrobe*, means to take off one's clothes.

10–D The answer closest in meaning to *insist* is choice D, *demand firmly*. To *insist* is to take a serious stand, be persistent and emphatic, and stand by your resolution to get your way. For example, if you *insist* on good manners from your children, if you're persistent and serious in your intentions, they're more likely to be polite.

11–C If you *expire,* your life ends and you *die.* Another familiar word, *expiration,* is a noun meaning the closing, finish, or end of something, as in the *expiration* date on your driver's license.

12–A To *pamper* is a verb that means to spoil, indulge, pet, cater to, humor, gratify, and give in easily to someone, like a *spoiled* or *pampered* child. It means to treat someone with extreme or excessive care and attention.

13–C The word *galoshes* is one you may remember from your childhood. It means *boots,* rubbers, or overshoes, as in shoes worn over regular shoes to protect them in bad weather.

14–D The answer closest in meaning to *nullify* is choice D, *cancel. Nullify* also means to negate, annul, or make invalid. For example, if your fishing permit has expired, your right to fish has been *nullified* or *canceled.*

15–B When you *rely* on your parents, you *depend* on them. It means you have confidence in them based on prior experience—in other words, your parents are people you can *rely* or *depend* on. A common related word is *reliance,* as in *putting your reliance on the commanding officer.*

16–C To be *precise* is to be *exact,* decisive, correct, or very carefully rigid. Related words are *precision,* meaning accuracy, and *precisely,* as in being at work *precisely* at 6 a.m. Choice B, *vague,* is the opposite in meaning, i.e., not clear, accurate, or *precise.*

17–D *Anonymous* means *unknown,* not recognized, or not named or identified. For example, some charity donors wish to remain *anonymous* in order to preserve their privacy.

18–A The answer closest in meaning to *vicious* is choice A, *malicious.* A *vicious* or *malicious* person is one who is dangerously aggressive, savage, fierce, really cruel, and very nasty. A *vicious* dog is one that will bite you without reason. Choice C, *virtuous,* means being without fault, or the exact opposite of *vicious.*

19–B Something *sinister* is *evil,* harmful, and scary. A *sinister* feeling is one of foreboding, one that makes you feel that you will have bad fortune or be threatened by a serious disaster. The movie *Frankenstein* is full of *sinister* events and scary or evil people.

20–C *Shrivel* means to *shrink,* dry up, contract, or dwindle in size or shape. It means to get wrinkled up due to loss of moisture, or to become small and helpless. A piece of bacon can *shrivel* as you cook it because it loses fat and moisture. A neglected plant will *shrivel* and die in time.

Practice Exercise 2

1. <u>Kindred</u> most nearly means
   - 1–A similar
   - 1–B fired
   - 1–C wooden
   - 1–D angry

2. <u>Vigilant</u> most nearly means
   - 2–A hardy
   - 2–B thick
   - 2–C moving
   - 2–D watchful

3. <u>Solemn</u> most nearly means
   - 3–A tearful
   - 3–B cheerful
   - 3–C lonely
   - 3–D serious

4. <u>Catalog</u> most nearly means
   - 4–A list
   - 4–B garment
   - 4–C merchandise
   - 4–D order

5. <u>Penal</u> most nearly means
   - 5–A wooden
   - 5–B punishment
   - 5–C last
   - 5–D common

6. <u>Toxic</u> most nearly means
   - 6–A smoky
   - 6–B drowsy
   - 6–C burdensome
   - 6–D poisonous

7. <u>Eccentric</u> most nearly means
   - 7–A difficult
   - 7–B circular
   - 7–C busy
   - 7–D odd

8. <u>Fatality</u> most nearly means
   - 8–A wound
   - 8–B illness
   - 8–C death
   - 8–D surrender

9. <u>Lanky</u> most nearly means
   - 9–A sneaky
   - 9–B bent over
   - 9–C tall and thin
   - 9–D short and fat

10. <u>Manned</u> most nearly means
    - 10–A carries a person
    - 10–B automatic
    - 10–C operated by robots
    - 10–D sent into space

11. <u>Probable</u> most nearly means
    - 11–A movable
    - 11–B likely
    - 11–C seldom
    - 11–D far-fetched

12. <u>Haphazard</u> most nearly means
    - 12–A flimsy
    - 12–B dangerous
    - 12–C unorganized
    - 12–D planned

13. <u>Pilfer</u> most nearly means
    - 13–A substitute
    - 13–B steal
    - 13–C translate
    - 13–D delay

14. <u>Mature</u> most nearly means
    - 14–A die
    - 14–B spray
    - 14–C ripen
    - 14–D network

15. <u>Abrasion</u> most nearly means
   - 15–A   descendent
   - 15–B   scrape
   - 15–C   cut
   - 15–D   lesson

16. <u>Oasis</u> most nearly means
   - 16–A   disease
   - 16–B   ancient god
   - 16–C   refuge
   - 16–D   desert

17. <u>Coherent</u> most nearly means
   - 17–A   abundant
   - 17–B   knowledgeable
   - 17–C   persuasive
   - 17–D   understandable

18. <u>Flimsy</u> most nearly means
   - 18–A   unsubstantial
   - 18–B   funny
   - 18–C   sturdy
   - 18–D   airborne

19. <u>Eligible</u> most nearly means
   - 19–A   capable
   - 19–B   educated
   - 19–C   receivable
   - 19–D   qualified

20. <u>Belittle</u> most nearly means
   - 20–A   praise
   - 20–B   applaud
   - 20–C   disparage
   - 20–D   admire

Answer Key

1. A	2. D	3. D	4. A	5. B
6. D	7. D	8. C	9. C	10. A
11. B	12. C	13. B	14. C	15. B
16. C	17. D	18. A	19. D	20. C

Answers and Explanations

1–A   *Kindred* means something that is *similar* in nature, something that is alike. *Kindred* also is used when speaking of people of the same ancestry, people who are related or have a *similar* family background.

2–D   To be *vigilant* means to be watchful, to pay attention, and to be alert. A store security guard must be *vigilant* and protect his employer's business. Words like *vigil, vigilance,* and *vigilante* are related.

3–D   A *solemn* occasion is one that is *serious,* somber, and often marked by the observance of established form or ceremony. Examples of *solemn* events are funerals, religious events, or swearing-in ceremonies. Choice B, *cheerful,* is opposite in meaning.

4–A   A *catalog,* sometimes spelled *catalogue,* is a *list,* a register, a systematic organized arrangement of items with descriptive details. For example, libraries always have a book *catalog,* which is a *list* of their books.

5–B   A *penal* institution, or prison, is one that exists for *punishment. Penal* is a word that involves punishment. Other familiar related words that you will recognize are *penalty, penal code, penance,* or *penalize.*

6–D   *Toxic* is a familiar word that means *poisonous*. Related words are *toxin*, which is something causing a toxic reaction, and *toxemia*, an illness that is caused by having *toxic* substances in the blood.

7–D   *Eccentric* means *odd*, unusual, or differing from established or usual conduct in strange, unexpected, or whimsical ways. An *eccentric* person may live strangely, or have tastes different from most other people.

8–C   The word *fatality* means a *death*, usually resulting from a disaster. For example, victims of deadly earthquakes are spoken of as *fatalities*. Victims of war are also spoken of as *fatalities*. Similar words are *fate*, *fatalism*, and *fatal*, which all are related to the idea of a predetermined destiny of some kind, as in "Their son was *fated* to be the king of England."

9–C   A person who is *lanky* is ungracefully *tall and thin*. The words *lean* or *slender* also refer to someone who is thin, but these words are not synonyms of *lanky* because they don't imply that he or she is ungraceful.

10–A *Manned* refers to something that *carries a person*, in other words, is run by a person. For example, a *manned* spaceship carries a human being. A *manned* factory is one that is operated by men and women, not robots. Choices B and C are therefore the opposite in meaning—something that is operated by robots or run automatically does not need to be *manned*.

11–B *Probable* is another word that will no doubt be familiar to you. It is related to words like *probability* and *probably* and means *likely*. Something that is *probable* is not completely certain, but is *likely*. When you see lightning it is *probable*, but not 100 percent certain, that you will also hear thunder. Choices C and D are opposite in meaning.

12–C A *haphazard* event is one that is *unorganized*, happening by chance, and lacking in planning, order, or direction. It is a *random* event. For example, "The students casually sat around the classroom in a *haphazard* manner." Choice D, *planned*, is opposite in meaning. Choice B, *dangerous*, may fool you since it is related to *hazard*, not *haphazard*.

13–B To *pilfer* means to *steal*, usually in small amounts over and over again to avoid detection. For example, an office employee may *pilfer* office supplies, like paper, pencils, or paper clips repeatedly in small quantities and not be caught for a long time.

14–C To *mature* is to *ripen*, develop, grow up, or become wiser and more experienced. It also means to *reach perfection*, especially when referring to fruit.

15–B An *abrasion* is a common medical term that means a *scrape*, or a wearing, grinding, or rubbing away by friction, such as an *abraded* area of the skin. It is not as bad as a full cut, but it can be just as painful.

16–C *Oasis* refers to a *refuge*, sometimes an unexpectedly green fertile place in an arid region, like a desert. An *oasis* is a pleasant place that provides rest and relief and is a *refuge*.

17–D Something that is *coherent* is *understandable*, meaning it is clear and intelligible. For example, when you do a presentation about a topic to an audience, it should be *coherent*, logical, easily understood, and consistent. While you should also be knowledgeable and maybe persuasive, these are not synonyms for *coherent*.

18–A An item that is *flimsy* is *unsubstantial*, badly made, inadequate, wobbly, or fragile. It is lacking in physical strength or substance because it might be made with inferior materials or workmanship. For example, plastic toys are *flimsy* in comparison with ones made of metal. Choice C, *sturdy*, which means strong and well made, is the opposite of *flimsy*.

19–D To be *eligible* means to be *qualified*. It means that a person is entitled, that he or she has the necessary skills, or is worthy of being chosen. For example, in order to be *eligible* to be in the U.S. Armed Forces, you must show that you can pass the four ASVAB tests in reading and math—that you are sufficiently *qualified*.

20–C When you *belittle* a man you *disparage* him, you cause him discomfort by making him feel smaller, you insult him by speaking slightingly to him. You make him feel less good about himself. Here is a hint for you: In answering this question, you can see that the other answer choices—*praise*, *applaud*, *admire*—are familiar words that mean more or less the same thing, so even if you are unfamiliar with the word *disparage* you can assume that it is the correct answer.

Practice Exercise 3

1. Suburban most nearly means
    - 1–A   inner city
    - 1–B   midtown
    - 1–C   downtown
    - 1–D   outskirts of a city

2. Abrupt most nearly means
    - 2–A   rough
    - 2–B   gentle
    - 2–C   ailing
    - 2–D   sudden

3. Detect most nearly means
    - 3–A   discover
    - 3–B   mistake
    - 3–C   slide
    - 3–D   move away

4. Oval most nearly means
    - 4–A   circular
    - 4–B   egg-shaped
    - 4–C   square
    - 4–D   rectangular

5. Merge most nearly means
    - 5–A   tip
    - 5–B   combine
    - 5–C   confuse
    - 5–D   spend

6. Thrive most nearly means
    - 6–A   complete
    - 6–B   save
    - 6–C   prosper
    - 6–D   argue

7. Faint most nearly means
    - 7–A   strengthened
    - 7–B   weak
    - 7–C   clumsy
    - 7–D   feverish

8. Reduce most nearly means
    - 8–A   argue
    - 8–B   conclude
    - 8–C   dispose
    - 8–D   diminish

9. Vain most nearly means
    - 9–A   dangerous
    - 9–B   useless
    - 9–C   deserving
    - 9–D   expensive

10. Hint most nearly means
    - 10–A   back
    - 10–B   suggestion
    - 10–C   ribbon
    - 10–D   paint

11. <u>Hermit</u> most nearly means
    11–A   crab
    11–B   traveler
    11–C   recluse
    11–D   inspector

12. <u>Keepsake</u> most nearly means
    12–A   memento
    12–B   heart
    12–C   price
    12–D   security

13. <u>Order</u> most nearly means
    13–A   participate
    13–B   shout
    13–C   command
    13–D   spin

14. <u>Shindig</u> most nearly means
    14–A   graduation
    14–B   leg injury
    14–C   party
    14–D   beach

15. <u>Mellow</u> most nearly means
    15–A   pleasant
    15–B   fruity
    15–C   biting
    15–D   nasty

16. <u>Bizarre</u> most nearly means
    16–A   market
    16–B   unusual
    16–C   mixed
    16–D   outspoken

17. <u>Verbal</u> most nearly means
    17–A   loud
    17–B   spoken
    17–C   charge
    17–D   confured

18. <u>Yowl</u> most nearly means
    18–A   wind
    18–B   free
    18–C   save
    18–D   wail

19. <u>Facsimile</u> most nearly means
    19–A   copy
    19–B   fact
    19–C   similarity
    19–D   partition

20. <u>Topnotch</u> most nearly means
    20–A   alert
    20–B   first-rate
    20–C   sleepy
    20–D   first cut

Answer Key

1. D	2. D	3. A	4. B	5. B
6. C	7. B	8. D	9. B	10. B
11. C	12. A	13. C	14. C	15. A
16. B	17. B	18. D	19. A	20. B

Answers and Explanations

1–D The word *urban* refers to a city, and *sub* means near, so *suburban* refers to a place near a city, or the *outskirts of a city.* The other choices all refer to different sections of the city itself so they are incorrect.

2–D An *abrupt* event is one that is *sudden,* unexpected, occurring without warning or preparation. For example, the weather can change *abruptly* in the tropics. Moody people can have *abrupt,* unexpected changes in mood.

3–A The word *detect* is related to *detective* or *detector* and means to *discover. Detect* means to uncover the true character, or the existence, presence, or fact of something, usually with a good deal of effort.

4–B Something that is *oval,* like a race track, is *egg-shaped.* The word *oval* comes from *ova,* which means egg. Related words are *ovary,* meaning the place an egg is developed, or *ovarian,* which refers to an ovary.

5–B When two or more companies *merge,* they *combine* and become one company. To *merge* is to blend or come together without any abrupt or noticeable change, as in *merging* traffic. Related words are *merger,* as in an industrial merger, or *immerse,* which means to surround something in water.

6–C To *thrive* is to *prosper,* flourish, grow vigorously, gain in wealth or possessions. When you say that someone is *thriving,* you mean that he or she is making good progress toward an important life goal. For example, a *thriving businessman* is a person who is successful in his business venture.

7–B To feel *faint* is to feel *weak,* dizzy, or lacking in strength or vigor. To actually *faint* is to lose consciousness because of a temporary lessening in the blood supply to the brain. Choice A, *strengthened,* is opposite in meaning.

8–D The word *reduce* means to *diminish* in size, amount, extent, or number. To *reduce* the chances of war means to lessen the likelihood that there will be war. The word *reduce* will sound familiar to you because of its frequent use in math; for example, *reducing* both sides of an equation. Related words are *reduction* and *redundant.*

9–B Something that is *vain* is *useless,* has no real value, or is foolish or silly. For example, in speaking of *prisoners making vain efforts to escape,* we mean that they had no real chance of being successful, that the odds were against them. Also, someone who overestimates his or her own attractiveness or accomplishments is spoken of as being *vain.*

10–B A *hint* is a *suggestion,* a clue. It refers to saying something indirectly, implying something, rather than saying it openly and explicitly. It means giving people a clue, or only a very small amount of information.

11–C A *hermit* is a person who has withdrawn from society, often for religious reasons, and lives by himself. The answer choice closest in meaning is choice C, *recluse.*

12–A *Keepsake* is a souvenir, a *memento,* kept or given by one person to another as a sentimental or loving remembrance.

13–C To give an *order* is to *command.* For example, the officer *orders* his unit to march. Other meanings for *order* are to arrange, organize, or put into a system. When used as a noun, *order* means appropriately arranged or a group of people united in a formal way, such as a religious *order* or a fraternal society.

14–C   A *shindig* is a funny-sounding word meaning a celebration, a social gathering, or a *party,* usually with dancing. While a graduation may be celebrated with a *shindig,* choice A is incorrect, as it is not a synonym.

15–A   Something *mellow* is *pleasant,* agreeable, laid-back. Listening to music that is pleasant and soothing makes people feel *mellow,* but listening to hard rock music usually does not. Things or experiences that are *mellow* are relaxing, not overly exciting. Choices C and D are opposite in meaning. Choice B, *fruity,* relates to the word *melon,* not *mellow.*

16–B   When something is spoken of as being *bizarre* it is regarded as being highly *unusual,* unexpected, odd, not typical, out of the ordinary. Having dyed blue hair is usually thought of as *bizarre.* Choice A refers to the word *bazaar,* which is an outdoor market.

17–B   The word *verbal* means relating to or consisting of *words.* It also means *spoken,* as opposed to written, language, so choice B must be the correct answer. Related words are *verb,* which forms the action center of the predicate of a sentence, and *verbatim,* which means word-for-word.

18–D   To *yowl* is to *wail,* to make a noise that sounds like a long mournful howl. For example, a cat will sometimes *yowl* at night when communicating with other cats. To *yowl* means to call out with a loud long cry expressing protest or feelings of pain, grief, or distress.

19–A   *Facsimile* is a twenty-first-century word that will be familiar to anyone who has worked in an office. It means an exact *copy* or reproduction of something, or *fax* for short. A *facsimile* or fax is also a system for instantly sending and reproducing written material by means of signals sent over telephone lines.

20–B   The word *topnotch* means *first-rate.* It's used when referring to something of the highest quality, like being a *topnotch* athlete, or doing a *topnotch* job on an assignment at work. A *topnotch* soldier is one who is courageous and dependable.

WORD SKILL 2: CONTEXT CLUES

Some of the words on the ASVAB Word Knowledge Test will be presented in the *context of a sentence*. The meaning of the sentence itself, or a few of the surrounding words in the sentence, called *context clues,* often give you clues as to the meaning of the word.

The following is an example of such a question:

Sample 1. The <u>pachyderm</u> was led into the arena blowing hot air from its huge trunk.

1–A   elephant
1–B   fish
1–C   luggage
1–D   clown

You are being asked for the meaning of the word *pachyderm.* The surrounding words, the *context clues,* are *arena* and *huge trunk.* These words suggest that the sentence may be about a circus and an animal being brought in. So, the correct answer must be choice A, *elephant.* The other choices can be quickly eliminated, since neither fish, luggage, nor clowns can logically be substituted for *pachyderm* in the sentence.

You must use *logic* and *common sense* in order to benefit from these context clues. It is important to remember, however, that you have only a few seconds to figure out the word using *context clues. Answer quickly* so you will have enough time left to answer all the questions that follow.

Now do Practice Exercises 4 through 6 to get accustomed to using *context clues.* For each question, choose the synonym, or answer that is closest in meaning, to the underlined word. After you complete each exercise, check your answers against the Answers and Explanations that follow. The Explanations will offer many techniques and examples of the way the context can help you, as well as additional related words that will help improve your vocabulary.

Practice Exercise 4

1. Because so few guests came, the hostess had a <u>surplus</u> of food.

1–A   roll
1–B   parcel
1–C   sail
1–D   excess

2. The <u>molten</u> steel was poured from the vat.

2–A   heavy
2–B   changeable
2–C   melted
2–D   slippery

3. The family ate the tasty <u>produce</u> that they grew in their back yard.

3–A   evergreens
3–B   vegetables
3–C   ponies
3–D   crafts

4. The <u>saga</u> of ancient Viking heroes is exciting to read.

4–A   silliness
4–B   boredom
4–C   ice
4–D   story

5. The <u>jarring</u> sound of the siren awakened everyone.
   - 5–A   confused
   - 5–B   harsh
   - 5–C   alert
   - 5–D   postponed

6. The wedding was a <u>festive</u> occasion.
   - 6–A   joyous
   - 6–B   decorated
   - 6–C   overloaded
   - 6–D   anxious

7. The pressure <u>gauge</u> was not working.
   - 7–A   hot pipe
   - 7–B   measurement device
   - 7–C   steam pipe
   - 7–D   bubble bath

8. She <u>resents</u> not being invited to the performance.
   - 8–A   is offended by
   - 8–B   likes
   - 8–C   sends back
   - 8–D   recalls

9. The lifeguard was unable to <u>rescue</u> both children at once from the water.
   - 9–A   save
   - 9–B   instruct
   - 9–C   resign
   - 9–D   resemble

10. The grandparent tried to <u>pacify</u> the crying infant.
    - 10–A   feed
    - 10–B   hold
    - 10–C   walk
    - 10–D   calm

11. <u>Partitions</u> were brought in to separate the warehouse into sections.
    - 11–A   dividers
    - 11–B   kitchens
    - 11–C   wheels
    - 11–D   workers

12. The dog's <u>muzzle</u> was filled with gray hairs.
    - 12–A   chain
    - 12–B   fencing
    - 12–C   snout
    - 12–D   leash

13. Ghosts supposedly <u>haunted</u> the abandoned house.
    - 13–A   visited
    - 13–B   yelled
    - 13–C   suggested
    - 13–D   spanked

14. The problem <u>baffled</u> even the experts.
    - 14–A   misled
    - 14–B   confused
    - 14–C   added
    - 14–D   rolled

15. The man's <u>shabby</u> appearance suggested he was homeless.
    - 15–A   talkative
    - 15–B   heavy
    - 15–C   seedy
    - 15–D   round

16. The uncooperative witness <u>evaded</u> the prosecutor's questions.
    - 16–A   attacked
    - 16–B   dodged
    - 16–C   encircled
    - 16–D   applied

17. The meteorite left a huge <u>crater</u> in the ground.
    - 17–A   burn
    - 17–B   rock
    - 17–C   hole
    - 17–D   mark

18. The animals were in a <u>frenzy</u> as the fire approached.
    - 18–A   agitation
    - 18–B   fence
    - 18–C   circle
    - 18–D   smoke

19. Breaking her leg was a <u>misfortune</u> that spoiled her summer.

    19–A   poverty

    19–B   silly mistake

    19–C   wealth

    19–D   bad luck

20. After he retired, he was too restless to remain <u>idle</u> for long.

    20–A   inactive

    20–B   curious

    20–C   worshipful

    20–D   ignorant

Answer Key

1. D	2. C	3. B	4. D	5. B
6. A	7. B	8. A	9. A	10. D
11. A	12. C	13. A	14. B	15. C
16. B	17. C	18. A	19. D	20. A

Answers and Explanations

1–D   The logic of the sentence tells you what *excess* means. The hostess bought too much food for her guests because she overestimated how many would come, so *surplus* means *excess*, or the amount left after all that is needed is used up. If you substituted any of the other choices, the sense of the sentence would be lost.

2–C   Here the context clue is *poured.* The steel must have been a hot liquid, or *melted*, in order for it to be poured, so *molten* means *melted.* A *molten* substance is one that has been heated enough to make it a seething fluid, with the purpose of forming or shaping it into something.

3–B   The context clues are *ate, tasty,* and *grew,* so *produce* is something you can grow and eat. Therefore, *produce* means *vegetables.* You can eliminate the other choices, since evergreens can be grown but not eaten, ponies also cannot be eaten, and crafts are made, not grown.

4–D   The context clues in the sentence are *exciting to read.* Regardless of what the *saga* is about, if it is *exciting to read* it is probably a *story.* A *saga* was originally the story of twelfth- or thirteenth-century historic or legendary figures in Norway or Iceland, and modern *sagas* are stories that resemble these.

5–B   The clues you will notice in this sentence are *sound* and *siren.* The fact that it *awakened* people suggests that it probably produced a *harsh,* or *jarring,* noise.

6–A   The context clue *wedding* will help you realize that *festive* means *joyous.* Most weddings are thought of as being *festive* or *joyous* occasions. The word *festive* is related to *feast, festival, festivity,* and *festoon.*

7–B   Here, the whole sentence serves as a clue for the meaning of *gauge,* which means *measurement device.* A *gauge* is a *measurement device,* in this case one that measures pressure.

8–A   The context clue here is *not invited.* If the girl was *not invited to the performance,* she is probably going to *resent,* or be *offended* by, the omission. In other words, she will feel bad, annoyed, *resentful,* and *offended.*

9–A   The context clues in this sentence are *lifeguard, both children, water.* What comes to mind is that two children were in the water and something happened to endanger them.

The lifeguard couldn't *rescue,* or *save,* both of them at once—perhaps they weren't near each other. To *rescue* means to *save,* deliver, reclaim, or redeem.

10–D Look at the context clues *grandparent* and *crying infant.* To *pacify* a crying infant means to *calm* him, or to soothe, placate, conciliate him. It means to calm him down, to perhaps feed him or do whatever it takes to ease the discomfort or upset that is causing him to cry.

11–A Notice that the context clues tell you that *partitions* serve the function of *separating the warehouse* into sections. In looking at the choices, the only one that could do this is *dividers. Partitions* or *dividers* are things that are used to create separate smaller spaces within a larger area.

12–C The clue given is the phrase *filled with gray hairs,* so we know that the sentence is saying something about the dog, or his *snout.* Since chain, fencing, and leash are not likely to be *filled with gray hairs, muzzle* must mean *snout.* A *muzzle* or *snout* refers to the projecting jaws and nose of an animal. A *muzzle* is also the name of a device put over an animal's *snout* in order to keep him from biting.

13–A The context clues are *ghosts* and *abandoned house.* So, *haunted* means *visited,* or to reappear constantly and spontaneously. While choice A, *visited,* does not have the same scary feel as the word *haunted,* which in this sentence implies something supernatural, it is the best, and thus the correct, answer.

14–B The context clues here are *problem, even,* and *experts.* In other words, something is a *problem* even for the experts. *Baffled* means *confused,* frustrated, defeated, or disconcerted. It means the problem was so difficult it could not be solved by people even though they were experts.

15–C The context clues in the sentence are *appearance* and *homeless,* suggesting that the man looked really poor, or *seedy.* Perhaps his clothing was very worn, dilapidated, and threadbare, and his grooming bad.

16–B The words that give you clues to the correct answer are *uncooperative* and *questions*—in other words, the witness was uncooperative in answering the questions, he *evaded* or *dodged* the questions. The implication is that he did not want to answer the questions; he *evaded* them, or escaped from answering them by giving roundabout or irrelevant and uninformative answers.

17–C The sentence describes what effect the meteorite had on the ground. A meteorite comes from outer space and obviously would leave a *crater,* or *hole,* if it hit the earth, or the ground. While it may also cause burning, rock formations, or some other marks, your answer needs to be a synonym, so choice C, *hole,* though not a perfect synonym, is the best answer.

18–A The context clues are *animals* and *fire approached.* You can assume that the animals were very frightened of the approaching fire. The word *frenzy* means *agitation,* an intense temporary madness and emotional upset. *Frenzy* means an extreme emotion, a wild and fearful excitement.

19–D Words that give you clues as to the meaning of *misfortune* are *breaking her leg.* Breaking your leg can be considered an unfortunate happening, a *misfortune,* or *bad luck.* While people can have a *misfortune* because of a *silly mistake,* choice B is incorrect because it is not a synonym for *misfortune.*

20–A The context clues here are *too restless,* meaning he was unable to remain *idle,* or *inactive* after he retired. *Idle* in this sentence means lazy, *inactive,* not doing anything, unoccupied. Choice C, *worshipful,* relates to the word *idol,* which is something you pray to, like a religious idol, or are devoted to, like a movie star idol.

Practice Exercise 5

1. The bad-smelling spray <u>repelled</u> the ants.
   - 1–A   attracted
   - 1–B   drove away
   - 1–C   confused
   - 1–D   amused

2. The difficult math problem <u>perplexed</u> him.
   - 2–A   puzzled
   - 2–B   solved
   - 2–C   helped
   - 2–D   surprised

3. She was <u>groggy</u> after the operation.
   - 3–A   talkative
   - 3–B   sleepy
   - 3–C   sad
   - 3–D   hopeful

4. She was eager to <u>refresh</u> the look of the room with bright new colors.
   - 4–A   reorganize
   - 4–B   reflect
   - 4–C   renovate
   - 4–D   redistribute

5. The <u>delightful</u> child brought joy to everyone who knew her.
   - 5–A   well-fed
   - 5–B   overactive
   - 5–C   underweight
   - 5–D   pleasure-giving

6. It is not good to <u>meddle</u> in other people's business.
   - 6–A   talk
   - 6–B   settle
   - 6–C   interfere
   - 6–D   muddy

7. He built an exact small-scaled <u>replica</u> of a World War II airplane.
   - 7–A   copy
   - 7–B   wood
   - 7–C   owner
   - 7–D   factory

8. She had the <u>option</u> to pay by check or by credit card.
   - 8–A   custom
   - 8–B   money
   - 8–C   choice
   - 8–D   plan

9. The police <u>barricade</u> prevented easy access to the house.
   - 9–A   plan
   - 9–B   force
   - 9–C   barrier
   - 9–D   troops

10. The plane's <u>erratic</u> flight showed that the pilot was having a problem.
    - 10–A   bumpy
    - 10–B   mistaken
    - 10–C   unusual
    - 10–D   noisy

11. It was hard to see the turtle in the deep <u>murky</u> water.
    - 11–A   cold
    - 11–B   dim
    - 11–C   bottomless
    - 11–D   colorful

12. The mansion's <u>upkeep</u> required three servants.
    - 12–A   maintenance
    - 12–B   hired help
    - 12–C   expenses
    - 12–D   top floor

13. The dog was <u>waterlogged</u> from swimming.
    - 13–A   heavy
    - 13–B   submerged
    - 13–C   soaked
    - 13–D   tired

14. The lake <u>abounds</u> with many, many fish.
    - 14–A   swims
    - 14–B   overflows
    - 14–C   bubbles
    - 14–D   dries

15. The large pot <u>simmered</u> and bubbled slowly on the stove.

    15–A   stewed gently

    15–B   rattled loudly

    15–C   slipped off

    15–D   swayed

16. The sad-faced men <u>grimly</u> searched the wreckage for survivors.

    16–A   forcefully

    16–B   quickly

    16–C   hopefully

    16–D   gloomily

17. The boy's <u>torrid</u> love letters embarrassed the shy girl.

    17–A   passionate

    17–B   careless

    17–C   lingering

    17–D   friendly

18. The oversized suit required an <u>alteration</u> to make it fit.

    18–A   pocket

    18–B   garment

    18–C   change

    18–D   color

19. He angrily <u>plunked</u> the money down on the counter.

    19–A   fell down

    19–B   dropped abruptly

    19–C   rolled over

    19–D   played with

20. She <u>whittled</u> a bird out of the piece of wood.

    20–A   carved

    20–B   called

    20–C   yelled

    20–D   hung

Answer Key

1. B	2. A	3. B	4. C	5. D
6. C	7. A	8. C	9. C	10. C
11. B	12. A	13. C	14. B	15. A
16. D	17. A	18. C	19. B	20. A

Answers and Explanations

1–B The words that give you the context clues here are *bad-smelling*. If the spray is bad-smelling, it will cause the ants to be *repelled* or *driven away*. Choice A, *attracted,* is the opposite in meaning.

2–A The context clues here are *difficult* and *math*. A person who is *perplexed* by a math problem is *puzzled* by it, is unable to understand it clearly, figure it out logically, or overcome the difficulty of it. The problem remains a *puzzle.*

3–B The clue words here are *after the operation*. How does a person usually feel after an operation? *Groggy* or *sleepy*, sometimes dizzy, out of it, often weak and unsteady on his or her feet. The word *groggy* is related to *grog,* which is an English alcoholic drink, like rum, which has been cut with water, sugar, and lemon juice, and is often served hot. This was a popular drink among sailors.

4–C The clues given in the sentence are *looks* and *new colors*. When you want to *refresh* the looks of a place, you want to *renovate* it. It means you are freshening up the room, renewing it. *Refresh,* when used in reference to *people* rather than places, means to restore strength, revive, or replenish. For example, you can *refresh* the tired runner by giving him water.

5–D   The definite clues that give you the correct answer are the words *brought joy.* Someone who is *delightful* is able to *give pleasure* to others. The child gave people pleasure because she was cute, funny, and enjoyable to be with. She was a *delight* for those who knew her.

6–C   The context clues are *not good* and *other people's business.* If it is someone else's business, then it is not good to *meddle* or *interfere* in it. It is better to mind one's own business than someone else's.

7–A   The context clues are *built, exact,* and *small-scaled.* A *replica* is a *copy,* an exact reproduction. A related word is *replicate,* which means to duplicate something, to produce a *replica,* or *copy.* He built a copy of the World War II airplane, an exact model.

8–C   The word that gives you a context clue is *or,* as in *by check or by credit card.* The word *or* tells you that she had an *option,* or a *choice* of paying one way or the other. An *option* implies the ability to choose among several choices.

9–C   The context clues here are the words *prevented easy access,* so a *barricade* must be something that gets in the way of entering a house, like a *barrier.* A *barricade* is an obstruction thrown up across a way or passage to prevent access, or entry.

10–C   The clues as to the meaning of *erratic* can be found in *having a problem.* Something was wrong with the way the plane was being flown—it was *erratic* or *unusual.* The plane might have had no fixed course, wandered from its path, or been inconsistent and not regular in its flight pattern, so its flight was *erratic.*

11–B   The clues given as to the meaning of *murky* are *hard to see* and *deep. Murky* water is *dim,* obscure, and darkly vague. If the turtle dives deep into the water, it will be difficult to see it because of the *murky* or *dim* water.

12–A   The context clues are *mansion* and *three servants.* Servants generally take care of homes and take charge of their *maintenance,* so *upkeep* means *maintenance.* The mansion was so large that it needed three servants to take care of it.

13–C   You can assume that since the dog had been swimming, its coat was wet—it was *water-logged,* or *soaked.* Its fur had *soaked* up water, making it *waterlogged,* or full of water.

14–B   The context clue for the meaning of *abounds* is *many, many*—the lake has *many, many fish,* so *abounds* means *overflows.* Words related to *abounds* are *bounty, bountiful,* and *abundant,* all meaning plentiful.

15–A   The context clue in this sentence is *bubbled slowly.* If something is bubbling slowly on the stove, it is cooking gently. *Simmered* means *stewed gently.* To *simmer* is to cook something *below* or *just at* the boiling point. It means to cook slowly and gently, as you would cook a stew.

16–D   The context clues here are *sad-faced, searched,* and *wreckage.* We know these men were not happy when they were searching the wreckage for survivors. *Grimly* means *gloomily.* The related word is *grim,* which in this sentence would mean serious, stern, or somber.

17–A   The context clues are the words *love letters* and *embarrassed.* If the letters were merely friendly, she would not feel embarrassed by them, but *torrid* here means *passionate,* ardent, overflowing with love and feeling. The word *torrid* also means hot, as in the scorching hot, or *torrid,* midday desert sun.

18–C The context clues are *oversized* and *fit*. To make an oversized suit fit, it is necessary to make an *alteration, change*, or modification. A related word is *alter*, which means to make something different without entirely changing it into something else, or to modify it.

19–B The context clues here are *angrily* and *down*. If he put the money down angrily, he *plunked* it down, or *he dropped it abruptly*. To *plunk* something down means to put it down suddenly, often making a hollow metallic *plunking* sound.

20–A The context clues here are *piece of wood*. To *whittle* or make something out of a piece of wood means to *carve* it. To *whittle* wood is to cut or pare off chips from the surface with a sharp knife, or to shape or *carve* it.

Practice Exercise 6

1. Everything was <u>chaos</u> in the new teacher's classroom.
   - 1–A screaming
   - 1–B confusion
   - 1–C beautiful
   - 1–D organized

2. The <u>exclusive</u> country club only admitted the very rich and clannish.
   - 2–A carefully chosen
   - 2–B colorfully illustrated
   - 2–C snobbishly aloof
   - 2–D painfully strained

3. The <u>former</u> teacher still enjoyed helping the students in the school.
   - 3–A previous
   - 3–B promoting
   - 3–C late
   - 3–D interesting

4. The children had been <u>included</u> in the planning of their party.
   - 4–A barred
   - 4–B involved
   - 4–C contacted
   - 4–D shunned

5. It was hard to <u>concur with</u> his many ridiculous statements.
   - 5–A forget
   - 5–B promote
   - 5–C agree with
   - 5–D laugh about

6. The <u>lack</u> of water caused constant thirst.
   - 6–A absence
   - 6–B taste
   - 6–C availability
   - 6–D nearness

7. The poor wording made the meaning of the order <u>obscure</u>.
   - 7–A painful
   - 7–B unnecessary
   - 7–C unclear
   - 7–D obvious

8. Even though his crime was serious, he received a <u>lenient</u> sentence.
   - 8–A strict
   - 8–B legitimate
   - 8–C unfair
   - 8–D light

9. The <u>urgent</u> message needed to be delivered immediately.
   - 9–A angry
   - 9–B covered
   - 9–C airtight
   - 9–D important

10. Because he was so tired, he <u>yearned</u> for his vacation.
    - 10–A longed
    - 10–B spoke
    - 10–C looked
    - 10–D slept late

11. The homeless people found temporary <u>ref-uge</u> in the church.

    11–A   prayer

    11–B   food

    11–C   salvation

    11–D   shelter

12. When becoming soldiers, they took a solemn <u>oath</u> to defend their country.

    12–A   testimony

    12–B   pledge

    12–C   strike

    12–D   song

13. The constant <u>drizzle</u> made everything wet.

    13–A   frost

    13–B   ice

    13–C   rain

    13–D   river

14. The kind and helpful Salvation Army is a <u>benevolent</u> organization.

    14–A   outgoing

    14–B   doing harm

    14–C   doing good

    14–D   armed

15. The sad children <u>mourned</u> for their dead parents.

    15–A   grieved

    15–B   thanked

    15–C   ignored

    15–D   yelled

16. It took strong men to work the oars of the <u>galley</u>.

    16–A   battle

    16–B   building

    16–C   boat

    16–D   buttons

17. It took several weeks for the package to be shipped <u>overseas</u>.

    17–A   by freight

    17–B   while refrigerated

    17–C   abroad

    17–D   by plane

18. The runners made slow <u>headway</u> because of the strong winds.

    18–A   rhythm

    18–B   progress

    18–C   exhaustion

    18–D   space

19. The jury's favorable <u>verdict</u> allowed the defendant to be freed.

    19–A   judgment

    19–B   trial

    19–C   summary

    19–D   question

20. He <u>flattered</u> the girl with numerous compliments.

    20–A   laughed loudly

    20–B   sang often

    20–C   praised excessively

    20–D   took advantage of

Answer Key

1. B	2. C	3. A	4. B	5. C
6. A	7. C	8. D	9. D	10. A
11. D	12. B	13. C	14. C	15. A
16. C	17. C	18. B	19. A	20. C

Answers and Explanations

1–B   Anyone who has gone into a class with a new teacher will know what the word *chaos* means—*confusion* and lack of order. The context clue words here are *new teacher.* When a new teacher does not know how to organize a class, there will be noise, confusion, and *chaos* in the classroom.

2–C   The context clues here are *only admitted* and *rich and clannish.* A place like a country club that only admits the rich is *exclusive* and *snobbishly aloof,* restricted, preferential, particular, and select. It means they pick and choose who is admitted. Related words are *exclude* and *exclusion,* both meaning the act of keeping away those who are not wanted.

3–A   The context clues are *still enjoyed,* implying that this teacher was no longer working in the school. *Former* means *previous,* preceding, or coming before in time. Even though this person is no longer a teacher, he/she still came to help.

4–B   The clue words here are *in the planning.* The children had participated, had been *included* or *involved* in the planning of the party. Choice D is opposite in meaning, and choice C, which would make sense in the sentence, is not a synonym of *included.*

5–C   The context clues here are *hard to* and *ridiculous.* If the statements were ridiculous, it would be hard to *concur* or *agree* with them. *Concur* means to be in accord with, *agree* with, or approve of. A dentist will *concur* that it is important to brush your teeth twice a day.

6–A   The context clue is *thirst.* If there is constant thirst, there must be no water. *Lack* means the state of missing something, or the *absence,* deprivation, paucity, or deficiency of something. For example, *lacking* common sense means you have little common sense, or if you are *lacking* in cash, you are broke.

7–C   The context clues here are the words *poor wording.* If something is poorly worded, or poorly written, the meaning becomes *obscure* or *unclear,* ambiguous, indistinct, or hard to understand. Choice D, *obvious,* is the opposite in meaning.

8–D   The words *even though* and *serious* tell you that the *lenient* sentence was not appropriate, that it was too *light,* that the criminal should have received a tougher sentence. *Lenient* means indulgent, or being treated too easily or softly.

9–D   If the message needed to get there immediately, then it must have been *important. Urgent* means *important,* critical, compelling, imperative, essential, and absolutely vital. For example, it is *urgent* that people treat each other with respect and fairness. It is *urgent* or *important* that wars be prevented if at all possible.

10–A   The words that give you the clue in this sentence are *tired* and *vacation.* Because he was very tired, he *longed* for his vacation. To *yearn* for something means to want persistently, wistfully or sadly, to have a tender or urgent *longing.*

11–D   The context clues here are *homeless* and *temporary,* which implies that the homeless people received some help—in this case, *refuge,* or *shelter,* protection, or relief from being out in the open. A related word is *refugee,* which means a person who flees to a foreign country to escape danger or persecution.

12–B   The words *solemn* and *defend their country* tell you that the soldiers were saying something important—they were giving an *oath* or *pledge,* meaning that they meant what they said. An *oath* is a declaration, vow, promise, and sworn statement. It is not given lightly or thoughtlessly by most people.

13–C   The phrase *made everything wet* gives you the clue that the sentence is speaking of *rain*. A *drizzle* is a fine, misty *rain*—in other words, rain that comes down in very small drops or very lightly.

14–C   Even if you've never heard of the Salvation Army, the context clues *kind and helpful* hint at the meaning of *benevolent—doing good.* A *benevolent* person or organization is there to *do good* for others. Related words are *benefit* or *benevolence*, which refer to the kindness or help that is given, and *beneficiary,* which refers to the person getting the *benefit*.

15–A   The context clues here are *sad* and *dead parents.* You would expect children who lost their parents to be sad and *mourn* or *grieve* for them. To *mourn* means to feel great sorrow, regret, anguish, and to weep and suffer because of the loss being experienced.

16–C   The context clue here is the word *oars,* which tells you that the sentence is talking about a *boat.* A *galley* is a ship or a boat that is propelled mainly by oars. *Galleys* were the long low ships used for war and trading, especially in the Mediterranean Sea from the Middle Ages to the nineteenth century.

17–C   The words *several weeks* and *shipped* tells you that the package is being sent far away, or *abroad. Overseas* means something relating to transport or communication over the sea, or a place situated in lands beyond the sea. For example, troops being sent *overseas* are being sent beyond the ocean to a faraway country.

18–B   The context clues are *slow* and *strong winds.* The runners are making slow *progress* or *headway* because of the strong winds that are slowing them down. *Headway* refers to the rate of motion while going in a forward direction.

19–A   The context clues are *favorable* and *freed.* The jury's *verdict,* or *judgment,* refers to the finding or decision made by a jury on a matter submitted to it in a trial. If a jury makes a favorable *verdict,* the defendant will be freed.

20–C   The context clue is *numerous compliments.* When a person *flatters* someone with numerous compliments, he is giving *excessive praise.*

WORD SKILL 3: WORD PARTS

Another way of finding the correct meaning of words given on tests such as the ASVAB Word Knowledge Test is to use your knowledge of *Word Parts*. Once you become familiar with commonly used Word Parts, you will be able to quickly figure out the correct meaning of many words.

There are three basic types of Word Parts: *prefixes, suffixes,* and *roots. Prefixes* attach to the beginning of a word to change its meaning or create a new word. *Suffixes* are put at the end of a word to change its meaning, help make it grammatically correct, or form a new word. And finally, every word must have a *root. Roots* are the basic elements of words that determine the meaning. Words *may* have a prefix, and they *may* have one or more suffixes.

Look at the list of commonly used Word Parts that follows. Learn a few each day, taking note of the examples given. Try and see if you can think of other words that you know with the same Word Part. Be aware that some of the Word Parts have several meanings. Also, you will notice that often different Word Parts may mean the same thing.

List of Common Word Parts

PREFIXES

Prefix	Meaning	Examples
anti-	against	antiwar—against war
auto-	self	automobile—self-moving vehicle
bene-	good, well	benefactor—one who does good deeds
bi-	two	bilateral—two-sided
circum-	around	circumnavigate—sail around
com-, co-, col-	with, together	cooperate—work together
contra-, contro-, counter-	against	contradict—speak against
demi-	half	demitasse—half cup (of coffee)
di-	twice, double	dichromatic—having two colors
equi-	equal	equivalent—of equal value
extra-	outside, beyond	extraterrestrial—beyond the earth
fore-	in front of, previous	forecast—tell ahead of time
		foreleg—front leg
homo-	same, alike	homophonic—sounding the same
hyper-	too much, over	hyperactive—overly active
hypo-	too little, under	hypothermia—too little body heat

in-, il-, ig-, im-, ir-	not	innocent—not guilty
		ignorant—not knowing
		illogical—not logical
		irresponsible—not responsible
intra-	within, inside	intrastate—within a state
mal-	bad, wrong, poor	maladjust—adjust poorly
mis-	badly, wrongly	misunderstand—understand incorrectly
mono-	single, one	monorail—train that runs on one rail
neo-	new	Neolithic—from the New Stone Age
non-	not	nonfactual—not a fact
omni-	all	omnipresent—present in all places
poly-	many	polygon—a many-sided figure
post-	after	postmortem—after death
pre-	before, earlier than	prejudice—judgment in advance
pro-	in favor of, forward	prowar—in favor of war
		proceed—go forward
re-	again, back	reimburse—pay back
semi-	half	semiawake—half awake
tele-	far	television—seeing things from afar
trans-	across	transport—carry across an area
un-	not	unaware—not aware or knowledgeable

SUFFIXES

Suffix	**Meaning**	**Examples**
-able, -ble	able, capable	acceptable—capable of being accepted
-age	total, sum of	frontage—total space in front
-al	like, of, suitable for	theatrical—like the theater
-ance	state of, act of	disturbance—the act of disturbing
-dom	the state of, belonging to	kingdom—belonging to the king
-er, -or	that which, one who	pacifier—one who pacifies
-hood	condition or state of	adulthood—condition of being adult
-ish	a bit like	foolish—like a fool
-ism	practice of, belief	racism—belief in racial superiority
-logy	study of	musicology—study of music
-ness	act or quality of	eagerness—quality of being eager
-ous	having, full of	amorous—full of love

| -ward | direction of | westward—in a western direction |
| -y | like, full of, somewhat | sporty—full of sport |

ROOTS

Root	Meaning	Examples
aqua	water	aquatic—having to do with water
auto	self	autograph—someone's own signature
biblio	book	bibliography—a reference list of books
bio	life, living things	biology—study of living things
cede, ceed	move, go with	precede—to go ahead of
chron	time	chronometer—tool for measuring time
clude	close or shut	include—close or shut in
cogn	know about	recognize—know again, remember
flect, flex	turn or bend	flexible—able to be bent
fract	break	fracture—a break or crack
hydr	water	hydrant—something for getting water
ject	throw, toss	eject—to throw out
junct	join	junction—joining parts of something
logue	speech, speaking	dialogue—speech between two people
mand	command, order	mandate—a command
manus, mani	hand	manicure—care given to hands
ped	foot	pedestrian—person who is walking
port	bring, carry	export—to bring trade out of a country
rupt	break	disrupt—to break up
scend	climb	ascend—climb up
sect	cut apart	trisect—cut something into three parts
serve	save, keep	preserve—hold on to something, save it
term	end, finish off	terminal—the end of the line

Now try Practice Exercises 7 and 8. Check your answers against the Answers and Explanations that follow each Exercise. Be sure to read the Explanations carefully to learn about how many English words are constructed, and also to revue many *additional words* that are related to the words in the questions.

Practice Exercise 7

1. <u>Impatient</u> most nearly means
   - 1–A   not patient
   - 1–B   very patient
   - 1–C   hospitalized
   - 1–D   not important

2. Because of the snowstorm, the meeting had to be <u>postponed</u>.
   - 2–A   avoided
   - 2–B   led
   - 2–C   delayed
   - 2–D   arrived

3. <u>Extraordinary</u> most nearly means
   - 3–A   unusual
   - 3–B   from outer space
   - 3–C   satisfactory
   - 3–D   pathetic

4. The <u>immature</u> boy was not ready for the responsibilities of marriage.
   - 4–A   awkward
   - 4–B   youthful
   - 4–C   grown
   - 4–D   loud

5. <u>Malformed</u> most nearly means
   - 5–A   slow
   - 5–B   beautiful
   - 5–C   misshapen
   - 5–D   sculpted

6. His shaky handwriting was <u>illegible</u>.
   - 6–A   not readable
   - 6–B   uninteresting
   - 6–C   not significant
   - 6–D   not clear

7. The <u>autobiography</u> of Benjamin Franklin is often read in schools.
   - 7–A   printing press
   - 7–B   story of someone else's life
   - 7–C   founding fathers
   - 7–D   story of one's life

8. <u>Reflex</u> most nearly means
   - 8–A   rejection
   - 8–B   responsibility
   - 8–C   reduction
   - 8–D   response

9. <u>Forehead</u> most nearly means
   - 9–A   backhand
   - 9–B   sidesaddle
   - 9–C   ears
   - 9–D   brow

10. The <u>mileage</u> indicator tells you when you need to fill up.
    - 10–A   total gas
    - 10–B   timing belt
    - 10–C   total distance
    - 10–D   system alert

11. <u>Conductor</u> most nearly means
    - 11–A   one who conducts
    - 11–B   electricity
    - 11–C   trainer
    - 11–D   player

12. <u>Homeward</u> most nearly means
    - 12–A   to be homeless
    - 12–B   in the direction of home
    - 12–C   long distance from home
    - 12–D   child going home

13. All of us must someday die since no one is immortal.

    13–A   indestructible

    13–B   listless

    13–C   friendless

    13–D   without illness

14. Exclude most nearly means

    14–A   trap in

    14–B   shut out

    14–C   finish off

    14–D   envelop

15. Geology most nearly means

    15–A   study of the earth

    15–B   geography

    15–C   landscaping

    15–D   social studies

16. His bad actions spoke of his malevolent intentions.

    16–A   ill-wishing

    16–B   good

    16–C   questionable

    16–D   funny

17. Automatic most nearly means

    17–A   basic

    17–B   self-starting

    17–C   underwater

    17–D   robotic

18. Beneficial most nearly means

    18–A   promoting good

    18–B   bending an ear

    18–C   berserk

    18–D   begging someone

19. With advanced age comes increased wisdom.

    19–A   being old

    19–B   state of being wise

    19–C   tendency to silliness

    19–D   confusion

20. Aquarium most nearly means

    20–A   athletic field

    20–B   bird feeder

    20–C   fish tank

    20–D   flying machine

Answer Key

1. A	2. C	3. A	4. B	5. C
6. A	7. D	8. D	9. D	10. C
11. A	12. B	13. A	14. B	15. A
16. A	17. B	18. A	19. B	20. C

Answers and Explanations

1–A The prefix *im,* which means *not,* makes the word *impatient* the opposite of *patient.* An *impatient* person is unable to be mild-tempered, serene, easy going, or accepting. For example, a hungry baby is *impatient* to have its mother feed him quickly.

2–C The sentence tells you that something—the bad weather—affected the timing of the meeting. *Postponed* has the prefix *post,* which means *after,* meaning the meeting had to be *delayed,* or scheduled for a later time.

3–A   The word closest in meaning is choice A, *unusual*. The word *ordinary* means something that is normal, customary, or an everyday occurrence. The prefix *extra* makes the word *extraordinary*, or *unusual*—remarkable, notable, something very different, unexpected, or special. An *extraordinary* baseball player is one who is way above his peers in ability to play ball.

4–B   The prefix *im* means *not*. The boy is *immature*, or *not mature*—he is *youthful*, not yet grown up, and young for his age, therefore not ready for marriage. Notice also that the sentence gives you a context clue for the meaning of *immature*, so that you can see that *immature* can't mean anything but *youthful*.

5–C   The prefix *mal* means *wrong, bad,* or *poor*, so something that is *malformed* is badly formed, or *misshapen*, distorted, abnormally put together, deformed, or twisted. For example, lack of proper nutrition causes plants to be undersized or *malformed*.

6–A   The prefix *il* is a negative meaning *not*, so something that is *illegible* is not legible, or *not readable*. So, the man's shakiness made his writing hard to read, or *illegible*.

7–D   The prefix of the word *autobiography* is *auto*, which means *self*, so an *autobiography* is the *story of one's life*. A *biography* is the story of someone else's life, with *bio*, as in *biology*, meaning life, and *graphy* being the writing or describing of something.

8–D   The root of *reflex* is *flex*, which means to bend or turn, and the prefix *re* means *again* or *back*, so *reflex* means a *response*, or a return movement. A tennis player must have quick *reflexes*—he must be able to turn back or return the ball quickly.

9–D   The prefix *fore* means *in front of*, or coming before. Your *forehead* comes before, or in front of your head and is therefore your *brow*, which is the area of your face above your nose and eyes. Words like *foreground, forecast, foremost, forefront,* and *forerunner* all have the prefix *fore* and refer to something that is *before*, in front of, or better than something else.

10–C   The suffix *age* means the *total*, or *sum* of something—in this case, the *mileage*, or total number of miles, or *total distance* the car has traveled.

11–A   The suffixes *or* and *er* mean *one who*, or *that which*. So a *conductor* is *one who conducts*. A *player* is *one who plays*, and a *driver* is *someone who drives*.

12–B   The suffix *ward* means *in the direction of*, so *homeward* means *in the direction of home*.

13–A   The prefix *im* means *not*, so *immortal* means *not mortal*, or *indestructible*. The sentence states that since none of us is *indestructible*, permanent, imperishable, timeless, everlasting, or perennial in their life expectancy, we will all eventually die.

14–B   The word *exclude* consists of the root *clude*, which means *shut* or *close*, and the prefix *ex* which means *out*. Therefore, *exclude* means to *shut out*. For example, an overbooked plane may cause some people to be *excluded* from it, or unable to board it.

15–A   The suffix *logy* means the *study of* something, so *geology* means the *study of the earth*, or earth science. Many words for various academic and scientific areas end with this suffix—for example, *biology, paleontology, zoology, psychology,* and *anthropology*. These words all mean the *study of* these different subjects.

16–A   The prefix *mal* means *bad* or *wrong*, so *malevolent* intentions are ones that are *ill-wishing*, badly meant, unkind, mean, or cruel. A person with *malevolent* intentions towards you is not your friend, but an enemy. The words *his bad actions* in this sentence also give you the clue that there is something bad about his intentions, that they are *malevolent.*

17–B The prefix *auto* tells you that *automatic* has something to do with *self.* Something *automatic* is *self-starting,* under its own power, already programmed, involuntary, spontaneous, unthinking, or mechanical. An *automatic* shift in a car is one that shifts *automatically,* in other words, by itself, without your help.

18–A The prefix *bene* means something *good,* so *beneficial* means *promoting good.* Something that is *beneficial* for our country's defense, for example, refers to activities or things that further our country's defense and that make our country a safer place.

19–B The suffix *dom* in this word means *the state of,* or *the condition of.* Therefore, *wisdom* means the *state of being wise.* The sentence states that as most people get older, they get wiser, they gain in *wisdom.*

20–C The root *aqua* refers to water, so an *aquarium* must mean something having to do with water, such as a *fish tank,* which is a container filled with water for keeping fish.

Practice Exercise 8

1. <u>Exceed</u> most nearly means
   - 1–A   outstrip
   - 1–B   speed
   - 1–C   run
   - 1–D   win

2. The speaker bored everyone with his lengthy <u>monologue</u>.
   - 2–A   irrelevant story
   - 2–B   severe criticism
   - 2–C   silly specifics
   - 2–D   one-person speech

3. <u>Mandatory</u> most nearly means
   - 3–A   optional
   - 3–B   required
   - 3–C   rural area
   - 3–D   heavy rock

4. He overwhelmed everyone with his <u>kindness</u> and generosity.
   - 4–A   stupidity
   - 4–B   holiness
   - 4–C   compassion
   - 4–D   brutality

5. <u>Glamorous</u> most nearly means
   - 5–A   full of glamour
   - 5–B   being thin
   - 5–C   feeling sad
   - 5–D   badly dressed

6. <u>Improper</u> most nearly means
   - 6–A   poorly done
   - 6–B   imprinted
   - 6–C   not correct
   - 6–D   immature

7. <u>Hydrotherapy</u> in swimming pools is helpful with elderly people.
   - 7–A   psychotherapy
   - 7–B   diving instruction
   - 7–C   running meets
   - 7–D   cure by water

8. <u>Biped</u> most nearly means
   - 8–A   large-wheeled
   - 8–B   two-footed walker
   - 8–C   three-wheeled car
   - 8–D   one-sided figure

9. Good music can <u>transcend</u> cultural and language differences between people.

9–A	focus on
9–B	discover
9–C	show up
9–D	get beyond

10. <u>Exterminate</u> most nearly means

10–A	eliminate
10–B	grow
10–C	mature
10–D	reverse

11. He had the <u>forethought</u> to save for his retirement.

11–A	factual knowledge
11–B	ability to count
11–C	advance planning
11–D	careful thinking

12. <u>Nonaggressive</u> most nearly means

12–A	inoperable
12–B	not combative
12–C	restrained
12–D	war-mongering

13. <u>Childhood</u> most nearly means

13–A	child's environment
13–B	growing pains
13–C	kindergarten
13–D	state of being young

14. The town is <u>equidistant</u> from St. Louis and Minneapolis.

14–A	on the equator
14–B	equally far
14–C	closer to
14–D	larger than

15. <u>Statehood</u> most nearly means

15–A	status of being a state
15–B	state laws
15–C	headgear
15–D	state of war

16. <u>Vegetarianism</u> most nearly means

16–A	love of fruit and fish
16–B	growing high-quality food
16–C	practice of eating no meats
16–D	genetic engineering

17. His habit of <u>predawn</u> waking tired out his roommate.

17–A	8 a.m. to 9 a.m.
17–B	late evening
17–C	before daybreak
17–D	after lunch

18. <u>Amateurish</u> most nearly means

18–A	in a professional way
18–B	like a beginner
18–C	foreigner
18–D	with a lisp

19. <u>Exclude</u> most nearly means

19–A	forget
19–B	exist on
19–C	close in
19–D	shut out

20. <u>Biology</u> most nearly means

20–A	study of living things
20–B	scientific inquiry
20–C	educating doctors
20–D	chemistry

Answer Key

1. A	2. D	3. B	4. C	5. A
6. C	7. D	8. B	9. D	10. A
11. C	12. B	13. D	14. B	15. A
16. C	17. C	18. B	19. D	20. A

Answers and Explanations

1–A   The root of the word *exceed* is *ceed,* which means to go or move. To *exceed* is to *outstrip,* outdo, outdistance, outrun, beat, or run circles around an opponent. Lance Armstrong was able to *exceed* or *outstrip* the nearest opponent's speed by many minutes and win his fifth French biking title.

2–D   The word *monologue* is made up of the prefix *mono,* which means *single* or *one,* and the root *logue,* which means *speech.* Therefore, the word *monologue* means a *one-person speech,* or a speech in which only one person is speaking.

3–B   The root of *mandatory* is *mand,* which means an order, or command, so something that is *mandatory* is *required,* compulsory, necessary, or an obligation. For example, when enrolled in the Armed Services, it is *mandatory* that the orders of superior officers be obeyed. Choice A, *optional,* is the opposite of *mandatory.*

4–C   The suffix *ness* means the *quality of,* so *kindness* means the quality of being kind, or *compassion,* good intentions, consideration, helpfulness, or goodness. For example, teachers usually show *kindness* to their pupils.

5–A   The suffix *ous* means being *full of* something, or *having* some quality, so *glamorous* means being *full of glamour.*

6–C   The prefix *im* is one of several that means *not,* so *improper* means *not proper* or *not correct.* Something that is *improper* is not generally factual, true, or correct. It can also mean something that shows poor taste, or poor manners. For example, wearing blue jeans to a dressy formal wedding is *improper.*

7–D   The root of *hydrotherapy* is *hydro,* which refers to water, and therapy refers to treatment, so *hydrotherapy* is a *cure by water.* Other examples of words using this root are *dehydrate,* which means to remove water from something, *hydrophobia,* meaning fear of water, and *hydrology,* which is the study of water.

8–B   The word *biped* consists of the prefix *bi* meaning *two,* and the root *ped,* which means *foot.* So a *biped* is an animal that walks on two feet (as opposed to those that walk on all four). Be careful of choices that don't make any sense; for example, there is no such thing as a three-wheeled car or one-sided figure. These kinds of choices can be quickly eliminated.

9–D   The prefix *trans* means *across,* and *scend* means *climb,* or getting over, so the word *transcend* means to *get beyond* something. The sentence states that even though people may come from different cultures and speak different languages, they can enjoy good music; it can *transcend* their differences.

10–A   The root *term* in the word *exterminate* means an *end* or *finish* of something, so to *exterminate* something is to put an end to it, *to eliminate* it.

11–C   The prefix *fore* means *previous,* or *in front of,* so *forethought* means thinking ahead, or *advance planning.* The sentence states that he thought ahead and saved money for his retirement. Also, an officer must show good *forethought* in showing concern for keeping his troops safe.

12–B   The prefix *non* in front of *aggressive* makes it a negative, or *not combative. Nonaggressive* means not offensive, or inclined to attack. A *nonaggressive* person is not inclined to be aggressive, or assaultive, towards others, while an *aggressive* person *is* so inclined.

13–D   The suffix *hood* refers to a *state* or *condition*, so *childhood* means the *state of being young,* the time of being a child.

14–B   The prefix *equi* means *equal,* so *equidistant* means *equally far,* or the same distance. In other words, the town is as far from St. Louis as it is from Minneapolis. Other common words using this same prefix are *equitable,* meaning fairness to all sides, and *equivalent,* meaning of equal value.

15–A   The suffix *hood* means the *state* or *condition of,* as in *statehood,* meaning the *state* or *status of being a state.* For example, when America got its independence from England, it was able to achieve *statehood,* to become a *state,* which is another word for becoming a *country.*

16–C   The suffix *ism* refers to the *belief,* or *practice* of something, so *vegetarianism* means the *belief in the practice of eating no meats,* the belief in the health benefits of eating foods derived from vegetables—in other words, the belief in being a *vegetarian.*

17–C   The word *dawn* refers to early morning when the sun is rising, and the prefix *pre* means *before,* or *earlier than.* Therefore, *predawn* means *before daybreak,* or before sunrise. The sentence states that his early rising habits disturbed and tired his roommate.

18–B   An *amateur* is a nonprofessional, a beginner, not an expert in a particular skill. The suffix *ish* means *a bit like,* so *amateurish* means *like a beginner,* in a nonprofessional way, without expertise. For example, *he pitched the baseball in an amateurish way* means he pitched *like a beginner,* not like a pro.

19–D   The root *clude* means to *close* or *shut,* so *exclude* means to *shut out,* reject, ban, or bar. For example, if the youngsters were *excluded* from the family wedding, it means they were unable to attend, they were not invited, they were *shut out* of the wedding.

20–A   The prefix *bio* means *life,* or *living things,* and the suffix *logy* means the *study of,* so *biology* means the *study of living things.*

THREE SAMPLE WORD KNOWLEDGE TESTS

This section contains three full-length sample Word Knowledge Tests that are similar to the ones on the ASVAB. Tear out this page and use the answer strips below to record your answers to the sample tests, just as you will have to do on the real test. Stick to the time limit so your practice is realistic. After you finish each sample test, check your answers against the Answer Key and Explanations that follow.

Word Knowledge Test 1

1. Ⓐ Ⓑ Ⓒ Ⓓ   2. Ⓐ Ⓑ Ⓒ Ⓓ   3. Ⓐ Ⓑ Ⓒ Ⓓ   4. Ⓐ Ⓑ Ⓒ Ⓓ   5. Ⓐ Ⓑ Ⓒ Ⓓ
6. Ⓐ Ⓑ Ⓒ Ⓓ   7. Ⓐ Ⓑ Ⓒ Ⓓ   8. Ⓐ Ⓑ Ⓒ Ⓓ   9. Ⓐ Ⓑ Ⓒ Ⓓ   10. Ⓐ Ⓑ Ⓒ Ⓓ
11. Ⓐ Ⓑ Ⓒ Ⓓ   12. Ⓐ Ⓑ Ⓒ Ⓓ   13. Ⓐ Ⓑ Ⓒ Ⓓ   14. Ⓐ Ⓑ Ⓒ Ⓓ   15. Ⓐ Ⓑ Ⓒ Ⓓ
16. Ⓐ Ⓑ Ⓒ Ⓓ   17. Ⓐ Ⓑ Ⓒ Ⓓ   18. Ⓐ Ⓑ Ⓒ Ⓓ   19. Ⓐ Ⓑ Ⓒ Ⓓ   20. Ⓐ Ⓑ Ⓒ Ⓓ
21. Ⓐ Ⓑ Ⓒ Ⓓ   22. Ⓐ Ⓑ Ⓒ Ⓓ   23. Ⓐ Ⓑ Ⓒ Ⓓ   24. Ⓐ Ⓑ Ⓒ Ⓓ   25. Ⓐ Ⓑ Ⓒ Ⓓ
26. Ⓐ Ⓑ Ⓒ Ⓓ   27. Ⓐ Ⓑ Ⓒ Ⓓ   28. Ⓐ Ⓑ Ⓒ Ⓓ   29. Ⓐ Ⓑ Ⓒ Ⓓ   30. Ⓐ Ⓑ Ⓒ Ⓓ
31. Ⓐ Ⓑ Ⓒ Ⓓ   32. Ⓐ Ⓑ Ⓒ Ⓓ   33. Ⓐ Ⓑ Ⓒ Ⓓ   34. Ⓐ Ⓑ Ⓒ Ⓓ   35. Ⓐ Ⓑ Ⓒ Ⓓ

Word Knowledge Test 2

1. Ⓐ Ⓑ Ⓒ Ⓓ   2. Ⓐ Ⓑ Ⓒ Ⓓ   3. Ⓐ Ⓑ Ⓒ Ⓓ   4. Ⓐ Ⓑ Ⓒ Ⓓ   5. Ⓐ Ⓑ Ⓒ Ⓓ
6. Ⓐ Ⓑ Ⓒ Ⓓ   7. Ⓐ Ⓑ Ⓒ Ⓓ   8. Ⓐ Ⓑ Ⓒ Ⓓ   9. Ⓐ Ⓑ Ⓒ Ⓓ   10. Ⓐ Ⓑ Ⓒ Ⓓ
11. Ⓐ Ⓑ Ⓒ Ⓓ   12. Ⓐ Ⓑ Ⓒ Ⓓ   13. Ⓐ Ⓑ Ⓒ Ⓓ   14. Ⓐ Ⓑ Ⓒ Ⓓ   15. Ⓐ Ⓑ Ⓒ Ⓓ
16. Ⓐ Ⓑ Ⓒ Ⓓ   17. Ⓐ Ⓑ Ⓒ Ⓓ   18. Ⓐ Ⓑ Ⓒ Ⓓ   19. Ⓐ Ⓑ Ⓒ Ⓓ   20. Ⓐ Ⓑ Ⓒ Ⓓ
21. Ⓐ Ⓑ Ⓒ Ⓓ   22. Ⓐ Ⓑ Ⓒ Ⓓ   23. Ⓐ Ⓑ Ⓒ Ⓓ   24. Ⓐ Ⓑ Ⓒ Ⓓ   25. Ⓐ Ⓑ Ⓒ Ⓓ
26. Ⓐ Ⓑ Ⓒ Ⓓ   27. Ⓐ Ⓑ Ⓒ Ⓓ   28. Ⓐ Ⓑ Ⓒ Ⓓ   29. Ⓐ Ⓑ Ⓒ Ⓓ   30. Ⓐ Ⓑ Ⓒ Ⓓ
31. Ⓐ Ⓑ Ⓒ Ⓓ   32. Ⓐ Ⓑ Ⓒ Ⓓ   33. Ⓐ Ⓑ Ⓒ Ⓓ   34. Ⓐ Ⓑ Ⓒ Ⓓ   35. Ⓐ Ⓑ Ⓒ Ⓓ

Word Knowledge Test 3

1. Ⓐ Ⓑ Ⓒ Ⓓ   2. Ⓐ Ⓑ Ⓒ Ⓓ   3. Ⓐ Ⓑ Ⓒ Ⓓ   4. Ⓐ Ⓑ Ⓒ Ⓓ   5. Ⓐ Ⓑ Ⓒ Ⓓ
6. Ⓐ Ⓑ Ⓒ Ⓓ   7. Ⓐ Ⓑ Ⓒ Ⓓ   8. Ⓐ Ⓑ Ⓒ Ⓓ   9. Ⓐ Ⓑ Ⓒ Ⓓ   10. Ⓐ Ⓑ Ⓒ Ⓓ
11. Ⓐ Ⓑ Ⓒ Ⓓ   12. Ⓐ Ⓑ Ⓒ Ⓓ   13. Ⓐ Ⓑ Ⓒ Ⓓ   14. Ⓐ Ⓑ Ⓒ Ⓓ   15. Ⓐ Ⓑ Ⓒ Ⓓ
16. Ⓐ Ⓑ Ⓒ Ⓓ   17. Ⓐ Ⓑ Ⓒ Ⓓ   18. Ⓐ Ⓑ Ⓒ Ⓓ   19. Ⓐ Ⓑ Ⓒ Ⓓ   20. Ⓐ Ⓑ Ⓒ Ⓓ
21. Ⓐ Ⓑ Ⓒ Ⓓ   22. Ⓐ Ⓑ Ⓒ Ⓓ   23. Ⓐ Ⓑ Ⓒ Ⓓ   24. Ⓐ Ⓑ Ⓒ Ⓓ   25. Ⓐ Ⓑ Ⓒ Ⓓ
26. Ⓐ Ⓑ Ⓒ Ⓓ   27. Ⓐ Ⓑ Ⓒ Ⓓ   28. Ⓐ Ⓑ Ⓒ Ⓓ   29. Ⓐ Ⓑ Ⓒ Ⓓ   30. Ⓐ Ⓑ Ⓒ Ⓓ
31. Ⓐ Ⓑ Ⓒ Ⓓ   32. Ⓐ Ⓑ Ⓒ Ⓓ   33. Ⓐ Ⓑ Ⓒ Ⓓ   34. Ⓐ Ⓑ Ⓒ Ⓓ   35. Ⓐ Ⓑ Ⓒ Ⓓ

WORD KNOWLEDGE TEST 1

TIME: 11 Minutes—35 Questions

This test has 35 questions about the meanings of words. Each question has an underlined word. You are to decide which one of the four choices is *closest in meaning* to the underlined word. Then mark the space on your answer form that has the same number and letter as your choice.

Your score on this test will be based on the number of questions you answer correctly. You should try to answer every question. Do not spend too much time on any one question.

1. Flatter most nearly means
   - 1–A   praise excessively
   - 1–B   fly away
   - 1–C   weave into rope
   - 1–D   beg

2. Because of his secretive nature, he was unable to impart the information.
   - 2–A   sell
   - 2–B   limit
   - 2–C   disclose
   - 2–D   sing

3. Ragged most nearly means
   - 3–A   prearranged
   - 3–B   settled
   - 3–C   musical
   - 3–D   torn

4. He had a valid driver's license.
   - 4–A   legal
   - 4–B   chauffeur
   - 4–C   continuous
   - 4–D   temporary

5. Bewildered most nearly means
   - 5–A   argued
   - 5–B   unsettled
   - 5–C   confused
   - 5–D   fumed

6. Obligation most nearly means
   - 6–A   tall structure
   - 6–B   duty
   - 6–C   fulfillment
   - 6–D   need

7. Relentless most nearly means
   - 7–A   forgiving
   - 7–B   grateful
   - 7–C   sinister
   - 7–D   persistent

8. Only a cruel person will abandon a helpless puppy.
   - 8–A   play
   - 8–B   urge
   - 8–C   beckon
   - 8–D   desert

9. The birds migrated south in winter.
   - 9–A   ate
   - 9–B   chirped
   - 9–C   sowed
   - 9–D   moved

10. The quarterly magazine was about science and technology.
    - 10–A   twice per year
    - 10–B   tri-monthly
    - 10–C   cut into fifths
    - 10–D   yearly

11. <u>Unusual</u> most nearly means
    11–A   rare
    11–B   dull
    11–C   marked
    11–D   frequent

12. <u>Backlash</u> most nearly means
    12–A   repercussion
    12–B   swelling
    12–C   helpfulness
    12–D   whipping

13. It is impossible to accurately <u>predict</u> the direction of a hurricane.
    13–A   refuse to say
    13–B   tell in advance
    13–C   guess
    13–D   predominate

14. Joe Louis <u>dominated</u> heavyweight boxing for many years.
    14–A   refused
    14–B   lessened
    14–C   ruled
    14–D   obliged

15. <u>Diverse</u> most nearly means
    15–A   thin
    15–B   spread out
    15–C   natural
    15–D   varied

16. <u>Sabotage</u> most nearly means
    16–A   secret airlift
    16–B   deliberate destruction
    16–C   old sailboat
    16–D   valuable antique

17. An <u>informal</u> meeting was held at lunch.
    17–A   casual
    17–B   light
    17–C   colorful
    17–D   noisy

18. <u>Comical</u> most nearly means
    18–A   clever
    18–B   shaped like a cone
    18–C   funny
    18–D   healthy

19. They were <u>unable</u> to lift the refrigerator.
    19–A   incapable
    19–B   unstoppable
    19–C   helpful
    19–D   unhappy

20. <u>Lament</u> most nearly means
    20–A   pray
    20–B   grieve
    20–C   bind
    20–D   sweeten

21. <u>Throng</u> most nearly means
    21–A   sandal
    21–B   crowd
    21–C   burden
    21–D   strap

22. No one was injured in the <u>scuffle</u>.
    22–A   bombing
    22–B   rush
    22–C   fistfight
    22–D   strife

23. The police will <u>ensure</u> your safety on your trip home.
    23–A   drive
    23–B   guarantee
    23–C   see
    23–D   sustain

24. <u>Glare</u> most nearly means
    24–A   harsh light
    24–B   sticky surface
    24–C   famous man
    24–D   brightness

25. <u>Omnipotent</u> most nearly means
- 25–A   insignificant
- 25–B   all powerful
- 25–C   loudly heard
- 25–D   printed

26. <u>Consume</u> most nearly means
- 26–A   prepare
- 26–B   authorize
- 26–C   use up
- 26–D   storm

27. Her voice was <u>hoarse</u> from yelling.
- 27–A   rough
- 27–B   distant
- 27–C   widespread
- 27–D   tremendous

28. The soldiers did not <u>realize</u> the seriousness of the opposition.
- 28–A   believe
- 28–B   begin to criticize
- 28–C   become aware of
- 28–D   state clearly

29. <u>Tenant</u> most nearly means
- 29–A   occupant
- 29–B   landlord
- 29–C   owner
- 29–D   caretaker

30. <u>Portion</u> most nearly means
- 30–A   medicine
- 30–B   share
- 30–C   half
- 30–D   berth

31. <u>Deceased</u> most nearly means
- 31–A   stated
- 31–B   lessened
- 31–C   dead
- 31–D   picked

32. <u>Nick</u> most nearly means
- 32–A   loud bang
- 32–B   surgeon's tool
- 32–C   deep gash
- 32–D   small cut

33. <u>Thrifty</u> most nearly means
- 33–A   banking
- 33–B   frugal
- 33–C   miserable
- 33–D   new

34. The tiger <u>mangled</u> its prey beyond recognition.
- 34–A   mutilated
- 34–B   devoured
- 34–C   enjoyed
- 34–D   showed

35. <u>Particle</u> most nearly means
- 35–A   large section
- 35–B   tiny fragment
- 35–C   large planet
- 35–D   unnecessary fuss

Answer Key

1. A	2. C	3. D	4. A	5. C
6. B	7. D	8. D	9. D	10. B
11. A	12. A	13. B	14. C	15. D
16. B	17. A	18. C	19. A	20. B
21. B	22. D	23. B	24. A	25. B
26. C	27. A	28. C	29. A	30. B
31. C	32. D	33. B	34. A	35. B

Answers and Explanations

1–A   To *flatter* someone is to *praise* him or her *excessively*, to give more praise than the person deserves. Often *flattering* is done with some other purpose in mind, as in wanting something from the person being *flattered*.

2–C   To *impart* something is to *disclose,* share, give, convey, communicate, or grant it. In this sentence, he was too secretive, too private a person to *impart,* or give out, the information to others.

3–D   Something that is *ragged* is roughly unkempt, *torn,* or worn and in tatters. For example, a child's favorite doll becomes *ragged*-looking with time and use.

4–A   A *valid* driver's license is one that is *legal.* The word *valid* can also refer to something being sound, well grounded, accurate, correct, and legitimate. A counterfeit ID is not a *valid* form of identification, for example, but a school ID is.

5–C   To be *bewildered* means to feel *confused*, perplexed, confounded, disconcerted, puzzled, or to lose one bearings. For example, the child felt *bewildered* by the many Christmas presents he received—in other words, he was *confused* and distracted by all the nice choices of gifts.

6–B   The word *obligation* refers to *duty,* responsibility, burden, or debt. For example, a soldier has the *obligation,* or the responsibility, to fulfill his *duty,* or the tasks that he has been assigned.

7–D   Something that is *relentless* is *persistent,* unyielding, or unmerciful. A *relentless* hurricane is one that shows no signs of stopping—it keeps going in intensity, strength, and duration. A *relentlessly* crying child is one who keeps on crying and doesn't stop.

8–D   To *abandon* a puppy is to *desert* it, to turn your back on it. To *abandon* something means that you are not only leaving it, but walking away from your responsibility to take care of it.

9–D   The context clues here are *birds* and *south*, indicating that *migrated* means *moved,* or relocated, to a different part of the world. Birds *migrate* from one climate to another in order to find food, reproduce, and raise their young.

10–B   A *quarterly* magazine is one that comes out four times a year. Since there are twelve months per year, that means *tri-monthly,* or every three months. Also, to *quarter* something is to divide it into quarters, or four parts.

11–A   The prefix *un* means *not,* so *unusual* means not usual, *rare,* or uncommon. *Unusually* cold weather means the weather is colder than usual, or not as warm as usual.

12–A   A *backlash* refers to a sudden violent backward movement, or reaction, or a *repercussion.* A strong negative reaction by the public to a political or social development is often called a *backlash.* For example, if the government raises taxes too much, there is often a *backlash,* or *repercussion,* from the voters, who will protest or vote to show their anger.

13–B   The prefix *pre* means *before,* or *earlier than,* and the root *dict* means *to say,* as in *diction,* so *predict* means to *tell* or *forecast* an event before it has occurred. The sentence also gives you some context clues—*impossible* and *direction.* The word *predict* means *tell in advance,* foretell, forecast, prognosticate.

14–C To *dominate* something means to *rule* it, control it, be on top of it, to exert the most important influence on it. Joe Louis was so important to boxing that he set the standard and *dominated* the sport.

15–D *Diverse* means *varied,* differing from one another, and being unlike in some important qualities. The residents of major cities like New York, for example, are of *diverse* backgrounds—there are all kinds of people in this city, so New York can be described as an international and *diversified* city.

16–B To *sabotage* something means to cause *deliberate destruction* of someone else's property, or to purposely hinder a project. Some workers who are dissatisfied have been known to *sabotage* their company by destroying property or preventing work from being done successfully.

17–A The prefix *in* means *not,* so *informal* means *not formal,* or *casual.* Something that is *informal* is often spontaneous, not planned, ordinary, *casual,* or easy. An *informal* lunch means the participants don't have to be dressed up and can be relaxed in their behavior.

18–C Something that is *comical* is *funny.* It is related to *comedy* and refers to something humorous that causes laughter. Related words are *comic* and *comic book.* Choice B refers to *conical,* which means *shaped like a cone.*

19–A The prefix *un* means *not,* so *unable* means *not able,* or *incapable.* The refrigerator was probably too heavy, so the men were *unable,* or *incapable,* of lifting it.

20–B To *lament* means to *grieve,* wail, or complain loudly. Related words are *lamentable,* meaning deplorable or regrettable, and *lamentation,* which refers to an act of *lamenting.* Also, in religious scripture, there is a poetic book on the fall of Jerusalem, called *Lamentations.*

21–B A *throng* is a large *crowd* of people, as in *crowding* together of a multitude, or *throng* of people.

22–D A *scuffle* is a minor confrontation, a short fight, *strife,* or struggle. Choice C is incorrect, because a fistfight is a more serious event than a *scuffle.*

23–B The words *ensure, assure,* and *insure* all mean making certain beforehand, taking necessary measures beforehand, making sure of something, or the removing of doubt from a person's mind. The police are *ensuring,* or *guaranteeing,* the person's safety.

24–A A *glare* is a *harsh light*—in other words, a light that is uncomfortably bright. For example, when you drive at night, oncoming cars can cause a *glare,* making it hard to see the road. A *glare* also sometimes means an angry or fierce look on someone's face.

25–B The prefix *omni* means *all,* and *potent* means *powerful,* so *omnipotent* means *all powerful.* In many religions, God is commonly referred to as being *omnipotent,* or having no limits to power.

26–C To *consume* is to *use up,* wear out, eat up, destroy, squander, destroy, or do away with completely. A bad fire can *consume* an entire forest. A hungry person will *consume* a huge meal. A hard and demanding job will *consume* a person's energies.

27–A A *hoarse* voice is one that is *rough,* or harsh and grating—in other words, one that has become unnatural and unpleasant as a result of too much use.

28–C When you *realize* something you are *aware of,* understand, perceive, or are conscious of it. To *realize* something also means to accomplish it, make good on it, or complete it, as in *realizing* an ambition.

29–A   A *tenant* is someone who temporarily *occupies* a piece of real estate, which he rents or leases from a landlord for a fee.

30–B   A *portion* is a person's part or *share* of something, like a person's fair share of an inheritance, for example. A pie gets cut into eight equal *portions* at the dinner table to give each person a fair *share*. Don't be fooled by choice A, *medicine*, which refers to the word *potion*, or a medicine in liquid form.

31–C   A *deceased* person has departed from life, ceased to exist, is no longer living, and is *dead*.

32–D   When you get a *nick* on your finger, you've gotten a *small cut*. The word *nick* is also a verb with the same meaning—indent, notch, slit, cut yourself a bit. A *nick* is a small wound, not as serious as a *deep gash*, choice C.

33–B   To be *thrifty* means to be very careful with your money, to spend it sparingly or in a *frugal* manner. It means that you tend to be economical and manage your money wisely.

34–A   *Mangled* means *mutilated*, torn apart, maimed, disfigured, butchered, or sliced up. To *mangle* something is to injure it with deep disfiguring wounds, like a shark attacking a person in the water, for example. The sentence tells you that the tiger *mangled* its prey, or victim, so badly that it no longer looked the same.

35–B   A *particle* is a very small quantity, a *tiny fragment*. It refers to the smallest portion or amount of something. Any of the basic units of matter and energy, such as a molecule, atom, proton, electron, or photon, are examples of *particles*.

WORD KNOWLEDGE TEST 2

TIME: 11 Minutes—35 Questions

This test has 35 questions about the meanings of words. Each question has an underlined word. You are to decide which one of the four choices is *closest in meaning* to the underlined word. Then mark the space on your answer form that has the same number and letter as your choice.

Your score on this test will be based on the number of questions you answer correctly. You should try to answer every question. Do not spend too much time on any one question.

1. <u>Captive</u> most nearly means
    1–A   clipped
    1–B   quiet
    1–C   confined
    1–D   exchange

2. The hurricane created a <u>disaster</u> the town could not recover from.
    2–A   injury
    2–B   calamity
    2–C   sickness
    2–D   fortune

3. <u>Offspring</u> most nearly means
   - 3–A   child
   - 3–B   parent
   - 3–C   plant
   - 3–D   mattress

4. His <u>blunder</u> cost him his promotion.
   - 4–A   stammer
   - 4–B   careless mistake
   - 4–C   spiteful behavior
   - 4–D   blindness

5. <u>Merchant</u> most nearly means
   - 5–A   advertiser
   - 5–B   shipbuilder
   - 5–C   captain
   - 5–D   storekeeper

6. <u>Abbreviate</u> most nearly means
   - 6–A   step down
   - 6–B   worsen
   - 6–C   shorten
   - 6–D   help

7. He showed his <u>defiance</u> by refusing to participate.
   - 7–A   fighting skills
   - 7–B   poor manners
   - 7–C   absurd tastes
   - 7–D   disposition to resist

8. Her <u>witty</u> remarks livened up the dull party.
   - 8–A   serious and informative
   - 8–B   amusingly clever
   - 8–C   sentimental and nostalgic
   - 8–D   insensitive and insulting

9. <u>Grapple</u> most nearly means
   - 9–A   drink
   - 9–B   tackle
   - 9–C   provide
   - 9–D   confuse

10. <u>Salvage</u> most nearly means
    - 10–A   save
    - 10–B   criticize
    - 10–C   water
    - 10–D   throw out

11. <u>Aggravate</u> most nearly means
    - 11–A   grumble
    - 11–B   gather
    - 11–C   worsen
    - 11–D   spread

12. It was <u>futile</u> for the employee to argue.
    - 12–A   helpful
    - 12–B   nervous
    - 12–C   spirited
    - 12–D   useless

13. The captain was able to <u>rally</u> his men and defeat the enemy.
    - 13–A   race ahead
    - 13–B   pay off
    - 13–C   renew strength
    - 13–D   call loudly

14. <u>Uproar</u> most nearly means
    - 14–A   upstart
    - 14–B   tornado
    - 14–C   downdraft
    - 14–D   commotion

15. <u>Commence</u> most nearly means
    - 15–A   move
    - 15–B   begin
    - 15–C   end
    - 15–D   remain

16. <u>Tactics</u> most nearly means
    - 16–A   followers
    - 16–B   strategy
    - 16–C   cleverness
    - 16–D   staples

17. The <u>abundant</u> rainfall made the crops grow tall.

    17–A   surplus

    17–B   overwhelming

    17–C   stored

    17–D   plentiful

18. <u>Backward</u> most nearly means

    18–A   up front

    18–B   sidesaddle

    18–C   reverse direction

    18–D   lined up

19. He was relieved to have <u>recovered</u> his lost wallet.

    19–A   retrieved

    19–B   spoken

    19–C   advised

    19–D   complained

20. <u>Waver</u> most nearly means

    20–A   dance

    20–B   curve

    20–C   hesitate

    20–D   combine

21. <u>Haggard</u> most nearly means

    21–A   bent over

    21–B   elderly

    21–C   professional

    21–D   gaunt

22. <u>Wary</u> most nearly means

    22–A   strange

    22–B   cautious

    22–C   tired

    22–D   thin

23. <u>Autopilot</u> most nearly means

    23–A   one driver

    23–B   jet plane

    23–C   self-steering

    23–D   stop and start

24. Math is a required course in high school, not an <u>elective</u>.

    24–A   optional subject

    24–B   difficult area

    24–C   freshman class

    24–D   final test

25. <u>Questionable</u> most nearly means

    25–A   respectable

    25–B   doubtful

    25–C   probable

    25–D   helpful

26. <u>Earmark</u> most nearly means

    26–A   hear of

    26–B   tick loudly

    26–C   bother

    26–D   set aside

27. <u>Mammoth</u> most nearly means

    27–A   camel-like

    27–B   small

    27–C   mocking

    27–D   gigantic

28. His sudden <u>lapse</u> in manners surprised everyone.

    28–A   drop

    28–B   surprise

    28–C   error

    28–D   silliness

29. The troops will stay for the <u>duration</u> of the war.

    29–A   length

    29–B   brightness

    29–C   spell

    29–D   battle

30. The horse <u>plodded</u> up the hill.

    30–A   snorted

    30–B   trudged

    30–C   slowed

    30–D   ran

31. <u>Limit</u> most nearly means
    31–A   small bit
    31–B   any amount
    31–C   maximum quantity
    31–D   unclear direction

32. <u>Hasten</u> most nearly means
    32–A   speed up
    32–B   uncover
    32–C   clasp
    32–D   confuse

33. <u>Nonresident</u> most nearly means
    33–A   occupying
    33–B   passing through
    33–C   not included
    33–D   not inhabiting

34. The game's <u>outcome</u> was decided in the final minute.
    34–A   ejection
    34–B   result
    34–C   postponement
    34–D   celebration

35. <u>Infect</u> most nearly means
    35–A   bounce off
    35–B   wash hands
    35–C   contaminate with disease
    35–D   injure carelessly

Answer Key

1. C	2. B	3. A	4. B	5. D
6. C	7. D	8. B	9. B	10. A
11. C	12. D	13. C	14. D	15. B
16. B	17. D	18. C	19. A	20. C
21. D	22. B	23. C	24. A	25. B
26. D	27. D	28. C	29. A	30. B
31. C	32. A	33. D	34. B	35. C

Answers and Explanations

1–C   To be *captive* means to be confined against one's will, locked up, or a *prisoner*. It refers to someone being held under the control of another, or having lost his/her independence.

2–B   A *disaster* like a hurricane is a *calamity,* or a sudden terrible event that brings very serious damage, loss, or destruction. It is a sudden or great misfortune or catastrophe.

3–A   An *offspring* is the youngster, *child*, product, offshoot, or result of something. It refers to someone or something that you produce or create.

4–B   To make a *blunder* means to make a *careless mistake,* usually through stupidity, ignorance, or thoughtlessness. A *blunder* can be serious or not, but it is not done purposely, so choice C, *spiteful behavior,* is incorrect.

5–D   A *merchant* is someone who buys, sells, or trades items. If he does this in a store, he is called a *storekeeper.*

6–C   To *abbreviate* something is to *shorten* it, to make it briefer, to abridge it, or reduce it to a shorter form intended to stand for the whole. For example, you can shorten *Mister* to *Mr.,* which then is called an *abbreviation*.

7–D   When someone shows *defiance* he is challenging authority, displaying his *disposition to resist,* or his tendency to not go along with those in command. The American colonists, for example, showed *defiance* of their English rulers by declaring their independence and fighting a war.

8–B   In this question, context clues can help you figure out the answer. The words *livened up* tell you that *witty* probably means *amusingly clever.* Only an amusing and clever person would *liven up a dull party.*

9–B   To *grapple* with something is to *tackle* it, to come to grips with it. For example, the math student *grappled* the difficult calculus question, he *tackled* it. A hand-to-hand struggle is also called a *grapple.*

10–A   The word *salvage* means *save,* retrieve, recover, or regain. To *salvage* something is to rescue or save it, especially from wreckage or ruin. The act of saving or rescuing a ship or its cargo from a storm, or saving property from destruction in a calamity such as a wreck or a fire, or extracting something from rubbish that might be useful or valuable, is also called *salvage.*

11–C   When you *aggravate* something, you *worsen it*—you make it more serious, more severe, and you intensify it unpleasantly. A serious problem, like a bad relationship, can get *aggravated,* or *worsen,* if you neglect it. An injury can get *aggravated* if you scratch it.

12–D   Something that is *futile* serves no useful purpose; is *useless,* ineffective, fruitless, or produces no results; or can't be done. For example, it is *futile* to try to change the inborn personality of a child.

13–C   From the context clue words, which are *defeat the enemy,* you can guess that the meaning of *rally* is *renew strength.* The captain was able to *rally* his men, to summon up their strength and courage after a period of weakness. A losing basketball team may *rally* in the final minutes of a game and win. A *rally* is a sudden and unexpected show of strength or courage.

14–D   An *uproar* is a state of *commotion,* excitement, confusion, turmoil, hassle, racket, or violent disturbance. A chaotic clamor is an *uproar.* For example, the class broke out in an *uproar* when the teacher announced that everyone had failed the final exam. Or, the crowd was in an *uproar* when the rock star failed to appear.

15–B   To *commence* is to *begin,* or start. The best-known related word is *commencement,* which refers to the ceremonies celebrating graduation, and means the *beginning* or the onset of a young adult's life.

16–B   *Tactic* refers to the *strategy,* maneuver, plan of attack, procedure, or approach of getting something accomplished. For example, the science and art of using military forces in combat is referred to as the *tactics* of war. The small actions that will serve a larger purpose, the *means to an end,* are also called the *tactics.*

17–D   The context words that give you the clue about the meaning of *abundant* are *grow tall.* In the logic of this sentence, only the word *plentiful* makes sense—because there was *plentiful* or enough rainfall, the crops were able to grow well. *Abundant* means ample, rich in, and *plentiful.*

18–C To have something *backward* is to have it in a *reverse direction,* towards the back, or with the back in front. The opposite of *backward* is *forward.* Sitting *backward* means you are facing back, not forward. Also, someone who is slow in developing skills is sometimes referred to as being *backward.*

19–A In this sentence, *recovered* means *retrieved,* found, regained, or reclaimed. The man *found* his wallet again, he *recovered* it after it had been lost. The word *recovered* can also mean having gotten better after an illness—a man with a bad heart *recovered* his strength after getting proper care.

20–C To *waver* means to *hesitate,* vacillate, dillydally, or hem and haw. When you are unsure of your next step, you *waver,* you stop and think before going on. When a person is lost in the forest, for example, he or she might *waver* or *hesitate* before deciding which way to walk. In answering a difficult test question, the student will *waver* before picking an answer.

21–D A *haggard* appearance refers to someone who is *gaunt,* tired or sickly looking, worn or emaciated in appearance. A person who has worked 18 hours in a row and not eaten regularly may have a *haggard* appearance. Homeless people often have a *gaunt,* thin, tired, or *haggard* look.

22–B To be *wary* of something means to approach it in a *cautious* manner. It means to be very careful, alert, guarded, a bit suspicious, especially in the face of possible danger. For example, shy children are *wary* of strangers. A guard dog is *wary* of strange noises or unfamiliar people.

23–C The prefix *auto* means *self,* so *autopilot* means *self-steering,* or self-driving. An *autopilot* is a device for automatically steering ships, aircraft, and spacecraft—eliminating the need for a live pilot to drive the vehicle.

24–A A class in school that you can take if you want to is called an *elective,* or *optional subject.* An *elective may* be taken but is *not required* for graduation. It is *optional.* The word *elective* also relates to political *elections,* as in an *elected* official.

25–B The suffix *able* means *capable* of, so *questionable* means something to be questioned, *doubtful* about, suspicious-sounding, inviting inquiry, or something that is uncertain and not totally logical. The soldier's *questionable* excuses for being AWOL, for example, will not satisfy his superiors, will be viewed *doubtfully,* or as not above suspicion.

26–D When you *earmark* something, you *set it aside.* For example, when a company *earmarks* funds for its pension system, the funds cannot be used for other purposes, only for pensions. Or, if a contract is *earmarked* for Company A, it cannot be given to Company B.

27–D *Mammoth* means of very great size, enormous, or *gigantic.* A *mammoth* is also the name of a very large extinct animal that is related to present-day elephants.

28–C A *lapse* refers to a slight *error,* usually due to forgetfulness, lack of attention, or an interruption. A *lapse* in manners means that the person's normally good manners changed temporarily, that he made a mistake he normally would not be expected to make. Also, if you don't pay your car insurance, your coverage will *lapse,* be interrupted, or be ended.

29–A The *duration* of something is the *length* of it, the time during which something exists or lasts—in this sentence, the *length,* or *duration,* of the war. A related well-known word is *during,* which means at a point in the course of something, like being in the war *during* the conflict, or while the conflict was going on.

30–B To *plod* means to *trudge,* or move heavily, slowly, and with great effort, to proceed slowly or tediously. To *plod* is also used in other contexts to mean *working laboriously and monotonously,* as in the *drudge plodded through the assignment with little enthusiasm or interest.*

31–C The *limit* of something is the outer boundary, the *maximum quantity,* farthest reach, extremity, or the end. For example, there is no *limit* or *maximum amount* of money a social security recipient may earn after the age of 65. You may not legally stay longer than 6 months at a stretch in most foreign countries—that is the *limit.*

32–A *Hasten* means to move or act quickly, accelerate, or *speed up.* People who are always late to work need to make *haste,* need to *speed up,* in order to be more prompt.

33–D The prefix *non* means *not,* and a *resident* is someone who lives or occupies a place. Therefore, *nonresident* means *not inhabiting,* or not living in a particular residence or place.

34–B The *outcome* is the *result,* upshot, consequence, end, or final event.

35–C To *infect* is to *contaminate with disease.* Bacteria can harm people by *infecting* them, by causing an *infection,* by spreading within their bodies and making them ill.

WORD KNOWLEDGE TEST 3

TIME: 11 Minutes—35 Questions

This test has 35 questions about the meanings of words. Each question has an underlined word. You are to decide which one of the four choices is *closest in meaning* to the underlined word. Then mark the space on your answer form that has the same number and letter as your choice.

Your score on this test will be based on the number of questions you answer correctly. You should try to answer every question. Do not spend too much time on any one question.

1. Delete most nearly means
   1–A   postpone
   1–B   print
   1–C   erase
   1–D   strike

2. Celestial most nearly means
   2–A   heavenly
   2–B   revolving
   2–C   strengthened
   2–D   meteoric

3. Matrimony most nearly means
   3–A   system
   3–B   marriage
   3–C   measurement
   3–D   friendship

4. Abolish most nearly means
   4–A   sign
   4–B   curse
   4–C   hurl
   4–D   repeal

5. The child <u>hesitated</u> before entering his new classroom.
   - 5–A   hid
   - 5–B   raced
   - 5–C   paused
   - 5–D   hiccupped

6. The house was built on the <u>brink</u> of the cliff.
   - 6–A   crack
   - 6–B   bottom
   - 6–C   ice
   - 6–D   edge

7. The birds <u>flitted</u> from one feeder to another.
   - 7–A   moved rapidly
   - 7–B   ate
   - 7–C   jumped
   - 7–D   landed

8. The high jumper <u>misjudged</u> the bar.
   - 8–A   raised
   - 8–B   lowered
   - 8–C   wrongly estimated
   - 8–D   took off

9. <u>Solitude</u> most nearly means
   - 9–A   crowd
   - 9–B   isolation
   - 9–C   solidity
   - 9–D   solemnity

10. The slippery snake was able to <u>elude</u> being put into the cage.
    - 10–A   evade
    - 10–B   emanate
    - 10–C   slip
    - 10–D   smell

11. <u>Huddle</u> most nearly means
    - 11–A   limp
    - 11–B   crouch
    - 11–C   mourn
    - 11–D   pray

12. <u>Secede</u> most nearly means
    - 12–A   postpone
    - 12–B   scrub
    - 12–C   steal
    - 12–D   withdraw

13. <u>Vaccinate</u> most nearly means
    - 13–A   inoculate
    - 13–B   infect
    - 13–C   prevent
    - 13–D   sting

14. He <u>excelled</u> at repairing small engines.
    - 14–A   yelled
    - 14–B   was superior
    - 14–C   balked
    - 14–D   worked hard

15. <u>Ominous</u> clouds came before the storm.
    - 15–A   heavy
    - 15–B   raining
    - 15–C   threatening
    - 15–D   huge

16. <u>Canyon</u> most nearly means
    - 16–A   rock
    - 16–B   mountain
    - 16–C   valley
    - 16–D   summit

17. <u>Ventilate</u> most nearly means
    - 17–A   capsize
    - 17–B   air out
    - 17–C   excite
    - 17–D   fly over

18. <u>Qualified</u> most nearly means
    - 18–A   helped
    - 18–B   quarreled
    - 18–C   busied
    - 18–D   competent

19. Conspiracy most nearly means
    19–A   plot
    19–B   convention
    19–C   trouble
    19–D   constitution

20. He prepaid the loan two months early.
    20–A   billed incorrectly
    20–B   delayed
    20–C   paid in advance
    20–D   stamped

21. The water fountain was accessible to everyone.
    21–A   essential
    21–B   available
    21–C   huggable
    21–D   avoidable

22. Duplicate most nearly means
    22–A   sweep
    22–B   serve
    22–C   storm
    22–D   copy

23. Implicate most nearly means
    23–A   trouble
    23–B   involve
    23–C   calm
    23–D   confuse

24. Gyrate most nearly means
    24–A   whirl
    24–B   bake
    24–C   carry
    24–D   weigh

25. Literate most nearly means
    25–A   wounded
    25–B   cut
    25–C   educated
    25–D   operated

26. Hangar most nearly means
    26–A   shed
    26–B   foreigner
    26–C   weapon
    26–D   intelligence

27. Dazzle most nearly means
    27–A   encircle
    27–B   shine brilliantly
    27–C   hose down
    27–D   foam

28. Food in most states is nontaxable.
    28–A   taxed lightly
    28–B   free
    28–C   exported abroad
    28–D   not taxable

29. Glacial most nearly means
    29–A   archaeological
    29–B   frigid
    29–C   showy
    29–D   huge

30. Not getting into college was a profound disappointment.
    30–A   expected
    30–B   programmed
    30–C   deep
    30–D   intellectual

31. Javelin most nearly means
    31–A   spear
    31–B   calm
    31–C   gown
    31–D   marmalade

32. A flamingo gracefully walked out of the water.
    32–A   prejudice
    32–B   hot food
    32–C   aquatic bird
    32–D   false friend

33. The sound of their laughter made it <u>evident</u> that the children had arrived home safely.

   33–A   postponed

   33–B   criminal

   33–C   promoted

   33–D   obvious

34. <u>Heave</u> most nearly means

   34–A   lift up

   34–B   shout at

   34–C   crumble

   34–D   shift

35. <u>Polyatomic</u> most nearly means

   35–A   atomic bomb

   35–B   many atoms

   35–C   polygamous

   35–D   chemical

Answer Key

1. C	2. A	3. B	4. D	5. C
6. D	7. A	8. C	9. B	10. A
11. B	12. D	13. A	14. B	15. C
16. C	17. B	18. D	19. A	20. C
21. B	22. D	23. B	24. A	25. C
26. A	27. B	28. D	29. B	30. C
31. A	32. C	33. D	34. A	35. B

Answers and Explanations

1–C To *delete* means to eliminate something by blotting it out, cutting it out, or *erasing* it. You correct an error in your composition by *deleting* it with an eraser.

2–A *Celestial* refers to something having to do with the *heavens* or skies. *Celestial* or *heavenly* bodies refer to stars, planets, or moons. *Celestial* or *heavenly* can also relate to other worlds, the unknown, or religious concepts.

3–B *Matrimony* means *marriage*, or the union of two people. Related words are *matron*, meaning a married woman, *matronly*, meaning having the characteristics of a married woman, or *matrilineal*, which refers to tracing family descent through the maternal line.

4–D To *abolish* something is to *repeal*, terminate, annul, end, cancel, or overturn it. For example, slavery in the United States was *abolished* after the Civil War—it no longer existed afterwards. Vaccinations for many childhood diseases have virtually wiped them out, or *abolished* them.

5–C To *hesitate* means to *pause*, hold back, stop, vacillate, think about, delay, or hang back. In the sentence, it means that the child was probably uncertain about what to do, was a bit nervous, and so waited a bit before going into his new classroom. *Hesitate* means to be cautious, to stop and think before going ahead.

6–D   The *brink* refers to the *edge* of a steep place—in this case, a cliff. The word *brink* also is used to mean being on the *verge* of something, as in being on the *brink* of war.

7–A   *Flit,* or flitter, means to *move rapidly* and abruptly from one place to another, to alter or shift position, or to move in an erratic fluttering manner. *Flit* is almost always used in reference to the movements of birds. Choice C, *jumped,* is incorrect because it doesn't mention the idea of speed—*flitted* infers a fast movement.

8–C   The prefix *mis* means *badly* or *wrongly,* so *misjudged* means to have *judged* or *estimated wrongly.* The jumper *misjudged* the height of the bar and probably missed jumping over it.

9–B   *Solitude* means seclusion, or *isolation*. It means a condition of being apart from all other human beings or of being cut off from one's usual associates. Related words are *solitary, solo,* and *soloist.* A prisoner who misbehaves while in prison may be put into a *solitary* cell, away from others. When you perform a *solo* you are performing by yourself, or as a *soloist.*

10–A   In this sentence, *elude* means *evade,* escape, get away from. The snake was hard to catch, too fast, or hard to see, so it *eluded* or *evaded* being captured. Also, failing to understand or grasp some piece of knowledge means it has *eluded* you. A related word is *elucidate,* meaning *explain.*

11–B   To *huddle* is to draw oneself down, to *crouch,* or to gather in a closely packed group. In football, the players *huddle,* they *crouch* down together briefly and plan their strategy secretly without being overheard.

12–D   To *secede* is to *withdraw,* as in *seceding* from an organization. During the American Civil War, the South wanted to *secede* from the rest of the States. Related words are *secession,* meaning the act of withdrawing, or *secessionist,* the person who joins in *secession.*

13–A   When a doctor *vaccinates* you, he *inoculates,* immunizes, protects you against illness. For example, if he *vaccinates* you against measles, the *vaccine* protects you from getting measles. The *vaccine* is a preparation that makes your body develop immunity to a particular illness.

14–B   To have *excelled* means to have been *superior.* To *excel* is to be distinguishable by surpassing others, to have *exceeded* others in skill or accomplishment. To have *excelled* in repairing small engines means to be better at this than most other people.

15–C   *Ominous* clouds are *threatening*, forbidding, menacing, dire, gloomy, or suggestive of the coming of bad weather. *Ominous* clouds *threaten* the possibility of a serious storm.

16–C   A *canyon* is a deep narrow *valley* with steep sides and often with a stream flowing through it.

17–B   To *ventilate* something is to *air it out,* freshen it, let in fresh air, circulate the air, open the windows and cool it. Related words are *vent* and *ventilation,* which both refer to the means or act of *ventilating* a space.

18–D   To be *qualified* means to be *competent,* or fitted because of training or experience for a given purpose. It means to be eligible, or to have complied with the specific requirements or necessary conditions.

19–A A *conspiracy* is a *plot,* an agreement among a group of *conspirators* who are *conspiring* together. When people *conspire* they are joining in a secret agreement to do an unlawful or wrongful act. Often a *conspiracy* will have a political end, such as *conspiring* to overthrow a disliked government.

20–C The prefix *pre* means *before* or *earlier than*, so *prepaid* means *paid in advance,* or paid early. The context clue words are *two months early,* which tell you that to *prepay* is to pay the loan off before the due date, to *pay it in advance*.

21–B When something like a water fountain is *accessible,* it is open, reachable, capable of being used, and *available.* It means that it is in a place that can make it usable by people of all sizes and capabilities. A related word is *access,* meaning the way, or path, of getting into a place.

22–D When you *duplicate* something you *copy,* or make an exact double, likeness, or reproduction of it. Related words are *duplicator,* or copier, meaning a machine for making copies, or *duplicity,* meaning deceiving or fooling someone by hiding one's true intentions.

23–B To *implicate* means to *involve,* connect, entwine, associate, link, relate, or compromise someone. When a person is *implicated* in a crime, he or she has something to do with it, is *connected* with it.

24–A To *gyrate* is to *whirl,* wind, coil, or revolve around a particular point. It means to oscillate or turn in a circular or spiral motion, as in a windmill that has a *gyrating* set of blades.

25–C The word *literate* means to be *educated,* able to read and write, cultured, polished, lucid, well-informed, or familiar with literature. The Armed Forces want men and women who are *literate,* which is why they administer the ASVAB, and a democracy depends on an electorate that is *literate*.

26–A A *hangar* is a kind of *shed,* a covered and usually enclosed area for housing and repairing aircraft.

27–B To *dazzle* is to *shine brilliantly,* to arouse great admiration by an impressive display, to overpower with brilliance. For example, a movie star who is very witty, charming, and beautiful can be described as a *dazzling* person with his/her wit and good looks.

28–D The prefix *non* means *not,* and *taxable* means something that is subject to taxes imposed by the government. So, *nontaxable* means *not taxed*.

29–B Something *glacial* is extremely cold, *frigid,* lacking in warmth or cordiality, or referring to the Ice Age, when the earth was mostly covered in *glaciers,* or ice. A *glacial* handshake is one that is cold, unfriendly, and lacking in real warmth. Or, certain snowy mountain ranges are remnants, or leftovers, of the *glacial* Ice Age.

30–C The sentence gives you *not getting in* and *disappointment* as context clues. The student was *profoundly* or *deeply* disappointed. *Profound* means extending far below the surface, deep-seated, or complete. In other words, the student cared *profoundly* about getting into college, so not achieving his wishes was a *deep* or *profound* disappointment.

31–A A *javelin* is a long, slender, light *spear* thrown at others as a weapon of war, or at animals in hunting. It dates from ancient times. Long distance *javelin*-throwing is also a field event in sports competitions such as the Olympics.

32–C   A *flamingo* is a striking-looking, large, graceful *aquatic bird* with long legs and neck, webbed feet, a duck-like bill, and usually with rosy-white feathers. In this question, you can quickly eliminate choices A, B, and D, since they make no sense when substituted in the sentence.

33–D   *Evident* means *obvious,* plain, clearly seen or understood, or apparent. Because they could be heard, it was clear that the children were safe. Related words are *evidence,* referring to a proof or indication of something, and *evidently,* meaning in an *evident* or unmistakable manner.

34–A   To *heave* is to elevate, *lift up,* raise, struggle, pant, or pull while using much effort. To *heave* is to *lift up* or pull at something very heavy. For example, an overturned car will require many men to *heave* it upright, or turn it right side up.

35–B   The prefix *poly* means *many,* and *atomic* means *atoms,* so *polyatomic* means *many atoms.* The human body, made up of millions of cells, is *polyatomic.* Choice C, *polygamous,* using the same prefix, means many mates, or having more than one mate at a time.

PARAGRAPH COMPREHENSION

COMPREHENSION SKILL 1: FINDING MAIN IDEAS

n the Paragraph Comprehension Test, you will be asked to answer questions about one or more paragraphs. You will need to understand the passage quickly and well. Before you read the passage, first *glance at the question below it.* Many of the questions will ask you to *find the main idea.*

Questions that focus on the *main idea* of the passage will often begin like this:

The best title for this passage is _____ .

This paragraph is mainly about _____ .

The passage best supports the statement that _____ .

The author's most important message is that _____ .

As you read the passage, ask yourself questions like: What is the author telling me? What is the main message? What is the idea that the author is trying to get across? What am I learning here? While reading, remember to look for the *main idea.* Sometimes, this is stated in the first, or *topic,* sentence. As you read the passage, try to carefully follow the logic or thinking of the writer.

303

The following three sample passages illustrate the kinds of *main idea* questions you may find on the ASVAB.

Sample 1.   Have you ever seen a red panda, spectacled bear, banded iguana, black tree monitor, bearded dragon, poison dart frog, Arabian oryx, spider monkey, or hooded merganser? These are some of the unusual residents of the beautiful St. Louis Zoo. Walking around, or riding the zoo train, you will marvel at the wonderful and varied birds and animals living there. The St. Louis Zoo is open daily all year round, and it's free. Visit it when you can.

The best title for the above passage is

    1–A   "Riding the St. Louis Zoo Train"

    1–B   "The St. Louis Zoo"

    1–C   "Caring for Birds and Animals"

    1–D   "Unusual Birds and Animals"

1–B   The best title is choice B, *"The St. Louis Zoo."* Notice that the main topic of the passage is the St. Louis Zoo and some of the wildlife that can be seen there. Choice A is incorrect because the train at the zoo is only mentioned in passing, so it is not a good title. Choice C refers to a topic not discussed, so it is also not a good title. While there are obviously a good number of unusual birds and animals listed as being in the St. Louis Zoo, choice D is also not a good title since it fails to mention that they are at the St. Louis Zoo.

Sample 2.   In 2003, LeBron James was the top high school basketball player in the country. At age 18, he was 6 feet 8 and 240 pounds of muscle, and the number one pick for the NBA draft. He is a smooth player, a skilled rebounder, possesses solid ball-handling ability, and passes the ball effortlessly while moving well. LeBron is an exciting young player who will possibly be the next basketball legend as he plays with the Cleveland Cavaliers.

This passage is mainly about

    2–A   the NBA draft.

    2–B   moving well in basketball.

    2–C   tall young players.

    2–D   LeBron James.

2–D   The passage tells us about LeBron James, the exciting young basketball player. You are introduced to him in the first sentence, then told of his skills as a player. Therefore, only choice D is the correct answer. Choices A, B, and C are incorrect because they are topics only mentioned in passing as they relate to LeBron James; they are not discussed in detail.

Sample 3.   The Academy of Motion Picture Arts and Sciences, begun in 1927, consists of the most important people in the movie industry. The main purpose of this professional organization, whose members are chosen by invitation according to their accomplishments and abilities, is to set good standards of professional filmmaking. This is done partly through the awarding of the prestigious Oscar, the most sought-after reward for prominence in filmmaking.

The main point expressed in the passage is that

    3–A   Hollywood is one of California's largest cities.

    3–B   the Oscars are heavier that most other awards.

    3–C   the Academy is important because it sets standards for films.

    3–D   only Academy members receive Oscars.

3–C   This is the correct answer because the passage mentions that the Academy sets standards, which is its most important function. The other choices given are either incorrect or not discussed in this piece.

> Now, do Practice Exercises 1 and 2 for additional practice with *main idea* questions. Choose the best answer for each question. As you finish each exercise, check your answers with the Answer Key and Explanations that follow.

Practice Exercise 1

1. Instead of commuting to a company office each day, thousands of Americans now "telecommute" from their homes. This means that they work at home with the use of modern electronic devices like computers, faxes, scanners, printers, and e-mail. They are able to stay in touch with clients or coworkers with such methods as teleconferencing and multiparty telephone calls and by sending written material electronically. Telecommuting is found to be an efficient, practical change in today's work scene.

The main idea above is that

    1–A   telecommuting is inefficient.

    1–B   all telecommuters use voice mail.

    1–C   a person's office is sometimes at home.

    1–D   clients will get better service from telecommuters.

2. Teddy Roosevelt, who became the 26th president of the United States after the assassination of McKinley, was known for his energy and many interests. He went on numerous hunting and exploring expeditions; published over 2000 works on history, politics, and his travels; and formed his famous volunteer cavalry troop, the *Rough Riders*. His most important achievement was his conservation program, which added over 250 million acres to the national forests.

The passage best supports the statement that

    2–A   Roosevelt had a wide range of accomplishments.

    2–B   the *Rough Riders* were a volunteer navy.

    2–C   politics and science don't mix.

    2–D   historians like Roosevelt make good presidents.

Questions 3 and 4 are based on the following passage.

The *Holocene* is the name given to the last 10,000 years of the Earth's history. This is the era since the end of the last major Ice Age and the one we are living in today. It is a relatively warm time, but humans have adapted to survive in both cold and warm climates. Volcanic eruptions and earthquakes tell us that the Earth's surface is continuing to change, with the continents we live on constantly moving around our planet. We are, however, not usually aware of this because of the slowness of the changes.

3. The main idea above is that
    3–A   the *Holocene* era is the beginning of the Ice Age.
    3–B   humans adapt with difficulty to change.
    3–C   the Earth changes with time and humans have adapted.
    3–D   humans cannot survive an Ice Age.

4. The best title here would be
    4–A   "The Ice Age."
    4–B   "Volcanic Eruptions."
    4–C   "Human Survival."
    4–D   "The *Holocene* Era."

5. Personal computers of the future will come with built-in safeguards against illegal tampering or copying of material. The safeguards are necessary in order to protect entertainment content, for example, or corporate data from being seen or taken by competitors. They are also needed by individuals to maintain the privacy of personal health records, bank accounts, and other financial information.

    The general idea in this passage is that
    5–A   privacy safeguards will be built into future computers.
    5–B   it is always illegal to look at other people's computers.
    5–C   only corporations are in need of these privacy safeguards.
    5–D   health records need to be open to everyone.

6. Historians are increasingly able to use science as a way of investigating ancient manuscripts that are otherwise unreadable. For example, a new digital technological process called *multi-spectral imaging* has been used to decipher burned scrolls from ancient Roman times that were buried by the eruption of Mt. Vesuvius in 79 A.D. This process is also being used to read more recently burned historical papers that have been damaged by the destruction of war.

    This passage best supports the statement that
    6–A   all ancient scrolls were buried by the eruption of Mt. Vesuvius.
    6–B   old manuscripts are being read by scientists.
    6–C   historians now sometimes use science in their work.
    6–D   old manuscripts are not useful to historians.

7. Every summer, there are reports of people drowning while swimming at ocean beaches. Sudden storms can kick up waves and create a dangerous undertow. Even strong, experienced swimmers can be at risk, especially when swimming in unfamiliar waters. Beware of warnings coming from lifeguards or from posted flags that are used at some beaches to signal degrees of danger as a result of changing weather.

   What is the author's main message?

   7–A   If you're a strong swimmer, you can swim in any conditions.

   7–B   It is important to take swimming lessons.

   7–C   If there are no posted flags, it is always safe to swim.

   7–D   Ocean swimming can sometimes be dangerous for anyone.

8. Yugoslavia is being targeted by bird poachers from other countries. Wildlife experts there have warned that forestry and customs officials are being bribed, while foreign poachers help themselves to some of the rarest protected species of birds, including birds of prey, and songbirds. Because the government shows little concern, time may be running out for many of these rare exotic species of birds in Serbia and Montenegro.

The author's most important message is that

   8–A   all wildlife species need protection.

   8–B   poaching is harmless.

   8–C   it is urgent that Yugoslavia's special birds be protected now.

   8–D   arrested poachers will be severely prosecuted.

9. In America, more people than ever are gaining weight. Why is this happening? Studies show that *fatty foods* are to blame. Many favorite everyday foods, like French fries, hamburgers, hot dogs, ice cream, and pizza, are heavily loaded with fat. Because the fat adds great taste, it's hard to let go of these foods. Getting more physical exercise helps, but more importantly, it is better to eat more carbohydrates, like pasta and rice, in preference to these fatty foods.

This passage is mainly about

   9–A   excess fat in American diets.

   9–B   eating too much bread and other carbohydrates.

   9–C   the effect of exercise on weight.

   9–D   heart attacks and calories.

Questions 10 and 11 refer to the passage below.

The *Concorde,* the world's only supersonic commercial transport, completed its last commercial passenger flight to Heathrow Airport in November 2003. It was a sad day for those who became used to flying at twice the speed of sound.

British Air and Air France, who had developed and flown this plane since 1976, retired the *Concorde* because its profitability never recovered after a horrific crash in Paris in 2000, in which 113 people died.

The beautiful droop-nosed *Concorde* is now on display in exhibits at the Intrepid Sea Air Space Museum on the Hudson River in New York City, as well as at the Museum of Flight in Seattle, and the Smithsonian's new National Air and Space Museum outside Washington D.C.

10. The best title for this selection is
   - 10–A   "The History of Flying."
   - 10–B   "The End of the *Concorde.*"
   - 10–C   "Fast Commercial Passenger Transport."
   - 10–D   "Flight Museums."

11. Which of the following statements is best supported by the passage?
   - 11–A   We will probably never see high speed flying again.
   - 11–B   All old planes are seen in museums throughout the country.
   - 11–C   The *Concorde* was a badly designed plane which is being studied at the Intrepid and at the Smithsonian.
   - 11–D   The *Concorde* was a much-admired plane that is no longer profitable for the airlines.

12. There is a crisis brewing in American public education—the growing shortage of qualified *teachers*. Many current teachers are reaching retirement age, and there are few young people eager to take their places. School districts are busily recruiting across the country, with new programs making it possible for people from other backgrounds to switch into teaching jobs. There are also lucrative incentives being offered to people with math or science backgrounds because of the special shortages in teachers competent to teach these subjects.

What is the main message of this passage?
   - 12–A   School districts are scrambling to fill teacher vacancies.
   - 12–B   There are few positions for science teachers.
   - 12–C   Teachers retire earlier than they used to.
   - 12–D   More young people are interested in teaching than years ago.

Answer Key

1. C	2. A	3. C	4. D	5. A
6. C	7. D	8. C	9. A	10. B
11. D	12. A			

Answers and Explanations

1–C   The main idea is that a person who works at home is a telecommuter. Thus, his or her home becomes an office, and choice C is correct.

2–A   The passage is mainly about Teddy Roosevelt and his accomplishments. The statement that is most clearly supported in the passage is choice A. Choices C and D are not related to the passage. Choice B is incorrect, since the *Rough Riders* were a cavalry troop, not a volunteer navy.

3–C   The main idea is that land masses move and climates change drastically, but humans have survived both warm and cold climates. The other choices are incorrect.

4–D Although the Ice Age, volcanic eruptions, and human survival are all mentioned in the passage, the overall topic of the piece is the *Holocene* era. This is therefore a good all-inclusive title for this passage.

5–A The topic sentence states that future computers will protect the user's privacy. Choice B is not supported by the passage. Choice C is contradicted by the passage, which states that individuals, not just corporations, also need to protect private information. Choice D is also contradicted by the passage, which *does* imply that most people would like to keep their health records private.

6–C The passage is about how *multispectral imaging* is now used to decipher old historical manuscripts, or readings—in other words, how science is sometimes used by historians. Choice A is incorrect—nothing is stated about *all* scrolls being buried by Mt. Vesuvius. Choice B makes no sense. Choice D is contradicted by the passage.

7–D The author's main point is expressed in the second and third sentences—that ocean swimming conditions can change unexpectedly and become dangerous, and that even experienced swimmers can be at risk. Therefore, the conclusion you can draw is that ocean swimming can sometimes be dangerous.

8–C The passage states that rare exotic birds in Yugoslavia are being poached, and that the problem is being ignored. The author's main point is that time may be running out, meaning these species will disappear if something isn't done quickly.

9–A The main idea here is that Americans are becoming overweight because they favor fatty foods. Choice B incorrectly states the opposite of the message in the passage. Choice C is incorrect because exercise is mentioned but is not part of the main point being made. Choice D is incorrect because these topics are not dealt with in this passage.

10–B This passage gives a brief story about the *Concorde* while focusing on its retirement from use, or its end. Therefore, the best title among the choices is "*The End of the Concorde.*" The other choices present only minor aspects of the information given in the passage.

11–D This statement is a good summary of what happened to the *Concorde*. The second sentence tells us that its end was sad for those who flew it, meaning it was liked and admired. The second paragraph tells us why the plane was no longer profitable, or able to make money, for the airlines. Choice A is not a reasonable inference, and choice B is not supported by the passage. Choice C is probably not accurate; since the *Concorde* flew for all those years, it was probably well designed in spite of the Paris crash.

12–A The main message is that there's a crisis because fewer people are going into teaching than are currently leaving the profession. Therefore, choice A is correct—districts are having a hard time filling teacher vacancies. Choices B and D are contradicted by the passage, and choice C is not discussed.

Practice Exercise 2

1. Many communities in the United States are dependent on one industry or even one company for their economic survival. For example, a large GE plant can provide tens of thousands of jobs and be the only source of income for many households in a particular city. If trouble hits that company, then many workers can lose their jobs. This has happened in cities with coal mining plants, steel producers, automobile manufacturers, or other specialized companies. In such difficult changing economic times, workers must move elsewhere or retrain for other employment.

This paragraph supports the statement that

1–A   people shouldn't work for GE for fear of being fired.

1–B   a recession creates joblessness and poverty.

1–C   people should get second jobs.

1–D   it is risky for an area to have just one large employer.

2. Have you ever tried tandoori chicken, lemongrass pork, sukiyaki, or blackened catfish? Most young people stay within a diet of hamburgers, fried chicken, hot dogs, French fries, or an occasional steak or pork chop. They don't know what they're missing by not being more adventurous in their eating habits!

This paragraph is mainly about

2–A   learning to cook.

2–B   improving nutrition.

2–C   trying new foods.

2–D   all the above.

3. Most old masterpieces in Italy need frequent work and restoration in order to maintain their beauty. In January 2002, after working for more than a quarter of a century, a team of 35 skilled art restorers put the finishing touches on Giotto's famous fresco paintings in the 700-year-old Scrovegni Chapel in Padua, in northern Italy. This masterpiece, consisting of more than 100 paintings covering the walls and ceiling of the chapel, was beginning to fade and lose its great colors.

The main message above is that

3–A   fresco paintings are 700 years old.

3–B   great old works of art need constant care.

3–C   there are 100 paintings in the Scrovegni Chapel.

3–D   Giotto was a great restorer of art.

4. Scientists are debating whether the currently warm temperatures on Earth are a permanent phenomenon or a passing phase. Some fear that we may be seeing evidence of the *greenhouse effect*. This refers to gases that become trapped in the Earth's atmosphere and are unable to escape, thereby keeping the Earth warm. Other scientists feel that this is part of a normal cycle of weather patterns and that there is no immediate danger.

The passage best supports the statement that

4–A   people around the world are experiencing heat waves.

4–B   the greenhouse effect started one hundred years ago.

4–C   controversy exists regarding whether the Earth's warming is temporary or permanent.

4–D   gases are trapped in the Earth's core.

Questions 5 to 7 refer to the following passage.

Every year, many fans flock to Cooperstown, New York, to visit the Baseball Hall of Fame and Museum.

Housing over 30,000 objects that represent many aspects of the game, the Museum displays baseballs, bats, uniforms, awards, tickets, collectibles, and other memorabilia. Several million more items are kept in archives in an effort to conserve this valuable material for future generations to enjoy. These include photographs, news clippings, films, and video- and audiotapes.

In addition, the Hall of Fame, currently consisting of 256 players, honors great athletes like Hank Aaron, Lefty Gomez, Reggie Jackson, Yogi Berra, Roy Campanella, Whitey Ford, Ty Cobb, and Joe DiMaggio.

5. The best title for this passage is

5–A   "Honoring Baseball."

5–B   "Remembering the Players."

5–C   "Cooperstown."

5–D   "American Sports."

6. This passage is mainly about

6–A   the history of baseball.

6–B   Ty Cobb and his accomplishments.

6–C   the many museums of Cooperstown.

6–D   the offerings of the Baseball Hall of Fame and Museum.

7. The passage best supports the statement that baseball

7–A   is not nearly as popular now as in the past.

7–B   is important to many people.

7–C   has been played since 1895.

7–D   is similar to rugby.

8. Both in civilian and military life, women have made great strides in gaining equality with men. Because of legal protections and social changes, women have entered all aspects of the world of work and culture. Women are now in law, medicine, government, universities, corporations, banking, and the arts in large numbers. While more progress needs to be made, opportunities for women have expanded and opened up their lives as never before in history.

Which of the following would the author most agree with?

8–A   Working women are in the worst shape ever.

8–B   Men need to protect their rights in the workplace.

8–C   There are now more opportunities for women than in the past.

8–D   The world is now perfect for women.

9. Michael Jordan is one of the greatest basketball players in NBA history. He played for the Chicago Bulls, winning three championships, retired to play minor league baseball, and then returned to the Bulls to win three additional titles. Jordan's retired number 23 hangs from the rafters in the Chicago stadium, and there is a statue of him outside the arena. During the summer of 2001, at age 38, he left his job as an executive and briefly put on a Wizards basketball jersey to once again play the game he loves. No matter what he does in the future, Jordan's place in sports history is secure.

The best title for this passage is

9–A   "The Chicago Bulls."

9–B   "Sports in the Contemporary U.S.A."

9–C   "The Washington Wizards."

9–D   "Michael Jordan's Career."

10. When thinking about weather patterns, meteorologists often speak of "El Niño," which is the name given to an abnormal warming of the waters in the equatorial Pacific. El Niño, which means "Christ Child" in Spanish, usually leads to a mild winter in the United States. The last severe El Niño occurred in the winter of 1997 to 1998, when it caused drought in Australia and Indonesia, and flooding in Ecuador and Peru.

This passage is mainly about

10–A   El Niño.

10–B   weather patterns.

10–C   droughts in Australia and Indonesia.

10–D   global warming.

11. The Perseid meteor shower, named after the constellation Perseus, is visible at certain times of the year. The best time for you to view it is between midnight and dawn. While lying on a blanket outdoors, point your feet towards the southeast and look up. If you avoid looking directly at the moon, your eyes will quickly adjust to the dark. Besides Perseid, you will also be able to find the bright planet Mars in the southeastern sky.

This paragraph best supports the statement that

11–A   Mars is part of the Perseid meteor shower.

11–B   at certain times, it is possible to see a meteor shower.

11–C   no one has ever seen the constellation Perseus.

11–D   astronomy is a romantic hobby.

12. *Globalization* is the name given to the ever-increasing tendency for very large companies to be multinational and to do business the world over. Many people feel that this is a good thing because these companies spread wealth to poorer countries, create work opportunities, and introduce technologies that raise living standards. Others feel hostile to these companies, which they view as enemies of poor developing countries and as destroying the environment by using up the world's natural resources.

What is the main idea of this passage?

12–A   It proposes an alternative to globalization.

12–B   It condemns the spreading of modern technology.

12–C   It explains the meaning and possible effects of globalization.

12–D   It tells how work opportunities are created in the United States.

Answer Key				

1. D	2. C	3. B	4. C	5. A
6. D	7. B	8. C	9. D	10. A
11. B	12. C			

Answers and Explanations

1–D The main idea is that if everyone in town works for only one company, thousands may be at risk of losing their jobs if the company has any financial problems or closes.

2–C The author urges the reader to try different kinds of foods rather than staying with the same choices, so choice C is the correct answer. Choices A and B are not discussed in the passage, so they are incorrect.

3–B The passage is mainly about how great works of art need careful and frequent restoration, with Giotto's paintings in Padua given as an example. This is therefore the best answer to this question.

4–C The main idea is that there is a controversy among scientists about why the weather seems warmer. Choice A mentions heat waves, which isn't the topic here. There is no discussion of when the greenhouse effect began, so choice B is incorrect. And choice D is contradicted by the third sentence, which states that the warm gasses are trapped in the atmosphere, not in the Earth's core.

5–A Because the passage is an overview of the Baseball Hall of Fame and Museum, which honors baseball and its players, the best title is choice A, *"Honoring Baseball."* Choices B and C both fail to mention baseball, which is the primary topic of this passage. Choice D doesn't mention baseball and is too general. Remember, a title has to encompass the general message and topic of the passage.

6–D The correct answer is choice D, *the offerings of the Baseball Hall of Fame and Museum.* Choice A is on a topic not discussed in the passage. Ty Cobb is only mentioned as being honored in the Hall of Fame but not otherwise discussed, so choice B is incorrect. Choice C is incorrect also, as Cooperstown's museums in general are not discussed.

7–B The most accurate conclusion, based on the passage, is choice B, *baseball is important to many people.* You can see this is the main message of the passage. No evidence is given to support choices A, C, or D.

8–C The author's main message is that opportunities for women have opened up as never before in history, so this is the correct answer. The author would not agree that everything is perfect for women, and he doesn't state that men's rights are threatened. Therefore, the other choices are incorrect.

9–D This passage is not about the Bulls, the Wizards, or sports in contemporary America, although they are mentioned, so choices A, B, and C are not correct. The piece talks about Michael Jordan and his current career in sports. Therefore, the title for this piece could be *"Michael Jordan's Career."*

10–A Since El Niño is mentioned in each of the three sentences of the passage, it is safe to assume that it is the main topic being discussed. While passing reference is given to the other choices, they are not the subjects of the paragraph.

11–B The main point of the passage is that Perseid, the meteor shower, can be seen at certain times of the year, and certain times of the night. The other choices are contrary to what is stated in the passage.

12–C The passage discusses the possible pros and cons of *globalization*, which is explained in the first sentence. Choice A is incorrect because no alternative is presented. Because the author remains neutral and does not take sides, choice B is incorrect. Choice D is on a topic not discussed in the passage.

COMPREHENSION SKILL 2: LOOKING FOR DETAILS

Another type of question in the Paragraph Comprehension Test will ask you about a *particular detail, fact, or specific piece of information* in the passage. Again, you must briefly glance at the question *first* to determine what kind of question you will need to answer after reading the paragraph. In this type of question, look at the *key words* in the question. This will tell you what to look for in the passage.

A *looking for details* question will often begin with specific *key words* from the passage, as in the following:

Aphrodite was _____.

The abalone shell is _____.

The Economic Opportunity Act _____.

The Klondike Gold Rush _____.

The three sample questions that follow illustrate typical *looking for details* questions.

Sample 1. In order to stop telephone solicitation, you can contact the Federal Trade Commission to be put on a "do not call" list. Telemarketers who ignore this list can be fined up to $11,000 per call. It is expected that 60 million homes will eventually be signed up to block these annoying calls. You may, however, still be bothered by getting increased junk mail as companies try to make up for these imposed restrictions on advertising.

Telemarketing is
    1–A   no longer legal.
    1–B   highly effective for advertisers.
    1–C   restricted by the Federal Trade Commission.
    1–D   only done by mail.

1–C   The first sentence tells us that telemarketing is being restricted by the list, so choice C is the correct answer. Choice A is contradicted by the passage, which states that only people whose names are on this list can't be called, but others can. Therefore, telemarketing is still *partly* legal. Choice B is not discussed. Choice D is incorrect; telemarketing is obviously *telephone* solicitation, not done by mail.

Sample 2.   According to a story from Greek mythology, a young man named Narcissus was incapable of loving others. He was only able to love himself. One day, as he sat next to a pond, he looked down at his reflection and fell in love with it. As a punishment, the gods turned him into a flower, the *narcissus*, which is often seen growing near water.

Narcissus, a young man in Greek mythology,

    2–A   was punished for loving only himself.
    2–B   was a god in Greek mythology.
    2–C   fell into a pond and became a god.
    2–D   is a Greek bush.

2–A   The third and fourth sentences tell you that Narcissus fell in love with his reflection and was punished by being turned into a flower.

Sample 3.   Scientists have long been interested in ways of studying the intelligence of animals. Currently, scientists measure their intelligence by observing how they solve problems or behave in their own social environments rather than in laboratories. Many studies concentrate on the intelligence animals use in dealing with others of their own kind and in solving group problems. It is believed that this *social intelligence* is an appropriate and logical way of judging an animal's capabilities.

According to this passage, scientists currently study the intelligence of animals by observing

    3–A   how they solve problems.
    3–B   the way they learn tricks.
    3–C   whether they can recognize numbers.
    3–D   how they relate socially to people.

3–A   The second and third sentences tell you that scientists are interested in observing how animals *solve problems*. Therefore, this is the correct answer. There is no mention in the passage that they are interested in observing their tricks, number recognition, or relations with human beings.

Now try Practice Exercises 3 and 4 for additional practice with specific detail questions.

Choose the best answer for each question. As you finish each exercise, check your answers against the Answers and Explanations that follow.

Practice Exercise 3

1. The United States has finally landed on Mars! The robot *Spirit,* which weighs 400 pounds and is the size of a golf cart, arrived there safely in January 2004. *Spirit* was equipped with a color camera, communications equipment, microscope, and an infrared instrument for classifying rocks from a distance. It was designed to roam the planet for several months and examine rocks in a mission to map out the possible history of water on Mars. The idea was to see if any form of life ever existed there.

The robot *Spirit* was looking for
    1–A   Earth.
    1–B   color cameras.
    1–C   evidence of water.
    1–D   maps of Mars.

Questions 2 and 3 are based on the following passage.

It is now over 50 years since Sir Edmund Hillary, the New Zealand mountaineer, first scaled the world's tallest mountain. On May 29, 1953, this one-time beekeeper teamed up with a Sherpa guide, Tenzing Norgay, for the historic climb of Mount Everest. Subsequently, Hillary led expeditions to the South Pole and up the Ganges River in India, as well as undertaking further exploration of the Himalayas.

2. Which of the following statements is TRUE according to this passage?
    2–A   Tenzing Norgay was a Sherpa guide from New Zealand.
    2–B   Mount Everest is the highest mountain in the world.
    2–C   Sir Hillary had always been a mountain climber.
    2–D   The Ganges River flows into the Himalayas.

3. Tenzing Norgay
    3–A   reached the top of Mount Everest.
    3–B   explored the South Pole.
    3–C   was a brother of Sir Hillary.
    3–D   All of the above

4. The two major federal law enforcement agencies in the United States are the CIA, which deals with international criminal activities like organized smuggling and terrorism, and the FBI, which works on crime within the borders of the United States. In recent years, these two agencies have streamlined ways of sharing information in order to increase their effectiveness in dealing with many issues more efficiently.

In what ways are these two agencies now more effective?

4–A   They both solve international crime cases.

4–B   They communicate better with each other.

4–C   They work under the same director.

4–D   They have each hired more employees.

5. Because of the prevalence of computers in modern life, it is possible to have a fast exchange of information. Today, anyone sitting at a computer has an unlimited personal library. He has a research tool to work with that can access most human knowledge. This is true whether the person is in a remote village in a third world country or in a modern capital city. Computers can empower people with knowledge and understanding of the world around them. In this way, they have made our world a much smaller place.

The author of this passage states that computers

5–A   are more trouble than they are worth.

5–B   can only be used in modern cities.

5–C   have a long history as a research tool.

5–D   are an important modern tool.

6. Sandra Day O'Connor was brought up in Arizona. By age eight she could already drive a truck around her family's ranch. She eventually changed her life by going to law school at Stanford University, where she graduated in 1952 near the top of her class. Thirty years later, she became the first woman appointed to the United States Supreme Court. In her autobiographical book, *The Majesty of the Law: Reflections of a Supreme Court Justice*, she shares some rare insights and interesting life experiences.

Which of the following is a TRUE statement according to this paragraph?

6–A   There are no other women on the United States Supreme Court.

6–B   Sandra Day O'Connor was born in Stanford, California.

6–C   There were no women on the Supreme Court prior to 1982.

6–D   All of the above are false.

7. France's latest outdoor project, erected in the Auvergne Volcanoes Park, is called *Vulcania*. Topped by a 28-meter cone, most of the amazing attractions are below ground. Visitors descend a spiral staircase built around an artificial crater, and then experience a variety of simulations and spectacles related to volcanic eruptions. There is a volcanic garden, and a vibrating movie theater with one of the world's largest projectors. *Vulcania* is expected to attract half a million visitors each year.

Most of the attractions at *Vulcania*

7–A   are seen from a 28-meter cone.

7–B   are underground.

7–C   vibrate.

7–D   revolve.

Questions 8 to 10 are based on the passage below.

In Iceland, which is heavily dependant on airline-borne tourism, the Keflavik International Airport is the first to introduce *face recognition technology*. The computer software works with security cameras to quickly scan the faces of thousands of passengers, examines eighty facial characteristics, and compares each person's unique "faceprint" to a database of suspected terrorists and criminals. If just twelve of the features match up, an alarm sounds.

This is just one example of *biometrics*, the process of identifying people by their unique characteristics, such as their DNA, or eye features like the retina or the iris. The effectiveness of using faceprints in deterring terrorism is still unknown, however.

8. Which of the following is NOT an example of biometrics?
   - 8–A   Inspection of luggage
   - 8–B   DNA evaluation
   - 8–C   Face recognition technology
   - 8–D   Retina identification

9. A face scan
   - 9–A   is potentially harmful.
   - 9–B   is known to be highly effective.
   - 9–C   takes a long time to perform.
   - 9–D   is done very quickly.

10. Each person's *faceprint*
    - 10–A   has twelve characteristics.
    - 10–B   matches the ones of his parents.
    - 10–C   is different from everyone else's.
    - 10–D   becomes part of a database.

11. Where can you find miles of sandy beaches, a championship baseball team, a 2700-plant rose garden, two major rivers, and Bengal tigers? The Bronx, in New York City, of course. This is the home of the New York Yankees, sweeping Orchard Beach on Long Island Sound, the stunning Botanical Gardens, the magnificent Hudson and Harlem Rivers, and the world famous Bronx Zoo. These are little-known facts about the only borough of New York City that is *not* on an island and is connected to the rest of the United States.

Which of the following is NOT true according to this passage?
   - 11–A   There are sandy beaches along the Hudson and Harlem Rivers.
   - 11–B   The Bronx is part of New York City.
   - 11–C   The New York Yankees are based in the Bronx.
   - 11–D   The Bronx Zoo is home to some Bengal tigers.

12. Americans enjoy many different types of restaurants. This is an outgrowth of our multicultural heritage. People have emigrated here from all parts of the world and brought their delicious foods with them. Besides the ever-popular Chinese and Italian restaurants, people can also try Latino, Japanese, French, Mexican, Indian, Middle Eastern, Thai, Russian, Irish, Vietnamese, and various African delicacies. You do not need to leave the borders of the United States to try exotic specialties from all over the world.

The tastes that Americans have for many different foods

12–A   come from good cookbooks.

12–B   are limited to Chinese and Italian specialties.

12–C   are related to our mixed cultural heritage.

12–D   can only be satisfied by travel.

Answer Key

1. C	2. B	3. A	4. B	5. D
6. C	7. B	8. A	9. D	10. C
11. A	12. C			

Answers and Explanations

1–C   The second to last sentence tells us that the purpose of *Spirit*'s mission was to look at rocks for evidence of water. The last sentence tells us why that would have been an exciting find—it would suggest that there had been life on Mars.

2–B   The first sentence tells you that Sir Hillary climbed "the world's tallest mountain," and the second sentence tells you the name of this mountain—Mount Everest. Choice A is incorrect since Hillary, not Norgay, came from New Zealand. Choice C is incorrect because we are told that Hillary was originally a beekeeper, meaning that he had not always been a mountain climber. Choice D is incorrect because we are told only that the Ganges River is in India, not that it flows into the Himalayan Mountains.

3–A   The first two sentences tell you that Norgay was one of the two people who reached the top of this mountain, so choice A is the correct answer. Choice B is incorrect—Sir Hillary, not Norgay, explored the South Pole. Choice C is not correct according to the information given.

4–B   Part of the last sentence, "*...these two agencies have streamlined ways of sharing information in order to increase their effectiveness...,*" gives you the answer to the question. Choice A is incorrect; only the CIA works on international cases. Choices C and D are not discussed in the passage.

5–D   The author states that computers are part of "modern life" and an important "research tool," making choice D the correct answer. Since computers are a recent invention, choice C is wrong. As they can provide information for the person in a "remote village" also, choice B is wrong. Choice A is the opposite of the point being made in this passage.

6–C   The passage states that O'Connor was appointed thirty years after graduating in 1952, meaning 1982, and there were no other women appointed before then. Choice A is incorrect because we are not told if there are any other women on the Court—notice, the tense means they're asking about the present time. Choice B is also false—she was born in Arizona, not California.

7–B   The second sentence indicates that most of the attractions are underground, so choice B is the correct answer.

8–A   Searching luggage is not a type of biometric screening, which refers to screening some aspect of a person's body, like his face, fingerprint, or DNA.

9–D   The second sentence states that the cameras can scan the faces of thousands of people quickly, so choice D is the correct answer.

10–C The second sentence states that each person's "faceprint" is unique, meaning it's different from everyone else's, just like a fingerprint or an iris or retina scan.

11–A The only untrue statement is choice A, since the beach mentioned is Orchard Beach, which lies along Long Island Sound, not the rivers.

12–C The second sentence tells us that people who came to America from many other countries brought their tastes for different kinds of foods with them. The assumption is that this then led to the opening of many different restaurants, giving Americans the chance to be exposed to many interesting foods without leaving their own country.

Practice Exercise 4

1.   The American alligator, currently found in Florida and other southern coastal regions, resembles a large lizard and is usually between 9 and 12 feet in length when fully grown. It swims by moving its tail from side to side and uses its short strong legs for walking. When first hatched, it is only about 9 inches long. Alligators probably live as long as 50 or 60 years. Large males sometimes kill dogs, pigs, or even cattle by dragging them underwater to drown, but luckily they seldom attack people.

The American alligator
   1–A   is brown and scaly.
   1–B   is found in Florida and southern coastal regions.
   1–C   has black teeth.
   1–D   feeds on swamp vegetation.

2.   The first feature film ever to be entirely made in Haiti came out in the fall of 2003. The movie, *Royal Bonbon*, directed by the French director Charles Najman, used nonprofessional actors. It is a comedy-drama about a villager who believes he is the reincarnation of King Christophe, who was a former colonial slave who led Haiti to independence by defeating French colonial forces in 1804.

The film *Royal Bonbon* was
   2–A   about the director Charles Najman.
   2–B   a travelogue about Haiti.
   2–C   the first to be made in Haiti.
   2–D   All of the above

3. The Mormon Tabernacle Choir, in existence for over 150 years, is a respected and world-renowned musical group. With over 360 volunteer and highly trained members, the Choir gives weekly free concerts at its home in Salt Lake City, Utah. It has also participated in five presidential inauguration ceremonies, made over a hundred recordings, and toured widely.

Which of the following is a TRUE statement according to this passage?

3–A	According to Mormon tradition, only women sing in the Choir.
3–B	The Choir gives infrequent concerts.
3–C	The Mormon Tabernacle Choir is based in Utah.
3–D	None of the above is true.

4. Everyone loves watching the Olympics, and many countries also want the prestige and economic advantages of hosting the games. After years of frustration, Beijing, China, finally won its long-standing bid to host the 2008 summer games. The games are alternated between applicant countries, with sites chosen by the International Olympic Committee. Athens is hosting the 2004 summer games, and Italy is hosting the 2006 winter games. The announcements are made years in advance to give the host countries plenty of time to prepare the many sports facilities that will be needed.

The site of the Olympic games is

4–A	announced two years beforehand.
4–B	prepared with little effort.
4–C	always in Athens, as in ancient times.
4–D	picked by the International Olympic Committee.

5. The Magna Carta, which was signed by King John of England in 1215, provided the ideas behind the most basic principles of our free and democratic society. These principles state that our country is governed by the rule of law, that no one is above the law, not even the government. They protect individual citizens against the great power of the government.

According to this passage,

5–A	no one is above the law in our country.
5–B	King John opposed the Magna Carta.
5–C	there is no historical background to our laws.
5–D	All of the above

6. Spain once controlled the largest empire the Western world had seen since the fall of Rome. In 1565, it had established St. Augustine, Florida, as its first permanent settlement in territory that would one day be part of the United States.

By 1607, when the British established their first successful American settlement at Jamestown, Virginia, Spain had already extended its dominion nearly 800 miles from Southern California to the Straits of Magellan. Today, the Latino population of the United States continues to grow and be increasingly important.

The author states that

6–A	Spain settled Jamestown in 1607.
6–B	St. Augustine was ruled by the British.
6–C	there is no longer a Spanish presence in the U.S.
6–D	Spain was already in America when the British established Jamestown.

7. Wimbledon, England, is well known as the site of one of the top yearly tennis tournaments. The other tournaments making up the "grand slam" quartet of top meets are the French Open, the Australian Open, and the U.S. Open. Some current top-seeded players are Venus and Serena Williams, Lleyton Hewitt, 6-foot-10 Ivo Karlovic from Croatia, and the youthful Maria Sharapova from Russia.

Which of the following is NOT one of the "grand slam" tennis tournaments?

7–A   The French Open
7–B   Wimbledon
7–C   The Russian Open
7–D   The U.S. Open

Questions 8 and 9 are based on the following passage.

The French are experimenting with a new means of quickly transporting large numbers of people over short distances. The *trattoir*, or TRR, which is being tried out at a subway station in Paris, is a fast-rolling pavement. It travels the average speed of a bus, is 180 meters long, and can carry 110,000 people per day. However, first-time users not following directions sometimes lose their balance and fall on their faces, so engineers are determining whether it is really safe and practical. Other countries are looking at it and seeing if it can be used elsewhere. If successful, the *trattoir* could revolutionize the way we get around big cities.

8. According to the passage, a *trattoir* is

8–A   a subway station.
8–B   a fast-moving pavement.
8–C   in New York City.
8–D   dangerous.

9. Which of the following statements is FALSE?

9–A   The rolling pavement is being tested and observed in Paris.
9–B   The device can carry large numbers of people for short distances.
9–C   The *trattoir* will shortly be used all over the world.
9–D   The TRR in Paris is 180 meters long.

10. American Samoa is a U.S. territory that lies in the South Pacific Ocean, about halfway between Hawaii and New Zealand. While it has a traditional Polynesian economy, with most of the land communally owned, it does have a thriving tuna fishing and processing industry that is the backbone of the private economy.

Samoa's remote location, its limited transportation, and its devastating hurricanes limit the development of a broader economy. Tourism, a developing sector, has been held back by the recurring financial difficulties in East Asia.

The passage states that

10–A   Samoa has terrible storms that limit economic growth.
10–B   the United States owns New Zealand and American Samoa.
10–C   swordfish export is Samoa's most important industry.
10–D   Hawaii lies between American Samoa and New Zealand.

Questions 11 and 12 are based on the following selection.

The 1,500-mile Alaska Highway, nicknamed *Alcan Highway,* is a two-lane road originally built by U.S. troops during World War II as a supply route. Today, many visitors combine this picturesque route with holiday trips on the Alaskan ferries. The road starts in Dawson Creek, British Columbia, then winds northwesterly through Canada's Yukon Territory into the heartland of Alaska, and ends just south of Fairbanks. It is open all year, well cared for, and able to offer a surprisingly smooth and exciting ride for visitors.

11. The Alaska Highway
      11–A   closes during the winter.
      11–B   is 1,000 miles long.
      11–C   was built by U.S. troops.
      11–D   is composed of cement and asphalt.

12. Which of the following statements is TRUE, according to this paragraph?
      12–A   This is a superhighway with eight lanes of traffic.
      12–B   The Alaska Highway provides access to Fairbanks.
      12–C   There are no posted speed limits on this road.
      12–D   The road only reaches the fringes of Alaska.

Answer Key

1. B	2. C	3. C	4. D	5. A
6. D	7. C	8. B	9. C	10. A
11. C	12. B			

Answers and Explanations

1–B   The first sentence states that alligators are found in Florida and other coastal regions of the South.

2–C   The first sentence tells you that the film was the first one to be entirely made in Haiti. Choice A is incorrect; Charles Najman was the director of this film, not its subject. Choice B is also incorrect; this is not a travelogue, but a comedy-drama.

3–C   The only true statement is choice C, *the Mormon Tabarnacle Choir is based in Utah.* This is supported by the second sentence, which mentions its "home" as being in Salt Lake City. Choice A is not supported by the passage. Choice B is contradicted by the passage, which states that the group gives "weekly" concerts and tours widely.

4–D   The third sentence tells us that the site is picked by the International Olympic Committee from among the countries who applied. It also states that the site is "alternated," which makes choice C incorrect. Choice A is wrong because the last sentence states that announcements are made "years" in advance. Choice B is also wrong since we're told that much time and many sports facilities are needed, implying that the effort is huge.

5–A   The second sentence tells us that *...our country is governed by the rule of law, that no one is above the law.* Choice B is contradicted by the first sentence. Choice C is incorrect, since the passage states that the Magna Carta *was* a basis of our laws and so provided a historical background for them.

6–D   The short passage presents a lot of facts that you must absorb quickly in order to answer this *detail* question correctly. The second and third sentences tell you that Spain was in America *before* the British. The third sentence tells you that Britain, not Spain, settled Jamestown, so choice A is incorrect. Choice B is incorrect according to the second sentence, which says that St. Augustine was Spanish, not British. Choice C is contradicted by the last sentence.

7–C   Of the choices given, only *"the Russian Open"* are not mentioned in the passage. The other choices are mentioned in the first and second sentences as being part of the "grand slam."

8–B   The second sentence gives you the answer. The *trattoir* is a fast-rolling pavement. While it is being tried out in a subway station, choice A is incorrect. Choice C is also incorrect—the TRR is currently in Paris, not New York City. Choice D is unsupported. The passage states that its safety is still being tested.

9–C   Choice C is the correct answer because the other three choices are TRUE. The last two sentences tell you that the *trattoir* is being studied by other countries, and that it may be used elsewhere but only if it is successful.

10–A   The second paragraph mentions devastating hurricanes as a serious drawback to a broader economy. Choice B is incorrect—the United States does not own New Zealand. Choice C is also incorrect; Samoans fish for tuna, not swordfish. Choice D is a muddled statement; it is American Samoa that lies in the middle, not Hawaii.

11–C   In the first sentence, we are told that this road was built by U.S. troops during World War II. The other choices are incorrect.

12–B   This is the correct answer because the passage tells us that the road ends just short of Fairbanks. There is no information about how many lanes it contains or about speed limits. Choice D is incorrect because the paragraph informs us that the road goes through the heartland of Alaska, not just the fringes.

COMPREHENSION SKILL 3: MAKING INFERENCES

A third type of Paragraph Comprehension question will ask you to make an *inference*, or *educated guess*, based upon the passage. In these types of questions, the answer is *not stated directly* in the passage. You must use your careful reading of the passage as well as your thinking abilities to determine the correct answer.

With *inference* questions, you must use logic and reasoning. You must use your critical thinking skills and the information from the passage to determine the correct answer. *Inference* questions are probably the most challenging category of English questions on the ASVAB.

The sample and practice passages that follow will give you plenty of practice and give you the confidence you need to succeed in doing these questions.

Inference questions often begin with:

It can be inferred from the above passage that _____.

The author probably believes that _____.

Which of the following is implied by the above passage? _____.

The three sample questions that follow are typical inference questions.

Sample 1.   In the Sierra Nevada areas that border California and Nevada, there are now two kinds of black bears: those that live in the wilderness, and those that live in cities and towns, where they patrol backyards and parking lots for nutritious garbage. The wilderness bears spend almost all of their time roaming over many miles of wild lands searching for pine cones, berry bushes, or occasional prey, while the city bears merely fish in dumpsters and garbage cans for their dinner.

Which of the following is a correct inference about the Sierra Nevada bears?

1–A   City and town bears are probably fatter than country bears.

1–B   Wilderness bears are more dangerous to humans than city bears.

1–C   The numbers of black bears are on the decline nationally.

1–D   All of the above are true.

1–A   Since the passage tells you that city and town bears merely go from garbage can to garbage can, while wilderness bears must "roam over many miles," you can infer that the city and town bears are probably fatter. This is because they have to work a lot less for their food than wilderness bears. Choice B is probably the opposite of the truth; since humans in cities are in closer proximity to bears, city bears are most likely more dangerous than wilderness bears. No support is given for choice C.

Sample 2.   Benjamin Franklin, who was the publisher of his own newspaper, *The Pennsylvania Gazette,* believed ardently in free expression, a free flow of ideas, and a free press. He felt that no tyrannical government with arbitrary power would exist for long if all points of view could be fearlessly and publicly expressed.

Which of the following would Benjamin Franklin NOT agree with?

2–A   One person should own all the newspapers in the state.

2–B   There are probably many sides to every important issue.

2–C   Public opinion can influence a government.

2–D   It is necessary for the people to know various sides of an issue.

2–A   You can infer that Franklin would not think it wise for one person to own all the newspapers, since he felt that all points of view needed to be heard. Therefore, choice A is the correct answer. He would agree with choice B, that there are many sides to every issue. Choice C is supported by the last sentence; Franklin felt a public expression of opinions *could* influence government. He would also agree with choice D; in order to have a free flow of ideas, people need to be exposed to different opinions.

Sample 3. A recent survey of consumers showed that many people put off buying modern technological gadgets, which they view as confusing, frustrating, and annoying. Often they are perplexed by the mysterious lingo. The foreign language of abbreviations and technical terms engineers have devised intimidates them. The gadgets most perceived as too complicated by consumers are digital cameras, handheld electronic organizers, and home personal computers.

According to this passage, modern gadget sales would increase if

3–A   they were less inclined to break.

3–B   they were advertised on television.

3–C   confusing directions were eliminated.

3–D   All of the above

3–C The passage mentions confusing *lingo*, or language, as annoying the consumer and causing him not to buy modern gadgets. Therefore, the inference is that if directions were simplified, sales would improve. Choice C is the correct answer. The issues of breakage and advertising are not related to the issue being discussed, so choices A and B are incorrect.

> Now, try Practice Exercises 5 and 6 for practice with *inference* Paragraph Comprehension questions. After reading each question carefully, use your common sense to find the best answer. As you finish each exercise, check your answers with the Answers and Explanations that follow.

Practice Exercise 5

1. Why did dinosaurs become extinct? The best known theories are that a large asteroid hit the Earth and killed them or that radiation from nearby exploding stars caused mass extinction of life on Earth. Some people believe that huge volcanic eruptions somehow contributed to their disappearance. There were also major changes in climate and sea level at the time of their demise, which led to the rise of mammals and flowering plants. How these factors might have been related to the downfall of dinosaurs is a subject of continuing debate.

Which of the following can be assumed from this passage?

1–A   Humans must have killed off the dinosaurs.

1–B   Dinosaurs caused massive volcanic eruptions.

1–C   The climate changed because dinosaurs became extinct.

1–D   Scientists don't really know why dinosaurs disappeared.

2. The residents of Michigan's Upper Peninsula consider the double-crested cormorant an enemy. The reason? This black duck-like bird was declared an endangered and protected species in 1972. Since then it has prospered and grown into a population of 2 million, and by 2001, this fish-gobbling bird was blamed for eating up a great number of the fish fishermen like to catch in the Great Lakes region. The number of perch caught by fishermen has dropped from 145,000 in 1986 to only 20,000 in 2001.

The author probably believes that

    2–A   the issue of protecting cormorants needs to be reexamined.
    2–B   cormorants require access to more fish.
    2–C   fishing in the Great Lakes region should be restricted.
    2–D   the Great Lakes district needs better nesting grounds for birds.

Questions 3 and 4 are based on the passage below.

To be an opera star means not only to have a spectacular voice and the steely nerves required to take that voice to its limit in front of thousands of listeners, but also to be an actor with a commanding stage presence and the ability to move gracefully.

   The story of the opera may require sword fighting, dying, climbing stairs, dancing, running, or writing letters. It also often requires knowledge of any one of half a dozen other languages, and a memory good enough to remember a score that is several hours in length.

3. From this passage, it is reasonable to infer that

    3–A   an opera singer must develop many skills and abilities.
    3–B   opera only appeals to very few listeners.
    3–C   all operas are written in Italian.
    3–D   All of the above are true.

4. The author probably believes that

    4–A   poise is not that important to a great singer.
    4–B   physical stamina is not an issue for singers.
    4–C   singers do not have to be well-educated.
    4–D   None of the above is true.

5. The 3,900-mile long Amazon River is the world's largest river in volume, and it is the second longest. It begins in the Andes Mountains of Peru and flows through the world's largest equatorial forest to the Atlantic Ocean. During flooding season, it can be 30 miles wide. Draining the water from almost half of South America, the Amazon pours an estimated one-fifth of all the water falling on Earth into the Atlantic Ocean, where its current extends 200 miles out to sea.

Based on the passage, the reader may conclude that the Amazon River

    5–A   floods most of the forests in Africa.
    5–B   supplies the water needs of most of South America.
    5–C   warms the waters of the Pacific Ocean.
    5–D   is the most important river in South America.

6. In 1960, natural forests covered 40 percent of Ethiopia, but by 2002 this figure dropped to less than 3 percent. This has prompted fears of an impending environmental disaster and a great loss of economic potential. Farmers who set small fires to prepare for planting have inadvertently caused the loss of the forests. The small fires get out of control and create massive forest fires that destroy crops, livestock, native plants, and animals. These forest fires also affect the chemical and biological nature of the soil of this agriculture-dependent country, which may create real problems for coming generations.

It is possible that

    6–A   by 2020, Ethiopia may have no natural forests left.

    6–B   Ethiopia's economy will not suffer.

    6–C   all forest fires occur during planting season.

    6–D   Ethiopia's forest fires may be the cause of global warming.

7. The Albanian capital of Tirana recently celebrated the inauguration of a new cathedral. *Tirana Cathedral* was built to replace several earlier churches in the capital that were destroyed by the former communist regime. In 1967, under communist rule, the country was declared to be atheist, or non-believing in God, and its churches were either destroyed or used for other purposes.

According to this passage, it can be inferred that

    7–A   many more churches will be rebuilt.

    7–B   the current government in Albania encourages religion.

    7–C   Albanians no longer are interested in religion.

    7–D   communists are still in power in Albania.

8. American manufacturers are increasingly moving their factories to foreign countries like China, India, Bangladesh, or Indonesia, where manufacturing costs are much more moderate. This has resulted in a permanent loss of more than 2 million factory jobs in the United States during the last two years. It is feared that this will make employment possibilities for many Americans much more difficult.

The author suggests that

    8–A   American factory workers will need to relocate to foreign countries.

    8–B   these jobs will be replaced easily.

    8–C   factory wages are probably higher in the United States.

    8–D   unions are ruining the American economy.

9. Some countries are regarded as being *heterogeneous*, meaning that they consist of citizens of many different backgrounds in terms of race, ethnicity, and religion. An example of such a country is the United States, which has a 200-year history of providing a homeland for all people looking for opportunity in a free new land. By contrast, countries like Japan or Norway are regarded as being *homogeneous*, meaning that their residents are largely of the same background.

From this passage, you might infer that

    9–A   Japan is a much older country.

    9–B   the Japanese are racially diverse.

    9–C   Japan and Norway have had limited immigration.

    9–D   the climate of Norway is considerably colder than the United States'.

Questions 10 and 11 are based on the following passage.

On January 1, 2002, the biggest monetary change in history occurred when twelve countries in Europe adopted the *euro* as their common currency. The residents of Austria, Belgium, Finland, France, Germany, Greece, Holland, Ireland, Italy, Luxembourg, Portugal, and Spain had to give up their familiar local currencies, which became worthless after February 2002. This entailed a huge operation, with the printing of 50 billion *euro* coins and 14.5 billion *euro* banknotes. Some people were sorry to see the disappearance of the many beautiful European paper notes in these countries.

10. Which of the following is inferred by the above passage?

   10–A   People were afraid that their currencies would be worth less than the *euro*.

   10–B   In England, people continue using their own currency.

   10–C   *Euros* became unavailable after February 2002.

   10–D   Everyone in these countries was happy with the monetary changes.

11. The author of this paragraph probably believes that

   11–A   having to "think" in another currency is a major adjustment for people to have to make.

   11–B   it is no big deal to change the currency of a country.

   11–C   the *euro* bills are really ugly.

   11–D   no one really likes using the *euro*.

12. In Sardinia, Italy, citizens are known for their very long life expectancy. Antonio Todde, a mountain shepherd listed by the *Guinness Book of Records* as the world's oldest man, died on January 5, 2002, just short of his 113th birthday. He attributed his long life to drinking a glass of good red wine every day. However, scientists have taken DNA samples from 337 Sardinian communities so that they can look into genetic and dietary factors that affect life expectancy.

It can be implied by reading this passage that

   12–A   everyone should drink good wine to live a longer life.

   12–B   everyone should move to Sardinia.

   12–C   Antonio needed to drink less wine.

   12–D   red wine may not be the reason for a Sardinians' long life expectancy.

Answer Key				
1. D	2. A	3. A	4. D	5. D
6. A	7. B	8. C	9. C	10. B
11. A	12. D			

Answers and Explanations

1–D   The last sentence of the passage, which mentions the "continuing debate," gives you the answer. As of now, there is no clear agreement as to why dinosaurs became extinct. Dinosaurs didn't create volcanoes or change the climate, so choices B and C are incorrect, and there is no support for choice A.

2–A   The author mentions the damage to local fishing caused by the overwhelming growth in numbers of this legally protected species. Therefore, it is logical to infer that the author is suggesting a reevaluation of the cormorant protection laws.

3–A   The passage summarizes all the things a great singer must do on stage in addition to singing, so choice A is the correct answer—you can infer that many skills are required of an opera star. Choice B is not related to the passage. Choice C is contradicted by the last sentence, which mentions that many languages, not just Italian, are used in opera.

4–D   None of the first three choices is a true statement, according to the passage, so choice D, *none of the above is true* is the correct answer. Poise and physical stamina are indeed important, so choices A and B are incorrect. You can also assume that singers really do have to be well-educated if they are to develop a knowledge of foreign languages, voice, music, etc. Therefore, choice C is incorrect also.

5–D   Of the four answer choices, the only reasonable inference you can make is that the Amazon is the most important river in South America. Choices A and C are factually incorrect, since the Amazon does not flow in Africa nor into the Pacific. No support is given for choice B, which is therefore also incorrect.

6–A   Since the passage doesn't mention any solution to the problem, you can infer that Ethiopia will probably lose all its forests to forest fires by the year 2020. The other choices are not supported by this passage.

7–B   The rebuilding of the cathedral at this time suggests that the current Albanian government supports and encourages religion. We don't know how many more churches will be rebuilt, so choice A is wrong. Choice D is incorrect because the second sentence mentions the *former* communist regime, meaning it is no longer in power. Choice C is also incorrect, because they would not have gone to the trouble and expense of rebuilding this cathedral if religion were no longer important to Albanians.

8–C   The first sentence tells you that *manufacturing costs*, which probably include wages, are *much more moderate* in these foreign countries, so choice C is the correct answer. Nothing is suggested about relocating workers abroad, so choice A is incorrect. Choice B is contradicted by the last sentence, which implies that replacing these jobs will not be easily done. Unions are not mentioned, so choice D is also incorrect.

9–C   You can infer that Japan and Norway have had very limited immigration as compared to the United States and that therefore they have remained *homogeneous* countries.

10–B   Since England is not mentioned as one of the twelve countries that have switched to the *euro*, you can infer that the English will continue to use their own currency, which is the British pound.

11–A   The statement by the writer that the people in these countries had to "give up their familiar local currencies" implies that he feels it might have been difficult for many people to make this change.

12–D   The last sentence indicates that scientists are studying the DNA of Sardinians to look into possible genetic and dietary reasons for their increased longevity. They probably wouldn't be doing this if they believed that red wine was the clear answer.

Practice Exercise 6

Questions 1 and 2 are based on the following passage.

The longest marked hiking trail in the world—the *Appalachian National Scenic Trail*—winds its way along the high crest of the Appalachian Mountains from Mt. Katahdin in Maine, to Springer Mountain in northern Georgia.

The Appalachian Trail, which is maintained by 4,000 volunteers, is a favorite with hikers. While some hike only a portion, there are others who are "through-hikers"—people who are able to hike the entire 2,167-mile length of the trail in one season. Along the way, these hikers will go through twelve additional states—New Hampshire, Vermont, Massachusetts, Connecticut, New York, New Jersey, Pennsylvania, Maryland, West Virginia, Virginia, Tennessee, and North Carolina.

1. Which of the following is implied by the passage?
    - 1–A   The fees make this trail a real luxury for most people.
    - 1–B   The Appalachian Trail is probably quite beautiful.
    - 1–C   The trail was named after Appalachia, a Native American.
    - 1–D   None of the above is true.

2. Based on this passage, you can assume that
    - 2–A   most people will not hike the entire length of the trail.
    - 2–B   most hikers must be from Maine, since the trail starts there.
    - 2–C   at least 4,000 people hike the Appalachian Trail each season.
    - 2–D   the trail is very expensive to maintain.

3. Parents complain that it seems to be taking longer for their children to leave home and set up their independent lives these days. While young people in the past generally left home for college, marriage, the working world, or the armed services at age 18, never to return, statistics show that the current generation now tends to stay at home much longer. There are frequent debates about whether this is due to the impact of the economy, which makes moving away very expensive, or whether young people now simply take longer to grow up.

It can be inferred from this passage that
    - 3–A   families are closer than they used to be.
    - 3–B   more kids are now dropping out of school.
    - 3–C   grown children now may take longer to find a high-paying job.
    - 3–D   housing is plentiful.

4. The Securities and Exchange Commission, or SEC, was created in 1934 to protect investors in stocks and bonds. It requires public companies to register and disclose how they are structured. The current head of the SEC has promised to crack down on wrongdoers in some companies and protect the small investor.

From this passage, you can assume that

    4–A   some companies must be engaging in fraudulent practices.

    4–B   the SEC is an unnecessary agency.

    4–C   all companies are corrupt.

    4–D   None of the above

5. The rodeo is a unique contest and entertainment well known in the United States and Canadian West. It dates from late nineteenth-century rancher meets, where contests were held by cowboys to celebrate the end of yearly cattle drives. A rodeo usually features five main events: calf-roping, steer-wrestling, bareback riding, saddle-bronco riding, and bull riding.

Which of the following is implied by this passage?

    5–A   Steer-wrestling is much harder than bareback riding.

    5–B   Cowboys needed to know a lot about handling horses and cattle.

    5–C   Bull riding is similar to the bull fights held in Spain and Mexico.

    5–D   Rodeos are a dangerous entertainment.

6. Tropical rain forests in Latin America are the source of many foods for the rest of the world—coffee, bananas, livestock, and fish. In recent years, new foods have been developed and exported. For example, a root vegetable called *ulluco,* and a potato substitute called *oca* have been introduced on some farms in the United States. Latin American rain forests have many other varieties of plants that may one day feed people in other countries.

The passage suggests that

    6–A   only rain forests are the source of new foods.

    6–B   people do not eat enough vegetables.

    6–C   *ulluco* and *oca* are probably tasty.

    6–D   Latin American rain forests are over-farmed.

7. At the beginning of the twentieth century, farmers from northern Florida moved south to avoid winter freezes. They chopped down large swaths of trees in South Florida and installed hundreds of miles of drainage canals in the wetlands. Since then, they have increasingly found their fields of sugar cane, tomatoes, bell peppers, and lettuce freezing over with little or no warning. Researchers now say that by draining the lush wetlands that once dominated South Florida's landscape, farmers have actually changed the climate there.

According to this passage, you can reasonably infer that

    7–A   the farmers needed to move back north.

    7–B   the former wetlands somehow kept southern Florida warmer.

    7–C   Florida is a poor state for farming.

    7–D   dairy farming is more profitable than vegetable farming.

8. The Dead Sea scrolls, among the most important discoveries in modern archaeology, are religious texts that were written more than 2,000 years ago. They give a picture of the beginnings of Christianity, but many of the hundreds of scrolls, which were found in 1940 in caves in Judea, in the Middle East, were poorly preserved and unreadable. Now scientists at NASA's Jet Propulsion Laboratory, employing special camera techniques used in space probes, are having success piecing together some of these text fragments.

This passage suggests that the Dead Sea Scrolls

8–A   confirm that Christianity began more than 2,000 years ago.

8–B   were found by scientists with special cameras.

8–C   are all unreadable and poorly preserved.

8–D   were written in caves by early Christians.

9. While holidays like Christmas and Thanksgiving are joyous yearly events, they also cause much anxiety and stress. Buying the right gifts, preparing meals, cleaning and decorating homes and yards, meeting time deadlines, seeing bothersome relatives, and being reminded of lost loved ones are only some of the causes of stress during the holidays. Experts advise that in order to minimize stress it is important to try to plan ahead, delegate duties to others, set priorities, and above all, keep a sense of humor.

Which of the following would the author agree with?

9–A   You should put off unnecessary tasks during Christmas.

9–B   Never let anyone do things for you during the holidays.

9–C   Eliminating all decorating and cleaning would make life easier.

9–D   All of the above

10. Cloning is a very interesting and sometimes controversial area of medical research. Dolly, the world's first cloned sheep, was born in 1996, and recently scientists announced the birth of cloned, genetically engineered pigs that may be suitable for animal-to-human transplants. However, along with many other young cloned animals, Dolly developed arthritis, and then died at an early age, suggesting that there may be genetic defects caused by the process of cloning.

This paragraph infers that

10–A   there is no medical reason for the cloning of animals.

10–B   it is impossible to clone many different species.

10–C   it is easier to clone pigs than sheep.

10–D   cloning is probably a difficult procedure.

Questions 11 and 12 are based on the following passage.

On January 21, 2002, delegates from about sixty countries and international organizations, including U.N. Secretary-General Kofi Annan, held a conference discussing the reconstruction of Afghanistan. They discussed the scope and specifics of aid and support to be given to the country. One of the donor countries, South Korea, is planning to give about 200 million dollars to support efforts focusing on rebuilding roads and hospitals. Overall, about 15 billion dollars will need to be spent over the next ten years to rebuild Afghanistan, according to United Nations estimates.

11. From this piece, you can assume that

    11–A   there is little hope for the future of Afghanistan.

    11–B   only roads and hospitals need rebuilding.

    11–C   much needs to be done to rebuild Afghanistan.

    11–D   Kofi Annan will be in charge of all efforts to rebuild Afghanistan.

12. It appears that

    12–A   only South Korea cares to help Afghanistan.

    12–B   Kofi Annan is the Secretary-General of Korea.

    12–C   Afghanistan can only rely on itself.

    12–D   there is considerable international concern about Afghanistan.

Answer Key

1. B	2. A	3. C	4. A	5. B
6. C	7. B	8. A	9. A	10. D
11. C	12. D			

Answers and Explanations

1–B   Choice B is suggested within the first sentence: "…*winds its way along the high crest of the Appalachian Mountains.*" The fact that it goes through the crests, or peaks, of all these mountains in 14 states means that the views must be spectacular in places. There is no support for choices A or C—neither fees nor the derivation of the name are discussed in the passage.

2–A   Based on its great length—over 2,100 miles—it is safe to assume that most hikers will not hike the entire Appalachian Trail. There is no reason to assume the truth of choice B. Choice C is incorrect; the 4,000 people are mentioned as being volunteers, not hikers. Choice D is also not supported by the passage; in fact, since volunteers care for the trail, it may not cost the states or federal government anything to maintain it.

3–C   You can infer that not being able to support themselves with a good salary might be a major reason that grown children are living longer with their parents today. The other choices are either not supported by the passage or unlikely.

4–A   The last sentence is your clue. The fact that the SEC has promised *to crack down* implies that there must be some companies that are *fraudulent,* or dishonest in their practices. Choice B is contradicted by the passage, and there is no evidence for choice C.

5–B   You can assume that cowboys needed to know a considerable amount about handling these animals, since all the events revolve around riding or controlling them. No support is given for choices A and C. Choice D may be partially true; however, nothing in the passage indicates that these are dangerous activities, so it is an incorrect inference here.

6–C   You can make the inference that since *ulluco* and *oca* have been imported from Latin America as possible food sources in the United States, they are probably tasty. Otherwise, this wouldn't have happened.

7–B   The second sentence states that the wetlands were drained by farmers in southern Florida, and the last sentence states that this caused the climate to change. So, it is reasonable to assume that wetlands somehow were able to keep the temperature at a more moderate and suitable level. Choice A would not have been a good solution, and no support is given for choices C and D.

8–A   The correct answer is choice A, because if the scrolls are 2,000 years old, and they speak of Christianity, they do confirm that this religion began sometime before. Choice B is incorrect; the scientists merely studied them *after* archaeologists had found them. Choice C is partly incorrect; the passage states that *many,* not all, of the scrolls are unreadable. Choice D is incorrect, since the passage does not tell us where the scrolls were written, only where they were found.

9–A   The author states in the last sentence that it is advisable to minimize stress by "setting priorities," meaning doing important things first, and less important tasks later. Therefore, the author would agree that tasks should be put off during a stressful time like Christmas if they are not that important. Choice B is contradicted by the last line, and while choice C may be true, it is not inferred from the type of suggestions made by the author.

10–D   Since cloning is causing serious problems, such as arthritis and early death in young cloned animals like Dolly, you can infer that it is a difficult and complicated process. Choices B and C are about subjects not dealt with here, and choice A is contradicted by the passage, which mentions the possibility of transplants to humans as a medical reason for the cloning of animals.

11–C   Since as much as 15 billion dollars is needed for the rebuilding of Afghanistan, the assumption can be made from this passage that much needs to be done there.

12–D   The passage mentions that about sixty nations and organizations met for this conference and will be involved in helping Afghanistan rebuild. This implies that there is much international concern for this country.

COMPREHENSION SKILL 4: FINDING WORD MEANINGS

The final type of question you will find on the ASVAB Paragraph Comprehension Test will ask you for the *meaning of a word* used in the passage. Again, remember to *glance at the question first* to determine what kind of question you will need to answer.

In *word meaning* questions, you will utilize *context clues*. This involves using words or ideas in the *surrounding sentences* to help you determine the meaning of unfamiliar words. This is another skill necessary for good reading ability. It enables you to understand the meaning of a passage even though you may not be entirely familiar with each of the words used.

Questions that focus on *finding word meanings* will often begin like this:

In this passage, the word <u>altered</u> means _____ .

As used above, <u>pretext</u> means _____ .

The word <u>expression</u> as used in the last sentence means _____ .

The three sample questions that follow illustrate the kinds of *word meaning* questions you may find on the ASVAB Paragraph Comprehension Test.

Sample 1.   Hawaii, our fiftieth state, consists of some 130 islands stretching over 1,500 miles in length. The most developed island is Oahu, which contains the naval base at Pearl Harbor, the capital, Honolulu, and over three quarters of the state's population. Three highly active volcanoes capable of causing massive destruction are also on Oahu Island.

In this context, the word <u>active</u> means

    1–A   extinct
    1–B   noisy
    1–C   flaming
    1–D   showing life

1–D   The word *active* means showing action or movement, or *showing life*. The context clue is the phrase that follows in the sentence—*capable of causing massive destruction*. Volcanoes that cause destruction are *active* and are *showing life*. Choice A is opposite in meaning, and choices B and C are not related.

Sample 2.   The American monarch butterfly is remarkable, not just because of its wonderful size and colors, but because it is one of those species that migrates. Each spring, the monarch flies thousands of miles north to Canada for the summer, returning south along exactly the same route in the fall. No one knows how the monarch manages to do this.

As used above, the word <u>remarkable</u> means

    2–A   vigorous
    2–B   extraordinary
    2–C   commonplace
    2–D   colorful

2–B   The correct answer is *extraordinary,* or something to be noticed because of its unusual nature. In the context of the passage, the butterfly is *remarkable* because it does something so *extraordinary* as to fly thousands of miles. While the monarch is certainly vigorous as well as colorful, these are not synonyms for *remarkable,* so choices A and D are incorrect. Choice C is the opposite in meaning; something *commonplace* is an ordinary event that would *not* be *remarkable.*

Sample 3.   Curling, a game originally from Scotland, is also played in the United States, Canada, Scandinavia, and Switzerland. In curling, you must propel granite stones of up to 3 feet in circumference on ice rinks 138 feet in length, and try to hit a "tee" at the other end. National championship games are held in Canada and thousands attend to watch.

The word <u>propel</u> in the second sentence means

    3–A   drive forward
    3–B   leave home
    3–C   come along
    3–D   roll down

3–A   The word *propel* means to *drive forward,* or move something ahead with the use of force. In this case, the curler *propels,* or hurls, the heavy stone along the ice. Choices B, C, and D make no sense in the context above and are therefore incorrect.

Practice Exercise 7 will help you become familiar with how *word meaning* questions are used in the Paragraph Comprehension Test. When you finish, check your answers against the Answers and Explanations that follow.

Practice Exercise 7

Questions 1 to 3 are based on the following passage.

The cost of buying a special puppy, ranging from a couple of hundred to several thousand dollars, is determined by several factors. Purebreds cost more than mixed breeds. The scarcity, or novelty, of a particular breed can make it expensive. If the puppy's lineage includes champion studs or females, the price for the puppy will be higher. Show-quality dogs will cost more than pet-quality dogs because of their superior temperament, build, and lineage. Dogs already trained for showing in prestigious shows, such as the Westminster Kennel Club Dog Show, will cost as much as $100,000. And finally, a breed made popular by a movie or a recent "best in show" prize will be more expensive.

1. The word scarcity in the third sentence means

    1–A   not liked

    1–B   not plentiful

    1–C   abundance

    1–D   over-breeding

2. In this context, lineage means

    2–A   posture

    2–B   position

    2–C   dignity

    2–D   derivation

3. Prestigious in the second-to-last sentence means

    3–A   snobby

    3–B   honored

    3–C   yearly

    3–D   handsome

4. The moon's surface includes mountains, plains, faults, and many craters that are believed to have been formed by the explosive impact of high-velocity meteorites or small asteroids. Other craters and domes were formed by volcanoes.

    There is no weather change on the moon because it has no real atmosphere. The temperatures there are extreme, ranging from 261 degrees Fahrenheit during daytime to –279 degrees Fahrenheit at night.

As used in the first sentence, the word impact means

    4–A   heat

    4–B   presence

    4–C   collision

    4–D   impudence

5. The decision about whether to buy a house or rent depends on many factors. If you're fairly settled and planning on staying in an area for a long time, if you have good credit so you will qualify for a mortgage, if you have enough money for a down payment, and if you have a dependable income that will support monthly mortgage payments, then you could plan on buying a house. If not, then you should probably rent.

In this context, the word <u>depends</u> means to be

    5–A   lowered, lessened, or sunk

    5–B   continued, extended, or prolonged to

    5–C   based, determined, or contingent on

    5–D   None of the above

6. A recent government report warned that the United States faces a shortage of skilled workers. The report also stated that many job applicants lack basic reading and math skills. It recommended that the education system be strengthened and that it work together with other social and governmental institutions in order to help meet the need for a well-trained work force.

In this context, the word <u>strengthened</u> means

    6–A   toughened

    6–B   continued

    6–C   lengthened

    6–D   stated

7. Forest firefighters must wear clothing that is heavy-duty enough to protect the wearer from temperatures often in excess of 1,000 degrees Fahrenheit. However, this clothing must also be cool, breathable, and lightweight so that the firefighter will be able to move comfortably without feeling overly encumbered.

The last word in the passage, <u>encumbered</u>, means

    7–A   hindered

    7–B   counted

    7–C   waited

    7–D   heated

8. A giant carnivorous lizard, the Nile monitor, which is normally only found in Africa, has been seen in Cape Coral, Florida. Easily growing to 5 feet in length, the monitor is thought to be a threat to native species. It can eat fish, armadillos, foxes, ground doves, reptiles, and amphibians, and it can hunt prey in the water, trees, or even underground. Worried biologists from the University of Tampa are studying options that might include relocating or killing this animal.

As used above, the word <u>native</u> means

    8–A   famous

    8–B   indigenous

    8–C   uncommon

    8–D   growing

9. Botswana, with a democratic multiparty system of government, is among Africa's most stable countries. It has an outstanding human rights record and a constitution that provides for freedom of expression. The country is sparsely populated, with 1.5 million residents who speak English and Setswana. The Kalahari Desert makes up much of the country, and most areas are too arid to sustain agriculture other than cattle farming. Botswana attained its independence from Great Britain in 1966.

In this context, the word <u>attained</u> means

    9–A   achieved

    9–B   wanted

    9–C   altered

    9–D   climbed

Questions 10 to 12 are based on the following passage.

Giorgio Vassari was a sixteenth-century artist who was born in Arezzo, in central Italy. He was an ardent follower of Michelangelo and apprenticed with him at an early age. He also was intimate with all the famous artists of his time.

During his lifetime he became a well-known and successful painter, but today we know him primarily as the author of *The Lives of the Artists*. This book offers an entertaining wealth of facts and anecdotes about the private lives of the greatest artists of the Italian Renaissance.

10. From the context of this passage, the word <u>anecdotes</u> means

    10–A   lies

    10–B   sources

    10–C   productions

    10–D   stories

11. The word <u>ardent</u> as used in the second sentence means

    11–A   youthful

    11–B   reluctant

    11–C   enthusiastic

    11–D   friendly

12. In this story, the word <u>primarily</u> probably means

    12–A   mightily

    12–B   clearly

    12–C   only

    12–D   chiefly

Answer Key

1. B	2. D	3. B	4. C	5. C
6. A	7. A	8. B	9. A	10. D
11. C	12. D			

Answers and Explanations

1–B   There are several clues as to the meaning of *scarcity*. First, the word *novelty* immediately follows the word *scarcity*. Second, the fact that you're told that its *scarcity* makes a dog more expensive, tells you that we're talking about a *rare* breed, one that is *not plentiful*. *Scarcity* means that something is rare, unusual, not common. Choice C is the opposite in meaning.

2–D   The word *lineage* means the descent from a common ancestor, the dog's *derivation*, possibly from a champion dog. Again, the passage states that this is related to the price of a dog.

3–B   The word *honored* is closest in meaning to *prestigious,* which means having prestige, or high estimation, in most people's opinion, or being very highly regarded or much liked.

4–C   In the sentence, the word *impact* is used as a noun and means *collision*. In other words, the meteorites or asteroids *impacted* or *collided* with the moon and formed some of its craters. While heat was no doubt a factor, choice A is not a synonym for *impact*.

5–C   If a decision about something *depends* on something else, it is *based, determined,* or *contingent on* this other thing. In other words, your ability to buy a house *depends on* or is *determined by* the factors mentioned—having a steady income, good credit, etc. Choices A and B do not make sense in this context and are incorrect.

6–A   A *strengthened* educational system is one that is *toughened,* harder, and more solid. *Strengthened* is the past tense of *making strong*. In this passage, a *strengthened* school system is one that probably has *tougher* and more demanding courses, so graduates will be better prepared for work.

7–A   To be *encumbered* is to be *hindered,* weighed down, burdened, or impeded. In other words, the firefighter needs to be able to run, chop, dig, carry things, and do all necessary physical tasks without being *encumbered* by clothing that is too heavy or uncomfortable.

8–B   The word *native* as used here means something *indigenous*, or occurring naturally in a region. In the passage, *native species* refers to the wildlife inhabiting, or found in, the Cape Coral area. Choice C, *uncommon,* is almost opposite in meaning.

9–A   From the context, *achieved* is the only word that makes sense in the sentence. To *attain* something means to reach a positive goal.

10–D   The word *anecdotes* refers to *stories* or accounts of humorous or interesting incidents. The other choices do not make sense in the context of this paragraph.

11–C   The word *ardent* means *enthusiastic*, passionate, fervent, or full of positive feeling. From the context, you can tell he was an early admirer of Michelangelo, who was one of the great artists of all time.

12–D   The word *primarily* means *chiefly* or principally. It is related to words like *primary, prime,* or *primal*, which refer to being the first or highest in rank or importance. In the paragraph, the author states that Vassari was a well-known artist while he lived but is better known now as the writer of an interesting book on artists of the Italian Renaissance.

THREE SAMPLE PARAGRAPH COMPREHENSION TESTS

This section contains three full-length sample Paragraph Comprehension Tests similar to the ones on the ASVAB. Tear out this page and use the answer strips below to record your answers to the sample tests, just as you will have to do on the real test. Stick to the time limit for realistic practice. After you complete each Paragraph Comprehension Test, check your answers against the Answer Key and Explanations that follow.

Paragraph Comprehension Test 1

1. Ⓐ Ⓑ Ⓒ Ⓓ   2. Ⓐ Ⓑ Ⓒ Ⓓ   3. Ⓐ Ⓑ Ⓒ Ⓓ   4. Ⓐ Ⓑ Ⓒ Ⓓ   5. Ⓐ Ⓑ Ⓒ Ⓓ

6. Ⓐ Ⓑ Ⓒ Ⓓ   7. Ⓐ Ⓑ Ⓒ Ⓓ   8. Ⓐ Ⓑ Ⓒ Ⓓ   9. Ⓐ Ⓑ Ⓒ Ⓓ   10. Ⓐ Ⓑ Ⓒ Ⓓ

11. Ⓐ Ⓑ Ⓒ Ⓓ   12. Ⓐ Ⓑ Ⓒ Ⓓ   13. Ⓐ Ⓑ Ⓒ Ⓓ   14. Ⓐ Ⓑ Ⓒ Ⓓ   15. Ⓐ Ⓑ Ⓒ Ⓓ

Paragraph Comprehension Test 2

1. Ⓐ Ⓑ Ⓒ Ⓓ   2. Ⓐ Ⓑ Ⓒ Ⓓ   3. Ⓐ Ⓑ Ⓒ Ⓓ   4. Ⓐ Ⓑ Ⓒ Ⓓ   5. Ⓐ Ⓑ Ⓒ Ⓓ

6. Ⓐ Ⓑ Ⓒ Ⓓ   7. Ⓐ Ⓑ Ⓒ Ⓓ   8. Ⓐ Ⓑ Ⓒ Ⓓ   9. Ⓐ Ⓑ Ⓒ Ⓓ   10. Ⓐ Ⓑ Ⓒ Ⓓ

11. Ⓐ Ⓑ Ⓒ Ⓓ   12. Ⓐ Ⓑ Ⓒ Ⓓ   13. Ⓐ Ⓑ Ⓒ Ⓓ   14. Ⓐ Ⓑ Ⓒ Ⓓ   15. Ⓐ Ⓑ Ⓒ Ⓓ

Paragraph Comprehension Test 3

1. Ⓐ Ⓑ Ⓒ Ⓓ   2. Ⓐ Ⓑ Ⓒ Ⓓ   3. Ⓐ Ⓑ Ⓒ Ⓓ   4. Ⓐ Ⓑ Ⓒ Ⓓ   5. Ⓐ Ⓑ Ⓒ Ⓓ

6. Ⓐ Ⓑ Ⓒ Ⓓ   7. Ⓐ Ⓑ Ⓒ Ⓓ   8. Ⓐ Ⓑ Ⓒ Ⓓ   9. Ⓐ Ⓑ Ⓒ Ⓓ   10. Ⓐ Ⓑ Ⓒ Ⓓ

11. Ⓐ Ⓑ Ⓒ Ⓓ   12. Ⓐ Ⓑ Ⓒ Ⓓ   13. Ⓐ Ⓑ Ⓒ Ⓓ   14. Ⓐ Ⓑ Ⓒ Ⓓ   15. Ⓐ Ⓑ Ⓒ Ⓓ

PARAGRAPH COMPREHENSION TEST 1

TIME: 13 Minutes—15 Questions

This test contains 15 items measuring your ability to obtain information from written passages. You will find one or more paragraphs of reading material followed by incomplete statements or questions. You are to read the paragraph(s) and select the lettered choice that best completes the statement or answers the question.

Your score on this test will be based on the number of questions you answer correctly. You should try to answer every question. Do not spend too much time on any one item.

1. The North Atlantic Treaty Organization (or NATO) was originally formed in 1949 to protect Europe from possible aggression by the Soviet Union. The United States, West Germany, England, and France were some of NATO's original members, with the treaty providing for their mutual defense. In recent years, after the fall of the Soviet Union, there has been a new spirit of cooperation between NATO and Russia. This is the result of Russia's growing friendship and economic relationship with Western Europe and the United States.

   The North Atlantic Treaty Organization (NATO)
   1–A   includes several European countries.
   1–B   invaded Russia shortly after 1949.
   1–C   is part of the United Nations.
   1–D   defends Asia from the Soviet Union.

2. The Internet is a wonderful place to follow up on many of your interests in sports. For instance, do you like basketball? The ideal place to look up news and information for NBA, college, or street basketball is InsideHoops.com. This is a site rated highly by many Web directories. It is full of amusing articles and unique features, and it has content from basketball experts as well as from fans.

   As used above, the word <u>unique</u> means
   2–A   interesting
   2–B   unparalleled
   2–C   many sided
   2–D   funny

3. It is now possible for you to take a continuous 32-mile bike path, the *Manhattan Waterfront Greenway*, around the perimeter of Manhattan Island. You will pass Battery Park; the old Fulton Fish Market; the East River; the beginning of 42nd Street; the Brooklyn, Manhattan, Triborough, and George Washington Bridges; the Harlem and Hudson Rivers; and the Intrepid Museum. Along the way, you will be in close touch with the different neighborhoods, sounds, and lifestyles that make New York such an unusual and enjoyable city.

   From this passage, you can infer that
   3–A   Manhattan is 32 miles in length.
   3–B   the author knows and admires New York City.
   3–C   42nd Street runs from Manhattan to Brooklyn.
   3–D   no bikes are allowed within Manhattan.

4. Every four years, the *International Culinary Olympics* is held in a different location. Champion cooks prepare their menus in glass-walled kitchens, closely watched by a jury that assesses technical skill, creativity of recipes, artful presentation, and taste. Among the contestants are national teams, military teams, and youth teams. Meanwhile, the delicious results of all this cooking can be tasted by visitors at several *Olympics* restaurants.

Which of the following is a TRUE statement according to the passage?

4–A   The contestants all cook in well-known restaurants.

4–B   Dishes are judged by presentation, not by taste.

4–C   The competitors probably represent many different countries.

4–D   Only established cooks may enter the competition.

5. The Northern Rockies is the only area in the lower 48 states that still contains all the animal species that existed at the time of the Lewis and Clark expedition, and it is therefore an ecological region that is one of America's most precious natural treasures. In these wild lands of Montana, Wyoming, Idaho, Oregon, and Washington, the Grey wolf is making a comeback, and grizzly bears, bison, mountain lions, and vast herds of elk roam the spectacular landscape.

The Northern Rockies are a *natural American treasure* because

5–A   Lewis and Clark explored the area.

5–B   all ecological areas are precious.

5–C   many new species of wildlife were developed there.

5–D   wolves, grizzly bears, bison, mountain lions, and elk still live there.

6. One of Russia's former rulers was Catherine the Great, who was in power during the eighteenth century. She set up a system of representation for most of the social classes of Russia. However, the system worked imperfectly and did not address the problem of great poverty among the masses. After a serious peasant revolt, she gave more power to the central government in order to keep better control over the dissatisfied peasants in Russia.

The best title for this passage is

6–A   "Catherine the Great and Her Advisors."

6–B   "Central Governments versus Local Governments."

6–C   "A Famous Russian Ruler."

6–D   "Peasant Revolts in Russia."

7. During times when it may be difficult to find a job, many people start a business of their own. Even with limited experience, training, or education, most people have skills or talents that they can put to good use. Examples of possible businesses for an adventurous entrepreneur to start are pet care services, after-school child care, lawn or property care, or driving and doing chores for handicapped or elderly people. Even when times seem hopeless, by looking around and trying to see what services people might need, many possibilities can be discovered for creating a job or business.

From this passage, you can infer that the author

7–A   looks down on businesspeople.

7–B   feels hopeless about earning a living.

7–C   is unemployed.

7–D   is an optimist.

8. Queen Victoria was born in 1819, becoming Queen of England when she was only 18 years of age. She quickly asserted her style and authority in spite of her youth and ruled as queen for sixty-four years. During this unusually long tenure, she saw many historic events and the growth of England into a global industrial power. Queen Victoria eventually became the grandparent of royalty in countries all over Europe, such as Russia, Germany, Sweden, Spain, Greece, Rumania, and Norway.

From this passage, you can assume that

8–A	Queen Victoria never married.
8–B	good queens are born, not made.
8–C	the industrial revolution started after her death.
8–D	many European royal families are related.

Questions 9 and 10 are based on the following passage.

The fabled intersection of Hollywood and Vine has been renamed *Bob Hope Square,* in honor of the famous comedian and movie star who died in 2003 at the age of 100. However, Bob Hope was as much loved for his kind and giving nature as for his ready wit. He gave lavishly to charity, and he traveled millions of miles to entertain servicepeople in field hospitals, jungles, and aircraft carriers from France to Germany, and from Vietnam to the Persian Gulf. Bob had a familiar joke for the many times his shows were interrupted by gunfire: "I wonder which one of my pictures they saw?"

9. What does the word <u>lavishly</u> mean as used above?

9–A	generously
9–B	carefully
9–C	mightily
9–D	None of the above

10. Bob Hope

10–A	lived on Hollywood and Vine.
10–B	drove aircraft carriers in France.
10–C	traveled extensively.
10–D	only entertained during peacetime.

11. Cell phones are becoming increasingly important. While a lot of people still rely on regular telephones or beepers, others find that cell phones fully satisfy their communication needs. Because of the portability of cell phones, this seems to be especially true of college students or others who are not yet in permanent living situations.

According to this passage, many college students

11–A	have beepers and cell phones.
11–B	rely just on cell phones.
11–C	live in dormitories.
11–D	think cell phones are portable.

12. Women who work and have children face increased pressures and responsibilities. Over 50 percent of mothers with young children are now working, more than double the rate in 1970. Help often comes from husbands who share the housework, responsible baby-sitters, and employers who are willing to give working mothers flexible work schedules.

According to the paragraph, working mothers probably

    12–A   seek higher wages.
    12–B   had mothers who also worked.
    12–C   find support from their employers helpful.
    12–D   have more divorces than mothers who don't work.

13. Because rock-and-roll frequently is geared to appeal to teenagers, the singers are often teenagers themselves. For example, Elvis Presley was only 19 years old when his first recording of nine songs was widely acclaimed by the public. Stevie Wonder and Mariah Carey are also examples of singers who recorded million-dollar records while still in their teens.

This paragraph is mainly about

    13–A   public demand for million-dollar records.
    13–B   Elvis Presley.
    13–C   young stars of rock-and-roll.
    13–D   the music industry.

14. At one time, most people were apprehensive about going to the dentist because of the pain and suffering they often experienced in the dental office. During the past twenty-five years, however, patients have become much more relaxed because there has been progress in the use of different anesthetics and because of technological advances, such as the invention of high-speed drills. Therefore, even the most serious procedures now cause very little pain or discomfort for the patient.

This paragraph is mainly about

    14–A   advances in dentistry.
    14–B   combating cavities.
    14–C   false teeth.
    14–D   dental anesthetics.

15. China promotes Internet use for business and education and now has the second-biggest population of Internet users in the world, estimated at 70 million. The biggest group using the Internet in China is male and between the ages of 18 and 24. However, much of this group's time online, averaging 13 hours per week, is spent playing games. Currently there are almost half a million Web sites in China.

Which of the following is the best title for this passage?

    15–A   "The Growth of the Internet"
    15–B   "Education and Business"
    15–C   "Chinese Education"
    15–D   "Internet Use in China"

Answer Key

1. A	2. B	3. B	4. C	5. D
6. C	7. D	8. D	9. A	10. C
11. B	12. C	13. C	14. A	15. D

Answers and Explanations

1–A   Since France, West Germany, and England were mentioned as being NATO members, and these are European nations, this is the correct answer.

2–B   The word *unique* here means that this site is *unparalleled* when compared to other sites—in other words, unusual or impossible to duplicate.

3–B   All the information given in the passage and the closing phrase, *an unusual and enjoyable city*, tells you that the author knows and likes New York City. Choice A is incorrect; the bike path *circling* Manhattan, not Manhattan itself, is 32 miles long. Choice C is incorrect; there is no statement about 42nd Street going into Brooklyn. Choice D is contradictory to the passage; if bikes were not allowed in Manhattan, a bike path would be unnecessary.

4–C   Both the name of the competition and the mention of national teams tell you that contestants from different countries compete. Choice A is not supported by the passage. Choice B is incorrect; the second sentence states that judges consider taste *and* presentation. Choice D is also incorrect, since the mention of youth teams suggests that young cooks as well as established cooks participate.

5–D   These animals still live there as they did in olden days—they have not died out. While Lewis and Clark *did* explore the Northern Rockies, choice A is not the correct answer to the question, which asks about *natural American treasures*. Choice B sounds true, but it doesn't answer the question. Choice C is incorrect, because the passage talks about the preservation of *old* species, not the creation of *new* ones.

6–C   When you are asked for the best title, you are looking for the title that gives the main idea of the passage. This passage is about a famous Russian ruler, Catherine the Great. The other options are not good titles because they do not reflect the main idea of the passage.

7–D   The author is an *optimist* because he expects things to turn out well. In other words, the passage states that a jobless person can often succeed in creating a job for himself. Choice B expresses the opposite view and is therefore incorrect, as is choice A. Choice C assumes something about the author regarding whom we have been told nothing.

8–D   This is the correct answer because, according to the last sentence, much of European royalty shared the same grandmother, Queen Victoria. In other words, many members of these royal families are distant cousins.

9–A   The context clue words are in the previous sentence—*kind and giving nature. Lavishly,* therefore, means *generously* or abundantly. Giving lavishly to charity means he gave a lot, he gave generously, frequently, and more than most other people.

10–C   Bob Hope traveled extensively. This is stated in the first sentence of the second paragraph—*he traveled millions of miles to entertain servicepeople.* Choice B is an incorrect statement; Bob entertained on carriers, he didn't drive them. Choice D is contradicted by the last sentence, which mentions gunfire, suggesting that he bravely entertained during wartime and probably close to the front.

11–B   The passage states that college students are especially likely to just use cell phones, which fully satisfy their needs. Choice A is only partially correct, because beepers are not mentioned in relation to college students. Choice C doesn't relate to the question, and choice D, while probably a correct statement, is not the best answer to this question.

12–C   The answer to this question can be gotten by eliminating the obviously incorrect choices. Since higher wages, mothers of currently working women, and divorce are not mentioned in the passage, choices A, B, and D can be eliminated. Choice C can be inferred to be the correct answer.

13–C   The main idea of this passage is that some rock-and-roll stars are young like their audiences.

14–A   Since the passage speaks mainly about improvements in the field of dentistry, choice A is the best answer. Anesthetics are mentioned, but not as the main idea, so choice D is incorrect. The other choices are incorrect because there is no mention of cavities or false teeth here.

15–D   The passage deals with the growth of Internet use in China—who uses it, what for, and how the government feels about it. So "*Internet Use in China*" is the best title. Choices B and C would be misleading, as the passage is not about the Internet, education, or business as such, and choice A is also not the topic of the passage.

PARAGRAPH COMPREHENSION TEST 2

TIME: 13 Minutes—15 Questions

This test contains 15 items measuring your ability to obtain information from written passages. You will find one or more paragraphs of reading material followed by incomplete statements or questions. You are to read the paragraph(s) and select the lettered choice that best completes the statement or answers the question.

Your score on this test will be based on the number of questions you answer correctly. You should try to answer every question. Do not spend too much time on any one question.

1.   Electric eels are 6 to 9 feet in length, shaped like snakes, and found in the marshy waters of the Amazon River Basin in South America. They can produce strong electrical currents reaching 650 volts that can stun or kill prey that they then eat whole. Their bodies are similar to a battery, with the tail end having a positive charge, and the head region negatively charged. By touching its tail and head to another animal, the eel sends electric shocks through its victim's body.

This passage best supports the statement that

      1–A   many fish are immune to the eel's electrical charge.

      1–B   Amazonian fish kill eels with electric shocks.

      1–C   electric eels are too small to do any harm.

      1–D   it is best not to swim in the marshy waters of the Amazon.

2. The Amish are one of the original American settlers who arrived from Europe seeking religious freedom. Currently, they number about 150 thousand and live on farms in 26 states. The largest communities reside in Ohio, Indiana, and Pennsylvania, where they live a simple, separate, and religiously observant life without the use of modern inventions such as electricity, automobiles, radio, or television. They often supplement their income by making and selling beautiful quilts and wooden furniture.

Which of the following would make the best title for this passage?

    2–A   "Who Are the Amish?"

    2–B   "The Amish of Pennsylvania"

    2–C   "Amish Farming"

    2–D   "Modern Amish Technology"

3. El Greco, or "the Greek," was a famous artist who lived in Spain. His paintings are easily recognizable, often depicting faces that are lengthened, giving them a dream-like quality. He tended to use strikingly dramatic dark colors in his paintings. El Greco influenced many succeeding generations of artists.

The paintings of El Greco

    3–A   often have faces that are lengthened.

    3–B   are found only in Spain and France.

    3–C   show dreams of different people.

    3–D   have no contrast in colors.

4. Putting down a beautiful new wooden floor has never been easier for the do-it-yourself homeowner. The floor can be made of solid wood or a new and cheaper longwearing wood laminate. Strips or planks of this wood can be nailed down to the subfloor or installed as a "floating" floor on top of a foam underlayment. Parquet floors are the easiest to install because the tiles simply are glued to the subfloor.

Which of the following statements would this author agree with?

    4–A   Ceramic tile floors are the most attractive and practical.

    4–B   Replacing your floor will require expert craftsmanship.

    4–C   A parquet floor is installed over a floating underlayment.

    4–D   If you have an old, worn-looking floor, replace it.

5. Judging by the large variety of vegetarian dishes that are now available in most restaurants, it seems that vegetarian diets are getting very popular. Usually, these dishes are presented as healthy alternatives to foods that are often rich in animal protein and fat. Vegetarian foods appeal to many people who are concerned about the unhealthy effects of animal fats and cholesterol, as well as those who are reluctant to eat the flesh of a once-living being.

In the context of this paragraph, the word <u>alternatives</u> means

    5–A   vegetables

    5–B   varieties

    5–C   options

    5–D   dishes

6. Americans work an average of nine weeks more each year than Europeans. While Europeans have made a tradeoff between quality of life and hours worked, Americans have chosen to trade increases in productivity for more belongings. In order to pay for their expensive lifestyle, Americans need to work even more. The result has been the creation of a lot of very stressed out, unhappy Americans, with not enough leisure time to enjoy the fruits of higher production.

Which of the following is implied by the above passage?

    6–A   Europeans are probably less stressed than Americans.
    6–B   Many Americans work harder but are not happier than Europeans.
    6–C   Europeans are more modest in their money-spending habits than Americans.
    6–D   All of the above

7. Sushi is a Japanese delicacy that is becoming increasingly popular in the United States. It is made with bite-sized amounts of rolled vinegar rice and may contain bits of raw or smoked fish, such as tuna, salmon, and mackerel, as well as vegetables such as avocado and scallion. These are often covered in dry seaweed and served with ginger, hot mustard, and soy sauce. The 12 to 15 pieces of sushi are then presented on a very colorful platter so that your appetite will be enhanced. Try some!

Which of the following is a TRUE statement according to this passage?

    7–A   If you can't eat raw fish, stay away from sushi.
    7–B   All sushi is made with rice.
    7–C   Sushi comes from China and Japan.
    7–D   Americans generally don't like ethnic foods.

Questions 8 and 9 are based on the following passage.

The new 120,000 square-foot Ratho Adventure Center, built near Edinburgh, Scotland, contains the world's biggest indoor climbing arena. The complex, which was constructed in a former stone quarry, is expected to attract up to 200,000 visitors a year, and it is hoped that it will become a world center for climbing and a host to international competitions.

  In addition to climbing facilities, the Ratho Center includes the Scottish Judo Federation's National Academy, BMX and mountain bike trails, a scuba diving school, a health spa, and a wide range of additional sports and fitness facilities.

8. Which of the following is an UNTRUE statement?

    8–A   Thousands of visitors will probably be attracted to Ratho.
    8–B   Many different activities can be enjoyed at Ratho.
    8–C   The Ratho rock-climbing wall is 120,000 feet high.
    8–D   There is a health spa at Ratho.

9. Ratho Adventure Center

    9–A   is in the center of the city of Edinburgh.
    9–B   will feature heavyweight boxing matches.
    9–C   is American.
    9–D   was built in a stone quarry.

10. On July 27, 1995, President Bill Clinton and South Korean President Kim Young Sam dedicated the Korean War Veterans Memorial at a site next to the Lincoln Memorial and directly across the reflecting pool from the Vietnam Memorial in Washington, D.C.

To honor the brave men who fought in Korea, nineteen huge sculptures and 15,000 Korean War photographs from the National Archives have been placed at this Memorial. There is also a beautiful 164-foot mural depicting Army, Navy, Marine Corps, Air Force, and Coast Guard personnel and their equipment.

According to this paragraph,

10–A   Kim Young Sam built the Memorial.
10–B   President Clinton is pictured on the mural.
10–C   the Korean War Memorial was built *after* the Vietnam War Memorial.
10–D   there are 15,000 photographs of this Memorial in the National Archives.

11. Most American children have much trouble learning foreign languages later on in life. Meanwhile, children in many other countries easily learn as many as four or five languages as toddlers and speak them throughout their lives. In Poland, for example, many children pick up Polish, Russian, Ukrainian, and German on a daily basis, and are also taught English in school.

What can you infer from this passage?

11–A   It is easier to learn foreign languages as a child than as an adult.
11–B   American children are not as smart as Polish children.
11–C   Children in Latin America speak Spanish.
11–D   Any adult can learn a foreign language easily.

12. *Frankenstein,* the classic novel about the creation of frightening artificial life forms, was written by Mary Shelley. While today it is regarded as complete fiction, this book dealt with some questions being asked by serious scientists of its time. Could the dead be brought back to life? Could life arise spontaneously from non-living things? Life-restoring blood transfusions had just been invented, and the mysterious effect electricity had on nerves was being observed, so many people in Shelley's time worried that scientists may one day create a real-life *Frankenstein* monster.

The main idea of this passage is that

12–A   Mary Shelley's book proved the dead could be brought back to life.
12–B   scientists have not always been very serious.
12–C   *Frankenstein* reflected some serious scientific questions of its time.
12–D   scientists will surely create a *Frankenstein* monster in time.

13. Being in the U.S. Military helps develop many changes in the character of the young people who enlist. The most important trait learned is self-discipline. Self-discipline enables people to learn difficult skills, overcome bad habits, and develop pride and purpose while serving their country. Young men and women also become more goal-oriented as a result of their increasing self-discipline and maturity. These traits form the basis of lifelong success.

Which of the following would make the best title for this passage?

13–A   "Serving Your Country"
13–B   "How to Overcome Bad Habits"
13–C   "Learning Self-Discipline in the Military"
13–D   "How to Be Successful in the Military"

14. Japanese scientists have developed a robot called *Aquarobot* that can be used for underwater tasks or exploration. It is computer operated and remote controlled. *Aquarobot* uses a six-legged spider-like concept that allows it to operate on very rough surfaces where wheel or caterpillar-type robots would have great difficulty moving.

The *Aquarobot*

   14–A   is a six-legged mountain-climbing robot.

   14–B   is operated by remote control.

   14–C   costs a lot of money.

   14–D   is the only underwater robot in existence.

15. Did you know that the United States has two parallel court systems, the state and the federal? The state system was put in place by the individual colonial states before the U.S. Constitution was written, and the federal system was developed and added afterwards.

As used above, what does the word <u>parallel</u> mean?

   15–A   similar

   15–B   difficult

   15–C   foreign

   15–D   legal

Answer Key

1. D	2. A	3. A	4. D	5. C
6. D	7. B	8. C	9. D	10. C
11. A	12. C	13. C	14. B	15. A

Answers and Explanations

1–D   You can reasonably infer that it would be unwise to swim in such waters since electric eels are found there. Choice A is incorrect—we are not told if any fish are immune. Choice B is a misstatement—electric eels kill Amazonian fish, not the other way around. Choice C is contradicted by the passage, which states that electric eels are large and *can* do considerable harm.

2–A   Since the paragraph is a summary of their origins and main characteristics, the best title is "*Who Are the Amish*?" Choice B is too restrictive. Amish farming as such is not discussed, so choice C is also incorrect. Choice D is clearly incorrect, since the third sentence states that technology has no place in the lives of the Amish.

3–A   The second sentence tells you that El Greco's paintings have faces that are lengthened.

4–D   The first sentence states that redoing a floor is now easy. Choice A is not mentioned. Choice B is contradicted by the passage, which states that this job can be done by a do-it-yourselfer. Choice C is incorrect, according to the last sentence; parquet floors are glued, not put on top of an underlayment.

5–C In this passage, the word *options* is the correct choice. People who object to fatty meats or other animal protein dishes in their diets often pick what they view as healthy *alternatives* to meat dishes, choices or *options* such as vegetarian selections.

6–D Choices A, B, and C are all correct inferences based on the passage, which indicates that Europeans work less, spend less, and have more leisure time than Americans. You can infer that working less makes them feel less stressed and happier than the average American.

7–B Sushi is always made with rice, according to the second sentence of the passage, although other ingredients may vary. Choices A and C are only partly correct, and choice D is contradicted by the passage.

8–C The correct answer, and UNTRUE statement, is that the Ratho climbing wall is 120,000 feet high. The first sentence tells you that this number refers to the square footage of the entire facility, not the height of the wall. Choices A, B, and D are correct statements, since the large number of expected visitors and the offering of many activities and facilities, including a health spa, are referred to.

9–D This question tests your ability to take in many facts correctly while reading quickly. The second sentence states that the sports center was built in a former stone quarry, so choice D is correct.

10–C This is the correct answer, since the first sentence tells us the Vietnam War Memorial was already there at the time of the dedication in 1995. The first two choices are wrong. The last choice is also wrong, since the photos depict the Korean War, not the Memorial.

11–A Since Polish children, unlike Americans, are exposed to these languages as toddlers and then speak them throughout their lives, you can infer that it is easier to learn languages as a child than as an adult. No support is given for choice B, choice C is not discussed, and choice D is contrary to the message of the paragraph.

12–C The main idea is that *Frankenstein,* which we now consider merely to be an example of fiction, actually deals with issues scientists were questioning at the time it was written. Choice A is incorrect, since *Frankenstein* was fiction and Mary Shelley a writer, not a scientist. Choice B is not supported by the passage, which speaks of those scientists having serious concerns. Choice D is an inference that is not supported by the passage.

13–C This is a main idea question. Since self-discipline is mentioned in three out of the five sentences of the passage, it is likely to be the main idea of the passage and a good basis for a title. The other choices mention less-important aspects of what a person learns by being in the military and therefore do not make good titles.

14–B The correct answer is given in the second sentence—*it is computer operated and remote controlled.* Choice A is incorrect; the robot does not climb mountains, but is used in water. Choice C is not discussed, and choice D is not supported by the passage.

15–A As used in the first sentence, the word *parallel* means *similar, comparable,* or *side-by-side*—there are two *similar, side-by-side* court systems in the United States.

PARAGRAPH COMPREHENSION TEST 3

TIME: 13 Minutes—15 Questions

This test contains 15 items measuring your ability to obtain information from written passages. You will find one or more paragraphs of reading material followed by incomplete statements or questions. You are to read the paragraph(s) and select the lettered choice that best completes the statement or answers the question.

Your score on this test will be based on the number of questions you answer correctly. You should try to answer every question. Do not spend too much time on any one question.

1. Sometimes, strange sea creatures that have never been seen before get washed ashore. Recently, a huge 40-foot long slimy blob of flesh appeared on a beach in Chile. Scientists from France and Italy thought that it might be from a rare type of giant octopus, resembling those reportedly seen from time to time, while others thought it was just some blubber from a dead whale. Tissue samples sent abroad for analysis will hopefully clarify what the creature actually was.

The 40-foot slimy blob
    1–A   floated from France or Italy.
    1–B   might be from a giant octopus.
    1–C   clearly was a dead whale.
    1–D   is seen regularly in Chile.

2. Tiny and beautiful, Monaco is a country at the foot of the Maritime Alps noted for a mild climate and magnificent scenery. Once a popular destination for aristocrats, it now receives more than two million visitors a year. Popular events include the Grand Prix, a world-famous car race that takes place in the streets of Monte Carlo in May, and the *Fête du Prince* on November 19, a celebration with fireworks, pageants, and yacht races.

From the context above, the word __magnificent__ means
    2–A   striking
    2–B   sweet
    2–C   mountainous
    2–D   flat

Questions 3 and 4 are based on the following passage.

Five-star U.S. Army General Douglas MacArthur was the highly decorated and brilliant commander who served in both world wars and in the Korean War.

The son of a Civil War hero, MacArthur graduated with highest honors from West Point. He commanded the 42nd "Rainbow" Division of the Allied Expeditionary Force in France during World War I. Later he became the U.S. Army Chief of Staff, and then was appointed Field Marshall of the Philippine Army.

During World War II, MacArthur was Supreme Allied Commander of the Southwest Pacific and accepted Japan's unconditional surrender in 1945. While leading UN forces in South Korea in 1951, he was relieved of his command because of outspoken disagreements with President Truman about policy.

General MacArthur died in 1962 at the age of 84.

3. General Douglas MacArthur

    3–A   died during World War II.

    3–B   attended the Naval Academy.

    3–C   was born in 1962.

    3–D   None of the above

4. What is this passage mainly about?

    4–A   American military history

    4–B   The military career of Douglas MacArthur

    4–C   The United States Army

    4–D   World War I and World War II

5. AIDS is still a major concern all over the world. According to estimates given by the United Nations for the past year, there were 3.2 million more dead and 5 million more persons with HIV infections than the previous year. There are currently a total of 43 million people now living with HIV or with AIDS. Of these numbers, 28 million infected people live in Africa. Urgently needed are prevention measures, sex education, better treatment access, and the allotment of large amounts of money to fight this devastating epidemic.

The best title for this passage is

    5–A   "Better Treatment for AIDS."

    5–B   "The United Nations and AIDS."

    5–C   "The Continuing AIDS Epidemic."

    5–D   "Sex Education."

6. The cuckoo, a large grayish-brown bird found in Europe, is a clever parasite. It lays its eggs in the nests of other birds, which then are fooled into hatching these eggs and rearing the offspring. The offspring cuckoo will throw out any other birds or eggs from the nest, leaving itself as the sole bird being fed by the nesting mother. The cuckoo chick will also use its call to lure birds other than its host parents to feed it.

Which of the following is a TRUE statement about cuckoo birds?

    6–A   They make good pets.

    6–B   Cuckoos are found in Europe and Asia.

    6–C   They have a funny whistle.

    6–D   Cuckoos survive on the efforts of other birds.

7. According to a survey done in 2001 by Freedom House, an independent agency that monitors political rights and civil liberties around the world, 121 of the world's 192 governments are now electoral democracies. Some 29 countries, including the United States, received a perfect score, while 86 other countries are considered genuinely free according to the survey.

   The agency measures areas like the right to form political parties representing a wide range of views; the protection of religious, ethnic, and economic rights; and protection of freedom of the press, belief, and association.

According to the survey, the United States is
   7–A   only partly free.
   7–B   an overseer of Freedom House.
   7–C   one of the freest countries in the world.
   7–D   genuinely religious.

8. According to the best seller *The Millionaire Next Door,* the way to become a millionaire is to live frugally and put as much of your earnings into savings or investments as possible. Studies of people who have become millionaires show that most have spent their lifetimes living in modest homes, driving inexpensive cars, not giving excessive money or support to their children, and never spending more than they earn. By developing these sensible habits of money management, you too may eventually become a millionaire!

The author of this paragraph would NOT agree with your
   8–A   putting a set amount into savings each year.
   8–B   sending your children to college.
   8–C   buying a new expensive car each year.
   8–D   living in a good neighborhood.

9. Global warming has caused coral bleaching in the tropical waters of places such as the Great Barrier Reef in Australia, Hawaii, Maldives, Sri Lanka, Kenya, and Tanzania. The delicate coral, which is normally a beautiful orange, yellow, pink, or blue color, turns white if it becomes stressed by elevated sea temperatures. Coral is also sensitive to high light intensity, pollution, and low salt levels in the water. If these conditions persist too long, the coral can die.

The most important message of this passage is that coral
   9–A   is seen all over the world.
   9–B   may disappear unless care is taken.
   9–C   is very beautiful.
   9–D   is probably too delicate to survive.

10. Giuseppe Verdi, the composer of many operas, such as *Aida,* was one of the most beloved personalities of his day. When he became old and was suffering from his last illness, Italians passing his mansion in Milan refrained from blowing their car horns or making any noises that might disturb the maestro. Verdi's death was a tragedy that saddened the whole world. Tens of thousands walked after his funeral procession, singing a famous chorus from one of his operas.

Which of the following can be inferred from this passage?

10–A   Verdi's music was widely known in Italy.

10–B   Opera was not much liked during Verdi's lifetime.

10–C   Italians are a naturally expressive people.

10–D   Verdi died in a little town in France.

11. In 2003, the five safest states to live in, according to data based on FBI crime figures and compiled by Morgan Quitno, were Vermont, North Dakota, Maine, South Dakota, and New Hampshire. These states had the lowest crime figures in the country. The states rated as being the furthest above the national average in crime were Louisiana, Nevada, Arizona, Florida, and Maryland.

Which of the following is a TRUE statement?

11–A   Maine and Louisiana are dangerous states to live in.

11–B   The CIA keeps careful and timely crime statistics.

11–C   You do not need to lock your doors in Maryland.

11–D   Florida and Nevada have an above-average crime problem.

12. Quebec, Canada is the home of the uniquely beautiful *Ice Hotel,* a structure made entirely out of ice and snow, with ceilings as high as 18 feet, 4-foot-thick walls covered with artwork, and furniture carved from ice blocks. The Ice Hotel has many guest rooms, theme suites, two exhibition rooms, a cinema, chapel, reception room, working fireplaces, hot tubs, and the famous Absolut Ice Bar. It takes five weeks and 400 tons of ice to make this architectural marvel each winter.

According to this passage,

12–A   the Ice Hotel is built for just one season.

12–B   there are several other Ice Hotels in Canada.

12–C   the hotel's walls are 18 feet thick.

12–D   the furniture is made of ash and pine.

Questions 13 to 15 are based on the following passage:

Many people are not hampered by their severe disabilities. One prominent example is Stephen Hawking, who is regarded as the most brilliant theoretical physicist since Albert Einstein. He has been confined to a wheelchair by Lou Gehrig's disease for several decades and has serious problems with his speech. Nevertheless, he has been teaching in Great Britain and writing about his important new insights into the universe and the nature of time.

13. From its use here, the word <u>hampered</u> means

13–A   embarrassed

13–B   held back

13–C   concerned

13–D   helped

14. The best title for this piece is
- 14–A   "The Bravery of Stephen Hawking."
- 14–B   "Lou Gehrig's Disease."
- 14–C   "Problems of the Disabled."
- 14–D   "Brilliant Physicists."

15. The reader may conclude that
- 15–A   Hawking is a determined person.
- 15–B   Hawking knew Albert Einstein.
- 15–C   Hawking's disability is not that serious.
- 15–D   Lou Gehrig's disease is treatable.

Answer Key

1. B	2. A	3. D	4. B	5. C
6. D	7. C	8. C	9. B	10. A
11. D	12. A	13. B	14. A	15. A

Answers and Explanations

1–B   Some scientists guessed that it *might* be from an octopus, so choice B is correct. Since scientists couldn't agree as to what it was or where it came from, choices A and C, which make unsupported statements about the blob, are incorrect. The blob was an unusual occurrence, both in Chile or elsewhere, as stated in the first two sentences, so choice D is also incorrect.

2–A   In the first sentence, it is stated that Monaco is a beautiful country, and the word *magnificent* indicates that it is really *striking*, or unusually grand and extraordinarily splendid in appearance.

3–D   The passage states that MacArthur died in 1962, and that World War II ended in 1945, so choices A and C are incorrect. He attended West Point, not the Naval Academy, so choice B is incorrect. Choice D, *none of the above*, is the correct answer.

4–B   The passage outlines the military accomplishments of Douglas MacArthur, so the correct answer is choice B, *the military career of Douglas MacArthur.* The other choices are mentioned but they are not what the passage is mainly about.

5–C   The passage gives current statistics about the AIDS epidemic, so this is the best title. Since treatment and sex education are only mentioned in passing, and the United Nations is only cited as a source of numbers about AIDS, the other choices would not make good titles for this passage.

6–D   The correct answer is found in the first sentence—"The cuckoo…*is a clever parasite*," meaning it lives on the work and effort of other birds. Choices A and C are not discussed in the passage. Choice B is only partly correct—the bird is found in Europe, but not in Asia.

7–C   The second sentence states that the United States received a perfect score. That means that, along with 28 other countries, it is among the freest of the 192 countries of the world. The other choices are incorrect according to this passage.

8–C   The book promotes living modestly and sensibly according to your means. This does *not* infer that children shouldn't be educated, or that living in a good neighborhood is bad. Choice C, *buying a new expensive car each year,* would suggest overspending, even for a millionaire, so it is something the author would NOT agree with.

9–B   The most important message is that coral is sensitive to things such as water temperature and pollution and may die out unless more care is taken. While coral is seen in many locations, as stated in the first sentence, and is probably beautiful, neither of these is the most important message, so choices A and C are incorrect. Choice D is not supported by the passage.

10–A   Part of the last sentence—*thousands walked…singing a famous chorus from one of his operas*—shows that Verdi's music was very widely known. Choice B is contradicted by Verdi being described as a most beloved personality in the first sentence. There is no support for choice C. The second sentence tells you that Verdi died in Milan, Italy, not in France, so choice D is incorrect.

11–D   The last sentence lists both Florida and Nevada as having above-average crime. Choice A is only partly correct. The FBI, not the CIA, keeps U.S. crime statistics, so choice B is incorrect. Choice C is incorrect, since Maryland is listed as a dangerous, not a safe, state.

12–A   According to the last sentence, the *Ice Hotel* is rebuilt *each winter,* meaning that it only lasts for one winter season. Obviously this is because the hotel will melt as the weather warms up in the spring. No other such hotels are mentioned, so choice B is incorrect. Choice C is also wrong—the 18 foot measurement refer to the height of the ceiling. Choice D is contradicted by the first sentence. The furniture is not made of wood, but of blocks of ice.

13–B   The paragraph is about not being *hampered, held back*, impeded, hindered, or encumbered by a serious disability. Stephen Hawking is not *hampered* from doing his work even though he has a severe disability.

14–A   The article certainly suggests that Stephen Hawking is brave, so this would make a good title. His disease, the problems of the disabled, and brilliant physicists in general are not dealt with at length in the passage, so the other choices would not make good titles.

15–A   The reader may conclude that since Hawking accomplished so much in spite of having such serious disabilities, he is a very determined person, so choice A is correct. There's no mention of Hawking ever having met Einstein, and the final two choices are not supported by the passage.

PART III

ASVAB RESULTS AND MILITARY CAREERS

YOUR ASVAB RESULTS

YOUR ASVAB STUDENT RESULTS

If you take the ASVAB in high school, your results consist of a combined Student Results Sheet and Counselor Summary for each student tested, as well as School Summary Reports.

The Counselor Summary contains all the information that is provided to the student, plus percentile scores for academic composites and tests by same grade/combined sex. General information of interest to counselors is given on the back of the summary form. After test interpretation, it can be detached and filed in the student's cumulative record. Your guidance counselor can then help you determine what career path you may choose to follow after graduation.

Note that your high school scores can be used to determine whether you qualify for entry into the military services, provided the scores are not more than two years old.

If you plan to enlist after high school, be sure to ask your school whether they release test results to the military. If they do not, you need to contact a recruiter to discuss your ASVAB results.

YOUR ASVAB ENLISTMENT RESULTS

If you take the ASVAB for enlistment purposes, no matter which military version of the ASVAB you take, any branch of the military can use your scores. You will be asked to sign a form called the 714A in order to convert your scores for use by that particular service. For example, if you take the production ASVAB for the Navy and then decide you would rather join the Marines, you do not have to take the ASVAB again.

Your ASVAB scores will enable military personnel to determine if you are qualified for enlistment and for which career fields you are suited.

Percentile Scores

ASVAB scores are reported as percentile scores. Percentile scores indicate your standing in relation to a national sample of students.

Since test results are not exact measures of ability, ASVAB percentile scores are reported within a score band. The score band indicates the range within which your true score probably lies. When bands for two tests overlap substantially, it is unlikely that the student has scored better on one than on the other. Where there is little or no overlap, it can be said with more confidence that the student's ability ranking is higher in one area than the other.

Both same grade/same sex and same grade/opposite sex percentile scores are reported. The scores that are most important are those for the student's same grade level and sex. These scores allow students to see how their performance compared to that of their peers.

The same grade/opposite sex percentiles are reported because men and women perform differently on some ASVAB tests. On those tests that make up the academic composites, the differences are slight. On the more technical tests, the differences are more significant. Men tend to perform better on the Electronics Information Test, for example, and women on tests that measure speed. That does not necessarily mean that women should be discouraged from entering electronics occupations nor men from entering an occupation where women seem to have an advantage on tests. In either situation, students may want to gain additional relevant experience through course work or independent study in order to compete effectively and achieve their career goals.

Composite Scores

The composite scores you receive are combinations of results of two or more parts of the ASVAB. The following indicates what each composite score measures and shows the various tests that contribute to each composite score.

Academic Ability

Academic Ability is a general indicator of future academic success. It is a measure of how well you did on the Verbal Ability and Math Ability sections combined.

$$\text{Academic Ability} = \left[\left(\begin{array}{c}\text{Word} \\ \text{Knowledge}\end{array}\right) + \left(\begin{array}{c}\text{Paragraph} \\ \text{Comprehension}\end{array}\right)\right] + \left[\left(\begin{array}{c}\text{Arithmetic} \\ \text{Reasoning}\end{array}\right) + \left(\begin{array}{c}\text{Mathematics} \\ \text{Knowledge}\end{array}\right)\right]$$

Verbal Ability

Verbal Ability measures your performance on the Word Knowledge and Paragraph Comprehension tests combined. It is a general indicator of your ability to learn from written material.

$$\text{Verbal Ability} = \left(\begin{array}{c}\text{Word} \\ \text{Knowledge}\end{array}\right) + \left(\begin{array}{c}\text{Paragraph} \\ \text{Comprehension}\end{array}\right)$$

Math Ability

Math Ability measures how well you did on the Arithmetic Reasoning and Mathematics Knowledge tests combined. It is a general indicator of your success in future math courses.

$$\text{Math Ability} = \left(\begin{array}{c}\text{Arithmetic} \\ \text{Reasoning}\end{array}\right) + \left(\begin{array}{c}\text{Mathematics} \\ \text{Knowledge}\end{array}\right)$$

ASVAB Codes

Your score report includes two ASVAB Codes, a primary ASVAB Code and a secondary ASVAB Code. These codes can be used with *Exploring Careers: The ASVAB Workbook* to identify occupations in which workers have aptitude levels similar to your own. The scores can be used to find the occupations most suited to your aptitude levels.

It has been found that a general measure of ability is a good predictor of success for nearly all jobs. The two ASVAB Codes summarize your level of general ability and, together with interest inventory results and personal preferences, can be used to evaluate different occupations as possible career choices.

Individual Test Scores

Individual test scores that are not used in computing ASVAB Codes—General Science, Auto and Shop Information, Mechanical Comprehension, Electronics Information, and Assembling Objects—can be used individually to provide additional direction for career exploration. Scores on individual ASVAB tests that are significantly higher or lower than the rest may point out particular strengths or weaknesses that might be considered in selecting the careers to explore.

Military Careers Score

The Military Careers Score may be used with material in the book *Military Careers* to help you estimate your chances of qualifying for enlisted occupations in the military. This score is a combination of the scores from the Academic Ability composite and the Mechanical Comprehension and the Electronics Information tests.

The Armed Forces Qualification Test

The Armed Forces Qualification Test (AFQT) is a composite score used to determine your eligibility for entrance into the military. It is derived from the raw scores obtained on the ASVAB, as follows:

$$\text{AFQT Raw Score} = 2\left[\text{Word Knowledge Raw Score} + \text{Paragraph Comprehension Raw Score}\right] + \left[\text{Arithmetic Reasoning Raw Score} + \text{Mathematics Knowledge Raw Score}\right]$$

This AFQT Raw Score is then converted into a Percentile Score to determine your eligibility. Applicants without prior military service who receive an AFQT percentile score of 10 or higher are eligible for continued processing at the Military Entrance Processing Station. However, the services usually reject those who fail to score in the top three categories. Typically, the services prefer applicants who score in the following categories:

Category I (Percentile score: 93 and over)

Category II (Percentile score: 65 to 92)

Category III (Percentile score: 31 to 64)

However, under certain circumstances and depending upon the needs of the service, they may accept a limited number of Category IV (percentile score: 10 to 30). Final determination of acceptability remains with the services.

CAREER OPPORTUNITIES IN THE UNIFORMED FORCES OF THE UNITED STATES

The military is the largest employer of high school graduates entering the work force full time. Each year, more than 200,000 young men and women, most of whom are recent high school graduates, join the enlisted forces of the Army, Navy, Air Force, Marine Corps, and Coast Guard. Note that military service in the United States is completely voluntary.

Besides being the largest employer in the nation, employing more than 1.4 million enlisted men and women, the military offers the widest choice of career opportunities. Together, the five services offer training and employment in more than 2,000 enlisted job specialties.

The following pages will give you an overview of all the exciting facts about the military, including general enlistment qualifications. The information is partly condensed from *Military Careers* and partly obtained from U.S. military Internet sites.

If you have access to a computer, more detailed and current information is available on the Internet. Information about applying and enrolling in the military can be obtained on www.mepcom.army.mil, and general information about opportunities in *all* five branches of the military is available on www.myfuture.com.

General Enlistment Qualifications*

Age

Must be between 17 and 35 years old. Consent of parent or legal guardian required if 17.

Citizenship Status

Must be either (1) U.S. citizen; or (2) an immigrant alien legally admitted to the U.S. for permanent residence and possessing immigration and naturalization documents.

Physical Condition

Must meet minimum physical standards listed below to enlist. Some military occupations have additional physical standards.

Height—For males:	Maximum—6'8"	
	Minimum—5'0"	
For females:	Maximum—6'8"	
	Minimum—4'10"	

Weight—There are minimum and maximum weights, according to age and height, for males and females.

Vision—There are minimum vision standards.

Overall Health—Must be in good health and pass a medical exam. Certain diseases or conditions may exclude persons from enlistment; for example, diabetes, severe allergies, epilepsy, alcoholism, and drug addiction.

Education

High school graduation is desired by all services and is a requirement under most enlistment options.

Aptitude

Must make the minimum entry score on the ASVAB (Armed Services Vocational Aptitude Battery). Minimum entry scores vary by service and occupation.

Moral Character

Must meet standards designed to screen out persons likely to become disciplinary problems. Standards cover court convictions, juvenile delinquency, arrests, and drug use.

Marital Status and Dependents

May be either single or married; however, single persons with one or more minor dependents are not eligible for enlistment into military service.

Waivers

On a case-by-case basis, exceptions (waivers) are granted by individual services for some of the above qualification requirements.

*Each service sets its own enlistment standards.

Service Obligation

The military agrees to provide a job assignment, pay, benefits, and occupational training. In return, the enlisted member agrees to serve for a certain period of time, which is called the *service obligation*. The standard service obligation is eight years, which is divided between active military duty and inactive reserve. Individuals on inactive reserve are non-participating, unless called to active duty.

Most first-term enlistments are for four years of active military duty, but there are also programs with two, three, and six years of active duty. It depends upon the service and the job for which you are applying. Some offer *enlistment bonuses* for specific assignments. There are also part-time opportunities in the Reserves and National Guard, where your obligation is generally one weekend a month plus two weeks of active duty a year, unless called to active duty. Reservists may also move to inactive reserve status.

Enlistment Programs

Enlistment programs vary by service. The services adjust the programs they offer to meet changing recruiting needs. Major enlistment options include cash bonuses for enlisting in certain occupations and guaranteed choice of job training and assignments. Currently, all services also offer a Delayed Entry Program (DEP), an option that is used by many high school students who wish to enlist now but wait a short while before entering into active duty. By enlisting under the DEP option, an applicant delays entry into active duty for up to one year. High school students often enlist under the DEP during their senior year and enter a service after graduation. Other qualified applicants choose the Delayed Entry Program because the job training they desire is not currently available but will be within the next year.

Enlistment Contracts

The enlistment contract specifies the enlistment program selected by the applicant. It contains the enlistment date, term of enlistment, and other options such as a training program guarantee or a cash bonus. If, for whatever reason, the service cannot meet its part of the agreement (for example, to provide a specific type of job training), then the applicant is no longer bound by the contract. If the applicant accepts another enlistment program, a new contract is written.

High School Graduates

The military encourages young people to stay in school and graduate. Research has shown that high school graduates are more likely to adjust to military life and complete an initial tour of duty. Therefore, the services accept very few non-high school graduates.

ENLISTING IN THE MILITARY

Enlisting in the military involves a four-step process.

Step 1: Talking with a Recruiter

If you are interested in applying to one of the military services, you must talk with a recruiter from that service. Recruiters can provide detailed information about the employment and training opportunities in their service as well as answer specific questions about service life, enlistment options, and other topics. They can also provide details about their service's enlistment qualification requirements.

If you decide to apply for entry into the service and the recruiter identifies no problems (such as a severe health problem), the recruiter will examine your educational credentials. The recruiter will then schedule you for enlistment processing.

Step 2: Qualifying for Enlistment

Enlistment processing occurs at one of more than sixty Military Entrance Processing Stations (MEPS) located around the country. At the MEPS, applicants take the Armed Services Vocational Aptitude Battery (ASVAB) if they have not already done so, and they receive medical examinations to determine whether they are qualified to enter the service. The ASVAB may also be administered at Mobile Examining Team (MET) sites.

ASVAB results are used to determine whether an applicant qualifies for entry into a service and whether the applicant has the specific Military Careers Score required to enter job specialty training programs. If you have taken the ASVAB at your school, you can use your scores to determine if you qualify for entry into the military services, provided the scores are not more than two years old. Applicants with current ASVAB scores are not required to take the ASVAB a second time.

Step 3: Meeting with a Service Classifier

A service classifier is a military career information specialist who helps applicants select military occupations. For example, if you were applying for entry, the classifier would inform you of service job training openings that match your aptitudes and interests. Specifically, the classifier would enter your ASVAB scores into a computerized reservation system. Based on your scores, the system would show the career fields and training programs for which you qualify and when job training would be available.

After discussing job-training options with the classifier, you would select an occupation and schedule an enlistment date. Enlistment dates may be scheduled for up to one year in the future to coincide with job-training openings. This option is called the Delayed Entry Program (DEP).

Following selection of a military training program, you would sign an enlistment contract and take the oath of enlistment. If you chose the DEP option, you would return home until your enlistment date.

Step 4: Enlisting in the Service

After completing enlistment processing, applicants who select the immediate enlistment option receive their travel papers and proceed to a military base for basic training. Applicants who select the Delayed Entry Program option return to the MEPS on their scheduled enlistment date. At that time, applicants officially become "enlistees" (also known as "recruits") and proceed to a military base.

In the uncommon event that your guaranteed training program, through no fault of your own, is not available on the reserved date, you have three options:

- Make another reservation for the same training and return at a later date to enter the service
- Select another occupation and job training option
- Decide not to join the service and be free from any obligation

MILITARY TRAINING

The military operates one of the largest training systems in the world. The five services sponsor nearly 300 technical training schools that offer more than 10,000 separate courses of instruction.

The military generally provides four kinds of training to its personnel:

- Recruit training
- Job training
- Advanced training
- Leadership training

Recruit Training

Recruit training, popularly called basic training, is a rigorous orientation to the military. Depending on the service, recruit training lasts from six to thirteen weeks and provides a transition from civilian to military life. The services train recruits at selected military bases across the country. Where an enlistee trains depends on the service and the job training to be received. Through basic training, recruits gain the pride, knowledge, discipline, and physical conditioning necessary to serve as members of the Army, Navy, Air Force, Marine Corps, and Coast Guard.

Upon reporting for basic training, recruits are divided into training groups of 40 to 80 people. They then meet their drill instructor, receive uniforms and equipment, and move into assigned quarters.

During basic training, recruits receive instruction in health, first aid, and military skills. They also improve their fitness and stamina by participating in rigorous daily exercises and conditioning. To measure their conditioning progress, recruits are tested on sit-ups, push-ups, running, and body weight.

Recruits follow a demanding schedule throughout basic training; every day is carefully structured with time for classes, meals, physical conditioning, and field instruction. Some free time (including time to attend religious services) is available to recruits during basic training. After completing basic training, recruits normally proceed to job training.

Job Training

Through job training, also called technical or skill training, recruits learn the skills they will need to perform their job specialties. The military provides its personnel with high-quality training because lives and mission success depend on how well people perform their duties. Military training produces highly qualified workers and, for this reason, many civilian employers consider military training excellent preparation for civilian occupations.

The type of job specialty determines the length of training. Most training lasts from ten to twenty weeks, although some nuclear specialties require more than one year of training.

Military training occurs both in the classroom and on the job. Classroom training emphasizes hands-on activities and practical experience as well as textbook learning. For example, recruits who will be working with electronic equipment practice operating and repairing the equipment in addition to studying the principles of electronics.

At their first assignments, enlisted members continue to learn on the job. Experienced enlisted members and supervisors help servicemembers further develop their skills. In addition, the military offers refresher courses and advanced training to help military personnel maintain and increase their skills. As personnel advance in rank, they continue their training with leadership and management courses.

Three services, the Army, Navy, and Marine Corps, offer apprenticeship programs for some job specialties. These programs consist of classroom and on-the-job training that meet U.S. Department of Labor apprenticeship standards. After completing an apprenticeship program, personnel receive a Department of Labor apprenticeship certificate. To military commanders and civilian employers, these certificates demonstrate that the worker has acquired specific skills and qualifications.

Advanced Training

Hundreds of advanced training courses have been developed by the services to improve the technical skills of the enlisted work force. These courses offer instruction in skills not covered in initial training. Advanced training also includes courses covering new or additional job-related equipment. Advanced training is especially important in high technology areas where military technicians are constantly being exposed to newer and more sophisticated equipment. Other advanced courses provide instruction in supervising and managing the daily operations of military units, such as repair shops or medical facilities.

Some advanced training involves classroom training, but the services also provide enlisted members with a wide choice of self-study correspondence courses. Some of these are general courses and address most duties of a job. Other courses are designed to cover highly complex tasks or job-related skills. Self-study courses are particularly important to individual career advancement.

Servicemembers Opportunity Colleges (SOC)

SOC enables military members and their families to get *college degrees* through a group of more than 1,200 colleges, universities, and technical institutes. SOC member schools all acknowledge and transfer your credits between them, which makes it possible for you to continue your college studies as you move to new duty stations. SOC features include the following:

- Your own degree plan and "home college"
- A program ensuring that no one SOC school needs to contribute more than 25 percent of total degree course work
- College credit for *both* your military experience and for accredited military training courses
- College credit for national tests such as CLEP (College Level Examination Program)

Hundreds of thousands of servicemembers—and their families—are enrolled each year in SOC. Course work can be done both in the classroom and at a distance by computer or correspondence. Two-year, four-year, and graduate-level programs are available, and the Army has a special version of SOC called the Concurrent Admissions Program (ConAP).

Leadership Training

Each service has schools and courses to help supervisors be more effective in managing the day-to-day operations of their units. These classes are designed primarily for noncommissioned officers. Courses include instruction in leadership skills, service regulations, and management techniques needed to train and lead other servicemembers.

MILITARY BRANCHES

The different branches of the military attempt to meet the desires of the individual servicemember and provide opportunities for career development. At the same time, they must meet the staffing needs of the uniformed services. Enlisted personnel are stationed in each of the fifty states and in countries all over the world! Many men and women join for the opportunity to travel, live in foreign countries, and see different parts of the United States.

The following will give you an overview of some of the exciting and unique offerings of the different branches of the U.S. military. Look through them to see which might be of interest to you.

Army

Today, Army jobs are divided into eight fields: Aviation, Air Defense Artillery, Infantry, Medical, Armor, Artillery, Signal Operations and Intelligence, and Chemical.

Within these fields, the Army can train you in more than 200 military occupational specialties, many of which are high-tech areas. This high-tech training makes Army soldiers more marketable in an information-based society. Today's soldiers operate technologically advanced aircraft, sophisticated battlefield air defense systems, hand-held computers to collect and relay data about their positions, Inter-Vehicular Information Systems, digital-burst radio systems, and fire-control computers.

Whether your specialty is exiting aircraft at 1,300 feet, enforcing law and order around the fort, or taking medical X-rays, you're sure to develop new skills and confidence in the Army.

Navy

The Navy is full of "hot" jobs—Air Traffic Controller, Interpreter, Sonar Technician, Radioman, Electronics Technician, Advanced Electronics Computer Field, Aviation Electronics Technician, Missile Technician, Fire Control Technician (submarine), and Sonar Technician (submarine), to name a few. There are jobs in more than sixty fields in the Navy.

The Navy's Apprenticeship Programs offer special opportunities. In many Navy fields, hours spent in the classroom and on the job translate directly to journeymen points in the civilian world. So even if you decide to leave the Navy, you're armed with the training and experience to get off to a fast start in the real world.

The Navy also has an associate's degree program, although it's limited to candidates for the nuclear power field. You earn up to a full year's salary (approximately $12,000) while you complete the final twelve months of an associate's degree. When you're done, you enter the Navy's Nuclear Engineering Program for a minimum of 4–7 years in the military after graduation from Nuclear Power School.

Air Force

The U.S. Air Force offers a unique training opportunity and the chance to earn an Associate in Applied Science (A.A.S.) Degree *free of charge*. This happens at the Community College of the Air Force (CCAF), the largest multi-campus two-year college in the world (more than 388,000 registered students).

The curriculum is divided into Aircraft and Missile Maintenance, Allied Health, Electronics and Telecommunications, Logistics and Resources, and Public and Support Services. A.A.S. degrees are offered in sixty-six fields, including Air and Space Operations Technology, Allied Health Services, Computer Science Technology, Financial Management, Information Management, Paralegal studies, Public Affairs, and Survival Instructor studies.

The CCAF has more than 6,000 experienced faculty members and 128 affiliated educational institutions in thirty-five states and seven countries. The Air Force is becoming increasingly technological and complex, and the CCAF is setting the pace.

Marine Corps

After basic training and a short break, Marines attend either the School of Infantry or Marine Combat Training. After that, they receive either formal school training or on-the-job training.

Jobs in the Marine Corps vary a lot, with new Marines attending more than 200 basic formal schools.

Marines assigned to combat specialty occupations mostly train outdoors. Marine training for more technical jobs is classroom-based. Training lasts from four weeks to over a year, depending on the level of technical expertise and knowledge required to become proficient in certain job skills. Emphasis is placed on hands-on training and practical skill application in every job. After completing entry-level training, most Marines are assigned to operational units of the Fleet Marine Forces.

The Marine Corps also has an Apprenticeship Program. In many Marine Corps fields, hours spent in the classroom and on the job translate directly to journeymen points in the civilian world. So even if you decide to leave the Marines, your training will qualify you to start at a higher point when you are back in civilian life.

Coast Guard

There are twenty-two enlisted job specialties in the Coast Guard, and each has one or more civilian equivalents. In fact, that's *one* way to approach a tour in the Coast Guard (or any military service). Think about what you'd like to do in the civilian world, and then find out which military jobs give you the training to prepare you for it!

Remember, after boot camp (or basic training) you go to an "A" (Advanced) school. That's the school where you're paid to learn the job that gives you a head start in civilian life. That's a very good deal!

In addition, the Coast Guard Reserve offers three jobs not available in the active duty Coast Guard: Port Security Specialist, Investigator, and Data Processing Technician.

PAY AND BENEFITS

Military personnel in all five services are paid according to the same pay scale and receive the same basic benefits. Military pay and benefits are set by Congress, which normally grants a cost-of-living pay increase once each year. In addition to pay, the military provides many of life's necessities, such as food, clothing, and housing, or pays monthly allowances for them. The following sections describe military pay, allowances, and benefits in more detail.

Enlisted Pay Grades

Enlistees can progress through nine enlisted pay grades during their careers. Pay grade and length of service determine a servicemember's pay. Figure 1 contains information on the relationship between pay grade and base pay during the first four years of service.

New recruits begin at pay grade E-1, except in some services where a few who have certain technical job skills enter at a higher pay grade. Within six months, enlistees usually move up to E-2. Within the next six to twelve months, the military promotes enlistees to E-3 if job performance is satisfactory and other requirements are met. Promotions to E-4 and above are based on job performance, leadership ability, promotion test scores, years of service, and time in the present pay grade. Promotions become more competitive at the higher pay grades.

Basic Pay

The major part of an enlistee's paycheck is basic pay. Pay grade and total years of service determine an enlistee's pay. The chart on page 377 contains information on annual basic pay as of 2004. Cost-of-living increases generally occur once a year. At the time of publication, a 3.5% increase in base pay is expected as of January 1, 2005.

Incentives and Special Pay

The military offers incentives and special pay (in addition to basic pay) for certain types of duty. For example, incentives are paid for submarine and flight duty. Other types of hazardous duty with monthly incentives include parachute jumping, flight deck duty, and explosives demolition. In addition, the military gives special pay for sea duty, diving duty, special assignments, duty in some foreign places, and duty in areas subject to hostile fire. Depending on the service, bonuses are also paid for entering certain occupations.

Allowances

Most enlisted members, especially in the first year of service, live in military housing and eat in military dining facilities free of charge. Those living off base receive quarters (housing) and subsistence (food) allowances in addition to their basic pay. Because allowances are not taxed as income, they provide a significant tax savings in addition to their cash value.

Employment Benefits

The Armed Forces has a powerful package of benefits programs that is strong enough to be the envy of Fortune 500 employees. This package includes:

- Tuition assistance for college
- Free medical and dental care
- Free job training
- Free on-base housing, if available
- Sports, recreation, and hobby facilities
- Tax-free basic allowance for housing
- Tax-free basic allowance for subsistence (food)
- Thirty days' vacation with pay each year
- Airfare savings
- Savings at base exchanges and commissaries
- Opportunities to travel on duty
- Complete retirement program

The dollar value of all these benefits to a soldier, sailor, aviator, or marine depends on family size, base location, rank, and time served in rank, but they can add thousands of dollars to your total compensation.

Figure 1: 2004 Military Per-Month Active Duty Base Pay

Enlisted: Years Served

Rank	Under 2	2	3	4
E-1*	$1193.40*	$1193.40	$1193.40	$1193.40
E-2	$1337.70	$1337.70	$1337.70	$1337.70
E-3	$1407.00	$1495.50	$1585.50	$1585.50
E-4	$1558.20	$1638.30	$1726.80	$1814.10

*With over 4 months' service; E-1 under 4 months' service earns $1104.00 per month.

OFFICER PAY SCALE

	Years Served			
Rank	Under 2	2	3	4
O-1	$2264.40	$2356.50	$2848.50	$2848.50
O-2	$2608.20	$2970.60	$3421.50	$3537.00
O-3	$3018.90	$3422.40	$3693.90	$4027.20
O-4	$3433.50	$3974.70	$4239.90	$4299.00

Retirement Benefits

For individuals who joined the U.S. military on or after August 1, 1986, there are two retirement options. After fifteen years of service, such a member must decide which of the two retirement plans he or she would prefer:

1. The first option is to receive a lump sum payment of $30,000 at this point, and then receive a pension after 20 years of service at the rate of 40 percent of the *average* of the highest three years' pay.

2. The second option is *not* to receive the cash bonus at fifteen years, but to wait and receive a pension after 20 years of service at the rate of 50 percent of the *average* of the highest three years' pay.

With either option, the percentage of pay increases if retirement is delayed beyond 20 years. The maximum percentage for retirement pay is 75 percent.

Today's military members may also contribute to a separate retirement plan in addition to the standard military retirement plan. Members contribute to the Thrift Savings Plan using "pre-tax" dollars. Unlike some plans, however, there are no matching funds from the government.

SUMMARY OF EMPLOYMENT BENEFITS FOR ENLISTED MEMBERS

Vacation	Leave time of thirty days per year
Medical, Dental, and Eye Care	Full medical, hospitalization, dental, and eye care services for enlistees and most health-care costs for family members
Continuing Education	Voluntary educational programs for undergraduate and graduate degrees or for single courses, including tuition assistance for programs at colleges and universities
Recreational Programs	Programs include athletics, entertainment, and hobbies: Softball, basketball, football, swimming, tennis, golf, weight training, and other sports
	Parties, dances, and entertainment
	Club facilities, snack bars, game rooms, movie theaters, and lounges
	Active hobby and craft clubs as well as book and music libraries
Exchange and Commissary Privileges	Food, goods, and services are available at military stores, generally at lower costs than regular retail stores
Legal Assistance	Many free legal services are available to assist with personal matters

Notes

Notes

Notes

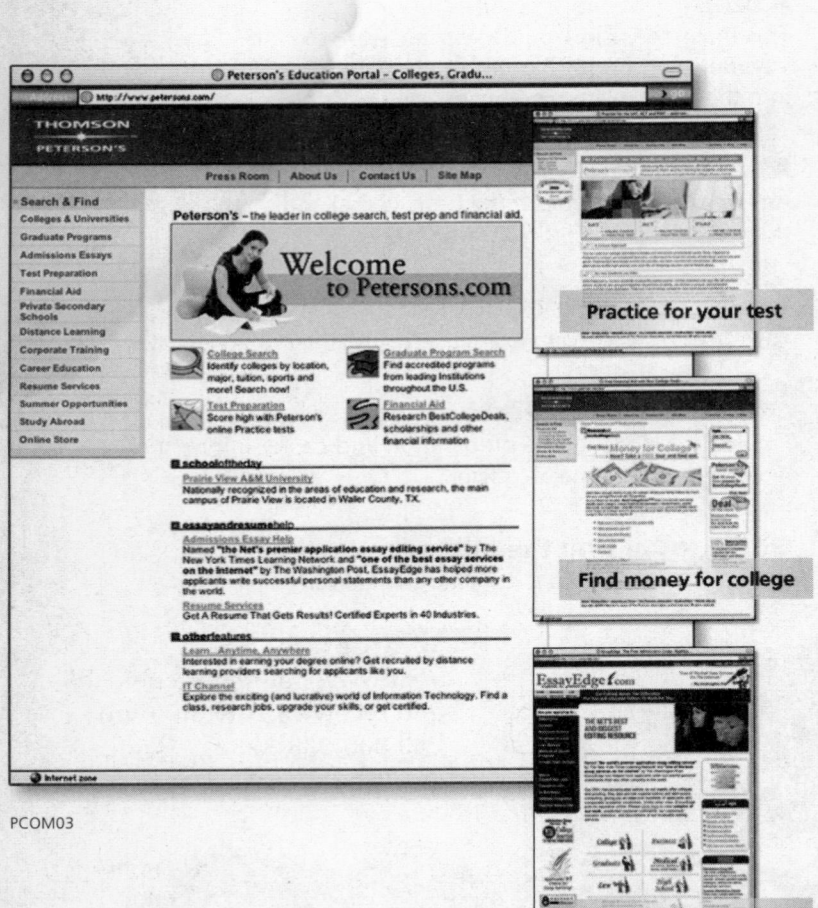